☀ INSIGHT GUIDES MUSEUMS AND GALLERIES OF Florence

APA PUBLICATIONS

Part of the Langenscheidt Publishing Group

ABOUT THIS BOOK

More than any other Italian city, Florence is defined by its artistic heritage, both blessed and burdened by a civic identity bound up with the Renaissance, and basking in its reflected glory. Equally suitable for the avid art-lover or the general enthusiast, this book is the key to exploring the city's treasures, guiding you around the maze of museums, galleries and churches.

While the focus of the book is obviously the historic heart of Florence, for those who want to venture further afield, a selection of nearby villas and gardens worth visiting is also included, together with a round-up of the best churches, galleries and museums in Tuscany.

Practical information, such as addresses, telephone numbers and transport details, is given at the beginning of each review, and the location of each museum is shown on a full-colour map. Most reviews end with one or two suggested refreshment stops in the vicinity.

In addition, authoritative background essays cover Renaissance art and architecture, a reminder that, in its 14th and 15th-century heyday, Florence was the most creative artistic centre in Europe. Other features focus on the city as a magnet for patrons of art from the Medici era onwards, and reveal its role as a restoration centre since the time of the grand-dukes.

For the latest museum news, check the special updates page of our website: **www.insightguides.com**.

The writing team

Lisa Gerard-Sharp is a writer and broadcaster with a long-standing interest in Italy who has contributed to most of Insight Guides' Italian titles. As a former Florence resident and regular visitor, she still has close ties with the city's contemporary architects, writers and art historians. She covered all the Major Collections and a number of the churches, and wrote the chapters on Public Palaces and Private Homes, Modern Arts and Ancient Crafts, and Villas and Gardens. She also wrote the features on The Brunelleschi Trail, Eccentric Philanthropists and Expatriate Collectors, and Restoration.

Christopher Catling is the author of more than 40 guides, including a number of Insight Guides. He fell in love with Italy as a student archaeologist and now looks for every excuse to visit – especially to the magical hilltowns and cities of Tuscany. He reviewed the majority of the religious buildings, and covered all the museums in the History and Archaeology and Science and Nature chapters. He also made the selection for the final chapter covering the best of cultural Tuscany and contributed the background essays on the Medici as Patrons of the Arts, Renaissance Art and Florentine Architecture.

The book was edited by London-based Italophile, **Cathy Muscat**. Thanks go to **Pam Barrett** for her help putting the book together, to **Emily Hatchwell** for proofreading, and to **Mario Carniani**, the President of Centro Guide (the Florentine guiding association) and **Roberta Berni**, of the Florence tourist board, for their help and support.

Editorial

Editor
Cathy Muscat
Design
Klaus Geisler
Picture Editor
Hilary Genin
Picture Research
Susannah Stone
Editorial Director
Brian Bell

Distribution

UK & Ireland
GeoCenter International Ltd
The Viables Centre, Harrow Way
Basingstoke, Hants RG22 4BJ
Fax: (44) 1256-817988

United States
Langenscheidt Publishers, Inc.
46–35 54th Road, Maspeth, NY 11378
Fax: (718) 784-0640

Canada
Prologue Inc.
1650 Lionel Bertrand Blvd., Boisbriand
Québec, Canada J7H 1N7
Tel: (450) 434-0306. Fax: (450) 434-2627

Worldwide
**Apa Publications GmbH & Co.
Verlag KG (Singapore branch)**
38 Joo Koon Road, Singapore 628990
Tel: (65) 6865-1600. Fax: (65) 6861-6438

Printing

Insight Print Services (Pte) Ltd
38 Joo Koon Road, Singapore 628990
Tel: (65) 6865-1600. Fax: (65) 6861-6438

©2002 **Apa Publications GmbH & Co.
Verlag KG (Singapore branch)**
All Rights Reserved

First Edition 2002

INSIDE FRONT COVER: Detail from the *Coronation of the Virgin* altarpiece showing angels, saints and apostles, by Giotto, *c.* 1330 (Santa Croce).

OPPOSITE: *Eleanor of Toledo with her son, Giovanni de' Medici*, by Bronzino, *c.* 1544–5.

BELOW: Donatello's Marzocco lion, emblem of Florence.

FEATURES

MAPS

The *Pitti Tondo* by
Michelangelo,
c. 1504 (The
Bargello).

FLORENCE MUSEUMS, CHURCHES & GALLERIES

Illuminated missal
by Fra' Angelico
(San Lorenzo).

The *Young Bacchus* by
Caravaggio, *c.* 1596
(Galleria degli Uffizi).

Brunelleschi's dome.

Donatello's
bronze *David*,
c. 1440–50
(The Bargello).

FOLLOWING PAGES: *The
Journey of the Magi*, by
Benozzo Gozzoli, *c.* 1460
(Palazzo Medici Riccardi);
The Birth of Venus, by
Sandro Botticelli, *c.* 1485
(Galleria degli Uffizi);
The Last Supper, by
Ghirlandaio, *c.* 1480
(San Marco).

THE MEDICI: PATRONS OF THE ARTS

Florentine history is inextricably linked to the Medici dynasty. Their tremendous wealth, accumulated through three centuries of banking and trading, largely financed the art which defines the Renaissance

Wherever you look in Florence you will encounter the Medici – their statues, busts and coat of arms are everywhere, as are the churches, the palaces and the works of art that they commissioned. To understand the role that each member of the Medici family played in the development of Renaissance art, it pays to know your Cosimo Il Vecchio from your Duke Cosimo I.

Father of the Medici clan was Giovanni di Bicci de' Medici (also known as Giovanni delle Bande Nere, 1360–1429). Although he does not figure largely in the annals of art history, he laid down the wealth and political power that enabled subsequent generations to play their leading role on the Florentine and European stage.

Giovanni was born without great wealth, but used his wife's dowry wisely to invest in wool workshops before setting up a modest banking business. Florence was undergoing such an economic boom in the late 14th century that it was difficult not to make money – though there was stiff competition from the hundreds of other small financial institutions based in Florence. The breakthrough came for the fledgling Medici bank when one of its clients, Cardinal Cossa, was elected Pope John XXIII.

The profligate Cossa had often borrowed money from the Medici in the past, and he continued to do so as pope, securing his loans by handing over quantities of papal jewellery and plate. It was not long before the Medici were handling the financial affairs of the whole papacy, and this continued even after John XXIII was deposed. In gratitude for his help, the Medici gave shelter to the deposed pope in the final years of his life, and when he died they commissioned Donatello to carve the magnificent funerary monument that is in the Baptistery *(see page 97)*.

Maiolica plate decorated with the Medici coat of arms, 16th century.

Cosimo "the Elder"

Giovanni brought his eldest son Cosimo into the business at an early age, and it was his intelligence and flair that turned the Medici bank into Europe's most profitable commercial organisation. Born in 1389, Cosimo was educated by monks and became fluent in Latin, Hebrew, Greek, Arabic, French and German, developing the respect for classical ideals that was to be the defining characteristic of the humanist movement which he did so much to foster later in life. At the age of 25, he spent two years learning the family

---

THE MEDICI COAT OF ARMS

Banking in the 14th century could be a risky business: when Edward III of England and Robert, King of Naples, both defaulted on their loans in the 1340s, financiers all over Europe went into bankruptcy. Shrewd bankers insisted on loaning against the security of family heirlooms, land or property. In that respect there was little difference between banking and pawnbroking, and that is exactly how the enemies of the Medici would taunt the family: by claiming that the six red balls of the Medici coat of arms were nothing more than the symbol of the pawnbroker, universally despised for the punitive levels of interest that they charged for small loans. The Medici themselves claimed that their name proved them to be the descendants of medical apothecaries – respectable, learned doctors, as symbolised by the six pills on their coat of arms. Later family members came up with a more fanciful explanation: the circles represented the dents in the shield of their ancestor, the legendary hero Everardo, a mighty warrior who defeated giants and tyrants wherever he went.

OPPOSITE: Portrait of a young man, possibly Piero or Giovanni de' Medici, with a medallion of Cosimo "the Elder", by Botticelli, c. 1475 (Uffizi).

business by working in branches of the Medici bank in Germany, France and the Low Countries, before taking over the all-important Rome branch in 1417. One benefit of his absence from Florence was that he avoided complicity in the political in-fighting of the day. Giovanni himself practised the art of sitting on the fence. He contributed to public causes, such as the funds set up to provide the Baptistery Gates of Paradise *(see page 19)*, the new Cathedral, and the Innocenti orphanage *(see page 136)*. But he carefully avoided ostentation, cultivated a reputation for modesty, and encouraged his son always to avoid commitment to any one faction, knowing that the price of popularity with one political group was the enmity of the other.

Founding father of humanism

Cosimo heeded the lesson well: throughout his life he gave the impression that he was too busy with his own business affairs to have time for matters of government. Instead he cultivated a close-knit circle of friends who shared a passion for classical literature. Wanting to travel to the Holy Land in search of Greek manuscripts, but too busy to do so, he paid the expenses of others, including Poggio Bracciolini, who scoured monastic libraries and made beautiful handwritten copies of his discoveries: such lost works as Lucretius's *De rerum natura*, *Quintilian's Treatises* on education, and the cookbook of Roman author, Apicius. Through his patronage, Cosimo had an enormous influence on the spread of humanism – and, in turn, on the art of the time, which reflected the tastes of like-minded patrons, fascinated by the stories they discovered in Homer and Livy.

Cosimo de' Medici the Elder (1389–1464) by Pontormo, c. 1518 (Uffizi).

Despite his efforts to avoid the limelight, Cosimo had many enemies: men who chose to believe that the new classical learning was heretical, and contrary to Christian teaching; rivals who were jealous of the Medici bank's success and who presented Cosimo's absences from the city and reluctance to serve in government as treachery. Accused of conspiring with Florence's enemies, even of plotting to invade the city and seize power, he was arrested in 1433, imprisoned in the tower of the Palazzo Vecchio, and sentenced to exile (a sentence meted out to so many others before him, including the unfortunate Dante).

King in all but name

In 1430, Cosimo had briefly agreed to serve on the Florentine war committee at a time when a series of costly battles with neighbouring states was bringing the city to the verge of economic crisis. He resigned shortly afterwards, having failed to win support for his idea of declaring a truce and ending the costly campaign. In 1434, Florence suffered its heaviest defeat to date, at the hands of Milan. Public sentiment swung heavily in favour of the peacemakers, and Cosimo's supporters saw the opportunity to revoke his sentence of exile: a year after leaving for Padua, he returned to the city to a tumultuous welcome.

From that time on, Cosimo never looked back. Frequently consulted about matters of state, although refusing ever to hold public office, he eventually came to wield enormous influence. The future Pope Pius II, the humanist Aeneas Piccolomini, described him as "king in everything but name... political questions are settled at his house, the man he chooses holds office... he decides peace and war and controls the laws".

Lorenzo "the Magnificent" (1449–92) as one of the Three Kings; detail from the *Journey of the Magi* cycle in the Palazzo Medici Riccardi, by Gozzoli, c. 1460.

Classical rigour

In matters of art and architecture, Cosimo poured money into public projects, and introduced a taste for classical simplicity and austerity. He commissioned Brunelleschi to rebuild San Lorenzo church, a model of mathematical rigour. He paid for the new San Marco monastery, with its public library (the first of its kind in Europe), and he maintained a bare monastic cell there for his own private use. When San Marco was finished, he asked Brunelleschi to design a new family palace but rejected the designs as too elaborate, bringing in Michelozzo to design something far simpler *(see page 111)*. Before his death he dictated that he did not want an elaborate funerary monument: just a simple grave slab. Historians have dubbed him Cosimo "Il Vecchio" (the Elder) to distinguish him from later Cosimos, but grateful Florentines bestowed upon him the honorary title Pater Patriae (Father of his People), a suitably classical epithet for a man who brought peace and prosperity to the city and presided over its rise to European pre-eminence in architectural, artistic and scholarly terms.

Piero "the Gouty"

Cosimo was succeeded by his son, the cultured Piero "il Gottoso" (the Gouty), who commissioned numerous works from the leading artists of his day, including Botticelli's *Adoration of the Magi* and Gozzoli's fresco on the same theme, which decorates the walls of the Medici palace chapel *(see pages 6–7, 161–2)*. Both works depict members of the Medici family as exotically attired kings and princes, and art historians have built whole careers on trying to identify precisely which Medici is which.

Argument rages particularly fiercely when it comes to identifying Lorenzo, Cosimo's grandson, who took over as the leading statesman of his day when Piero died in 1469. Lorenzo was strikingly ugly, with a huge lower jaw and a beak of a nose – nothing like the figure of Mercury (often claimed as a portrait of Lorenzo) who dances with the Three Graces in Botticelli's *Primavera*. On the other hand, Lorenzo was certainly blessed with Mercury's gifts of eloquence and reason. He was an outstanding poet, and one of the lasting legacies of his reign was the elevation of Tuscan – the *volgare*, or common tongue – to the status where it challenged Latin as a language fit for use by poets and scholars. Lorenzo promoted the study of Dante's poetry, written in the Tuscan dialect, at university, and he sponsored lectures on Dante (given by Boccaccio, among others) and public readings of his work in the Duomo (one of the few occasions when the Cathedral was packed to capacity).

Lorenzo "the Magnificent"

Although he commissioned no works of art himself, Lorenzo presided over the golden age of Renaissance art and architecture in Florence. The man dubbed "il Magnifico" (the Magnificent) also used his gift for words to good effect as a diplomat and statesman, helping old enemies to heal their rifts and draw up lasting treaties that brought peace to the warring city states of the Italian peninsula. The concept of a united Italy would not be realised for another four centuries, but Lorenzo came close with his aim of creating an alliance of states powerful enough to resist the growing power and ambition of Italy's external enemies – notably the Holy Roman Emperor – and its internal ones – Naples and the Papacy. At his death in 1492, Pope Innocent III declared prophetically that "The peace of Italy is at an end".

Savonarola

Ironically, it was the Medici themselves who upset Lorenzo's carefully created equilibrium. With their family having ruled Florence for so long behind the scenes, subsequent Medici grew ambitious for direct power, and used their influence to penetrate other seats of power, notably the papacy. As one Medici after another alienated their fellow citizens by adopting authoritarian practices, undermining the power of the city council, and giving themselves semi-regal titles, the city grew disillusioned with its rulers, especially when they proved ineffective in fending off the sacking of the city by the troops of the French King, Charles VIII. As the inscription written above the Palazzo Vecchio declares: "God alone is our ruler". Republican sentiment swept the Medici from the city and Savonarola, prior of San Marco and a persuasive orator, took over as leader.

Savonarola convinced himself and his supporters that Charles VIII's attack on the city was a warning from God, and a punishment for the Florentine obsession with fine clothes, profane art and pagan philosophy. He convinced Botticelli to destroy his classically inspired paintings. Born again as a devout Christian, Botticelli painted only religious subjects from that time onwards, though in his own inimitable style. "Bonfires of Vanity" were lit in the squares of Florence and citizens were encouraged to throw their fine clothes, their jewellery and mirrors, their obscene works of art and their books into the cleansing flames.

Execution of the fanatical reformist, Savonarola (1452–98) on Piazza della Signoria, 16th century (Museo di Firenze Com'era).

The Republic under siege

Florence was, of course, far too important to be left in the hands of renegade Republicans. The Medici regrouped, plotted and planned. In 1498, Savonarola was condemned by the Church as a heretic, and the city placed under excommunication until the Grand Council agreed to his arrest, trial and execution. The Republic survived under Soderini, with Machiavelli as Chancellor, until the Medici returned to rule the city, with the help of the Spanish, in 1512. The Medici Popes, Leo X and Clement VIII, then ruled Florence from Rome through the agency of their Medici cousins, and the city witnessed the blossoming of the talent of Michelangelo, who was kept busy through numerous commissions – including the New Sacristy at San Lorenzo, and the Laurentian Library.

The Medici Popes proved tricky allies, however, seeking to neutralise the power of the French and Spanish by playing one off against the other. Frustrated by Clement VIII's duplicity, Charles V of Spain sacked Rome in 1527 to "teach the Pope a lesson". Florence took advantage of the situation to make one last bid for independence: they expelled the Medici once again and prepared for the consequences, putting Michelangelo in charge of strengthening the city's defences *(see page 115)*.

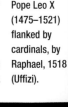

Pope Leo X (1475–1521) flanked by cardinals, by Raphael, 1518 (Uffizi).

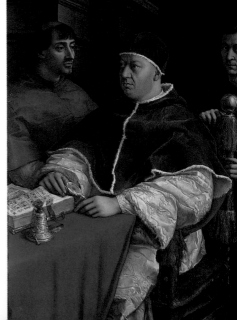

The response was three years in coming, but this time was decisive. Pope and Emperor made up their differences and, in 1529, jointly besieged Florence. The city bravely withstood the siege for nearly a year, but in August 1530 the gifted and inspiring Florentine commander, Francesco Ferrucci, was ambushed and hacked to death. Florentine resistance collapsed, the city was taken, and the Medici, in the person of Lorenzo the Magnificent's great grandson, Alessandro, were put in charge of the city government once again. Deeply unpopular for his tyrannical use of torture and execution to eradicate all his enemies, Alessandro was not mourned when he was assassinated in 1537 by his cousin, Lorenzaccio.

Cosimo I, Duke of Tuscany

The assassination did pose the problem of succession, however. The choice revolved around Alessandro's illegitimate four-year-old son, or Cosimo de' Medici, the immensely capable son of Giovanni delle Bande Nere, himself the great grandson of Cosimo Il Vecchio's brother. Cosimo was the clear choice, and once handed the reigns of power, he lost no time in making himself utterly master of Florence. He turned the Palazzo Vecchio, the city's town hall, into a private palace, commissioned Vasari to build the Uffizi as a home for the city administration, then bought the Pitti Palace and turned it into a semi-regal home, with state apartments for the reception of foreign dignitaries. With the military precision that is celebrated by Vasari's great ceiling painting in the Palazzo Vecchio, he subjugated most of the previously independent city states of Tuscany under Florentine dominion, receiving the title of Grandduke of Tuscany from Pope Pius V in 1570.

The end of the line

By the time of Cosimo's death in 1574, nobody challenged the family's right of succession; the Medici were now a royal family in all but name. Successive Medici Grand-dukes continued to collect works of art to embellish their palaces, they created the Boboli gardens, gave shelter and support to Galileo (1564–1642), and mounted lavish musical celebrations out of which modern opera was to develop.

By the 18th century, the Medici line was exhausted. There were only two surviving descendants: the homosexual and childless Gian Gastone, and his ageing and now infertile sister, Anna Maria Lodovica. Even before Gastone's death (in 1737), the European powers met to decide the question of the "Tuscan Succession" in favour of Francis, Duke of Lorraine, husband of the Empress of Austria.

When Anna Maria became the last surviving member of the House of Medici, she made her will. Declaring that her entire family property belonged to Florence, she bequeathed her palaces and works of art to successor Grand-dukes on the strict condition that nothing was ever to be removed beyond the borders of Tuscany. This remarkable step – which even more remarkably has been respected by subsequent powers – means that the vast body of Renaissance art and architecture has stayed in the city that gave it birth.

Alchemy by Jan Stradanus, 1570; one of a series of paintings in the study of Cosimo's son, Francesco I, who had a keen interest in science (Palazzo Vecchio).

RENAISSANCE ART

In its 15th-century heyday, Florence was the most creative centre in Europe. As birthplace of the Renaissance, the city led the artistic revolution inspired by ancient art and the "rebirth" of classical ideals

Art in Europe came to a full stop when the western Roman Empire collapsed in the 5th century, but many essential techniques survived and were fostered in the Eastern, or Byzantine, Empire, with its capital at Constantinople. These same skills were then imported back to the West by Byzantine artists who were routinely employed in 13th-century Italy to create frescoes, paintings and mosaics. Out of their skills, the Renaissance was born.

Giorgio Vasari (1512–74), himself an artist and architect of prodigious output (responsible for the design of the Uffizi and the paintings on the dome of Florence Cathedral), bequeathed to future generations a series of biographies of his contemporaries, called *Lives of the Artists* (published from 1550). In it, he gives credit to the Florentine painter Cimabue (1240–c.1302) for reviving art in Europe. Cimabue frequently played truant from school to watch the Greek painters at work in the Gondi Chapel in Santa Maria Novella. He eventually persuaded his father to let him serve an apprenticeship under the Greeks, and the skills he learnt from them he passed on to future generations as a teacher of, among others, his fellow Florentine, Giotto (1266–1337).

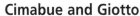

Cimabue and Giotto

Of course, anyone who knows anything about medieval European art will at this point interject that many wonderful Gothic sculptures, stained-glass windows, frescoes and illuminated manuscripts were produced in Europe before this date. But Vasari has an answer. To him, art before Cimabue and Giotto was "crude, stiff and mediocre". It was the result of "blindly following what had been handed down year after year by painters who never thought of trying to improve their drawing", and it was far removed from the "fine antique style" that he valued.

If you want to see what sort of difference Vasari was talking about, compare Cimabue's *Crucifix* (now sadly damaged by the 1966 flood, *see page 36*) in the Museo dell' Opera di Santa Croce, where the influence of Byzantine art is still evident in the stylised, almost abstract, patterning of loin cloth and musculature, and then look at Giotto's much more human figure on the newly restored *Crucifix* in Santa Maria Novella. But although he made major strides, Cimabue is still rooted in the past in style and in the choice of medium – he was one

The beginnings of realistic representation can be seen in Giotto's *Ognissanti Madonna, c.* 1310, (Uffizi).

of the last artists to work in mosaic, creating the apse of Pisa Cathedral and the dome of the Baptistery in Florence. Giotto, by contrast, rejected stylisation and – haltingly at first but with growing assurance – sought a return to that realism in art that was familiar to Giotto and his contemporaries from the Roman sculpture that lay all around them.

The Pisano masterpieces

Just as Vasari attributes the revival of drawing, painting and fresco to Cimabue and Giotto, he credits Nicola (1220–84) and Giovanni Pisano (1245–1313), the father and son team from Pisa, with creating a distinctive new style in sculpture. Nicola, he says, was greatly inspired by the antique sarcophagi (today in the Campo Santo in Pisa) that were brought back as spoils of war from the Holy

Land by the Pisan fleet. The influence is plain to see in his marvellous pulpit of 1260, carved with scenes from the Life of Christ in Pisa's Baptistery, matched in brilliance by Giovanni's pulpit with similar scenes in the adjacent Cathedral.

Confusingly, another father and son team with the same surname, Andrea (1290–1349) and Nino Pisano (died 1368), unrelated to Nicola and Giovanni, were also making waves at the same time and in the same field. Andrea Pisano's masterpiece is the south door, the earliest of three sets of bronze doors for the Baptistery, completed in 1330. Its panels depict scenes from the Life of St John the Baptist, the patron saint of Florence *(see page 95)*.

The Quattrocento (1400s)

A hiatus then occurred in artistic development that is perfectly understandable given the conditions that prevailed all over Europe during the mid-14th century. To the misery of constant warfare was added the privations of a series of very wet and unseasonably cold summers, failed harvests, and the ravages of the Black Death. A third of Europe's population died from

Sacrifice of Isaac, bronze relief panel for the Baptistery Doors, by Brunelleschi's rival, Ghiberti, 1402.

the disease, and towns and villages were abandoned on flooded low-lying land and on cold uplands. Defeated monarchs and warlords defaulted on loans, merchants, bankers and landlords went bankrupt. The times were not propitious for artistic production.

As conditions improved towards the end of the 14th century, Florence announced a series of architectural and artistic competitions, mainly associated with the Cathedral, dome, campanile and Baptistery. Perhaps the most symbolic of all was the competition of winter 1400 to find a designer for the Baptistery doors, which pitched the goldsmith Lorenzo Ghiberti (1378–1455) and the architect Filippo Brunelleschi (1377–1446), two of the most temperamental and gifted artists of their day, against each other as the finalists, chosen from scores of aspiring entrants. The panels that these two artists submitted as evidence of their skill both hang in the Bargello *(see page 60)*, and it is interesting to compare their different approaches to the same subject – Abraham's sacrifice of his son Isaac. Both represent a huge leap forward in terms of the artists' ability to convey the emotional and psycho-

Trinità by Masaccio, the pioneer of perspective, *c.* 1424 (Santa Maria Novella).

logical impact of a dramatic moment, and in the realistic modelling of the human and animal figures. To Brunelleschi's disgust, Ghiberti was awarded the commission (technically his was the better piece, and it was more economical to cast, a point that appealed to the financially astute judges), but it was not long before Brunlleschi was preoccupied with an even bigger commission – the Cathedral dome. Both artists thrived and – along with Donatello (1386–1466) – established major workshops in which many young artists served their apprenticeships.

Masaccio's perspective

In the early years of the 1400s, it was in the fields of sculpture and architecture that the greatest artistic advances were made, but out of Donatello's workshop emerged a pupil whose paintings were to show the way to subsequent artists. Masaccio (1401–28) managed to achieve the solidity, bulk and three-dimensional roundedness in his painted figures that hitherto had eluded artists working on flat surfaces – whether consciously or not, he seems to have imitated sculpture to do this: his strikingly memorable *Adam and Eve* in the Brancacci Chapel *(see page*

The Visitation, from a fresco series by Ghirlandaio, 1485–90 (Santa Maria Novella).

123), for example, are modelled on Hercules and Venus (Eve's attempts to cover herself up are exactly those of Venus emerging from her bath in countless antique statues). He, too, absorbed and applied to paint the mathematics of perspective, drastically foreshortening figures that were to be viewed from a distance, and surrounding his pictures in an architectural frame to increase the illusion of depth and space. He applied these new laws of perspective to his *Trinity* fresco in Santa Maria Novella, a ground-breaking work that marks a turning point in European painting.

Economic boom

By contrast with the previous century, 15th-century Florence was booming economically, and the demand for works of art from churches, abbeys, trades guilds and private patrons was so great that artists were never short of work. Artists were held in such esteem that Cosimo Il Vecchio requested that he and Donatello should, when the time came, be buried in the same part of San Lorenzo church. The ready flow of work did not lead to complacency: individual artists strove to impress each other with ever-new innovations, and to persuade their clients to pay for ever more costly colours and pigments.

There emerged from this period a distinctively Florentine style of fresco painting, which can best be described as having a spring-like clarity of line and colour. That quality is found at its freshest in *Primavera* and *Birth of Venus* by Botticelli (1444–1510), but is also found in the deeply spiritual *Annunciation* and *Crucifixion* frescoes of Fra' Angelico (1395–1455) in San Marco; in the portraits of his mistress purporting to be the Virgin, surrounded by smiling, cheeky cherubs; in the paintings of Fra' Lippo Lippi (1406–69) in the Uffizi; in the gorgeous *Journey of the Magi* fresco of Benozzo Gozzoli (1420–97) in the Palazzo Medici-Riccardi; and in the *Life of the Virgin* frescoes of Ghirlandaio (1449–94) in Santa Maria Novella. All these artists, and many others influenced by them, produced pictures that convey a sense of fresh wonderment at the astonishing richness and beauty of the world and its denizens.

Noah as pictured in Uccello's fresco cycle of *The Deluge*, c. 1440 (Santa Maria Novella).

Some artists also experimented with deliberate exaggeration, pushing the boundaries even further, creating work that is so expressive as almost to be avant-garde. Donatello, who was capable of producing such a realistic work as his famous *St George* (in the Bargello) could also produce the penitent *Magdalene* in the Museo dell'Opera del Duomo, which lies just within the bounds of realism. Donatello's soulmates include Filippino Lippi (1457–1504), so in love with the bizarre and exotic (see his frescoes in Santa Maria Novella) as almost to be camp, and Uccello (1397–1475), whose frescoes on the *Story of Noah* in the cloister of Santa Maria Novella are a work of pure imagination, powerful even in their damaged state.

The issue of how far you should go in art was played out in a disagreement, recorded by Vasari, between Donatello and Brunelleschi. The latter disliked a Crucifix that Donatello created for the church of Santa Croce because he said that the sculptor had made Christ look "like a mere peasant on a cross". To Brunelleschi, this was going too far in the direction of realism: Christ should look noble, dignified, the archetype of humanity, and he created his own version, carved in wood and now in Santa Maria Novella, to show how it should be done. Brunelleschi had a point: the main thrust of the 1400s was in the direction of realism, modelled on classical precedents, the so-called "Rebirth" of classical ideals that is so well represented by the huge quantities of lesser art to be found in Florence: the countless bronzes, cameo brooches, small *objets d'art* – and in the many marvellous funerary monuments of the era that fill the city's churches with their realistic portraits of the deceased.

The age of perfection

As always, Vasari had his own views on the differences between Donatello and Brunelleschi. Donatello was, quite simply, out of his time: a pioneer whose work foreshadows the later Renaissance (which Vasari calls the "age of perfection"), closer in spirit to that of the great Michelangelo (1475–1564), who, for Vasari, was the ultimate artist.

By "perfection" Vasari meant art that could finally stand comparison with the best of the antique, or Roman, era. Ironically, that art has nothing to do with photographic realism, and everything to do with deliberate distortion. Michelangelo's best-known work in Florence, his heroic figure of the young *David* (1504) is a perfect example: judged in exact anatomical terms, David's head and limbs are too big for his body – he doen't conform at all to the ideal proportions represented in Donatello's bronze *David* (in the Bargello). But judged in artistic terms, *David* is a triumph: naked, he prepares to meet the tyrant Goliath, trusting in his own bravery and youthful vigour to achieve what armies had not. He is a heroic statement of belief in the power of good, free people to triumph over tyranny and that ability to convey the essentials of the human spirit in stone is what won Michelangelo so many admirers.

Just how difficult it was to achieve that monumentality is exemplified by some of the other statues that decorate the area in front of the Palazzo Vecchio: Bandinelli (1493–1560) tried it with his *Hercules* (1534) and Ammannati (1511–92) with his *Neptune Fountain* (1575), only to have their efforts ridiculed by Florentines who invented crude rhymes to describe these mock-heroic statues. None could compare with Michelangelo, who towers so far above his contemporaries that even his unfinished works (the *Four Slaves* in the Accademia, for example) elicit more admiration for their elemental qualities than the finished works of lesser sculptors.

Michelangelo's triumphant *David*, 1501–4 (Accademia).

Mannerism

Michelangelo's use of heightened and exaggerated effect had enormous influence on the artists who followed, long after he himself had left Florence for Rome. Those artists have been given the unfortunate label "Mannerist" and are often derided by those who are unsympathetic to the passion that they poured into their work. At its best – in the work of Andrea del Sarto (1486–1530) and his fellow artists who decorated Santissima Annunziata, or in the paintings of Rosso Fiorentino (1494–1541) – the degree of exaggeration is scarcely noticeable. When it is thrust into your face, it can achieve astonishing effects. The *Martyrdom of St Lawrence* (1565–69) by Bronzino (1503–72) is a bravado masterpiece of contorted poses *(see page 108)*. Dismissed by author Mary McCarthy as febrile, the *Deposition* by Pontormo (1494–1556) in Santa Felicità bowls you over with its heightened emotion and astonishing colours *(see page 121)*. Perhaps Mannerism is at its best when dealing with such tragic subjects as the Crucifixion and Deposition, where heightened colour and emotion are appropriate. Certainly, there are lesser works in the Uffizi – such as the *Virgin of the Long Neck* by Parmigianino (1503–40) – where anatomical elongation seems only to be a stylistic quirk, serving no obvious artistic purpose.

The Martyrdom of St Lawrence (detail), by Bronzino, 1565–9 (San Lorenzo).

The development of oil painting

Another great difference between Early and High Renaissance art was in the development of oil painting. The artists of the 1400s worked with fresco and tempera, both of which use water or gum as the binding medium for the pigments. Both give a crisp, clean line, perfect for fine details of hair and fur. Modelling is achieved by laying down blocks of colour, tricking the eye into seeing folds of soft cloth instead of what are really hard geometric shapes, almost abstract in design. Experiments made by Leonardo da Vinci (1452–1519) led to some disasters (his now terminally ruined *Last Supper* in Milan) but also to the perfection of oil-based paints that liberated 16th-century artists to produce the infinitely subtle shading and gradation of colour that characterises, for example, human flesh.

Without oil paints, some of the very fine nudes and portraits that grace the walls of the Uffizi and the Pitti Palace would not have been possible – among them the *Madonna of the Goldfinch* by Raphael (1483–1520), the sensual *Venus of Urbino* by Titian (1485–1576; *see page 90*), and the *Bacchus* of Caravaggio (1579–1610; *see page 91*). But these are paintings produced outside Florence, for patrons in other parts of Europe. By the middle of the 16th century, very few artists of note remained in Florence – it was as if the artistic fever of the previous two centuries had exhausted the city's stock of talent. Among the few artists of note still working in Florence were the sculptors Giambologna (1529–1628) and Cellini (1500–71) – both well represented in the Bargello.

Portrait of a Gentleman (or The Englishman), by Titian, c. 1535 (Palatine Gallery).

Vasari's judgement

And last but not least there is Vasari (1511–74) himself – a man who aspired to that same monumentality he so much admired in Michelangelo. Vasari's prodigious energy and productivity is in no doubt, seen in the acres of paint that he applied to the huge ceilings of the Palazzo Vecchio and the dome of the Cathedral – he considered his *Last Judgement* scenes here to be the Florentine answer to Michelangelo's Sistine Chapel frescoes. But Vasari's real achievement does not lie here: instead it is in the books that he wrote – scurrilous, unreliable and gossipy but nevertheless the first, and some of the best, art criticism ever penned – and in the building that he created for the display of the city's best art: his brilliant and airy design for the Uffizi is the prototype for all subsequent art galleries, and has more than stood the test of time and use.

FLORENTINE ARCHITECTURE

Clarity, rigour, geometry – these are the sober classical values to which
Florentine architects aspired. Within their constraints, they created
remarkable buildings that remain an inspiration to modern architects

The earliest buildings that survive in the city already show the Florentine preference for geometric patterning. Making the most of the colours of the local building stones, the Baptistery was clad in green and white marble in 1174. When the basilica of San Miniato al Monte was completed shortly afterwards (in 1207) its façade was similarly decorated with white Carrara marble (from northern Tuscany), with geometric panels in contrasting, green, verde di Prato stone (from quarries just to the east of Florence).

These beautiful buildings are not unique to Florence. They belong firmly to the Tuscan Romanesque tradition, which reached its zenith in Lucca and Pisa. In these two cities the style is executed with enormous zest and vitality. Churches such as San Martino in Lucca are covered in hunting scenes and exotic monsters, whereas the façades of Pisa have arabesques and knots copied from Islamic carpet designs.

The relatively low-key nature of Florentine Romanesque was quite deliberate. In medieval Tuscany, the battle for supremacy between one city-state and the next was fought on a number of fronts, including the often-unprovable claim to be the region's oldest city. Siena traced its foundation to the son of Remus, making the city second in antiquity only to Rome herself. Even today Siena reminds visitors that it is built (like Rome) on seven hills, which appear on the city's coat of arms, along with a representation of the she-wolf that suckled Romulus and Remus.

Symbols of Florence

Florentines fostered the idea that their city was founded on swamps drained by Hercules, the mythical hero whose statue stands in front of the Palazzo Vecchio, and whose image formed the city's official seal. In the propaganda battle to establish which city was the true heir to the intellectual and artistic heritage of ancient Rome, the Baptistery in Florence was a key building: a genuine Roman Temple of Mars, built to celebrate the conquest by Roman Florentines of their Etruscan neighbour, Fiesole, and later converted to Christian use. The Baptistery therefore had to look antique and not an upstart *nouveau riche* structure like the frilly Pisan Baptistery.

The much-revered Baptistery provided the inspiration for the design of the new Cathedral that was built alongside from 1294. Although the latter took more than 150 years to complete, all the architects who worked on the building stayed faithful to the design principles established by

Arnolfo di Cambio's austere Palazzo Vecchio, the heart of Civic Florence.

the first architect, Arnolfo di Cambio. If you mentally block out the façade, which is a 19th-century neo-Gothic design, you can see just how strongly the rectilinear marble patterning reflects the simple but harmonious facing of the Baptistery.

Arnolfo di Cambio's other great building – the Palazzo Vecchio – conveys the same Florentine values of strength and austerity. Those who could afford it built palaces in similar style, copying its imposing proportions, although it is difficult to appreciate this fully today, since most of the sky-reaching towers that Florentines built for status and defence have been demolished. Visiting San Gimignano *(see page 210)* is the best way to understand how Florence looked in the 13th century.

View of the palazzo-lined Arno and the Ponte Santa Trinità, a 17th-century engraving by Giuseppe Zocchi.

The Florentine palazzo

Another much-copied feature of the Palazzo Vecchio was the use of rusticated stonework – rough-hewn in the style of a rustic farmhouse, or of the Cyclopean walls that surround many of the region's oldest cities. As a result, Florentine palaces often look fortress-like, forbidding and dour – especially by contrast with the more feminine and delicate brick buildings of Siena. Inside is a different story; elegant courtyards and stairways, well-proportioned and light-filled rooms, painted ceilings and frescoed walls made Florentine palaces some of the most luxurious and appealing buildings in medieval Europe – as you can see by visiting the Palazzo Vecchio itself, or the Davanzati Palace *(see page 159)*.

Veduta d'una parte di Lung'Arno col Ponte a S. Trinita presa dal Palazzo del Sig. March. Roberto Capponi.

During the 15th century, the pretence at least of austerity and honest simplicity continued to be a Florentine civic virtue, which is why Cosimo Il Vecchio rejected Brunelleschi's designs for the new Medici family palace (today's Palazzo Medici-

---

FLORENTINE PIAZZAS

"Piazza" is a term used very loosely in Florence for any public space enclosed by buildings. Piazzas come in all shapes and sizes – ovoid, triangular, L-shaped and rhomboid. The one thing they very rarely are is square, though this is how the word "piazza" has traditionally been translated. Many have statues or memorials, justifying the claim that Florence is one big open-air scuplture gallery.

The square that most deserves this name is the huge Piazza della Signoria *(see page 146)*, once capable of accommodating all the citizens of Florence, who would gather to hear new laws promulgated from the stone platform in front of the Palazzo Vecchio.

At the opposite end of the scale in terms of size is the tiny Piazza San Martino, located in the warren of medieval alleys just round the corner from Dante's birthplace. It has the splendid 13th-century Torre della Castagna to one side, one of the very few medieval towers left in a city that once bristled with such private fortifications.

One of the oddest-shaped squares in Florence is the Piazza di San Firenze, a short distance away, which extends from the Bargello southwards. Recent excavations have finally explained its irregular shape: digging in 1994,

archaeologists found that the square reflects the line of the ancient Roman walls, built in 30 BC.

Of all the squares whose shapes were dictated by their former functions, the Piazza Santa Maria Novella stands out. Annual chariot races were held here in the 16th century and the race track is preserved in the shape of today's road and gardens, while two great granite obelisks set up in 1608, resting on the backs of Giambologna's bronze tortoises, mark the turning points at each end of the course.

One block east of Santa Maria Novella is a tiny piazza called Croce del Trebbio. It is named after a Roman pillar, now topped with a cross and symbols of the Evangelists, marking the meeting of three streets. Another Roman pillar, a magnificent monster of granite topped by Francesco del Tadda's figure of Justice (1581), stands nearby in the triangular Piazza Santa Trinità. This column is not local, however – it came from the Baths of Caracalla in Rome and was presented to Duke Cosimo I by Pope Pius IV. Surrounding the square are some of Florence's finest medieval palaces, including the fortress-like Palazzo Spini-Feroni, now the headquarters of the Ferragamo shoe empire, and the Palazzo Gianfigliazzi (both 13th century).

Riccardi). It was not politically expedient to flaunt one's wealth and power, and Brunelleschi's design was considered too splendid and ornate. Cosimo's preference was for the monastic simplicity of San Marco, designed by his favourite architect, Michelozzo.

Michelozzo's design for the Palazzo Medici Riccardi *(see page 160)* became the prototype of the typical Renaissance palace. The Palazzo Pitti, the Palazzo Strozzi and many other city mansions built for the rich and powerful Florentine families, all share the same basic design: a cubic building of three clearly defined storeys (for defensive purposes, the bottom storey was the tallest, and made of rusticated stonework with few small windows placed high up) enclosing a courtyard surrounded by colonnades.

Renaissance Man

Brunelleschi was so incensed with Cosimo's rejection of his plans for the Medici family seat that he smashed his model into thousands of pieces. But, by then, he was used to having his ideas dismissed. He had already lost to Ghiberti in the competition of 1400–1 to design doors for the Baptistery (despite producing what many, in retrospect, consider to be the more exciting and innovative design). He faced his rival yet again in 1418–19 in the competition to find a design for the Cathedral dome, a building challenge that many Florentines had come to see as impossible. Undeterred, Brunelleschi spent many months at his own expense studying the Pantheon and other domed buildings in Rome.

While he was there, he imbibed more than just the solution to an engineering problem. The classical vocabulary that he studied and mastered in Rome was to bear fruit in the new commissions he received while waiting to hear the outcome of the dome competition, including the design of the Old Sacristy *(see page 108)*, in San Lorenzo church, and the Spedale degli Innocenti *(see page 136)* – a home for foundlings and orphans.

For both of these buildings, Brunelleschi produced structures perfectly attuned to Florentine sensibilities: deceptively simple, yet based on the rigorous application of mathematical principles of ratio, proportion and perspective, with details based on antique precedents. Perhaps the most endearing feature of both buildings was the choice of building materials, with the soft blue-grey of *pietra serena* sandstone contrasted with white stucco. These were to become Brunelleschi's signature colours, used again for the lovely Pazzi Chapel (the chapterhouse of Santa Croce), and the churches of San Lorenzo and Santo Spirito *(see* The Brunelleschi Trail, *page 27).*

Brunelleschi finally won the contract to build the Cathedral dome, although subject to the condition that Ghiberti supervise his work. How much Ghiberti actually contributed to the structure we will never know, partly because Brunelleschi himself was very secretive, and the detail of the dome's structure is not fully understood even today. In 1434, Pope Eugenius IV visited the city to see the near-complete dome; among those in his entourage was Leon Battista Alberti, who described the dome as "a structure so great, rising from the skies, large enough to shelter all the people of Tuscany in its shadow, built without the help of centring or scaffolding, of such workmanship as perhaps not even the ancients knew".

Brunelleschi's fame rests upon his engineering achievement in constructing the dome, but his lasting influence is to be found in his smaller buildings, which reminded Florentines of the vocabulary of classical architecture that they had at their disposal. Alberti himself added to that vocabulary by writing the first modern treatise on perspective, in a book called *De Pictura* (1436), followed up by further treatises on architecture *(De Re Aedificatoria)* and sculpture *(De Statua)*. Dedicated jointly to Brunelleschi, Ghiberti, Donatello, Luca della Robbia and Masaccio, these books codified the practices of the greatest innovators of their age and became the influential source manuals for generations of Florentine artists and architects.

Arguing strongly that there is a rational, mathematical basis to beauty that was fully realised by the architects of classical antiquity, Alberti did much to spread those quintessential Florentine values, as did his own designs, including the façade of Santa Maria Novella, the Palazzo Rucellai and the little Loggia Rucellai that stands close by.

The original Tuscan Romanesque façade of Santa Maria Novella was embellished by Alberti, who completed it in 1470.

The rural villa

Most of the buildings erected in Florence over the next 150 years were based on the Brunelleschi model and the teachings of Alberti, although such architects as Guiliano da Sangallo (Palazzo Gondi) and Cronaca (Palazzo Strozzi) came up with their own bold designs. Guiliano da Sangallo, in particular, was the inventor of the Renaissance villa, a very important development in Renaissance architecture. To the cultured circle surrounding the Medici, the word "villa" conjured up all sorts of associations – rural tranquillity, a refuge, an oasis where the intellectual élite could meet, read, take exercise, write poetry and music. This ideal of the villa as a place where men (and it always was a place for male society) of refined sensibilities could recharge their intellectual batteries in the company of like-minded friends, was fostered by the letters and writings of such villa-owning classical writers as Horace, Cicero and Virgil.

Alberti, as ever, supplied the essential rules for the archetypal villa (basing his own views on those of the 1st-century AD author, Vitruvius): it must be built on top of a hill, to take advantage of the views, he said, with its rooms radiating off an atrium or central hall, and its windows large and numerous to admit light and air. So much for theory: it was up to Guiliano da Sangallo to put these principles into practice, which he did with the pioneering villa at Poggio a Caiano (also known as the Villa Medicea), built in 1480–85 for Lorenzo "Il Magnifico". Here, the Florentine ruler, inspired by the Georgics of Virgil, extolling the seasonal work of the countryside, threw himself into gardening, raising pigs, poultry, Sicilian pheasants and racehorses – and even experimenting with new ways of manufacturing cheese.

Villa Careggi, one of the Medici family's favourite retreats, designed by Michelozzo, 1440.

Today, the villa, almost more than the church or palace, has survived as the lasting legacy of the Florentine Renaissance – for although our secular age has little time for churches, and few aspire any more to own or live in a palace, a villa in Tuscany remains an ideal to which many aspire – if only for the duration of a short summer holiday – coupled with a desire to return to the basics of the rural "good life".

THE BRUNELLESCHI TRAIL

The quintessential Renaissance man, Brunelleschi was tireless in his quest for architectural perfection. His legacy is an awe-inspiring ensemble of domes and churches that still define the cityscape

"In daring, the Florentines excelled; that is why their sculpture and much of their architecture have such a virile quality." Critic Mary McCarthy was thinking of Brunelleschi's dome, the taut, sinewy structure that best symbolises his genius. Filippo Brunelleschi (1377–1446) created some of the purest Renaissance architecture in the city, buildings which are striking in their simplicity and pared-down loveliness. Using rigorous geometry based on classical forms, they are the perfect expression of a rational use of space. The rediscovery of perspective is often attributed to Brunelleschi, even if Alberti provided the fuller academic interpretation. Certainly, Brunelleschi shared his peers' obsession with producing a perfect illusion of the three-dimensional world and was the first architect to use perspective in his buildings. He led the way in his understanding of geometrical space and in the use of mathematical proportions. The architects of the Western world happily followed him for the next five centuries.

Florence's skyline has changed little since the Renaissance. Brunelleschi's landmarks are as prominent today as they are in this, the earliest known image of the city (19th-century copy of a woodcut *c.* 1470; Museo di Firenze Com'era).

Brunelleschi began his working life as a goldsmith and sculptor in Florentine workshops. In time, he became the quintessential Renaissance man, an architect and painter, mathematician and naval engineer, an inventor of musical instruments and a master of ceremonies for Medici entertainments. However, it is as the first Renaissance architect that he will best be remembered. Brunelleschi had a practical bent and acquired some of his classical knowledge by visiting Rome to study the ancient masterpieces *(see page 27)*. He was also influenced by the grace and elegance of Romanesque buildings in Tuscany, unique in medieval Europe.

A change of direction

Brunelleschi's triumphant command of theory and practice hastened the transition from the medieval concept of master-builder to the Renaissance concept of architect. Brunelleschi straddled both functions, although his successors separated the roles. While medieval builders solved on-site problems empirically and contingently, the Renaissance architect was also a theoretician who could refer to plans, and modify them accordingly. He also recognised that the art and science of making something were part of the same coin, and that beauty and functionalism could co-exist.

After the failure of his competition entry to design the Baptistery doors in 1401 *(see pages 19 and 25)*, Brunelleschi turned his attention to architecture and returned to sculpture only in the 1420s. Nonetheless, his talent as a sculptor served him well, both in his familiarity with the sculptural devices he incorporated into buildings, and in his selection of the city's foremost sculptors to embellish his projects. Luca della Robbia and Donatello were two of the great sculptors he cultivated. Donatello, a lifelong friend, accompanied him on visits to Rome to learn the lessons of antiquity.

Brunelleschi first made his architectural mark with the Old Sacristy in San Lorenzo and the Spedale degli Innocenti (1419), the first secular building of the Renaissance. Yet it was his success in building the dome of Florence Cathedral that led to commissions all over the city. The Medici, the guilds and powerful bankers vied with each other to employ him on their pet projects. He was commissioned to work on the Pazzi Chapel in Santa Croce and on Santo Spirito and the church of San Lorenzo. Most of his projects were not completed in his lifetime but it is a tribute to his reputation that his designs were generally faithfully respected by his followers.

Decoration and innovation

Decorative simplicity was a guiding principle of Brunelleschi, who rejected the multi-coloured munificence of the Cathedral, with its glittering, patterned, geometrical surface. Instead, he looked to the precepts of the Greek philosophers, who stated that a sacred building should be "chaste", plain and well-lit. In keeping with this, Brunelleschi interiors tend to be in ungilded white plaster or, as in the case of Santo Spirito, complemented by soft grey columns in *pietra serena*. However, the grey stone is generally used to emphasise architectural forms rather than decorative devices. Yet given the bond with Donatello, some of Brunelleschi's architectural projects meld architectural and sculptural features perfectly, as seen in the decoration of Santa Croce. Here, as elsewhere, Brunelleschi's rationalism and eye for the big picture are complemented by Donatello's decorative skills.

The serene, three-naved interior of San Lorenzo, the Medici family church, with the Medici coat of arms on the ceiling.

Brunelleschi's borrowings from both the Roman and Romanesque traditions are legendary, but so, too, were his powers of invention and his talent at combining old and new in harmonious forms. On the first floor of the portico, in the Spedale degli Innocenti, pedimented windows, an authentic Roman motif, make an appearance. The architect also often incorporated elements from Florence's Romanesque buildings, notably cylindrical columns and semi-circular arches. Another favoured device took the form of slender Corinthian columns, which feature in the Spedale degli Innocenti, San Lorenzo, and in the cloisters at Santa Croce. In its harmony and simplicity, the Pazzi Chapel in Santa Croce, which took the form of a squared circle, captures the spirit of early Renaissance architecture. As for Santo Spirito, Brunelleschi's swansong, the harmonious proportions were a triumph of his synthesising approach.

Building the Cupola

After failing to design the Baptistery doors, Brunelleschi looked for a field in which Ghiberti, the victor by default, could not rival him. The design of the cupola for the Duomo was just such a challenge. He delved into the Florentine past to find a Classical style more in keeping with his aspirations than the Gothic style of most of the city's great churches. In his eyes, the Baptistery and San Miniato were mistakenly seen as Roman rather than Romanesque, which spurred him on in his quest to reassess the past and re-create the elements of Roman architecture he admired.

His vision ultimately triumphed in the creation of the cupola, recognised as the greatest civil engineering feat of the Renaissance. To build a dome over 50 metres (165 ft) in diameter was a major challenge equalled only by the Pantheon in Rome and Santa Sofia in Constantinople. The traditional costly and labour-intensive method involved wooden hoops and presumed a skilled workforce trained in such techniques; but Florence lacked both the expertise and the tradition of building in this style. Instead, Brunelleschi looked to the ancient Romans and the Pantheon for his solution. The dome may be Gothic in form but is essentially Renaissance in its engineering technique and conception. Its creation transformed Florence from a vertical city of medieval bell-towers to a horizontal Renaissance city on a more human scale. Unlike a Gothic cathedral, which overshadows the rest of the city, Brunelleschi's cupola becomes the central unifying force and makes endless connections, its harmonious form gently floating above the

Aquatint
etching of the
Duomo, by
Andrew
Ingamells,
1991.

skyline, repeating the rhythms of the encircling hills. Philosophically and politically, this democratising effect was supposed to reflect the new world order, from man's more elevated place in the universe to a greater demand for liberty. As a perfectly proportioned structure, the cupola became the confident symbol of the Renaissance.

In practical terms, the dome's octagonal shape is defined by eight marble ribs, matched by 16 ribs on the inside, with the structure strengthened by bands of stone and herring-bone patterned brickwork in the ancient Roman manner. Constructed without scaffolding, the cupola was built by means of a cantilevered system of bricks that could support itself as it ascended. As in Imperial Roman buildings, the brickwork was placed in a framework of stone beams.

Brunelleschi's other stroke of genius was to devise a system of an inner skeleton and outer dome to distribute the weight of the cupola, with thick walls negating the need for further buttressing. The space between the two concentric shells made the structure supple and light yet highly resistant. A staircase between the double domes gives a heady view of this architectural triumph. From the lantern extend views of rolling hills which take on the sensual contours of a supine body. Here is the ultimate proof of Brunelleschi's genius: the dome is at once an architectural masterpiece, an engineering marvel, an evocation of the Florentine countryside and a poetic symbol of Renaissance grace.

Brunelleschi's Florence

A stroll around Brunelleschi's Florence could begin outside the Spedale degli Innocenti, which represents his earliest façade (1419) and first significant building. From here, it is a short walk to the market district of San Lorenzo to admire the church and Old Sacristy of the same name. Just south is the Duomo, whose magnificent cupola is visible from all over the city, and, inside, a simple tombstone to the architect, the only Florentine honoured with burial here. The adjoining Baptistery *(see page 95)* represents one of the Romanesque works which inspired the architect, and is a reminder that Brunelleschi's original panel for the doors is now on display in the Bargello.

From the Cathedral, zigzag south to the river across the heart of medieval and early Renaissance Florence, dotted with landmarks known to Brunelleschi, from Dante's House *(see page 149)* to the Badia Fiorentina *(see page 103)* and the Bargello *(see page 55)*. After passing the Palazzo Vecchio *(see page 141)* and the Loggia dei Lanzi, the archetypal medieval loggia, turn right off Por Santa Maria to glance at the Palazzo di Parte Guelfa, attributed to Brunelleschi but greatly altered over the years.

The arcade of
the Spedale
degli Innocenti,
supported by
Brunelleschi's
slender
Corinthian
columns and
topped by
Della Robbia's
roundels.

The bustling Ponte Vecchio leads to Palazzo Pitti *(see page 62)*, whose central façade is supposedly based on Brunelleschi's designs. Staying in the Oltrarno means continuing west to Santo Spirito *(see page 131)*, Brunelleschi's austere last work, before re-crossing the Arno at the Ponte alle Grazie to appreciate the imposing Santa Croce and the Pazzi Chapel *(see page 119)*, a masterpiece by the Renaissance man.

ECCENTRIC PHILANTHROPISTS AND EXPATRIATE COLLECTORS

Florence in the 19th century was an open treasure-house for foreign collectors and philanthropists who settled in the city and turned their homes into virtual museums

"**G**od who created the hills of Florence was a goldsmith, engraver of medals, sculptor, bronze smelter and painter; He was a Florentine." Novelist Anatole France's description evokes the city wonders in the calculating tones of an auctioneer's catalogue. By then, acquisitiveness rather than God-given creation was the order of the day. Florence in the 19th century was a bottomless treasure pit for foreign collectors, with the patronage of the Medici replaced by the passion of private collectors. Renaissance paintings and priceless *objets d'art* could be acquired with great ease, and few questions were asked about provenance. While the Tuscan masterpieces were the obvious choices, Florence was also a centre for the burgeoning antiques trade and foreign art dealing. Not that all antiquities were spirited abroad: a cluster of collectors and philanthropists devoted their lives to safeguarding the city's artistic heritage or selfishly amassed an array of treasures before selflessly donating the collection to their adoptive city.

The beauty of Florence was a source of inspiration to poet Elizabeth Barrett Browning, captured here by John Brett in 1855.

Patrons and philistines

Anna Maria Gastone, the last of the Medici, left centuries of art treasures and palaces to the city in perpetuity. Then came a succession of patrons who, despite whimsical ways and self-indulgence, bequeathed a lasting legacy in the form of quirky museums and beguiling galleries. Some expatriates left little: the Sitwells built a "Gothick" pile on top of a genuine Gothic castle, and the romantic novelist, Ouida, behaved like the worst of English expatriates by founding nothing more than a dogs' cemetery on her death in 1909. Since the Medici heyday, however, the city institutions have mostly been enriched by non-Florentine donations. Natives tend to take their cultural heritage for granted, but outsiders have fallen in love with Florence and left their mark by founding distinctive collections.

The proverbial "paradise of exiles", Florence in the 19th century was the haunt of foreigners with tenuous reasons for settling in the city. Elizabeth Barrett Browning praised Florence as "cheap, tranquil, cheerful, beautiful, within the limits of civilisation, yet out of the crush of it". This celebrated poet aside, many genteel anglophiles were profound philistines, in Florence for reasons of economic retrenchment, there because one could live well so cheaply, "sipping champagne on a tightrope", as one wit put it. "They toil not, neither do they spin" was the cool judgement on his contemporaries by Irish novelist, Charles Lever (1806–72). Lever's biographer, William Fitzpatrick, damns the expatriate circle as "the society of diplomats and demireps, swells and snobs, princes and pretenders, wits and worthies, snarlers and social men". The writer Norman Douglas placed himself firmly in the philistine camp, curtailing Nancy Cunard's gushing over art and architecture with the snub: "Isn't all that rather Cinquecento, my dear?"

Yet there were wealthy, high-minded foreigners here for high-flown aesthetic reasons: the city was where they could best indulge their gentle bohemianism and passion for art. As early as

Bernard Berenson (1865–1959), the American art critic and expert on Italian Renaissance art, lived in Italy from 1900.

1699, the traveller Joseph Addison praised the place as a repository of "cabinets and curiosities, and vast collections of all kinds of antiquities". In sensitive eyes, the centuries of striving for artistic beauty must have soaked the walls of the city with a sense of the sublime. As the writer Francis King says: "If human nature could be redeemed through beauty, as Ruskin believed, then Florence was the ideal location for such a miracle." By association, these foreign residents felt that they owned the imaginative freehold on Florence as well as the mere property rights. And where cultural élitism led, snobbery was not far behind, with Anglo-Florentine collectors creating their own family crests and aspiring to the mantle of the Medici.

Anglophile city

As the most anglophile city in Italy, Florence has long been a magnet for English-speaking collectors and philanthropists. Consequently, the influence of the British and Americans is particularly marked in both the core collections and the quirkier museums. Foreign academic rigour also played a part in presenting Tuscan art to a new public and re-evaluating its place. This was formalised by the creation of history of art as an academic discipline, a process which started in the 1870s in England, with professorships founded in Oxford and Cambridge. In Vasari, Tuscany may have produced one of the first recognised art historians, but in the modern era John Ruskin, the English art critic and aesthete, was influential in helping to turn the tide in favour of Renaissance art. Despite the school-marmish tone of his *Mornings in Florence*, Ruskin's championing of the "Tuscan Primitives" bore fruit, both with art dealers and museum curators. In 1845, for instance, Ruskin counselled London's National Gallery against acquiring more works by Guido Reni and Rubens while it contained not a single work by Ghirlandaio or Fra' Angelico, and virtually nothing by Bellini or Perugino.

John Ruskin (1819–1900), art critic, social reformer and champion of Renaissance art.

Among connoisseurs and collectors, the 19th-century race for progress produced an artistic backlash, a desire for escapism coupled with nostalgia for an idealised past. In response, foreign collectors in Florence embarked on the pursuit of a private arcadia. Often the reaction took the form of romanticisation of the Gothic era, a period perceived as a heady amalgam of medieval chivalry and costume romp. Other collectors were inspired by the Florentine heyday, conjuring up a Renaissance stage set upon which the sun never set. Yet whether Gothic Revivalism or neo-Renaissance fervour, the desire was for works steeped in traditional values. In this context, collectors could convince themselves they were not pursuing eccentric private dreams but striving for a lost harmony in art. The Pre-Raphaelite movement tapped into the Zeitgeist, fuelling interest in sculpture of an exquisitely mystical sensibility or historical paintings in praise of famous men. In short, medieval and Renaissance works were sought after, spurring connoisseurs and dealers to cooperate to fulfil their dreams as well as make a profit.

Passion and profit were inextricably connected for all but the most prosperous collectors. Consolidating a private collection inspired by one period necessarily meant selling peripheral works that mattered less. Hence collector Herbert Horne's decision to part with his valuable English watercolours to concentrate on Tuscan treasures.

Horne and Berenson, aesthetes and collectors

Herbert Percy Horne (1864–1916) was a reclusive English architect and art historian who became an avid connoisseur of medieval and Renaissance art and an expert on Botticelli. After settling in Florence in 1896, Horne worked as an art dealer in order to fund his passion, notably the re-creation of an idealised Florentine Renaissance palazzo, perfect in every particular. The fastidious aesthete settled on the so-called Palagetto and set about restoring his new home to its Renaissance splendour, removing any later additions. Supported by Bernard Berenson, his American co-conspirator, Horne sold works to London dealers between 1899 and 1910, thereby

providing for the purchase of his palace, which he turned into a museum *(see page 154)*. In keeping with the Pre-Raphaelite tastes of his time, Horne favoured Tuscan medieval and Renaissance works, art in accord with the period of the palace. Renaissance furniture, ceramics, utensils, coins and seals were installed, and incongruous windows replaced with authentic, 15th-century, leaded glass. Today, the harmonious atmosphere is more impressive than the art within, although the works are far from negligible.

Bernard Berenson (1865–1959) dubbed Horne "the great man of the next generation", but the American was far more famous, and lionised by artistic circles in Tuscany. His autocratic reputation helped him acquire a fortune as an adviser to major museums and private collectors, and strengthened his links to the distinctly shady art dealer, Lord Duveen. Aided by Horne and British painter and critic, Roger Fry, Berenson formed core collections for the Metropolitan Museum in New York and for prestigious private collectors, including millionaire American financier, J.P. Morgan. Secure in his splendid Florentine villa, the frail yet acerbic aesthete was besieged by dealers in later years, yet continued to hold court to British and American travellers. Such was Berenson's over-refined sensibility that a manservant had to warm his wristwatch each morning lest the metal chill his skin. His art collection is an equally precious affair, favouring early Renaissance paintings by Domenico Veneziano and Cima da Conegliano as well as works by Luca Signorelli and Lorenzo Lotto. Since Berenson pioneered Renaissance studies, it is fitting that his villa, I Tatti *(see page 197)* should be Harvard University's Centre for Renaissance Studies.

The legendary wealth of American tycoon J.P. Morgan (1837–1913) made him a popular figure among satirists of the day. With Berenson's help, Morgan built a fine Italian collection, most of which is now in New York's Metropolitan Art Museum.

Stibbert's Gothic obsession

Exoticism formed a key strand in foreign collections, compounded by the colonial nostalgia of Anglo-Florentines. A taste for chinoiserie, dreamy Moorish minarets and ancient Egyptian temples was *de rigueur* in bohemian circles in late 19th-century Florence. Frederick Stibbert (1838–1906) was the classic case of a collector who succumbed to *fin de siècle* aestheticism. The inveterate traveller had agents around the world who supplied him with Ottoman armour from Constantinople, ceremonial silk robes from China, and Mogul swords from India. While no Egyptologist, he attended the opening of the Suez Canal in 1869 and luxuriated in the decadent atmosphere of ancient Egypt. His enthusiasms translated into orders for sphinxes and sarcophagi from Thebes, matched by an authentic mummy of an Egyptian priestess, all designed to adorn his Florentine temple. Nor did he overlook spoils from India, where his grandfather had served.

Born into a British colonial background in Florence, Stibbert inherited the family fortune acquired by his grandfather, a former governor of Bengal, who came back laden with Indian booty. As commander of the army of the East India Company, General Giles Stibbert was dismissed as a rich *nabob* on his return to England and his son, Thomas, married an Italian and settled in Florence. Thomas's son, Frederick, was deemed an insider in terms of social status and influence yet remained an outsider in his tastes and temperament. He distinguished himself in Garibaldi's service before abandoning the army for military spectacle and the creation of one of the world's finest collections of armour.

A dandy, soldier and dreamer, Stibbert relished historical re-enactments and took part in historical balls at the Palazzo Vecchio, but as an aesthete and gentleman of his age, his greatest passion was for the Gothic era. Blessed with a collector's nose, he was often ahead of the market: his late-Gothic wooden sculptures from Germany and the Tyrol represented a deeply unfashionable field at the time. Gothic and exotic strands are interwoven in his delicious museum, a villa steeped in decadent gloom. More than any other private collection in the city, Stibbert's villa is an anatomy of an obsession masquerading as a museum *(see page 156)*.

Atlas by Giovanni Francesco Barbieri, 1645 (Museo Bardini).

The role of philanthropists

Collectors such as Frederick Stibbert were equally committed to philanthropic gestures towards their beloved city. The Duomo's neo-Gothic façade, added in 1887, was partly paid for by Stibbert and benefactors from the foreign community. Sir Francis Sloane (of London's Sloane Square) paved the way by financing the earlier neo-Gothic façade of Santa Croce in 1857–63. Other foreign philanthropists were keen to leave their collections to landmark buildings. In 1928, Charles Loeser, an American connoisseur and heir to Macy's department store, left to the Palazzo Vecchio his art collection, including paintings and sculpture ranging from the 14th to the 16th century, especially Tuscan Old Masters by Bronzino, Cellini, Giambologna, Pontormo and Lorenzetti. His French counterpart, Louis Carrand, a benefactor from Lyons, left his collection of the decorative arts, primarily ivories and miniatures, to the Bargello in the 1880s *(see page 61)*.

Italian collectors of the era tended to play second fiddle to their more flamboyant foreign counterparts. However, Stefano Bardini (1836–1922) proved the exception. As one of the country's most important art dealers at a time when Renaissance art was under-valued, Bardini provided core Italian collections for a number of European and North American institutions, from the Isabella Stuart Gardner Museum in Boston and the National Gallery of Washington to the Hermitage and the Louvre. In Florence, his grand palace was embellished with architectural features salvaged from churches and palaces, from doors and windows to carvings and ceiling panels. Bardini's (currently closed) collection of religious paintings and Renaissance sculpture, wedding chests and weaponry was bequeathed to the city *(see page 152)*.

On a smaller scale, other Italians have contributed to the safeguarding of the city's heritage; in general, these were outsiders rather than Florentines. Salvatore Romano was a Neapolitan naval officer who loved Florence enough to save Santo Spirito and the refectory *(see page 134)* while Alberto della Ragione, a naval engineer from Livorno, was another self-taught art-lover who became an expert on modern art. He not only founded the modern collection that bears his name but supported artists such as de Chirico, de Pisis and Carra, who had fallen out of favour with the Fascist regime. Like the best of collectors, he operated on instinct, and, by no means wealthy, he chose to invest in a Modigliani rather than an apartment *(see page 171)*.

Secret agent Siviero

From the fascist period onwards, the war years created a crisis for Florentine art and architecture, not least because of the threat posed by Nazi bombing and looting. Yet the troubled era witnessed acts of heroism by curators and collectors in their attempts to safeguard the Medici collections. The city also saw curious anomalies, from a German consul who did his utmost to save art treasures from wanton destruction to a Fascist sympathiser in charge of the British Institute. Beyond all the individual gestures was the unstinting contribution made by Rodolfo Siviero (1901–83), the Tuscan art investigator, who dedicated his life to recovering stolen Italian masterpieces. The Siviero museum *(see page 151)* fancifully bills him as the James Bond of the art world, and this is not far from the truth, although few people ever knew whether this 007 was a double agent doing a bit of business for himself on the side.

Pisan-born Rodolfo Siviero studied at Florence University before reading history of art in Berlin and embarking on a life of adventure as an art detective. His methods ranged from subtle diplomacy to secreting works of art in the Pitti Palace, from armed ambushes to the halting of enemy trains en route to Germany. The Nazis were planning to remove most of the treasures from the Uffizi but Siviero

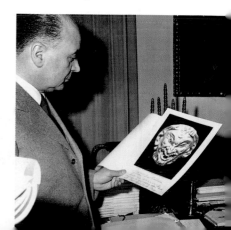

Rodolfo Siviero studying a photograph of Michelangelo's sculptured fauna mask. 1968.

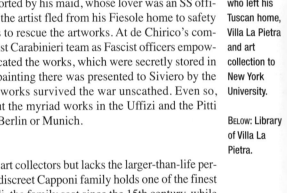

stopped a train laden with art from crossing the border into German-controlled Bolzano. On another occasion, Roman mosaics were concealed in a freight train which reached Switzerland; Siviero's agents promptly had the carriage decoupled and sent back to Florence attached to an Italian train. After the war, Siviero was made a minister with special powers for enforcing the return of looted Italian art-works.

Works pilfered by the Nazis were recovered and, until recently, were on display in the Palazzo Vecchio, but are due to be re-hung in the expanded Uffizi by 2004. Paintings hand-picked by Hitler and Goering were stolen to order. Hitler hankered after such mythological erotica as Leonardo da Vinci's *Leda and the Swan*, as well as the *Greek Discus-thrower*, which he saw as the perfect embodiment of the Aryan race. Among other works saved by Siviero were masterpieces by Titian, Leonardo, Masaccio, Veronese, Tintoretto and Cranach. His work did not end with the war: in America in the 1950s, he recovered Raphael's portrait of *Eleanora Gonzaga* and Pollaiolo's *Labours of Hercules*, which had been sold on the black market.

ABOVE: a young Harold Acton (1904–94), the Anglo-Florentine writer and benefactor who left his Tuscan home, Villa La Pietra and art collection to New York University.

Saving de Chirico

The Giorgio de Chirico painting in the Siviero Museum is a reminder that the art investigator saved the painter's works from being spirited off to Nazi Germany or destroyed as subversive. In 1943, de Chirico, who had a Jewish wife, was reported by his maid, whose lover was an SS officer based in Florence. Helped by the Resistance, the artist fled from his Fiesole home to safety with the parish priest, leaving Siviero's partisans to rescue the artworks. At de Chirico's commandeered home, Siviero presented his anti-Fascist Carabinieri team as Fascist officers empowered to search out "anti-Fascist Jews" and confiscated the works, which were secretly stored in the Pitti Palace stables. Whether the de Chirico painting there was presented to Siviero by the grateful artist himself is not known, but all the works survived the war unscathed. Even so, Siviero's real legacy is not his small museum but the myriad works in the Uffizi and the Pitti Palace, masterpieces that would otherwise be in Berlin or Munich.

BELOW: Library of Villa La Pietra.

Contemporary collectors

Contemporary Florence has a number of low-key art collectors but lacks the larger-than-life personalities of Siviero, Stibbert and Berenson. The discreet Capponi family holds one of the finest private collections, in their palace in Via de' Bardi, the family seat since the 15th century, while the patrician Corsini collection has a higher profile *(see page 158)*. In recent times, the city's most famous Anglo-Florentine benefactor was the engaging aesthete and writer, Sir Harold Acton (1904–94). Villa La Pietra, home of Acton and of his art collection, was left to New York University *(see page 196)*, while his Palazzo Lanfredini on the Arno, which serves as an English library, was left to the British Institute *(see page 175)*. Eccentric private collectors have now given way to corporate patrons, with banks, airlines and fashion houses increasingly becoming the new benefactors. Some firms are less faceless than others: the Ferragamo family are the city's most high-profile entrepreneurs, with a reputation for patronage and a portfolio ranging from fashion to property. Yet given Florentine history, it is ironic that the Ferragamo showpiece Gallery Art Hotel should display contemporary art and photography without a Michelangelo or Botticelli print in sight.

RESTORATION

Florence is Italy's conservation capital, with experts in every field of restoration – from Old Masters, sculpture, inlaid reliefs and ceramics, to frames, furniture and fabrics

If the glory of Florence is that it contains the world's greatest concentration of Renaissance art and architecture, the price is responsibility to future generations, and perpetual restoration. The American critic, Mary McCarthy, puts the dilemma forcefully: "Historic Florence is an incubus on its present population. It is like a vast piece of family property whose upkeep is too much for the heirs, who nevertheless find themselves criticised by strangers for letting the old place go to rack and ruin."

Yet there is much to celebrate, both in the city and in Tuscany as a whole. The (slightly straighter) Leaning Tower of Pisa has been unveiled to the public after a 12-year closure, while, in a grime-encrusted oratory in Siena Cathedral, the discovery of a fresco cycle that pre-dates Duccio (*c*. 1270) looks set to rewrite the Tuscan chapter in the history of art. In Florence, recent restoration triumphs include the Mannerist statuary on Piazza della Signoria and restored masterpieces by Giotto and Masaccio in Santa Maria Novella. As for the Duomo, both the façade and the frescoes in the cupola were restored in time for Holy Year 2000. The major city churches have also been well-restored, from the Strozzi chapel in Santa Maria Novella to the de Bardi and Pazzi chapels in Santa Croce.

Restoration of Fra' Angelico's *Crucifixion* in the church of San Marco.

In recent years, major rooms in the Palazzo Vecchio have been given a facelift, and the façade may soon be shrouded in scaffolding for a two-year cleaning programme. As for the Pitti Palace, although the carriage museum remains closed, an impressive rolling programme has seen most of its other galleries refurbished since 1985, matched by the gradual restoration of the grottoes and statuary in the Boboli Gardens. Elsewhere in the city, the Bardini and Davanzati museums are being revamped, but their closure is compensated for by the re-opening of the Vasari Corridor and by the restoration of artworks in the Uffizi Gallery. Even so, restoration is never-ending in Tuscany, with each significant project accompanied by public scrutiny from some of the most artistically aware citizens in Europe. In the recently restored Piero della Francesca's fresco cycle in Arezzo, for instance, the restorers have been accused of repainting rather than simply restoring.

Schools of thought

Restoration controversies are not simply a contemporary concern. Henry James reminds us that the Bargello, which we see as a wholly medieval work, was, in fact, given a neo-Gothic patina in 1865, finished shortly before his visit. The fastidious novelist found it hard to approve of these "furbished and renovated chambers" because "beautiful and masterly though the Bargello is, it smells too strongly of restoration".

Other Victorian visitors went further in their distaste for restoration, and revelled in the sense of a ruined civilisation languishing into oblivion. Charles Dickens was rather taken by the Palazzo Vecchio during its period of neglect, "a great saloon, faded and tarnished in its stately decoration, and mouldering by grains, but recording yet, in pictures on the walls, the triumphs of the Medici and the wars of the old Florentine people".

In fact, restoration has been going on since Classical times: Roman copies of Greek master-pieces were in turn considered masterpieces, and, depending on their state of repair, were restored or remodelled by Renaissance sculptors. Since then, the concept of restoration has evolved from a free interpretation of the spirit of the work to a rigorous academic study. Yet, within the restoration field, two schools of thought prevail: a modest, relativist approach that respects the damage of time, and a more daring, interventionist style that seeks to restore the work to its original state of perfection. The dangers of the latter approach range from over-restoration to a risk of obscuring the artist's original intentions. However, the finest restoration work respects the intentions of the artist while revealing new, hitherto hidden details. A case in point is Leonardo's *Annunciation* in the Uffizi, which reveals the artist's grasp of perspective and gorgeous landscape details.

A chapter of disasters

A section of Cimabue's semi-restored Crucifix – a poignant symbol of the 1966 flood (Santa Croce).

The city's restoration skills have been sorely challenged in the past 50 years, by both natural and man-made disasters. When the Arno broke its banks in 1966, the havoc caused to the city's heritage was immediate: Santa Croce was soon under water; the Duomo lost sections of its marble façade; panels from the Baptistery doors were swept away; statues from the Arno bridges were lost; over a million antiquarian books and illuminated manuscripts were destroyed; and countless artworks were damaged. Although most works have been restored to their original state, Cimabue's *Crucifix* in Santa Croce was controversially left semi-restored. Instead of re-creating the missing sections of the work, restorers simply painted in the spaces with patches of neutral colour, intended to symbolise the city's "wound". The devastating effects of the flood have encouraged conservation experts to reduce all risks. In 1990, in keeping with this policy, Ghiberti's east doors on the Baptistery were removed for safety to the Museo dell'Opera del Duomo and replaced by casts. Disaster struck again in 1993, when a Mafia bomb exploded close to the Uffizi, killing five people and gravely damaging the gallery, the Vasari Corridor and a number of works of art. It has taken the Uffizi almost a decade to recover completely.

Cloning culture

Even without disasters, Florence's perennial restoration polemics often monopolise the national arts pages. On Piazza della Signoria, the civic heart of the city, the replacement of famous statues by copies has fuelled a debate about the feasibility of displaying masterpieces outdoors. In response, the art critic of the respected *Corriere della Sera* thundered that "at this rate all the great statues in Florence will be hidden away in museums and replaced by clones".

The cloning issue divides critics, with realists opting for copies and romantics preferring the works to grow old gracefully, or disgracefully, as the case may be. The realists currently have the upper hand, arguing that the original statue can best be protected indoors whilst the outdoor replica at least re-creates the right mood and context for the work. Even so, Mary McCarthy makes a perceptive point about the inappropriateness of placing civic monuments in museums, instead of in their rightful public setting: "The civic spirit, the ghost of the republic, is imprisoned like a living person, in the marble, bronze and stone figures which appear like isolated, lonely columns, props and pillars of a society whose roof has fallen in".

The threat of pollution means that cloning carries the day, with restored statues generally replaced by copies. In a sense, the pattern was set by the removal of Michelangelo's *David* to the Accademia. The cloning process is already underway in the Loggia dei Lanzi, where Giambologna's mesmerising *Rape of the Sabine Women* should soon be replaced by a copy. The Bargello tells a similar story, with sculptures from the courtyard being moved to the museum loggia as soon as restoration is complete. In the case of newly restored sculpture from the Loggia dei Lanzi, the Bargello represents the natural home but the Accademia, given its Michelangelo link, makes a strong case for inclusion. Donatello's heraldic lion, known as the Marzocco, now resides in the Bargello, leaving its pale leonine shadow in the Loggia dei Lanzi. Cellini's *Perseus*, a work of bravura brilliance restored in 2001, is expected to move to a museum, probably the Bargello, since the original pedestal is already on display there. Meanwhile, the bronze sculpture is being monitored, on the assumption that bronzes tolerate pollution better than marble. Equally logical is the decision to move Donatello's restored *Judith and Holofernes* into the Palazzo Vecchio, leaving a copy on view in the Piazza della Signoria below.

Return to the churches

Cellini's Perseus (1554) in the Loggia dei Lanzi on Piazza della Signoria, was restored to its former glory in 2001.

A welcome trend in conservation is the return of artworks to the churches for which they were created. Until recently, it was considered more important to display the works stripped of context in easily accessible museums. Reflecting this shift in policy, Michelangelo's wooden *Crucifix* has recently been restored to Santo Spirito, its original location, much to the delight of the resident Augustinian friars. In Santa Maria Novella, Masaccio's trailblazing fresco of the *Trinity* (*c*. 1424; *see page 19*) has returned to view after a two-year restoration, while Giotto's equally revolutionary *Painted Cross* (1288–90) has also returned to the nave after a 12-year absence. Both the Santa Maria Novella masterpieces were restored by the Opificio delle Pietre Dure, Italy's foremost restoration centre, which has its origins in the craft workshops created by the Medici (*see page 169*).

The angel in Leonardo's beautifully restored Annunciation (pictured fully on pages 86-7).

Positive moves

Architecturally, one of the most significant projects is the mooted restoration of the city's Roman walls, allowing for walks along the stretch by Porta Romana. However, in this clubby and recalcitrant city, official decisions are slow to materialise. In the meantime, virtually all the major museums and galleries are seeking funds to take masterpieces out of storerooms and put them into the public domain. The pressure on display space means that various collections fall into limbo and disappear for decades. The Uffizi has recently decided to confront the problem head-on, in an exhibition entitled "I Mai Visti" (Never Before Seen), a display of long-hidden treasures, including works purloined by the Nazis (*see page 34*).

In terms of glamour, Florentine restoration projects cannot compete with the seductive allure of Venice, slowly sinking beneath the waves, and a "Florence in Peril" fund would not wring the tears or funds from foreign benefactors. Even so, Florence has been reaping the rewards of foreign involvement. The Friends of Florence have been active in restoring statuary on the Piazza della Signoria, boosted by the introduction of the Florence in the World Card, created in association with the tourist board. Membership is a way of contributing to specific restoration projects and also confers benefits such as free entrance to museums. The city is set to expand its cultural role, with conservation and restoration declared core values. As a move to decentralise Rome's lumbering cultural bureaucracy, Vittorio Sgarbi, a media-friendly art historian and Italy's controversial minister for culture, is planning to set up a permanent office in the Pitti Palace. The justification is that "Florence has the greatest concentration of art in Europe," but the less charitable see it as a ploy to acquire a sumptuous new office. If he does so, the Pitti should not have to look far for restoration funding.

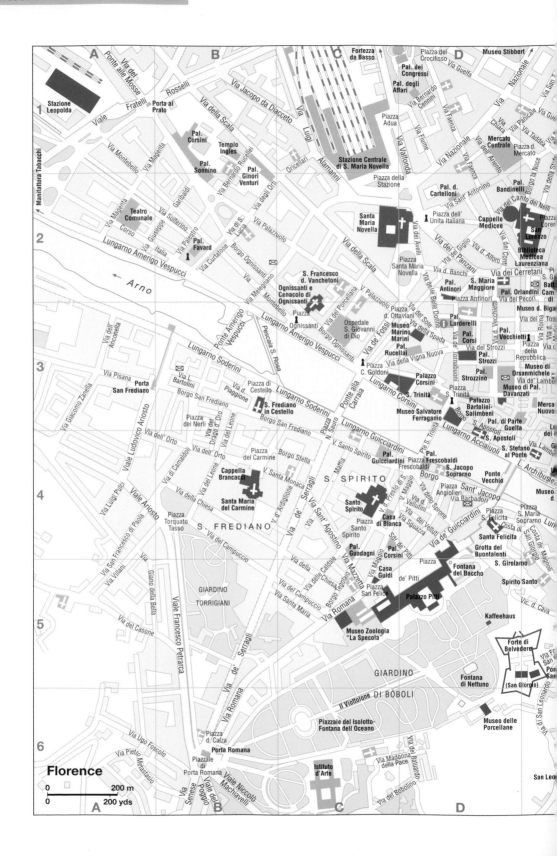

Florence

0   200 m

0   200 yds

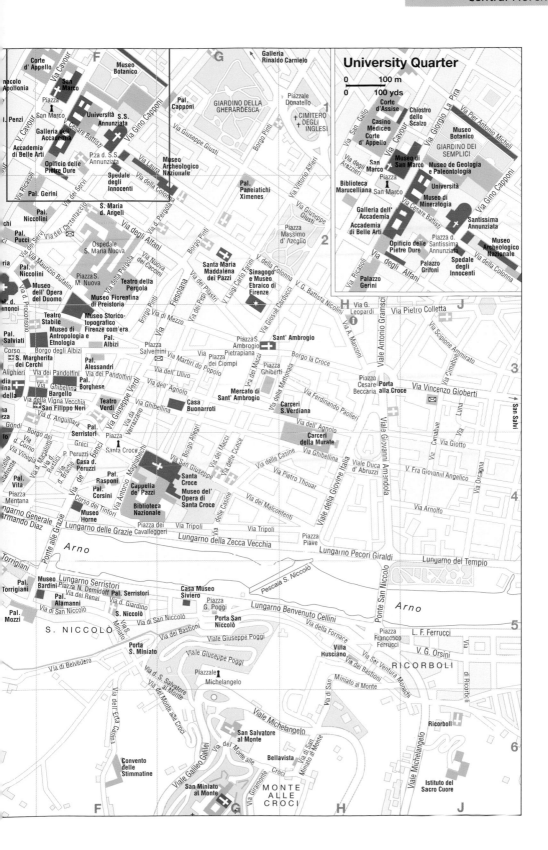

University Quarter

0   100 m

0   100 yds

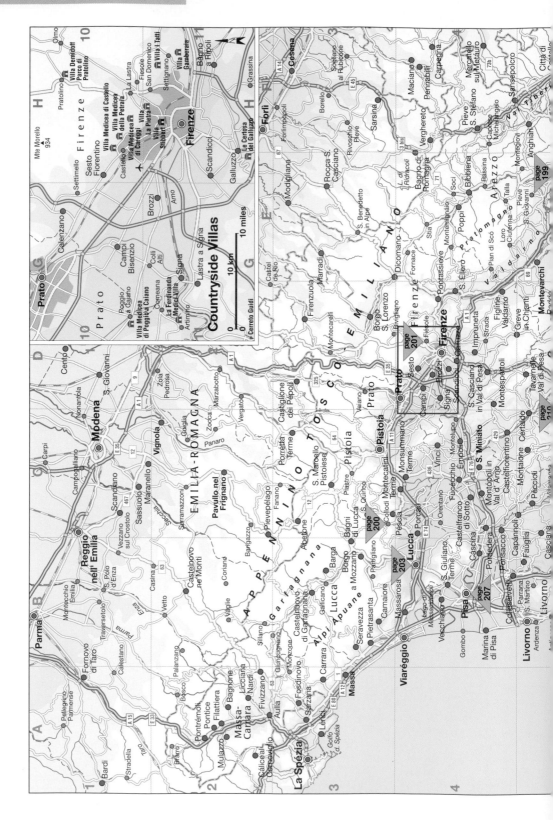

Countryside Villas

0   10 km
0   10 miles

Villa Demidoff
Parco di
Pratolino

Villa Medicea di Castello
Villa Medicea
della Petraia
Villa Medicea
di Careggi
La Pietra
Villa
Stibbert

Villa I Tatti
Bagno
a Ripoli
Gamberaia

Firenze

Le Certosa
del Galluzzo

Villa Medicea
di Poggio a Caiano
La Ferdinanda
Medici Villa

Cerreto Guidi

Map (main region)

EMILIA-ROMAGNA

Modena

Parma

Reggio
nell' Emilia

Vignola

Pavullo nel
Frignano

APPENNINO TOSCO - EMILIANO

Garfagnana

Alpi Apuane

Massa-
Carrara

Massa

La Spézia

Viaréggio

page 200
page 203
Lucca
page 207
Pisa
Livorno

Pistóia
Prato
Firenze
Sesto

page 201

Pratomagna
Val d'Arno
Arezzo

Forlì
Cesena

S. Miniato

page 210

page 199

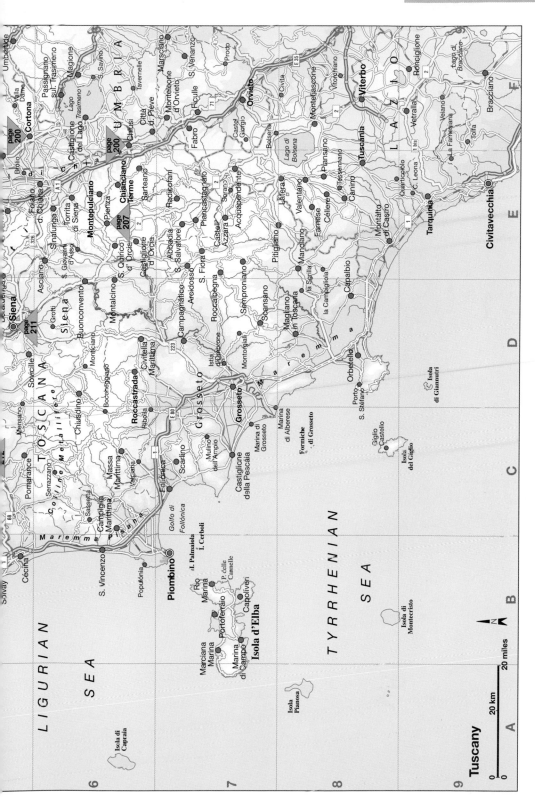

Tuscany

0   20 km
0   20 miles

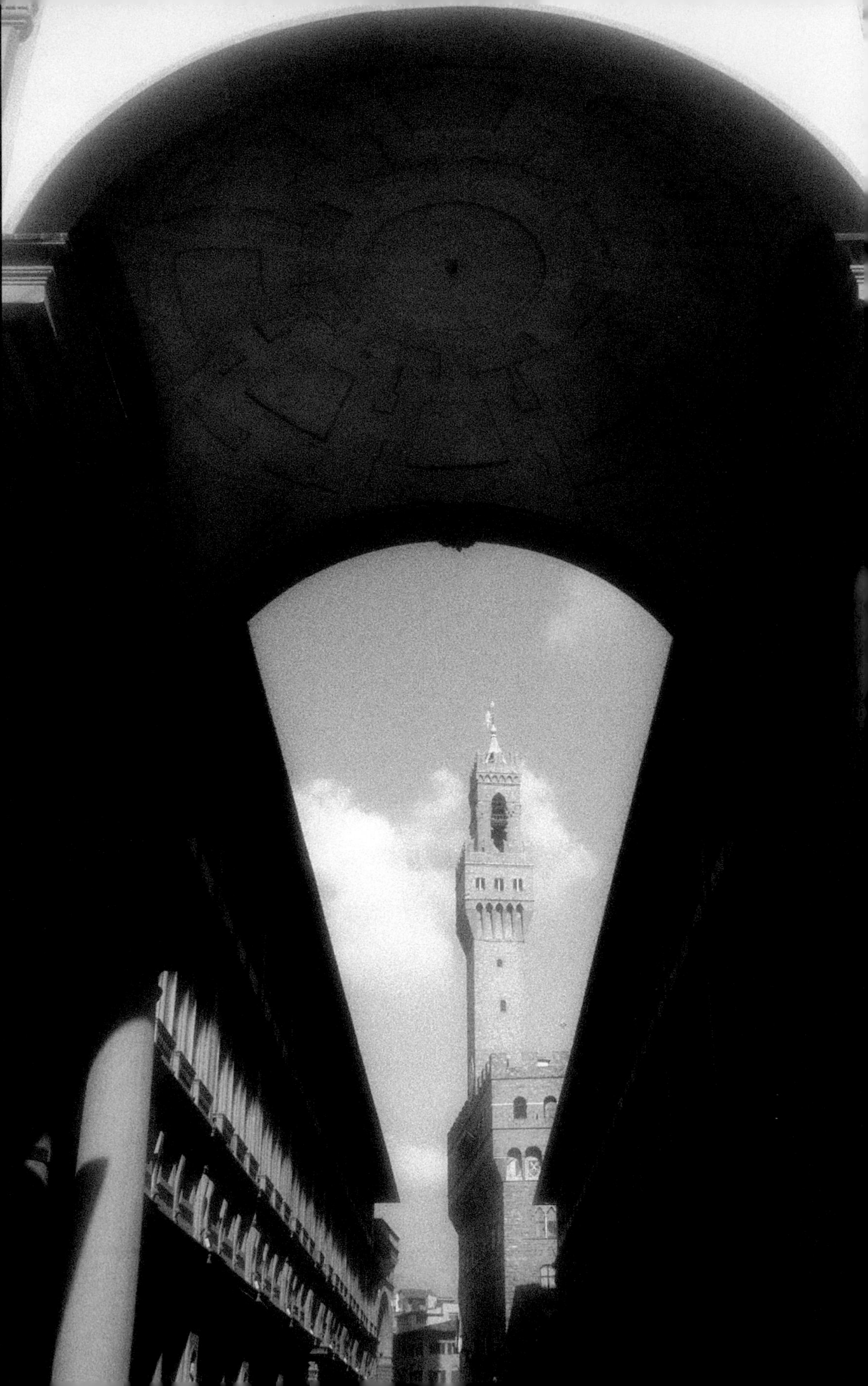

THE FLORENTINE MIRACLE

The essence of Florence is art and artistry, a glittering legacy linked to Renaissance riches and the patronage of the Medici dynasty, further enriched by underrated collections of medieval and modern art

As the birthplace of the Renaissance, Florence witnessed a flowering of the human spirit that has left a lasting artistic imprint. As a result of this "Florentine miracle", financed largely by the Medici rulers, the city's countless churches, palaces and galleries are guardians of the world's greatest concentration of Renaissance art and sculpture. Yet Florence has also been shaped by the passion of the many foreign and Italian collectors who subsequently settled in the city and turned their homes into virtual museums. Over the course of centuries, eccentric philanthropists and languid aesthetes, from Horne and Stibbert to Bardini, Berenson and Acton have greatly enriched the Florentine treasure-house.

The heart of this book belongs to the collections themselves, classified for convenience into the following categories. First and foremost are the "Major Collections", which embrace the Uffizi Gallery, the Pitti Palace, the Accademia and the Bargello, and represent the city's most prestigious painting and sculpture galleries. "Religious Buildings" is a section devoted to art in the service of spirituality, even if the lavish art collections on display rival any in the material world. Apart from the Duomo (Cathedral) and the Baptistery, special emphasis is given to the artistic treasures in San Marco, San Lorenzo and the Carmine, as well as to the landmark churches of Santa Maria Novella, Santa Croce and Santo Spirito. Peculiar to Florence is the role of the "Public Palaces and Private Homes", a category which embraces collections in historic buildings worthy of attention in their own right.

The chapter on "Modern Arts and Ancient Crafts" puts the spotlight on post-Renaissance art and craftsmanship, so often forgotten, reminding us that Florentine art did not die with the Medici dynasty. This includes a short section on "Exhibition Centres" focusing on the city's multi-functional showcases for art and antiques, fashion and photography, cinema and culture.

Often dismissed as minor museums, the city's lesser-known museums and galleries are not simply retreats for a rainy afternoon. All satisfy special interests while the best serve as engaging haunts which provide a break from the relentless outpouring of Renaissance art. The museums featured in the short "History and Archaeology" chapter are dominated by prehistoric, Roman, Egyptian and Etruscan artefacts, antiquarian books and topographical paintings. (The Florentine historian, Francesco Guicciardini, 1483–1540, is considered one of the founders of modern history). Equally underrated are the university-run museums of "Science and Nature" featuring botanical, geological and zoological collections that are a testament to Florentine inventiveness.

The final two chapters take you out of the claustrophobic heart of Florence to the beautiful villas and gardens of its outskirts and further afield to the art treasures of the historic Tuscan towns of Arezzo, Lucca, Pisa, Siena, San Gimignano and Volterra.

PRECEDING PAGES: View of the Piazza del Duomo, the religious heart of Florence; the skyline of San Gimignano, one of Tuscany's best-preserved medieval towns.
LEFT: The Palazzo Vecchio belltower framed by the Uffizi galleries.

The Major Collections

When it comes to Renaissance art, Florence has no rival. From Cimabue to Caravaggio, the sheer number of masterpieces held in the Uffizi, the Accademia, the Bargello and the Pitti is overwhelming

Galleria dell' Accademia

Home of Michelangelo's best-known sculptures (*David* and the *Four Slaves*) as well as of Florentine and Tuscan art from the 14th to the 16th century

Map reference: page 43, F1
Via Ricasoli 60
Tel: 055-2388609 (general information); 055-294883 (reservation line – for a small fee you can fix an entry time slot; lines open Mon–Fri 8.30am–6.30pm, Sat 8.30am–noon)
Bus: 1, 6, 7, 17
Open: Tues–Sun 8.30am–6.50pm ; Sat until 10pm in summer; last entry 45 mins before closing.
Bookshop. Audio-guide. Admission charge.

Michelangelo's original *David* (1504) takes centre stage in the Accademia.

Most visitors dutifully come to gasp over Michelangelo's *David* and then call it a day, scarcely realising that this is one of the city's finest galleries. The collection dates back to a school of fine arts founded by Cosimo I de' Medici in 1563, with the gallery consolidated in 1784 by Grand-duke Pietro Leopoldo, the most enlightened of the Lorraine dynasty. Although many treasures have been moved to the Uffizi and San Marco, the remaining array of Florentine, Byzantine and Gothic art justifies a visit, without the added inducement of Michelangelo. Yet there is no denying the fact that the foremost sculptor of his age, or arguably of all time, is well represented by the authentic *David*, the centrepiece of the museum, and by his magnificently unfinished *Four Slaves*.

The first two ground floor rooms currently focus on Michelangelo's works, framed by sculpture and paintings by his contemporaries. However, since newly restored statuary from the Loggia dei Lanzi on Piazza della Signoria (*see pages 146–7*) is due to be displayed here, the collection may be re-arranged; even so, *David* is certain to stay in his present position. Giambologna's impressive plaster cast for the *Rape of the Sabine Women* (1582) is expected to be joined by the newly restored marble sculpture itself, which is currently on Piazza della Signoria.

Sculpture has been a Florentine art form since the Middle Ages, when citizens boldly carried statuary into battle, rather than a mere standard. As for Renaissance times, even the city's greatest rivals admitted that the Florentines produced the foremost civic sculpture, work intended to convey the values of the city-state for centuries to come.

Product of an heroic age

In the work both of Donatello and, especially, that of Michelangelo, admirers were awed by the restraint, the control, the Classicising spirit of the sculpture. It is therefore no coincidence that *David*, the city's most deified statue, was produced in an heroic age of sculpture. In public-minded Florentine fashion, it was placed in front of the Palazzo Vecchio (*see page 146*), intended to teach a civic lesson.

In keeping with the city rulers' dissimulation of power, ostentation and self-aggrandisement were publicly frowned upon in Florence, as was the glorification of the individual. Yet the statue became both the symbol of liberty and a symbol of the artistic aspirations of the city.

Seen in meditative pose, preparing for his fight with Goliath, *David* evokes the patriotic image of a small state challenging, and defeating, a supposedly superior foe. The youth's traditional sling is barely visible, reinforcing the impression that David owes his victory to innocence and grace rather than to brute strength.

David, a celebration of the nude

As the most famous sculpture in Western art, *David* has immediate appeal, thanks both to the sculpture's recognition factor and to its accessibility. To most modern visitors, *David* is a celebration of the nude, a timeless icon of virility, stripped of his original cultural and political significance. It is therefore remarkable that, even without any artistic background, the average high-school student is still awed into an appreciation of Renaissance art through Michelangelo's boyish ambassador.

OPPOSITE: *Adoration of the Magi* by Gentile da Fabriano, 1423 (Galleria degli Uffizi).

MICHELANGELO IN FLORENCE

Michelangelo Buonarroti (1475–1564), the quintessential Renaissance man, sculptor, architect and poet, has left an enduring legacy in his home city. To their foes, Florentines were known for their self-righteousness, ferocious independence and boundless ambition, characteristics that come together in Michelangelo. As an artist, he was an unfettered spirit, but his fellow citizens and patrons often found his work arrogant, daring and demanding. Michelangelo the man was even more problematic: he was considered ungracious, irascible, stern and suffering from a persecution complex.

For his part, Michelangelo was intensely envious of Raphael and Bramante, whom he felt found more favour with patrons. In Florence, he progressed from working under his mentor, Ghirlandaio, to fulfilling commissions for his Medici patrons, Lorenzo the Magnificent and Leo X. The sculptor worked for the Medici dynasty until 1494, after which Julius II, the warrior Pope, commissioned the tortured genius to work on his mausoleum in 1501, then on the Sistine Chapel. Summoned back to Florence by Giuliano de' Medici in 1520, Michelangelo worked on the Medici chapel in San Lorenzo, but remained characteristically critical of his fellow citizens, including his patrons: "I never had to do with a more ungrateful and arrogant people than the Florentines."

Although the Accademia is considered the temple to Michelangelo, his works are also on display in the Bargello *(see page 57)*, the Medici Chapels *(see page 109)* and the Michelangelo Museum – Casa Buonarotti *(see page 148)*.

The Awakening Slave (1519–20), one of Michelangelo's four "unfinished" slaves, intended for the tomb of Pope Julius II in Rome.

Sculpted between 1501 and 1504, the masterpiece was made out of a huge block of marble that had been bungled by a lesser sculptor. Undeterred, the 29-year-old sculptor took up the challenge of carving the largest statue made since classical times. Although, as already mentioned, the colossal sculpture was originally erected in front of the Palazzo Vecchio, in 1873 it was installed, with much pomp, in a specially created Tribune in the Accademia.

When criticising the gigantism of the work, as some do, it has to be remembered that the statue was intended for a large civic space, not designed to be cooped up in a corner of a museum. Even at the time of the move, critics complained that the cramped space and the fragmented, fussy background detracted from the majesty of the sculpture. However, English essayist, William Hazlitt, who had the good fortune to see the original statue outside the Palazzo Vecchio in 1821, was still unimpressed: "It looks like an awkward overgrown actor at one of the minor theatres without his clothes; the head is too big for the body; and it has a helpless expression of distress." Despite any such reservations about its proportions and setting, modern critics conclude that the sculpture remains one of the most powerful works in Western art. Giorgio Vasari, Michelangelo's reluctantly admiring contemporary, concurred, praising its grace, serenity, proportion and harmony: "This figure has overshadowed every other statue, ancient or modern, Greek or Roman."

The Four Slaves

David may be the centrepiece of the museum but the so-called *Nonfiniti (Unfinished) Slaves* illustrate the magnitude of Michelangelo's talent and ambition. Also known as *The Prisoners*, these four sculptures were intended for the tomb of Pope Julius II in Rome. Instead, the statues were presented to the Medici and placed in a grotto in the Boboli Gardens until 1909, when they joined the Michelangelo collection here. These four muscular works, sculpted between 1519 and 1536, range from the virtually finished to the barely blocked out. Critics are divided as to whether the works were left unfinished because the sculptor was dissatisfied with them, or whether Michelangelo's restless genius simply moved onto new challenges.

These works emphasise the sculptor's epic humanity, his concentration on the human body alone, devoid of impediments. In the brooding intensity of his figures we sense the laying bare of the innate idea, the eternal truth that his art strove to

Deposition from the Cross, begun by Filippino Lippi and completed by Perugino, 1503–5.

attain. More clearly than in other masterpieces, these works reveal Michelangelo's philosophy: the genesis of a sculpture is not the classic shaping of art out of chaos but the struggle to free a creature that already exists. If the *Four Slaves* are struggling to free themselves from inert matter, it is a metaphor for Michelangelo's vision of the sculpture as a prisoner in stone, just as the soul is prisoner of the body. The sculptor referred to this paring down as a prerequisite for all his statues: "By sculpture, I understand an art that takes away superfluous material; by painting, one that attains the result by laying on."

Even though Michelangelo's paintings have a rare sculptural quality, only the sculpted naked body can express his most sublime concepts.

As a tortured artist who saw only God as his rival, Michelangelo was an unfettered spirit, or, more accurately, an artist fettered to his fearsome talent. Flattery in marble was never his aim; indeed, the sculptor liked to leave signs of roughness on his finished work, perhaps to leave clues as to his creative technique, to show the torment behind creation, or simply to highlight his imperfect perfection. In fact, when Michelangelo so chose, his technique was equal to recreating classical perfection.

The Florentine master not only stands comparison with the great sculptors of antiquity, but his work has been occasionally mistaken for Greek or Roman statuary. Yet, given the tyranny of his genius, Michelangelo felt that all creation was stacked against him. As Vasari said, "Michelangelo detested to imitate the living person unless it were one of incomparable beauty".

Unfinished masterpiece

Despite its unfinished state, *The Awakening Slave* (*pictured opposite*) most clearly shows the struggle of the enslaved man to free himself from his marble prison. His face is sketchily blocked in, but dramatic tension is created by his straining limbs. By comparison, *The Young Slave*, the first statue on the right, is less virile, less tormented, and depicted with his arm wearily shielding his head. *St Matthew*, the next statue on the right, is not part of the *Slaves* group but was designed as the first of *Twelve Apostles* to adorn the columns of Florence Cathedral. However, this statue was left unfinished and the others never attempted.

Next is *Atlas*, bent under the burden of his huge unformed head, and, facing him, *The Bearded Slave*, the statue closest to completion. His brooding energy is matched by the clear, relief modelling of his muscular body, which shows Michelangelo's intimate understanding of the male nude. The final statue of the group is a touching *Pietà*, which was traditionally ascribed to Michelangelo but whose attribution is disputed by modern critics.

Turn to the paintings

After circling *David* in the Tribune, the specially designed section at the end of the Gallery of the Slaves, turn your back on sculpture for the rest of the visit. Michelangelo's contemporaries are represented by well-chosen paintings in the same section of the gallery. Apart from Andrea del Sarto's poignant fresco, *Christ as a Man of Sorrows*, the highlights are Fra' Bartolomeo's *The Prophets*, influenced by Michelangelo's Sistine Chapel frescoes in Rome, and a gorgeously coloured *Deposition*, begun by Filippino Lippi but finished by Perugino.

The adjoining Florentine rooms offer a complete change of mood, replacing Michelangelo's muscular realism with the dignified formality of Florentine madonnas. The artworks complement the early masterpieces in the Uffizi *(see page 89)*, putting flesh on the bones of the Florentine Gothic tradition. A recent rearrangement allows for a fresh approach to the period running from Giotto (*c.* 1266–1337) to Masaccio (1401–*c.* 1428).

Sale del Duecento e Trecento

Set off the Tribune and the Gallery of the Slaves, the earliest of these adjoining rooms are known as the Sale del Duecento e Trecento and display 13th- and 14th-century works, a collection of gilded altarpieces and panels amassed from Florentine churches and monasteries. The late 13th-century works, the earliest art on display, are termed Byzantine paintings, thanks to their gold backgrounds, static postures and solemn expressions. The *Mary Magdalene* by an anonymous artist depicts a typically static central figure framed by livelier side scenes which show the innovative influence of Cimabue.

By comparison, *Saint Cecilia*, painted by a contemporary of Giotto in soft, luminous colours, shows far greater expressiveness. Opposite is the intriguing *Tree of Life* by Pacino di Buonaguida, a complex and highly decorative genealogy of Christ, with Christ on the Cross as its centrepiece. Above Christ's head is a pelican, a symbol of self-sacrifice, maternal and divine love, and a reminder that, just as the pelican will tear open her own breast to feed her young, so Christ sacrificed himself to save humanity. The other highlight in this room is a 13th-century wooden cross which adorned the church of Santa Maria del Carmine until 1956. Previously attributed to Duccio or Cimabue, it is now thought to be the work of Gaddo Gaddi.

Sala dei Giotteschi

The adjoining room, the Sala dei Giotteschi, is devoted to contemporaries and followers of Giotto, notably Taddeo Gaddi and Bernardo Daddi. The latter's *Painted Cross* is modelled on a late medieval tradition which held that the gilded image should be placed above the iconostasis. In Giotto's day, painted crosses were generally placed over the high altar and were intended to foster communion with the faithful. Giotto's painted cross for Santa Maria Novella became the model for such works as Daddi's. The Giotto-esque painter is also represented here by his *Coronation of the Virgin*, distinguished by its narrative detail. Taddeo Gaddi, Giotto's closest follower,

Front panel of a *cassone*, or wedding chest, painted by Lo Scheggia, depicting a wedding scene in front of the Baptistery *c.* 1450

is responsible for a *Madonna and Child* and for *Scenes from the Life of St Francis*, painted for Santa Croce. These lively episodes show a painterly understanding of perspective that was gleaned from Giotto's innovative approach.

Sala degli Orcagna

The following room, the Sala degli Orcagna, is dedicated to the Orcagna school, a family of 14th-century artists defined by their rigid monumentality and decorative repertoire. Andrea Orcagna's *Pentecost* is a triptych whose traditional colouring made it a perfect adornment for a Romanesque church. Given that artists of the period were expected to double as sculptors and architects, it is perhaps unsurprising that this painting shows an almost architectural spatial sense. Orcagna's brother, Iacopo di Cione, is responsible for the more animated *Episodes from the Childhood of Christ* and the flamboyantly decorative *Coronation of the Virgin*.

Fifteenth-century paintings

Also on the ground floor are the (often closed) Sale del Quattrocento Fiorentino, rooms dedicated to 15th-century Florentine painting, including a mysterious Paolo Uccello masterpiece. Entitled *Scenes of Hermit Life*, the painting depicts spiritual trials and a meditative path of truth. Here, too, is the masterpiece known as the *Cassone Adimari* by Lo Scheggia, Masaccio's brother. The vividly painted scene, depicting a sumptuous wedding procession, has much in common with the decorative detail in works by Carpaccio in Venice. Another highlight is the lovely *Annunciation* by Neri di Bicci, which depicts an accomplished painting within a painting. Equally striking is the majestic altarpiece, *Saints Stephen, James and Peter*, which is now attributed to Domenico Ghirlandaio, who ran one of the most productive workshops in 15th-century Florence.

Botticelli is credited with two works here, of which only one, the lovely *Virgin and Child*, seems certain to be his. The other, the more affecting *Virgin at the Sea* could conceivably have been painted by Filippino Lippi.

Tree of Life by Pacino di Buonaguida, c. 1305–10.

The survey continues

From here, a glass corridor leads to the exit and the stairs to the first floor, where the survey of late Gothic Florentine painting continues. The first room is dominated by a Giotto-esque *Christ as a Man of Sorrows* by Giovanni da Milano, a poignant panel of greater depth than the Orcagna works displayed on the floor below. The Como-born artist was considered a Florentine and painted this work for Santa Croce.

The second room contains works which are as much a tribute to the quality of Florentine Gothic craftsmanship as they are to the city's artistic tradition. In particular, Giovanni del Biondo's complex panel painting is composed and carved with supreme craftsmanship. However, the greatest painting in his section is Pietro Gerini's *Christ as the Man of Sorrows*, which is currently being restored. The panel refers to the practice of flagellation which was widespread in Florence: visible behind Christ are the grim instruments of torture, ranging from a whip, a lance, a hammer and nails to a sponge dipped in bile.

Monaco's masterpieces

The next room contains masterpieces by Lorenzo Monaco (1370–1425), considered the greatest exponent of Florentine Gothic. His best paintings clearly show the transition from Gothic to Renaissance, a bridge that is at the heart of Florentine art. His *Christ as a Man of Sorrows* is just such a work, as is his *Virgin Enthroned with Saints*, which combines the artist's decorative skills with a new fluidity and expressiveness.

Monaco's *Annunciation* sees him at the peak of his powers yet also displays the love of colour and gilding that betray his origins as an illustrator of illuminated manuscripts. The gallery ends on a slight anti-climax, with the rooms devoted to International Gothic style and, somewhat incongruously, to a collection of Russian icons amassed by the acquisitive Grand-dukes of Lorraine.

FOOD AND DRINK: Fiaschetteria (Via degli Alfani 70r, corner of Via dei Servi; Mon–Sat 9am–7pm) is a rough and ready wine bar for pasta, Tuscan snacks and local wines. See also San Marco, page 113.

Virgin and Child with Two Angels and St John by Botticelli, *c.* 1468.

The Bargello

A major collection of Renaissance and Mannerist sculpture (from Donatello and Michelangelo to Giambologna and Cellini) in one of the city's most historic palaces. Also holds a fine decorative arts collection, from ivories to arms and ceramics

Map reference: page 43, F3
Via del Proconsolo 4
Tel: 055-2388606 (general information); 055-294883 (reservation line: for a small fee you can fix an entry time slot; lines open Mon–Fri 8.30am–6.30pm, Sat 8.30am–noon)
www.sbas.firenze.it
Bus: A, 14 and 23
Open: Tues–Sat 8.15am–1.50pm, also 2nd and 4th Sun of month and 1st, 3rd and 5th Mon of month; last entry 45 mins before closing time
Bookshop. Wheelchair access. School visits on request. Admission charge.

U nlike the Accademia or even the Uffizi, the Bargello would be a major site even without its museum full of treasures. As the oldest surviving seat of government in Florence, the Bargello was the predecessor of the Palazzo Vecchio *(see page 141)*. Both were symbols of civic power but the earlier building is a more fortified affair, with its forbidding façade chiselled out of square blocks of stone in 1250.

Designed as the headquarters of the Capitano del Popolo, the Ghibelline ruler, the palace then became the seat of the rival, ultimately victorious, Guelf faction, which controlled the city. (Throughout the 13th century, Florence was torn apart by the Guelf–Ghibelline conflict, a ferocious struggle for territory and power. In broad terms, the Guelfs supported the Pope and the Ghibellines the German Holy Roman Emperor.) The battlemented fortress remained the seat of the Podestà, the governing magistrate, until 1502 *(see box)*. In 1547, in a later incarnation, the building became known as the Bargello, when it housed the military arm of the city-state, including the police force and prisons.

Today, signs of its grim past are scarce: a pleasant well occupies the site of the former scaffold. However, as if to confirm Florentine gallows humour, the side of the palace facing Via Ghibellina was once frescoed with portraits of condemned traitors. This gruesome practice continued until the death penalty was

Florence Victorious over Pisa by Giambologna, 1575.

FROM PODESTÀ TO PRISON

The Bargello became the Palazzo del Podestà, the seat of the city's chief magistrate, in 1260. The office of Podestà came into being in 1193, willed by the merchants and the people, who resented the domination of the *magnati*, the landowning nobility and military class. As the de facto head of the commune, the Podestà was charged with maintaining the peace and mediating between the city's rival factions. To ensure impartiality, the ruler was generally a non-Florentine. Yet the political irony was that power ultimately went to the Medici, whose appeal was originally predicated on support for the *popolo minuto*, the powerless lower classes. The Medici made short shrift of any democratic niceties: the office of Podestà was promptly abolished by Cosimo I and the Bargello became a prison and the headquarters of the chief of police.

Badia Fiorentina and the Bargello, when it was still a prison, by Giuseppe Zocchi (1711–67).

abolished in 1786. The Bargello then benefited from 19th-century Romanticism and the revival of interest in medievalism. After the discovery of frescoes attributed to Giotto in the chapel, the fate of the Bargello was sealed, and an impressive museum was born.

Probably built by the Dominican friar responsible for Santa Maria Novella, the oldest part of the palace dates from 1255 and faces onto Via del Proconsolo, with the rear of the building modelled on the original designs but built a century later. The stern Gothic structure is dominated by a crenellated corner tower containing the bell that once summoned Florentines to battle or warned of an imminent siege. The top storey is crowned by crenellations added in 1323, with the graceful ground-floor staircase connecting to a first-floor loggia added shortly afterwards. The Gothic courtyard, centred on the well, staircase and Mannerist statuary, is the most appealing part of the building.

Beneath a colonnade in the courtyard is the impressive sculpture *Oceanus* (The Ocean), by Giambologna (1529–1608), the Flemish-born Mannerist; a copy of this work is in the Boboli Gardens (*see page 76*). Under the adjoining colonnade stands a group of statues intended for an allegorical fountain in the Palazzo Vecchio. However, these mythological works by Ammannati (1556–63) eventually languished in the Boboli Gardens, moved there for the delectation of the Grand-dukes.

A sense of the Renaissance

The Bargello is the best place to gain a sense of the inter-connectedness of Florentine Renaissance sculpture. Even if the Uffizi and the Accademia offer complementary collections, the Bargello provides the clearest overview, with works of art by the greatest masters, from Donatello to Michelangelo. Moreover, despite the virtuosity of Michelangelo, the Bargello is more of a shrine to his predecessor, Donatello, the only sculptor to lay claim to equal, if less-acclaimed gifts.

As for the array of work on display, its importance has as much to do with the changing role of collecting and patronage as to the outpouring of artistic talent in 15th-century Florence. The collection shows the transition between statuary flaunted as public symbols and sculpture appreciated as private treasures.

The sculpture is the mainstay of the museum; the rest of the collection is composed of various miniature worlds, from medieval and Renaissance ivories and enamels to period jewellery and fabrics.

Compared with the city's other major museums, the Bargello is poorly labelled, but this should not detract from one's pleasure. More detrimental, however, is the closure of numerous sections of the museum and the loan of works to other collections. The loggia, which displays some of Giambologna's finest statues, is currently being restored, while the arms collection is closed indefinitely, with other rooms often out of bounds in summer, in most cases due to staff shortage.

Sala del Cinquecento

The main sculpture gallery off the courtyard, the Sala del Cinquecento, is guarded by heraldic lions that once graced the Piazza della Signoria. The room is a testament to the wealth of Florentine sculpture, from statuettes and models to busts and bas-reliefs in bronze and marble by masters such as Michelangelo, Cellini and Giambologna. Works by Giambologna (1529 1608) are dotted throughout the museum, with one of his masterpieces, *Mercury*, on display here. This delicate, influential statue, designed to adorn a fountain, has become the definitive image of the winged messenger.

An earlier master of bronze, Benvenuto Cellini (1500–71), a goldsmith turned sculptor, was celebrated for his refined yet expressive works inspired by Hellenistic models. His convoluted sculptures often border on the ostentatious and his vision falls far short of Michelangelo's, but Cellini's works are not to be dismissed. His *Narcissus* may border on the fey but his *Ganymede* is impressive, composed of a Hellenistic torso to which he added a convincingly naturalistic head and arms. This work was a favourite of Cosimo I, as was Cellini's bronze *Perseus*, a masterpiece created for the Piazza della Signoria *(see page 147)*. Given the importance of his patron, Cosimo I, it is fitting that Cellini should also have created a fine bust of the Medici ruler, with a breastplate studded with decorative detail.

A handful of Michelangelos

Michelangelo is represented by a handful of sculptures here, including his leitmotif male nudes in movement. As a solitary, troubled individualist, he was torn between the call of pagan philosophy, Classicism and Christian values, themes which find an echo in his works. His *Bacchus Drunk*, which ended up in the Medici collection, is a youthful work showing considerable grace and artistry, as well as the influence of classical models. The contrast is between the sober-

looking young god of wine who holds a drinking goblet aloft and the cloven-hoofed satyr impishly nibbling grapes behind him.

By contrast, the *Pitti Tondo*, depicting a Madonna and Child with a young St John, is a slightly more evolved work. The marble bas-relief, an example of the *schiacciato* (lit. squashed or flattened) technique, allows the sculptor to play with the blurred outlines and subtle shading that characterise his later work.

Apollo is a more mature work and gives some sense of Michelangelo's evolution, even if the work was relegated to the Boboli Gardens after the death of Cosimo I. The sculptor's creative torment is hinted at in the typical tension of the pose, known as a *contrapposto* (or serpentine) pose, seen in Apollo's graceful stretching behind his head to grasp an arrow from his quiver. In this statue there is a foretaste of how, as a classically inspired artist, Michelangelo became the first Mannerist sculptor and then paved the way for baroque. Finally, *Brutus*, the only known bust by Michelangelo, is a virtuoso model of masterful determination, commissioned by an opponent to the Medici and imbued with political significance.

Donatello

Those single-mindedly in pursuit of Renaissance sculpture would do well to head straight for the so-called Donatello Gallery, situated on the first floor, followed by the Verrocchio and della Robbia rooms, on the floor above. To appreciate the sculpture in its entirety, don't be waylaid by the distracting displays of unrelated decorative arts. The Donatello section contains many of the greatest works in the Bargello.

Unlike Michelangelo's work, Donatello's betrays little sign of creative torment and virtuosity for virtuosity's sake, which accounts, at least in part, for his less glittering reputation. In the Bargello, however, Donatello is the undoubted star. As an exponent of the principles of Hellenistic sculpture and a believer in the perfection of the classical world, he shared Greek ideals of beauty yet was blessed with his own highly individualistic and enigmatic take on life.

After visiting Rome to study classical sculpture, in the

The *Pitti Tondo* by Michelangelo *c.* 1504.

Donatello's bronze
David, c. 1440–50.

company of his friend, Brunelleschi, Donatello revived techniques in bronze not used since antiquity. Inspired by Brunelleschi's use of perspective to create a sense of depth, he quickly mastered perspective and became the first artist to apply it to sculpture. Donatello's constant experimentation made him the most modern of sculptors but meant that he often ran counter to the prevailing orthodoxy. For instance, his first attempt at *David*, modelled in marble, shows late Gothic influence in the highly stylised face; it is a static image in direct contrast to his dynamic pose – one more in tune with Renaissance experimentation.

Impressions of David

The Bargello's tantalising calling card is Donatello's coquettish *David*, a rival to Michelangelo's more virile version in the Accademia *(see pages 49–50)*. Few statues provoke such startlingly different responses. To art critics, Donatello's small bronze *David* is a landmark work of art, fêted as the first life-size, free-standing nude since antiquity. To the sculptor's Italian contemporaries, the statue seemed authentically Greek, so convincingly did Donatello breathe new life into classical sculpture. However, later critics have remarked on the statue's vein of melancholy, coquetry and coyness rather than its Olympian grandeur.

The French novelist, André Gide, visiting the Bargello in 1895, was enraptured by *David*'s enigmatic sex appeal: "the flatness of his loins; the ornamented nudity; the oriental grace; the shadow of the hat over the eyes, in which the source of his glance is lost or becomes immaterial". In another vein, a

---

RENAISSANCE SCULPTORS

In the 15th century, sculpture finally shook off its purely decorative role and gained its rightful place as an elevated art form on a par with painting. Florentine sculptors traditionally started out as goldsmiths before turning to sculpture in bronze, often supervised by Venetian masters. Greek rather than Roman sculpture was their role model, inspired as they were by its dynamism, fluidity and homo-erotic appeal.

Ghiberti, Donatello and Luca della Robbia were the best-known sculptors of the day, but Michelozzo, Verrocchio and Cellini also had their admirers, while Michelangelo later came to be considered the most singular artistic genius of all *(see page 50)*. Ghiberti (1378–1455), the link between late Gothic and Renaissance sculpture, never sought a clean break with the past, unlike his more radical followers. He founded a workshop where Donatello and Michelozzo learned their craft. They took up the

torch – Michelozzo, who was drawn to abstraction and simplification, and Donatello (*c.* 1386–1466), the greatest sculptor of the 15th century. In Vasari's estimation, his grace and sense of composition emulated the achievements of classical sculptors more closely than any of his contemporaries.

As a group, the Florentine sculptors favoured monumental works underscored by a sense of perspective and skilful chiaroscuro effects. These talents were allied to a profound, often eroticised, understanding of male anatomy and, in the case of Michelangelo, of the body in motion. Critic Mary McCarthy was not alone in believing that in a virile, highly sexed society, boys become objects of desire. In the case of Florentine painters and sculptors, in particular, lust often lit upon a brazen or coquettish boy: Michelangelo, Leonardo, Donatello, Verrocchio and Pontormo were all susceptible to such boyish charms.

character in Aldous Huxley's *Time Must Have a Stop* is breezing through the museum, "his head full of heroic bronze and marble", when his progress is halted by Donatello's statue, which conjures up dignity rather than erotic promise: "Nobility without affectation. Serenity combined with passionate energy. Dignity wedded to grace."

By contrast, writer and critic Mary McCarthy sees the statue with clearer, female eyes: "Donatello's *David* is a transvestite's and fetishist's dream of alluring ambiguity".

Donatello's *St George*, created in marble for Orsanmichele *(see page 106)*, is an equally significant early work, even if, unlike *David*, it was not designed to be viewed from all sides. Even so, the statue shows a deep understanding of classical sculpture which shines through any tendency towards late Gothic idealisation. As the saviour of Christendom, St George demanded to be portrayed with all due valour, a task Vasari felt Donatello accomplished with ease. At the same time, given the ideals of Renaissance Florence, the statue was also given an heroic air and a strong sense of individuality. Technically, the work represents a leap forward: the stylised, static face is offset by the creative assertiveness of the sculpture as a dynamic work of art in its own right, not merely decorative.

St George Killing the Dragon, intended for the pedestal, provides the finishing touch to the theme. Considered to be the first example of a freestanding flattened bas-relief, the sculpture shows a clear sense of chiaroscuro and perspective. Other fine works include the captivating *Atys*, a dancing cherub (currently being restored) which shows Donatello's sense of fun; and a highly naturalistic terracotta *Bust of Niccolò da Uzzano*. Nearby, Donatello's majestic lion stands sentinel: the *Marzocco*, the city's leonine symbol, projects all the gravitas required of such a powerful heraldic device. This seated lion, which holds a shield depicting the Florentine lily, once stood guard on Piazza della Signoria.

Della Robbia and Ghiberti

Luca della Robbia (1400–82), a follower of Donatello, and the founder of the terracotta-sculpting dynasty, is represented by works here, with the rest of the family featured on the floor above. As a daringly creative sculptor, Luca della Robbia progressed from working in gold and marble to his preferred medium of terracotta, glazed with tin and other minerals.

The art of enamelled terracotta remained a family industry until the 16th century. Luca della Robbia's luminous madonnas in the Bargello stand out for their purity, clarity of composition and expressiveness of the faces. His *Virgin with an Apple* is a typically pure work. Unlike his followers, Luca

Mercury by Giambologna, *c.* 1576.

della Robbia favoured a narrow palette of colours: white figures are framed by blue backgrounds, complemented by occasional details of fruit and flowers picked out in yellow and green. Another follower of Donatello, Settignano, revived the Roman art of portraiture in stone, and is represented here by his luminous *Bust of a Young Woman*.

Also on display are the rival gilded bronze panels for the Baptistery doors created by Ghiberti and Brunelleschi in 1402. The competition is often considered the defining moment when the Renaissance was born. Ghiberti's elegant trial panel is essentially late Gothic in its realism, with a rich decorative patina, but reveals a degree of Renaissance naturalism and skilful chiaroscuro effects. While Brunelleschi's panel is still dependent on Gothic notions, it combines naturalism with a dawning sense of perspective, and shows greater dynamism than Ghiberti's work. By a narrow majority, Ghiberti won the commission to create the north door, leaving Brunelleschi, the apparent loser, free to devote his energies to the greater challenge of forging the Cathedral dome *(see page 19)*.

If the adjoining loggia is open, make time to appreciate a collection of Giambologna's most memorable works. The airy space is currently undergoing refurbishment but the bronzes by the Flemish-born sculptor are expected to remain in situ. Most appealing are the sculptures of animals which he designed for the grotto of the Villa Medici at Castello *(see page 195)*. The highlights are the tufted *Owl* (1567) and the craggy *Turkey* (1567), the latter significant since turkeys had recently been introduced to Europe from the New World.

The Verrocchio room

On the floor above, the Verrocchio room displays late 15th-century Tuscan sculpture, Medici works and historical portraits, as well as works by Verrocchio himself. Although best-known as a sculptor, Andrea del Verrocchio (1435–88) was also a goldsmith, painter, and master to Leonardo da Vinci. As a sculptor, he is noted for his balanced and formally perfect style and for his skilful use of chiaroscuro, clear in his *David*. This bronze shows great technical skill and a degree of monumentality surprising for such a small-scale work, but there is no escaping an air of kitsch. Writer Mary McCarthy is kinder, likening it to Donatello's more famous version: "There is something of the same allure in Verrocchio's bronze *David* , with its ambiguous Leonardo-esque smile."

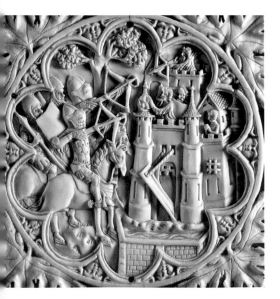

ABOVE: Ivory relief depicting *The Battle at the Castle of Love*, French, *c.* 1390.

RIGHT: *Acquamanile*, from Germany, interpreted as St George and the Dragon, *c.* 1400.

Facing the effeminate boy is a *Bust of a Noblewomen with Bouquet* (1475–80), a radiant sculpture originally attributed to Donatello, but now reassigned to Verrocchio, even if some critics also see the hand of Leonardo da Vinci. Equally lovely is Verrocchio's painted *Crucifix*, a masterpiece in pathos and subtlety.

Prolific dynasty

Adjoining rooms are dedicated to the prolific della Robbia dynasty, especially the father and son duo of Andrea and Giovanni. Although of a less classical bent than his uncle, Luca, Andrea della Robbia (1435–1525) was almost his match in inspiration and style, as well as arguably surpassing him in technique.

Andrea is best known for his sweet *tondi* (roundels) of foundlings in swaddling clothes on the Spedale degli Innocenti (*see page 136*), but his tender portraits of madonnas in the Bargello show great delicacy, only slightly marred by idealisation. Andrea's work shows greater sophistication but less purity than that of Luca; he was more interested in narrative sculpture and large polychrome reliefs. His son, Giovanni (1469–1529), in charge of the family workshop after Andrea's death, was a lesser sculptor but achieved renown for medallions and friezes. To modern eyes, his works seem proficient if over-coloured, including his vivid *Pietà* and a Nativity framed by pine cones and pears.

Bronze Gallery

On the same floor, the chaotically presented Gallery of Bronzes contains the finest collection of bronze statuettes in Italy, most by major sculptors and originally in Medici hands. The themes embrace mythology and Greek history but the objects themselves are often distinctly utilitarian, ranging from lamps and candelabra to bells and garden ornaments. Among the Renaissance bronzes are delightful statuettes by Giambologna, including *Morgante the Dwarf*, depicting Cosimo I's court dwarf riding a monster, and designed for a fountain.

Also on display is Giambologna's model for *The Rape of the Sabine Women*. Equally fine is his

Madonna and Child, bas-relief panel by Giovanni della Robbia (1469–1529).

Kneeling Nymph, a poised and accomplished work balancing the spiral of the nymph's body with the myth of Venus. Pollaiuolo (1433–98) is represented by *Hercules and Anteneas*, a sinewy work which, in dramatic tension, foreshadows Mannerism. The neighbouring Baroque Sculpture and Medals room contains late Gothic and Renaissance medals collected by Lorenzo de' Medici, as well as a charming baroque bust of a noblewoman by Bernini, modelled on his mistress.

Decorative arts

After taking your fill of sculpture, consider a return to the decorative arts collections, housed on the first floor. The Carrand collection was bequeathed to the city in 1888 by Louis Carrand, a wealthy art collector from Lyons. The frescoed ivories room was divided into cells during the Bargello's time as a prison but now displays Roman, Byzantine, French and Islamic *objets d'art*, dating from the 5th to the 17th century and including boxes, figurines, statuettes, combs, a medieval chessboard, and even an ivory fly-swatter.

Elsewhere in the collection are Longobard brooches, jewel-studded caskets, medieval miniatures, Spanish wrought-ironwork and French Gothic gold-work. Decorative Burgundian cameos and noble seals give way to Limoges enamels, Flemish goblets, Murano glass goblets and Bohemian crystal, by way of ceramics from Faenza, Urbino and Moorish Spain. Some of the most treasured objects include an exquisite medieval French diptych, a study in miniature, as well as an extravagant hatpin by Cellini, and the *Acquamanile*, a beautifully finished German bronze horse and rider. The Islamic room holds an eclectic collection of 16th-century Persian and Turkish tiles, breastplates and helmets, Anatolian carpets, Syrian incense-burners and mosque lamps.

FOOD AND DRINK: Dino (Via Ghibellina 51r; tel: 055-241452; closed Sun eve, Mon) serves traditional Tuscan cuisine in a 14th-century palace.

See also Palazzo Vecchio, page 147, the Uffizi, page 93, Casa Buonarroti, page 148 and Badia Fiorentina, page 103.

PALAZZO PITTI

Palatial residence of the Medici Grand-dukes and houses of Lorraine and Savoy. The museum complex, in the royal and state apartments, comprises two picture galleries, collections of porcelain, costumes and a treasure house of Medici *objets d'art*. The various museums can be found on the following pages:

Map reference: page 42, C–D 5–6
Piazza de' Pitti
Tel: 055-294883. This is the state museums' reservation line. You can avoid queues by getting a fixed entry time-slot for a small fee.
Bus: line D, 37
See individual museum entries for opening times. The Pitti is subject to periodic room closures Facilities: Bookshops. Cafés. Concerts. Theatrical events. Wheelchair access to Galleria Palatina, Appartamenti Reali and Galleria d'Arte Moderna; partial wheelchair access to the Galleria del Costume and the Museo degli Argenti.
Admission: combined tickets available for some or all of the Pitti Palace museums and Boboli Gardens, valid for a three-day period.

The Pitti Palace is the focal point in the Oltrarno, dominating its surroundings and drawing in visitors as inexorably as a Venus fly-trap. Designed by Brunelleschi and commissioned by Luca Pitti, a great rival of the Medici, Palazzo Pitti nonetheless retained its name when it became the foremost residence of the Medici rulers. Eleonora di Toledo, the wife of Cosimo I, bought the palace in 1549, after finding the Palazzo Vecchio too cramped for her family of nine. The other consideration was the need to live close to Piazza della Signoria, the centre of political power. The Medici swiftly shaped the palace in their own image, establishing summer and winter apartments, private picture galleries and libraries.

The rusticated façade of the massive Palazzo Pitti was extended over the centuries to a width of 200 metres (670 ft).

The end of the Medici line saw the palace pass to the house of Lorraine and the royal house of Savoy, each dynasty influenced by the decorative tastes of the day. The city's ruling families continued to live there until 1919, when Vittorio Emanuele III, Italy's last ruling monarch, presented the palace to the state. Ever since, the royal and state apartments have welcomed visitors, following the example of the Pitti's Palatine Gallery, which first opened its doors to the public in 1828.

Brunelleschi (1337–1446) produced bold plans for the new palace shortly before his death. Set on a slope to create more impact, and built on solid rock to support the weighty foundations, the Pitti was the first private palace to be built commanding its own piazza. Since the building was designed to be admired from the front, it comes as no surprise that, because of the steep slope at the rear, the second floor is level with the gardens.

Because of the massive size of the palace, the enterprise ruined the Pitti family; however, the Medici completed the project according to Brunelleschi's plans, with the façade enlarged to its present mammoth proportions in 1620. The landscaping of the Boboli Gardens, following the natural slope of the hill, provided the perfect complement to the palace, and became the model for Italianate gardens for centuries to come.

By 1565, the Vasari Corridor *(see page 85)* across the Arno was completed and, by linking the political seat of power with the private residence, symbolised the reality that, even from afar, the city was permanently and irrevocably ruled by the Medici family.

All the Pitti museums are worthwhile and have been recently restored, except the Carriage Museum, which is closed for the foreseeable future, and the Palatine Gallery, where restoration of the royal apartments is nearing completion. To appreciate the sumptuous Medici art collection and the lifestyles of the Grand-dukes, the Palatine Gallery and royal and state apartments are the obvious choice. The Museo degli Argenti (Grand-ducal Treasures Museum) comes a close second, more for the magnificently decorated rooms than for the contents, although those with specialist interests will appreciate the *objets d'art*.

In terms of art history, the Modern Art Museum takes up the story where the Uffizi leaves off, and gives a sense of the lavish, but somewhat dubious, decorative tastes of the last residents, the rulers of the houses of Lorraine and Savoy.

By comparison, the Porcelain Museum and the Costume Museum are more for connoisseurs. For light relief, any museum visit should be combined with a stroll in the beguiling Boboli Gardens, once a pastoral Medici pleasure dome. The pedestrian modern equivalent is the piazza in front of the palace, which, as a late afternoon sun-trap, is a popular meeting place for jaded locals and culture-sated tourists alike.

Galleria Palatina and the Appartamenti Reali

The palace's major picture gallery: High Renaissance, Mannerist, baroque and neoclassical art in a stately setting that was for centuries the main residence of the city rulers

Palazzo Pitti, Piazza de' Pitti
Tel: 055-2388614/2388611/2388613
Open: Tues–Sun 8.15am–6.50pm; Sat until 10pm in summer; last entry 45 mins before closing time. Temporarily closed rooms are listed at the entrance to the gallery.
Bookshops. Cafés. Compulsory cloakrooms for large bags. Lift or stairs to first floor.
Separate or combined admission fee.

The writer Arnold Bennett thought that the Pitti Palace "looked like a rather expensive barracks"; from within, however, any military comparisons are banished by the magnificence of the Palatine Gallery. This picture gallery is a testament to Medici self-glorification and acquisitiveness. The patronage of artists was both a cultural statement and part and parcel of collecting and commissioning prestigious work for the family's dynastic seat. As a gallery of works repre-

ABOVE: Self Portrait by Giorgio Vasari (1511–74).
RIGHT: The Jupiter Room.

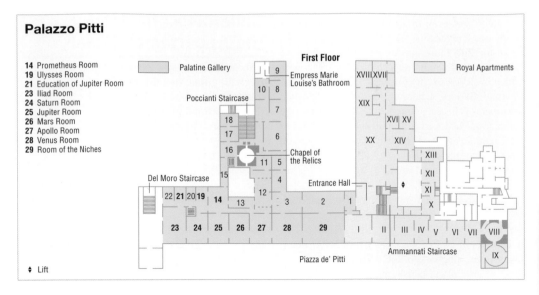

Palazzo Pitti

14	Prometheus Room
19	Ulysses Room
21	Education of Jupiter Room
23	Iliad Room
24	Saturn Room
25	Jupiter Room
26	Mars Room
27	Apollo Room
28	Venus Room
29	Room of the Niches

Palatine Gallery

Poccianti Staircase

Del Moro Staircase

First Floor

Empress Marie Louise's Bathroom

Chapel of the Relics

Entrance Hall

Royal Apartments

Ammannati Staircase

Piazza de' Pitti

♦ Lift

---

senting the greatest periods in Florentine and Italian art history, the quality of the core collection is beyond dispute, even if a disgruntled Stendhal, visiting in 1817, was far from impressed by the taste of Ferdinand III, the Grand-duke of the day: "Year by year, it is his habit to commission some thirty thousand francs' worth of pictures from the studios of those excruciating painters whom the public sees fit to designate for such an honour."

Art-lovers owe a debt of gratitude to a Medici prince who never ruled but devoted his life to collecting. The core High Renaissance, Mannerist and baroque collection was founded by Crown Prince Ferdinando (1665–1715), the eldest son of the long-lived Cosimo III de' Medici. The Crown Prince lived in the grand section of the palace that became known as the royal apartments upon the succession of the house of Savoy *(see below)*. His predecessor, Cardinal Leopoldo, brother of Grand-duke Ferdinando II (1610–70), had already installed his Venetian school collection in his palatial apartments so these masterpieces also came into the clutches of the Medici dynasty and joined the Tuscan, Bolognese, Umbrian and Flemish works now on display. Ferdinando II was also responsible for the most magnificent decorative schemes in this part of the palace: five vaulted ceilings were frescoed in the 1640s, to designs by Pietro da Cortona, the founder of the Roman baroque school of painting.

Apart from consolidating the collection, the contribution of the pragmatic Lorraine Grand-dukes was to create a private gallery in the richly decorated rooms that the collection occupies today. The

greatest paradox of the gallery is that although conceived as a private princely collection, the Palatine became one of the first public galleries, and has been welcoming the plebeian hordes since 1833.

Tracing the collection

The collection essentially follows the re-hang of 1833, although some paintings have been moved to the Uffizi, including masterpieces by Raphael and Rembrandt. Yet rather than following on from the Uffizi collection, the Palatine Gallery overlaps and echoes the larger one. Trecento and Quattrocento works may be the preserve of the more famous gallery, but the Palatine collection includes some fine works from the 16th and 17th centuries, including *tondi*, the circular paintings popular in Florence, and produced by such masters as Filippo Lippi and Raphael.

Indeed, one of the pleasures of this picture gallery is to see the interplay of artists working in the same period or tradition. In particular, we sense the foreshadowing of later artists, as in the relationship between Perugino and his most gifted pupil, Raphael, or between Fra' Filippo Lippi and Botticelli, Andrea del Sarto and Caravaggio, Giorgione and Titian, or Rubens and van Dyck.

The position of paintings reflects the dictates of the day, when, according to a whimsical interior decorator's logic, harmony of shape, size and colour prevailed over subject matter, tone and coherence. The result is a densely packed display in which the sumptuous setting and gorgeous frames risk overshadowing the works themselves. Even so, the subjectivity of this chaotic romp through post-Renaissance art is a delightful treat, far from the clinical, thematic or chronological displays of most international galleries.

Ongoing restoration means that the route is subject to change, an inconvenience exacerbated by the familiar Florentine problem – unpredictable closure due to lack of personnel. In particular, rooms in the royal apartments are often closed in summer, as are the minor rooms (Nos 4–11) in the Volterrano wing.

Setting the tone

All the rooms are named after the ceiling frescoes, which set the tone for the artworks within. Unless coming from a temporary exhibition, visitors enter through the Footmen's Antechamber (1), which has lovely views over the Boboli Gardens. Next comes the Gallery of the Statues (2), a former guards' room and now a repository of classical and Medicean statuary transferred from the Villa Medici in Rome. Despite Roman busts and a 17th-century likeness of Cosimo II, there is no disguising the fact that the best statues are on display in the Uffizi.

Beyond is the frescoed Castagnoli Room (3), dominated by a 19th-century table, one of the finest inlaid marble works in Florence. The frequently closed Volterrano wing only became part of the picture gallery in 1928, and was requisitioned to accommodate the influx of works that resulted from the suppression of neighbouring churches and monasteries. Until then, these had been the private apartments of the Grand-duchesses, from the 16th century onwards. These decorative minor rooms are more notable for their sumptuous frescoed and stuccoed ceilings than for their works of art.

Music Room and Poccetti Gallery

The Music Room (12), decorated in stately neoclassical style, was used for musical gatherings from Napoleonic times onwards. A *trompe l'oeil* frieze is matched by a frescoed neoclassical ceiling illustrating the 1683 Siege of Vienna.

The adjoining Poccetti Gallery (13) is more impressive, even if the decorative sweep is more satisfying than any specific work of art. In Medici times, this was a loggia connecting the apartments of the Grand-duke and Grand-duchess but, since being enclosed in 1813, the space has lost much of its charm.

An early 17th-century frescoed ceiling and red damask walls provide the backdrop for works of art as diverse as Furini's dreamlike *Hylas and the Nymphs*, influenced by Leonardo's smoky *sfumato* technique, and placid pastoral scenes by Dughet, Poussin's less talented brother-in-law. Another highlight is the superb *pietra dura* table designed for Cosimo III in 1716: a symphony of entwined flowers, fruit and leaves is picked out in marble, ebony, bronze and semi-precious stones.

The gallery's oldest works

Beyond is the frescoed Prometheus Room (14), an inviting showcase for the gallery's oldest works, which include an array of 15th-century Florentine *tondi* and portraits. On the right, set against golden yellow silk walls, is Pontormo's *Adoration of the Magi*, notable for its draughtsmanship and soft, rich colouring. The gravely beautiful *Tondo Bartolino* is a Filippo Lippi masterpiece, depicting a Madonna and Child against a busy narrative; the painting's fluidity and sense of perspective are reminiscent of the artist's innovative pupil, Botticelli (1444–1510). On the left is Botticelli's *Portrait of a Young Man*, a confident, youthful work influenced by Uccello. This sunny room, redecorated by the Lorraine Grand-dukes, displays neoclassical Sèvres vases and *pietra dura* tables.

Mary Magdalene by Titian, c. 1535.

Portraits of Agnolo and Maddalena Doni by Raphael, 1506.

Treasures worth seeking out

The adjoining apartments (15–18) were occupied by the Electress Anna Maria Luisa (1667–1743), who withdrew from the world after the death of her husband. Restored by the house of Lorraine, these rooms are often officially closed in summer, but it is worth appealing to a sympathetic custodian for a brief glimpse of the treasures within. The Corridor of the Columns (15) displays 17th- and 18th-century Flemish and Dutch miniatures acquired by Cosimo II and Cosimo III, who both had a particular interest in Flemish realism.

The Justice Room (16) is a return to mainstream Italian art, with portraits by Veronese and Titian, including the latter's penetrating *Portrait of Tommaso Mosti*, a sombre study in black and grey of a young courtier in Urbino. The Flora Room (17) displays Perugino's serenely captivating *Mary Magdalene* and Allori's *Madonna and Child*, a study in courtly elegance reminiscent of Bronzino, the painter's uncle. The Flemish influence reappears in *Flight into Egypt* by Rubens' most gifted pupil, van Dyck, created while the cosmopolitan artist was working at the English court of Charles I.

The Room of the Cupids (18) displays more Flemish and Dutch works, ranging from the meticulously crafted *Still Life* by Rachel Ruysch, one of few women court painters, to Rubens' *Three Graces*, a *grisaille* of predictably Rubenesque nudes.

The over-ornate Ulysses Room (19) was frescoed in honour of the Lorraine Grand-duke Ferdinando III's return after the Napoleonic interlude. On the left is a long Filippino Lippi painting intended as a panel on a wedding chest *(see Horne Museum, page 155)*. Entitled *Death of Lucrezia*, the vivacity and narrative power are reminiscent of Botticelli, Lippi's

RAPHAEL, UNIVERSAL ARTIST

The quintessential High Renaissance painter, Raphael (1483–1520), was, like Michelangelo, considered a divine artist, with a gift from the gods. The prodigy grew up in the Urbino court and was influenced by his Umbrian master, Perugino. In Raphael, Umbrian placidity was transmuted into a grandeur, subtlety and harmony surpassing that of his predecessors.

After moving to Florence in 1504, he came under the spell of Leonardo da Vinci and Michelangelo but his greatness was immediately recognised by his peers, from the lyrical sweetness of his figures to his sublime grace and synthesising genius. For Vasari, Raphael was the universal artist, a master of harmony, beauty and serenity. Raphael, like Mozart, died at 37 and, similarly, was mythologised immediately after his death. His influence on later artists was huge. As a supreme classical painter, only Titian has received greater accolades.

Even disregarding Raphael's Roman works in the Vatican, his Florentine legacy is remarkable *(see page 69)*. The Palatine Gallery has the portraits of *Maddalena Doni* and *Agnolo Doni*, which were designed as a pair, much like Piero della Francesca's *Duke and Duchess of Urbino (see Uffizi, page 83)*. As the prototype of the Renaissance portrait, these works became the model for generations of painters. As for religious works, Raphael's *Madonna della Seggiola (see page 70)* has been admired over the centuries as the embodiment of maternal love.

near contemporary. Above is a graceful Andrea del Sarto altarpiece. Also on the left is Raphael's famous *Madonna dell'Impannata*, named after the cloth covering the window in the background, and notable for its harmonious composition.

On the wall facing the Raphael is an intense *Ecce Homo* by Cigoli (1559–1613). In the eyes of his contemporaries, Cigoli's interpretation was greater than Caravaggio's painting on the same theme. Cigoli acted as master of ceremonies at the Medici court, yet was also devoted to his art.

Disturbing works

A brief respite from art is provided by Napoleon's Bathroom (20), designed by his sister, Elisa Baciocchi, and decorated with neoclassical stucco-work representing mythological scenes. Beyond is the Education of Jupiter Room (21), complete with several disturbing works, including Caravaggio's *Sleeping Cupid*. The innocuous title belies the fact that the artist used a dead baby as his model, one medical experts agree was suffering from a fatal disease. The realism is heightened by the dramatic addition of wings and an arrow, confirmation that Caravaggio has broken the conventions of his day: a sweet cherub is transformed into a pale and chilling corpse.

On the opposite wall is Allori's powerful *Judith with the Head of Holofernes*, self-consciously sensual but none the less provocative: the Mannerist artist persuaded his mistress to pose as Judith while the head of Holofernes is modelled on himself.

The adjoining Stove Room (22) formed part of the Grand-ducal winter apartments. Complete with vaulted ceiling and an inlaid majolica floor, this room was named after its advanced under-floor heating system. The room is frescoed by the baroque master, Pietro da Cortona, with allegorical scenes ostensibly depicting the Four Ages of Man but effectively glorifying the Medici dynasty.

The most splendid apartments

As custom dictates, the most splendid apartments are on the *piano nobile* above, overlooking the main piazza. The regal setting of these six rooms is matched by masterpieces on the walls, by Raphael, Rubens and Titian. The Iliad Room (23) is one of the most sumptuous in the palace, with a frescoed neoclassical ceiling inspired by Homeric myths. Two large Andrea del Sarto altarpieces face one another and are characterised by striking colours and a revolutionary use of space.

Artemisia Gentileschi, one of the few significant female painters of the period, is represented by her dramatic *Judith*, which shares Caravaggio's striking realism. By contrast, Justus Sustermans (1597–1681), court painter to the Medici, shows an utterly Flemish realism, emulating van Dyck's skill at portraying dress in minute detail. His *Portrait of Mattias de' Medici* shows a spaniel-eyed prince clothed in all his finery. In an equally intimate vein, Raphael is represented by his *Portrait of a Lady*, depicting a pregnant, placid-looking woman, an accomplished work which inspired Ridolfo del Ghirlandaio's similar portrait, which is also on display.

The Saturn Room (24) is arguably the most splendid in the gallery, and certainly the one most weighted down in masterpieces. However, the 17th-century ceiling, depicting an Olympian scene in gilt and stucco-work, is currently swathed in scaffolding and, until restoration work is complete, between 2003–5, most of the Raphael masterpieces have been moved to the Room of the Niches *(see page 69)*. The adjoining Jupiter Room (25) has the grandeur befitting a Medici throne room and is decorated by Pietro da Cortona's frescoes glorifying

The Three Graces by Rubens, *c.* 1620–23.

the young Prince Ferdinando. The ceiling is supported by a seething mass of nymphs, gods and entwined cherubs while the far door is framed by masterpieces painted by Raphael and Giorgione.

Raphael's *Portrait of a Lady* is a study of formal perfection, marked by the luminosity of the sitter's face and the virtuosity with which the portraitist captures the shimmering detail of her ruched sleeve and veil. By contrast, Giorgione's *Three Ages of Man* is either an allegory of youth and the gaining of wisdom or, more prosaically, a concert rehearsal. In the same room is a virile *John the Baptist* by Andrea del Sarto (1486–1531), a talented draughtsman with a grand style and smoky colour schemes. Beside it is a Fra' Bartolomeo *Pietà*, a poignant scene in soft Venetian-style colours. Also displayed is a *Madonna* by Perugino (*c.* 1445–1523), who painted religious works of poetic piety, mainly madonnas, suffused with a gentle mysticism and melting landscape.

Martial art

The Mars Room (26) is named after the ceiling's turbulent allegory of war and peace, alluding to a Medici victory improbably signalled by nude warriors and manic cherubs. Flemish and Italian masterpieces, set against vibrant red damask walls, include Rubens' martial masterpiece, *The Consequences of War* (1637) referring to the Thirty Years' War that was wreaking havoc in his homeland. The vibrant colours, fluidity and narrative sweep also show how marked Rubens was by the Italian High Renaissance. Rubens is also represented by his *Four Philosophers*, a rich and complex portrait in memory of his philosopher brother and his master, the humanist Justus Lipsius, both of whom had just died. Beside the Rubens is a Murillo *Madonna*, influenced by Raphael.

Apart from two tantalisingly animated panels by Andrea del Sarto, the remaining masterpieces are all portraits. In stature, there is little to choose between Titian's portrait of *Cardinal Ippolito de' Medici*, the cruel-looking grandson of Lorenzo de' Medici, and van Dyck's *Cardinal Bentivoglio*, an elegant symphony in red. In any lesser company, attention would be focused on two impressive Venetian portraits: Veronese's decorative *Man in Furs* and Tintoretto's sombre *Alvise Cornaro*.

Titian's masterpieces

The frescoed Apollo Room (27) is equally ornate and dotted with statuary. Framing the entrance doorway are masterpieces by Titian (*c.* 1485–1576), who was described by art historian Bernard Berenson as "the most complete Renaissance artist; his range remains unsurpassed in Western art". His ineffable technique and polished High Renaissance style are clear in his *Mary Magdalene*, a nude wreathed in the artist's trademark Titian hair *(see page 65)*.

The Three Ages of Man, by Giorgione, *c.* 1500.

The Silver Age, from the *Four Ages of Man* fresco by Pietro da Cortona (1596–1664) that decorates the Stove Room.

By contrast, his *Portrait of a Gentleman (see page 22)* is less painterly but psychologically penetrating; critics identify the nonchalant nobleman with the steely, grey-eyed gaze as the haughty Duke of Norfolk. In the same room are two major religious works by Andrea del Sarto: a monumental *Pietà* foreshadows Mannerism; while his *Holy Family* is a lesson in art history; the work owes its *sfumato* shading to Leonardo, its composition to Raphael, and its design to Michelangelo.

The Venus room

The Venus Room (28) is named after Canova's *Venus Italica*, commissioned by Napoleon as a replacement for the *Venus de' Medici*, which he had spirited away to Paris. This masterpiece of neoclassical statuary, all sweet curves and coyness, is the companion piece to the *Venus de' Medici*, which has now returned to the Uffizi.

Titian is represented by several portraits, including his *Julius II*, inspired by Raphael, and his gorgeous *Portrait of a Young Lady*, as well as by the powerful *Portrait of Pietro Aretino*. However, his undoubted masterpiece is the enigmatic *Concert*, originally attributed to his elusive master, Giorgione.

Nearby, Rubens, the master of Flemish baroque, is represented by a serene pastoral scene, *Peasants Returning from the Fields*, which is more than a match for his contemporary, the Neapolitan Salvatore Rosa, whose luminous seascapes are also on display.

A grand finale

While the Saturn Room is being restored, the Room of the Niches (29) provides a fitting grand finale, thanks to masterpieces by Raphael *(see page 66–7)*. Raphael's greatest portraits are here, notably *Maddalena Dono* and *Agnolo Doni*, two panels intended as a diptych, influenced by Ghirlandaio but painted with Flemish realism. The background, an idealised springtime landscape, unifies the pair of portraits, with Agnolo Doni's Florentine shrewdness contrasted with his wife's bovine placidity. The portrait of *Tommaso Inghirami*, appointed Cardinal by Pope Leo X, shows psychological insight and monumentality. Raphael's *Madonna della Seggiola* (named after the chair) is one of the most celebrated paintings in the city, an intimate family portrait painted with perfect assurance.

Apart from this *tondo*, Raphael is represented by two other madonnas. The moving *Madonna del Granduca* is named after the Grand-duke Ferdinando III, whose favourite work of art this was. The soft mood is enhanced by the dark background and the Leonardo-esque use of *chiaroscuro*. By contrast, the canopied *Madonna del Baldacchino* is more of a technical triumph, with its architectural grandeur to the fore. A complete change of mood is provided by Perugino's masterpiece, a *Lamentation*. The dreamy landscape and soft colouring betray the artist's Umbrian origins and his debt to Piero della Francesca.

Venus by Antonio Canova, 1810–11.

The Royal Apartments

The Room of the Niches leads to the so-called Appartamenti Reali, decorated in lugubrious taste. Even if garish French carpets and a surfeit of gilt overshadow the fine Florentine marble tables, frescoed ceilings and period portraits, the apartments reflect the ostentatious tastes of the times. Set on the first floor of the west wing of the palace, these monumental apartments were used for ceremonial occasions, such as ambassadorial receptions. "Royal apartments" is an historical misnomer, even if the city's ruling families lived in the palace for four centuries. These monumental apartments originally housed the princely Medici dynasty and the Grand-dukes of Tuscany, before passing to the house of Lorraine in 1734, when the Medici

RIGHT: *The Madonna
of the Chair (Madonna
della Seggiola)* by
Raphael, *c.* 1516.

FAR RIGHT:
The Throne
Room.

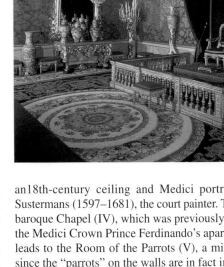

line died out. Only after the Unification of Italy, when Florence became the national capital in the city's final burst of glory, did these apartments become home to the royal house of Savoy (1866–70).

Despite the terms of the last Medici will, leaving everything in perpetuity to the city of Florence, the Habsburg-Lorraines used the proceeds of secret sales of Medici masterpieces to fill Austrian war chests. Even so, the Lorraine Grand-dukes brought their own neo-baroque tastes to bear on the palace, particularly in the choice of tapestries, silk fabrics, Flemish carpets and French furniture. That said, the present arrangement reflects the eclectic taste of the house of Savoy, who filled these over-stuffed rooms with treasures from their palaces in Parma and Lucca, including portraits of the French royal family. Since the shutters are often closed to protect the furnishings, many apartments feel unduly gloomy. Moreover, until the restoration of the apartments is complete, a number of rooms remain closed.

Rooms of many colours

The Green Room (I), named after the colour of its silk furnishings, contains a Caravaggio portrait and French paintings, as well as 17th-century ebony cabinets and marble busts. The grandiose red-damask Throne Room (II) was used as an audience chamber in the Medici era but became the court chamberlain's quarters during the Lorraine period, even if the royal house of Savoy's taste prevails in this display of chinoiserie and Oriental porcelain vases. The Blue Room (III) is slightly more subdued, with

an18th-century ceiling and Medici portraits by Sustermans (1597–1681), the court painter. The late baroque Chapel (IV), which was previously part of the Medici Crown Prince Ferdinando's apartments, leads to the Room of the Parrots (V), a misnomer since the "parrots" on the walls are in fact imperial eagles. The elegant room is adorned with 16th-century portraits, period tapestries and furnishings that once belonged to the Grand-dukes of Lorraine. The Queen's apartments (VI–VII) reflect the eclectic decorative tastes of the 17th–19th century while the King's apartments (X–XI) are decorated with 18th-century French and Tuscan furniture. Visitors generally leave through the Room of Bona (XIV), frescoed by Poccetti, the only room to retain its original 17th-century appearance. Beyond is the Sala Bianca (XX), the vast stuccoed ceremonial state room used for balls, exhibitions and fashion shows (*see Pitti Exhibition Centre, page 175*).

FOOD AND DRINK: **Pitti caffeteria** *(in the museum complex): clinical but convenient, with outside tables.* **Kaffeehaus** *(Boboli Gardens): over-priced café with forgettable food but good views; the only chance to eat in the gardens (unless you bring a discreet picnic).* **Caffè Pitti** *(Piazza Pitti 9; tel: 055-2396241; open late): facing the Pitti Palace, an appealing spot for cocktails, coffee, tea, or a light lunch; live music at weekends; over-priced, but good atmosphere and setting.* **Osteria del Cinghiale Bianco** *(Borgo San Jacopo 3r; tel: 055-215706; closed Wed): a cosy, rustic-style inn serving typical Tuscan dishes at reasonable prices.* **Celestino** *(Piazza Santa Felicità 4r; tel: 055-2396574; closed Sun in winter): old-fashioned restaurant halfway between the Pitti and the Ponte Vecchio; soup, risotto, grills and fish served on a garden terrace.*

Museo degli Argenti

Grand Ducal Treasures Museum (formerly known as the Silver Museum). Medici collection of treasures in the dynasty's frescoed summer apartments

Palazzo Pitti, Piazza de' Pitti
Tel: 055-2388709/055-2388710
Open: Tues–Sat 8.15am–1.50pm; 1st, 3rd and 5th Sun of the month and 2nd and 4th Mon of the month; last entry 45 mins before closing time. Bookshop. Café. Cloakrooms for large bags. Combined ticket with Costume Gallery.

The collection is a clear display of the power and wealth of the vainglorious Medici dynasty. Yet there is nothing systematic or coherent about the content of the collections: the treasures were amassed to bedazzle rivals and fellow rulers. Bric-à-brac was also required to embellish the monumental apartments, including inlaid marble table-tops incorporating semi-precious stones *(see Opificio delle Pietre Dure, page 169)*. There are cabinets for displaying jewellery and antiques, curios and keepsakes. Gold-work, silver-work, enamel-work and Japanese lacquer-work compete with Chinese porcelain and crystal vases, classical cameos and baroque jewellery. The magpie collection also includes gold goblets, terracotta busts, engraved pearl jewellery, ivory, ebony and amber curios, religious reliquaries, Roman vases and Viennese silver platters.

The Pitti's dynastic collection was founded by Cosimo the Elder in the 15th century and continued by his son Piero and grandson, Lorenzo the Magnificent. Consolidated by Cosimo de' Medici in the 16th century, it was boosted by the creation of the Grand-ducal workshops, which produced treasures for the Medici palaces. Under Francesco de' Medici and Ferdinando I de' Medici, sophisticated craft workshops were set up in the Uffizi in 1588; these later found a home in the Opificio, where restoration work continues today. Many of the *objets d'art* on display originated in these workshops and were the product of intense rivalry between inventive gold-cutters and silver-smiths, marble-cutters and cameo-makers, frame-makers and decorators.

Individual tastes

Each wave of rulers brought their individual tastes to bear on the collection, which accounts for its eclectic nature. The 17th-century Prince Mattias

de' Medici collected cameos from Germany while Anna Maria Luisa, the last of the line, favoured jewellery, commissioned from the Grand-ducal workshops or purchased from European collectors. The Medici also collected treasures to demonstrate prestige, even if frequent lapses in taste led to displays of decadence. As the most proprietorial of collectors, Lorenzo de' Medici stooped so low as to inscribe his name on the largest antique vases. Not that the Lorraine dynasty was slow in imposing its distinctive taste. As cousins to the Austrian Habsburgs, they knew their Sèvres from their Meissen, their Bohemian reliquaries from their German drinking beakers. After Grand-duke Ferdinando III's return from exile after the brief Napoleonic period, the Pitti became the repository of his collection of gold plates, drinking horns and silver beakers.

At its best, the collection is a magnificent display of the minor arts that confirmed the city as a major craft centre. At its worst, the sternest critics argue that the collection of such fripperies hastened the demise of Florentine culture, although it would be truer to say that while execrable lapses of taste represent the excesses of a decadent regime, the Renaissance heyday was unsustainable.

Vessel made from a nautilus shell studded with pearls, rubies and turquoise from the collection of Francesco I de' Medici, *c.* 1570.

Detail from the frescoes that decorate the Grand-duke's reception room, painted by Angelo Colonna, 1638–44.

Summer apartments

The museum occupies the high-windowed summer apartments of the Medici. Architecturally, the ground floor is the most rewarding, with richly frescoed monumental apartments. While an array of Medici treasure is displayed in side rooms on the ground floor, the main collection lies on mezzanine level above, which was designed as a treasury.

The first room, the Sala di Luca Pitti, named after the first owner of the palace, is decorated with portraits and terracotta busts of the Medici rulers. The adjoining Salone di Giovanni da San Giovanni is a splendidly frescoed room that connected the suites of the Grand-duke and Grand-duchess. As well as serving as an anteroom to the public audience chamber, it was used for banquets and receptions.

The room is named after the artist who painted it in honour of the dynastic marriage between Ferdinando II and Vittoria della Rovere in 1634. The marriage between the cousins is depicted on the ceiling in a lavish allegory which does not reflect the Medici's disappointment at Vittoria for not bringing the duchy of Urbino as her dowry. The blow was softened by the transfer of Urbino's Renaissance masterpieces to the Pitti art collection. The walls are frescoed with an apotheosis of the Medici:

the grandiose allegory evokes the glories of ancient Greece and Rome through the legacy of Lorenzo the Magnificent, the revered leader who made his princedom a paradise for the arts.

The Sala Buia, used as a public audience chamber by previous Grand-duchesses, is a shrine to the spirit of Lorenzo the Magnificent (1449–92). As well as displaying his death mask, the room contains Lorenzo's prized collection of antique vases, ranging from Roman and Byzantine masterpieces to Persian, Egyptian and Venetian models. The adjoining (but often closed) Grotticina opens onto a whimsical pastoral scene: dancing birds adorn the 17th-century frescoed ceilings; below is a fountain and a *pietra dura* marble inlaid floor.

Beyond lies the main public audience chamber, the Sala d'Udienza, which is one of the most impressive state rooms, despite the disappearance of the Grand-ducal throne. Seated below illusionistic frescoes depicting balconies and loggias, the ruler surveyed the massed ranks of courtiers and supplicants, who all had to remain standing. The impressionistic frescoes create a world within a world, from a young man pointing to the court musicians to a servant peeking out from behind a curtain. Lest anyone forget his place, a motto set in the centre of the illusory circular staircase advises supplicants to "Talk little, and be brief and witty". By contrast, the allegorical ceiling contains advice on the vanity of human wishes that the Medici should have heeded: "Fortune is illusory and transient; only Merit and Virtue survive."

Equally fine is the private audience chamber. Within these frescoed walls, the Grand-duke received ambassadors and discussed state secrets. Illusionistic frescoes re-create an elaborate loggia complete with quirky details such as a boy looking through a telescope, a sly tribute to Galileo and the scientific achievements of Renaissance Florence. The convoluted barrel-vaulted ceiling is cunningly drawn into the optical illusion to create a dizzying effect of constantly shifting columns.

Grand-ducal splendour

The next spectacular state room served as an anteroom to the Grand-dukes' summer apartments: given its original position overlooking the Boboli Gardens, it was here that visitors arriving by coach first encountered Grand-ducal splendour. After being ushered into a *trompe l'oeil* scene of loggias and flying cherubs, visitors were expected to be overawed by the lofty 17th-century frescoes glorifying the Medici dynasty. The bedroom belonging to the uncouth Gian Gastone (1671–1737), the last Medici ruler, contains a portrait of the plump, bewigged Grand-duke, as well as more impressive gilded wood cabinets and lapis lazuli ornaments.

The state apartments contain lovely *pietra dura* tables while the side rooms display silverware, crystal and glassware. The so-called Ivory Room is awash with sacred and secular *objets d'art*, from reliquaries to a 17th-century ivory lapdog and an accomplished spread-eagled nude.

Upstairs, the former treasury displays a collection of cameos studded with different stones. The craft of cameo-making flourished in classical Greece and Rome and was revived in Renaissance Florence. While the ancients were inspired by mythological scenes, Florentine cameos tended to be portraits, such as the one of Lorenzo's son, Pope Leo X, on display here.

The adjoining jewel collection was largely amassed by Gian Gastone's sister, Anna Maria Luisa, the Electress Palatine. As she bestowed the entire Medici heritage on the city, she can be forgiven for her taste in engraved pearls.

The eclectic Grand-ducal collection continues with Ferdinando III's Viennese gold and silverware. The following rooms are housed in the former loggia, frescoed with scenes of foliage and exotic beasts. Beyond is the compact porcelain collection, divided into three predominant colours, blue, green and rose. The highlight is the remarkable collection of blue Ming china (1368–1644) and the 16th-century *blanc de chine*, produced in South China on the orders of Louis XIV.

The collection closes with displays of jewellery, from baroque and rococo Sicilian and Spanish pieces to Roman cameos and brooches. After such a visual assault, even the most acquisitive of visitors may wish to defer a visit to the Porcelain Museum (*see page 74*).

FOOD AND DRINK: See Galleria Palatina, page 70.

Cameo depicting a triumphal procession of Philip II, King of Spain and Portugal, c. 1580.

Galleria del Costume

Italian fashion and costumes from the 18th-century to the present day

*Palazzina della Meridiana, Palazzo Pitti
(2nd floor, through Modern Art Museum)
Tel: 055-2388713
Open: Tues–Sat 8.15am–1.50pm; 1st, 3rd and
5th Sun of the month and 2nd and 4th Mon of
the month; last entry 45 mins before closing
time. Bookshop. Café (near main museum ticket office). Fashion shows. Combined ticket with
Museo degli Argenti.*

The costume gallery is housed in the Palazzina, quarters commissioned by Grand-duke Leopold in 1776 and finished in 1840. The rooms, furnished in the florid styles favoured by the houses of Lorraine and Savoy, present a counterpoint to the costumes. Many historical costumes come from the Grand-dukes, but the core collection has been enriched by private donations of period fashion, theatrical costumes, and contemporary couture. One section focuses on fashion of the 1920s, '30s and '40s, from frivolous frocks to sheer glamour. Displays generally rotate every two years, allowing for costumes to be refurbished and space to be made for different items and new donations.

The museum celebrated its complete overhaul with a lavish exhibition dedicated to designer Gianfranco Ferre in 2000. The Milanese designer's couture and prêt-à-porter clothes now form part of the permanent collection, proof that contemporary designers are not ignored. However, the main section of the museum displays costumes and accessories from the 17th–20th century, plus several fine 16th-century garments. Most of the courtly costumes come from the Medici collections, including the 16th-century funeral garments worn by Grand-duke Cosimo I de' Medici, Eleonora di Toledo, and her son, Don Garcia; Eleonora's costume can be seen in Bronzino's portrait of her in the Uffizi *(see page 2)*.

This is Italy's only fashion museum, a reminder that Florence has an honourable tradition in the cloth trade and should not be overlooked in the fashion stakes. The museum includes a tribute to Giovanni Battista Giorgione, known as "the father of Italian fashion" thanks to his successful launching of the modern fashion industry in 1951.

FOOD AND DRINK: See Galleria Palatina, page 70.

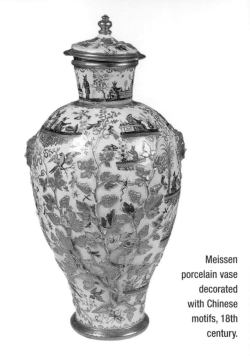

Meissen porcelain vase decorated with Chinese motifs, 18th century.

Museo delle Porcellane

China used by the city's ruling families, from the Medici to the house of Savoy

*Casino del Cavaliere, Giardino di Boboli,
Palazzo Pitti
Tel: 055-2388709
Open: Tues–Sat 9am–1.30pm; 1st, 3rd and 5th
Sun of the month and 2nd and 4th Mon of the
month; last entry 45 mins before closing time.
Bookshop. Café. Compulsory cloakroom for
large bags (facilities near ticket office at
entrance to main museums). Admission charge.*

Set on top of the Boboli hill, the museum overlooks the ramparts of the Forte di Belvedere *(see page 174)* and enjoys one of the loveliest rural views from the city. The collection occupies a 17th-century folly that served as a Grand-ducal retreat from the burdens of state, or from the burdens of excess in the case of the more decadent rulers.

The tableware on display was used by the ruling dynasties, from the Medici and Lorraine Grand-dukes to the royal house of Savoy. The collection, which comprises French, Italian, Austrian, German and English chinaware, is mostly from the 18th century, and includes dinner services, tableware and *objets d'art*, from vases to figurines. The writer, Mary McCarthy, was dismissive of the "torrent of bad taste – if there had been Toby jugs and Swiss weather clocks, the Medici would have collected them. For the diligent visitor who wants to see everything, the Pitti is pitiless."

Even so, amid the kitsch Viennese figurines lurk exceptional pieces of classic Sèvres porcelain and Meissen chinoiscrie. Other highlights are an English Worcester dinner service and a lavish, 19th-century Italian pictorial cup with a view of the Pitti Palace. The Italian chinaware includes pieces from the prestigious Doccia manufactory in Emilia Romagna, as well as elaborate Neapolitan pieces and frivolous Capodimonte figurines. The Meissen collection includes services used by Gian Gastone (1671–1737), the last Medici Grand-duke. He had little interest in collecting but his wife was keen on *mitteleuropean* chinaware. Her collection reflects the fashion for chinoiserie in 18th-century Europe.

Particularly fine is the Sèvres porcelain, originally intended for the court of Versailles, and noted for its translucence, durability and narrow palette of colours. The rest of the French booty on display represents a rare example of treasure taken to Italy by Napoleon, rather than carried away by him to Paris. He presented the collection to his sister, Elisa Baciocchi, who was Grand-duchess of Tuscany from 1809–1814.

FOOD AND DRINK: See Palatine Gallery, page 70.

Giardino di Boboli

An open-air museum, with landscaping and architecture spanning four centuries

Palazzo Pitti (ticket and access through gate at end of the inner courtyard)
Open: 9am–dusk; closed 1st and last Mon of the month; last entry one hour before closing. Admission included in combined Pitti museums ticket, otherwise separate ticket necessary.

The Giardino di Boboli is the most attractive garden in Florence, spanning four centuries and as many styles, from the Renaissance to Mannerism, baroque and neo-classicism. At every turn, classical and Renaissance statues give way to whimsical Mannerist grottoes dotted with grotesque sculpture.

Commissioned by Cosimo I, the gardens were to cover the hillside from the Pitti Palace to the ramparts of Forte di Belvedere *(see page 174)*. The steep slopes were landscaped by some of the greatest figures of the day, from

Vasari in the 1550s to Ammannati in the 1560s, and Buontalenti in the 1570s. The essential form of the gardens was finished under the rule of Ferdinand I (1587–1609), but in the 17th century it was extended to the west and beyond the ramparts, culminating in the creation of the majestic cypress avenue leading to the atmospheric island pool.

The house of Lorraine added new buildings and statuary, from a hothouse for citrus fruit to the folly known as the Kaffeehaus and an Egyptian obelisk.

Exploring the gardens

The gateway to the gardens lies off Ammannati's grotesque rustic courtyard, a Mannerist masterpiece, now the setting for summer concerts. The middle archway in the walls conceals a 17th-century grotto and pool, dominated by a statue of Moses, complete with a Roman torso. The gateway opens onto a terrace surmounted by a baroque fountain encrusted with cupids. Beyond is the panoramic amphitheatre, intended as an arena for Medici entertainment; Cosimo II replaced the amphitheatre's trees with six-tiered stands adorned with classical statuary, and, in 1790, the Lorraine Grand-dukes added an Egyptian obelisk of Ramses II in the centre. Taken from Heliopolis by the Romans in 30 BC, the obelisk, which rests on a bronze turtle, was transferred to Florence from the Villa Medici in Rome. In 1840, it was joined by an equally impressive ancient artefact: a Roman granite basin from the Caracalla Baths in the capital.

Further up the slope a couple of Roman statues mark the path to the ornamental pool known as the *Bacino di Nettuno*, named after the slimy statue of

ABOVE: Every green nook shelters a statue.

BELOW: *Strolling through the Boboli Gardens*, an illustration from 1860.

Neptune who brandishes his trident at threatening sea-monsters. The path climbs upwards past the towering statue of *Abundance*, begun by Giambologna in 1608. At the summit is the enchanting *Giardino del Cavaliere* rose garden, abutting the Porcelain Museum *(see page 74)*.

Set on bastions designed by Michelangelo, the garden overlooks one of the loveliest rural views imaginable: beyond stretches a truly Tuscan scene, made up of churches, cypresses, olive groves, ochre-coloured villas and grey-green hills. From here, a path leads to the Boboli café, the Kafeehaus, a rococo folly with an exotic domed roof.

Follow the steep cypress avenue known as Il Viottolone, lined by Roman studies of Greek statues, which leads downhill to the most romantic part of the gardens. At the end lies the *Vasca dell'Isola* (Island Pool), conceived as a citrus grove and flower garden. There are carp and turtles in the pool, and an allegorical *Ocean Fountain* sculpted in granite by Giambologna. The central figure of *Neptune* is now in the Bargello *(see page 56)* but the 17th-century statues of *Perseus on Horse-back* and *Andromeda* are original.

Staying on the lower level, follow the avenue that hugs Via Romana back towards the Pitti Palace, passing the 18th-century rococo *Lemon House*, which still houses pots of rare citrus trees in winter. From here, continue along the lower avenue, ignoring tempting tunnels of greenery that lead back into the gardens. After passing the façade of the Pitti Palace, follow sporadic signs to the grottoes, passing a hanging camellia garden and neat parterres.

Even if closed, the *Grotticina di Madama*, the oldest architectural feature in the gardens, can be admired through its gates. A path leads to the *Grotta del Buontalento* (currently being restored). One chamber houses replicas of Michelangelo's *Slaves*; the originals were moved to the Accademia in 1908 *(see page 50)*. Supervised by Vasari in the 1550s, the folly was finished by Ammannati and Buontalenti. Take the side exit from the gardens, passing the pot-bellied *Bacco*, representing Cosimo I's favourite dwarf sitting astride a giant turtle.

FOOD AND DRINK: Kaffeehaus; see the Galleria Palatina, page 70.

Galleria degli Uffizi

The finest concentration of Renaissance art in the world. Includes paintings by Giotto, Botticelli, Piero della Francesca, Michelangelo, Leonardo da Vinci, Raphael, Titian and Caravaggio

Map reference: page 42, E4
Piazzale degli Uffizi
Buses: Line B, 23
Galleria degli Uffizi
Tel: 055-2388651/238852 (general information); 055-294883 (Uffizi reservation line)
www.uffizi.firenze.it; www.cosi.it/principe
Open: Tues–Sun 8.15am–6.50pm; Sat until 10pm in summer; last entry 45 mins before closing. Bookshop. Café. Research library. Wheelchair access. Audio-guide. Guided tours and school visits by arrangement.
Corridoio Vasariano (Vasari Corridor)
Tel: 055-2654321/238699 (book a month ahead). Open. Tues–Sun at agreed times; closed in summer
Collezione Contini Bonacossi
Tel: 055-2388651/2654321
Open: Wed and Fri, variable times

Madonna and Child with Angels by Fra' Filippo Lippi, c. 1455.

As the world's greatest collection of Italian art, the Uffizi is both a feast for the senses and an indigestible banquet. What you are moved by will depend on your mood. As Henry James said, musing on the "merciless multitude" of masterpieces in the Uffizi and Pitti: "So it is that in museums and palaces we are alternate radicals and conservatives; on some days we ask but to be somewhat sensibly affected; on others, Ruskin-haunted, to be spiritually steadied." Solitude is also out of the question. The contrast with the gallery's genteel hush in the 1860s could not be more marked: "Sometimes there were not more than two or three figures standing there, *Baedeker* in hand, to break the charming perspective," said James. However, a tranquil contemplation of great works of art is still possible, away from the Botticelli bottleneck, the Giotto genuflection, the Leonardo da Vinci line and the Michelangelo muster station. Given the fickle nature of popular taste, Fra' Angelico, Perugino, Pollaiuolo and Mantegna, to name but a few, are often left to sleepy custodians and connoisseurs.

Although Tuscan art reigns supreme, the full panoply of Italian art is also well-represented, particularly painters from Umbria, Urbino, Emilia and the Veneto. Moreover, since most visitors come to see the Early Renaissance works, the High Renaissance rooms are far more peaceful and, by the time Titian and Veronese finally make way for Caravaggio and Tiepolo, Rubens and Rembrandt, the crowds have faded miraculously away. By the same token, the wonderful classical and Cinquecento statuary in the corridors is often overlooked in the stampede to see specific Renaissance paintings. Conversely, the vagaries of fashion mean that the *Medici Venus*, the famous nude statue displayed in the Tribune, can now be seen with relative ease.

A little history

While Rome epitomised the splendid maturity of the Renaissance, the Quattrocento belonged to Florence, which fostered the most original artists and thinkers. Even earlier, Giotto was one of the few painters to be praised as a revolutionary genius in his own lifetime. Rivalry and pride spurred Florentine artists on to greater heights as each sought not only to surpass previous standards of excellence but to lay down the gauntlet to contemporaries. In the *Divine Comedy*,

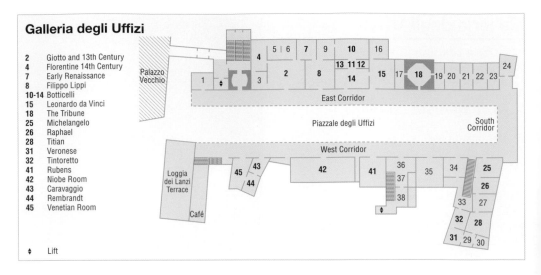

Galleria degli Uffizi

2	Giotto and 13th Century
4	Florentine 14th Century
7	Early Renaissance
8	Filippo Lippi
10-14	Botticelli
15	Leonardo da Vinci
18	The Tribune
25	Michelangelo
26	Raphael
28	Titian
31	Veronese
32	Tintoretto
41	Rubens
42	Niobe Room
43	Caravaggio
44	Rembrandt
45	Venetian Room

✦   Lift

Dante muses that "Cimabue thought he had the field to himself but now the word is Giotto, who has cast him into the shade."

Vasari relates how Florence was a hotbed of invention, a daring city in which art and science converge in the creation of a painting. In innovation, Masaccio, with his monumental majesty and sense of perspective, paved the way for Uccello, with both artists inspired by Brunelleschi's rediscovery of vanishing point and the illusion of deep space *(see pages 19, 122, 126)*.

In the Uffizi collection, Cimabue and Giotto prefigure Masaccio and Fra' Angelico, the Early Renaissance masters, who, in turn, give way to Fra' Filippo Lippi and Botticelli, Leonardo and Michelangelo. Tuscan art oscillates between the austere and essential and the decorative and flowery, a distinction transcending school and period. Artists at one end of the spectrum engineer pioneering works of perspective, or paintings of monumental majesty, while those at the other end produce works which, to modern sensibilities, may seem fey or sugary.

Yet the design of the Uffizi collection makes for a richly woven tapestry: the sweetly graceful Sienese school is followed by the poetic Umbrian school and the painterly Venetian tradition. With the Cinquecento, Florentine art declines into provincialism and the baton passes to Venice, particularly to Titian, Veronese and Tintoretto, all of whom are represented here. Consequentially, the circuitous path from the limpid sweetness of Duccio and Simone Martini to the mysteries of Leonardo and Perugino or the fullness of Raphael and Titian is only part of the story that the Uffizi tells so well.

The Uffizi was created as the administrative nerve centre of the grand duchy, reinforcing the chain of command between the Palazzo Vecchio, the Medici power-base, and the court at the Pitti Palace. In 1560, Vasari was charged with the project, although it was only completed by Buontalenti 20 years later. Vasari opted for a U-shape plan enclosing a rectangular piazza, with the Uffizi later linked to the Loggia dei Lanzi by Buontalenti. Although not a particularly graceful palace, it is still a remarkable engineering feat, planted as it is on unstable, sandy ground. The building work involved truncating the Romanesque church of San Pier Scheraggio, which Vasari cunningly incorporated into the Uffizi; it now forms part of the exhibition space.

In addition, a passageway across the river was created in a record five months in order to be ready for the marriage of Cosimo's son, Francesco, in 1565. The south and east corridors of the Uffizi, which linked the offices of state with the Palazzo Vecchio and Pitti Palace, were gradually lined with statuary.

In his turn, Francesco de' Medici (1541–87) decided to transform the second floor of the Uffizi into a museum, coincidentally paying tribute to the Medici's dynastic glory. For the introverted ruler, the gallery was essentially his private playground "for walking, with paintings, statues and other precious things." Work began in 1580 and, four years later, the gallery's octagonal centrepiece was ready. Known as the Tribune, it was designed as a temple-like showcase for the greatest artworks of the age. The core collection revolved around classical busts, Renaissance statuary and portraits but, in time, paintings from all periods enriched the collection.

The gallery's survival is due to Anna Maria Luisa, the last Medici, who left the gallery to the city as "public and inalienable property", a stipulation respected by the grand-dukes who succeeded her.

Exploring the collections

If you are visiting the Uffizi for the first time, it makes sense to go straight to the historical collection on the second floor. On a later occasion, consider booking a visit to the Vasari Corridor *(see page 85)*, the Contini Bonacossi Collection *(see page 89)* or the Prints and Drawings Collection *(see page 92)*.

If a leisurely visit is in order, then one gentle approach is to admire the sculpture in its entirety, simply by following the U-shaped second-floor corridor. Restored by art-free views in the café off the West Corridor, tackle the first 24 rooms, which all lie off the East Corridor, facing the café. These are the key rooms devoted to Gothic, Early Renaissance and High Renaissance artists. Bottlenecks tend to occur by Giotto (Room 2), Botticelli (10–14), Leonardo da Vinci (15) and the Tribune (18). Ideally, return to see rooms 25–45 after lunch or on another day, beginning with Michelangelo (Room 25) and continuing chronologically with the High Renaissance and Mannerist Venetian or Emilian painters, notably Raphael (26), Titian (28), Veronese (31) and Tintoretto (32).

After this, Tuscan and Venetian art loses its vigour, as may you. However, flagging spirits are revived by the diversity and cross-fertilisation of the rest of the collection, dedicated to 17th- and

THE REBIRTH OF THE UFFIZI

Although officially opened in 1765, the Uffizi Gallery welcomed the public by request two centuries earlier, with the first visitor guide to the collection written in the 16th century. Privileged to be one of the oldest museums in the world, the Uffizi pays the price in terms of planning and efficiency. As a result, the gallery has embarked on an ambitious renovation programme. The aim is to give the collection a facelift, to increase museum space, and enable the stockpiled works in the vaults to see the light of day. Much has already been accomplished, despite setbacks provoked by the terrorist bombing in 1993, which damaged the gallery and paintings. Since then, the premises and artworks, including the Vasari Corridor, have been restored and, although sections still tend to be closed for "lack of personnel" reasons, the major rooms are always open.

The expansion is being carried out in stages until 2005–8, leaving the historic core collection (described here) virtually as it is. The enlarged collection will continue to be displayed chronologically and by school, with the art historical development presented more clearly as new space becomes available. The increased space will allow the permanent collection to be tripled in terms of the number of artworks on display.

On the ground floor, the most tangible rewards should be new exhibition space, multi-media and conference facilities and the creation of a tapestry gallery. This is in addition to improved access and visitor services, including a new bookshop, bar and restaurant. A controversial new exit is being created on Piazza dei Castellani, but has provoked criticism for the huge scale of the projecting roof and a style out of keeping with the city character. While the second floor should undergo only minor reshuffling, the first floor will offer more gallery space, a permanent sculpture collection, and rooms for temporary exhibitions. Sixteen rooms have already been opened for temporary exhibitions, with much to follow before Botticelli's *Venus* can burst out of her shell with renewed wonderment.

View of the Tribune, designed by Bernardo Buontalenti, *c.* 1580.

ABOVE:
*Madonna and
Child
Enthroned*
(detail) by
Cimabue,
c. 1280.

ABOVE RIGHT:
*The
Annunciation*
by Simone
Martini, 1333.

18th-century art. Rubens (Room 41) makes a vibrant appearance, as does Rembrandt (44). The last great Italian flourish is provided by Caravaggio (Room 43) and Tiepolo (45), with 18th-century Italian architecture and classical sculpture beautifully showcased in the newly restored Niobe Room (42).

If time is limited, focus on the first 19 rooms of the gallery, with an obligatory visit to Michelangelo and Raphael (Rooms 25–26), before sampling the sculpture on the East Corridor. A welcome café terrace faces the beginning of the East Corridor and is the right place to take stock of the Renaissance.

Chronological route

The deconsecrated church of San Pier Scheraggio by the museum entrance, a victim of the 1993 terrorist bombing, is fully restored but currently closed. On display are frescoes of famous Florentines by Andrea del Castagno (*c.* 1420–57), including a portrait of Dante and Boccaccio. However, the main picture gallery is ranged over the second floor, reached via a staircase lined with classical busts. The Vestibule marks the entrance to the gallery, at least while the Archaeological Collection (Room 1) remains indefinitely closed. The Vestibule is dotted with classical sculpture, including a statue of a Hellenistic dog and two sarcophagi. Beyond is the East Corridor and a sculptural feast *(see page 92)* as well as the entrance to the picture gallery.

With no preamble, Florentine art explodes into life in the Giotto and the Duecento (13th-Century) Room (2), where masterpieces vie for attention. As the father of modern painting, Giotto (1266–1337) is the undoubted star, credited with laying the foundations of Western art by abandoning stylised medieval conventions.

His *Ognissanti Madonna (see page 18)*, an altarpiece for the Florentine church of the same name, enchants with its radiant colours and realistic facial expressions, while dazzling in its early use of perspective. In technique, subtlety and luminosity, Giotto's genius casts into the shade the *Maestà* of his master, Cimabue (1272–1302).

Part of a movement working towards greater naturalism, Cimabue represents the shift from a static Byzantine style to a more fluid one. His *Maestà* – a Madonna and Child enthroned with angels and saints – is still, in its grave majesty, a masterpiece of Western art. The same is true of the *Maestà* by the Sienese artist, Duccio di Boninsegna (1260–1319). This more static yet intense work is painted in the soft pinks and glistening golds associated with the Sienese school, which favoured a subtler, warmer palette than their cooler Florentine peers.

The Sienese School

Duccio is the perfect prelude to the Sienese Trecento (14th-Century) Room (3) dedicated to works from the city that, with Florence, symbolises the yin and yang of the artistic spirit. If Florentine art favours perspective, intellectual rigour and innovation, the Sienese tradition represents sensitivity and conservatism. Critic Mary McCathy is one of many to see Sienese art as the feminine foil to Florentine masculinity. Compared with the softer, sweeter Sienese madonnas, which place mood and colouring over composition, the Florentine character favours formal perfection, rigorous attention to composition and draughtsmanship. Yet within Florentine paintings there are several strands that cut across schools: the sterner, innovative, more rational approaches of Masaccio, Uccello and Michelangelo compared with the softer, sweeter approach of Benozzo Gozzoli, Fra'Angelico, Fra'Filippo Lippi and Botticelli, leaving Leonardo da Vinci to synthesise the styles.

A similar distinction can be made between the poignancy and lyricism of most Umbrian art compared with the more rational Florentine approach, underscoring the difference between the mystical spirit of Perugia and the stony heart of Florence.

The Sienese paintings serve to emphasise the difference from the Florentine sensibility. Sienese madonnas are all rapt devotion and doe-eyed glances, sinuous figures shimmering on brilliant surfaces. Simone Martini (c. 1284–1344) is represented by a delightful *Annunciation*, which may be flat and one-dimensional compared with Giotto's art, yet has compensations in the form of delicacy and detail; the lyrical angel prefigures Botticelli.

In the same room, the brothers Ambrogio and Pietro Lorenzetti show some understanding of Giotto but share the Sienese love of soft colouring, linear forms and decorative surfaces. Ultimately, however, a fascination for storytelling takes precedence in these scenes of everyday life. Ambrogio's *Life of St Nicholas*, in particular, is a doll's house of inviting effects, including a view of boats and unfurled sails, one of the earliest marine scenes in Western art. In Ambrogio's *Presentation of the Virgin*, the decorative detail and lively curiosity of the painter make a sharp contrast with the starker, more focused Florentine approach.

A Florentine feast

The Florentine Trecento (14th-Century) Room (4) is a visual feast, even if these proto-Renaissance painters still inhabit the medieval world. In these solemn works, decoration and the accumulation of detail are enriched by Giotto-esque touches. *Santa Cecilia*, painted by an unknown master, shows a tentative grasp of perspective while *San Pancrazio*, the graceful panel-painting by Bernardo Daddi (c. 1312–48) reveals Giotto-esque influences and dazzling colours. The *St Matthew Triptych* by Orcagna (1344–68) is typical of the period's severely elegant style, while Giottino's *Pietà* is a complex, luminous and expressive work.

International Gothic

The International Gothic Room (5/6) tells the traditional side of the Tuscan story, lingering in a golden tapestry world of no weight, depth or solidity, a style dismissed by writer Aldous Huxley as "repulsive Gothic architecture and its acres of Christmas card primitives." Compared with the revolutionary approach of Giotto and his followers, it is a conservative art form rooted in the medieval mindset. In this courtly art of vivid colours, flat figures shimmer against a formalised landscape or weave graceful arabesques over golden surfaces.

The main practitioners were Masolino (1383–c. 1440), Lorenzo Monaco (1370–1423) and Gentile da Fabriano (c. 1370–1427), represented by one his most beguiling works, the *Adoration of the Magi*, a kaleidoscope of faces, horses and harnesses. Lorenzo Monaco's *Adoration of the Magi* and *Adoration of the Virgin* altarpiece also owe much to the medieval world, with miniaturist skills in one work matched by the decorative scale of the huge altarpiece.

One of four scenes from the *Life of St Nicholas* by Ambrogio Lorenzetti, c. 1327–30.

The Battle of San Romano, depicting Florence's victory over Siena, by Paolo Uccello, 1432.

Early Renaissance room

The Early Renaissance Room (7) is an introduction to the leading figures of the Quattrocento. The innovative Masaccio (1401–*c.* 1428) is often considered the founder of Renaissance art, the master of a measured and monumental style peopled by solid figures who move in three-dimensional space. His most memorable work is in the *Brancacci Chapel (see page 122)*, but the Uffizi displays his *Santa Anne Materza*, painted with Masolino, his older, more traditional cousin, still mired in late Gothic conventions. Masaccio is thought to have painted the static *Madonna and Child*, as well as the more animated angel at the top. Venetian-born Domenico Veneziano (*c.* 1405–61), Florentine by adoption, can also be considered an innovator, as shown by his *Saint Lucy* altarpiece, a harmonious, softly glowing masterpiece, and one of his few surviving works.

Paolo Uccello (1397–1475) put Masaccio and Brunelleschi's lessons in perspective into practice in his *Battle of San Romano*. This work, which forms part of a famous trio, with companion pieces in London's National Gallery and the Paris Louvre, is ostensibly a study in warfare between two historical enemies, depicting a Florentine victory over the Sienese. Yet under the guise of warfare, the painter conducts a more cerebral campaign, a game of perspective between puppet-like knights battling on geometrical chargers, as stylised as hobbyhorses. The foreshortening devices embrace a thicket of lances, toppling heroes and fallen horses, plumed helmets and a heraldic breastplate set out like a backgammon board. With his sense of solid geometry, mathematical rigour and feel for colour, Uccello was a worthy successor to Masaccio.

Divine vocation

Fra' Angelico (*c.* 1395–55), commonly known as Beato Angelico in Italian, because of the divine or "blessed" nature of his artistic vocation, felt less free to innovate. As a devout Dominican, his duty was to glorify God and to obey the church hierarchy. Nonetheless, the luminosity and intensity of his work set him apart from his less joyous peers. Here, his *Coronation of the Virgin* shows a sly sense of perspective in the clouds, as well as the quality Henry James praised as "passionate pious tenderness". Piero della Francesca (1416–92) shares Fra' Angelico's ability to state great religious truths but extends this to a capacity for conveying psychological truths, as in his famous diptych. The *Portraits of the Duke and Duchess of Urbino (see page 83)* display matching aquiline profiles against a landscape that owes much to Flemish realism. These portraits offer an insight into how the Uffizi collection was enriched through dynastic marriage: just as wealth begets wealth, art begets art. Grand-duke Ferdinando II inherited the portraits through his wife, Vittoria della Rovere.

Filippo Lippi

The Fra' Filippo Lippi Room (8) introduces a more worldy note. Artistically, Lippi (*c.* 1405–69) followed in Fra' Angelico's footsteps, even if the Dominican friar was in thrall to celestial love while the lapsed Carmelite, Fra' Filippo, was more carnal. The purity may have gone, but the lyricism remains in his sweet *Madonna and Child*, supposedly based on the nun with whom he was scandalously in love. In this much-admired work, the realism of the landscape prefigures Leonardo, while the fine draughtsmanship, heightened by his sense of colour and movement, influenced his follower, Botticelli. His *Coronation of the Virgin* is a crowded scene, memorable for the sweetness of expression visible in the faces. Filippino Lippi (1457–1504), the product of the lascivious friar's eventual marriage to the nun, lacks his father's lyrical sweetness in his otherwise competent *Adoration of the Magi*. His *Young Boy in Red*, in the next room, is a more involving and mysterious portrait.

The Pollaiuolo brothers

The Pollaiuolo Room (9) is dedicated to Antonio (1443–96) and Piero del Pollaiuolo (1433–98), brothers whose talents have always been overshadowed by more singular painters. As decorative all-round artists, they lack a distinctive spark, even if Antonio's *Portrait of a Lady* is a pleasing work, matched by the dynamism and muscularity of his small *Hercules* panels. Also on display is the newly restored cycle of *Virtues*, commissioned by the powerful merchants' guild. Botticelli and Piero Pollaiuolo were asked to create six *Virtues* for their tribunal, works inspired by pagan sibyls. However, Botticelli's *Fortitude*, also displayed here, is infinitely superior to Pollaiuolo's works. While his *Fortitude* feels far from a coura-geous figure, she is depicted as majestic, seated on a throne, and has a clear gaze unlike the gauzy, unseeing women painted in his later work.

The Botticelli Rooms

The Botticelli Rooms (10–14) represent the world's best collection of works by Sandro Botticelli (1444–1510) and are the most popular in the Uffizi. Created in the upper section of the former Medici theatre, the space is devoted to the master of the evanescent. The ethereal beauty of voluptuous nymphs in chiffon veils has helped make Botticelli the best-loved of artists. Walter Pater was one of many Victorian critics moved by Botticelli's "sympathy for humanity in its uncertain condition", while Henry James admired his inventiveness: "his imagination is of things strange, subtle and complicated," comparing the Florentines favourably with the pre-Raphaelites – artists simply reproducing "diluted Botticellis". Other critics see Botticelli's painting as the product of a private, enclosed world, a place of semi-allegorical pagan spirits in which sweetness is mingled with unrealised emotion.

Botticelli began as a pupil of Fra' Filippo Lippi but gradually moved from painting wistful madonnas to idealised classical gods and goddesses. The *Sant'Ambrogio* altarpiece and *Madonna of the Magnificat* are fine examples of his religious work and show characteristic sweetness. Unlike many of his peers, Botticelli was sensitive to feminine beauty, even if his women resemble classical statues swathed in loose drapery. Yet he preferred a decorative and artificial composition to the illusion of reality, and deliberately distorts figures to give a

Battista Sforza and Federigo da Montefeltro, the *Duke and Duchess of Urbino* by Piero della Francesca, *c.* 1465.

Primavera by
Sandro Botticelli
(detail), *c.* 1478.

lovelier, languid shape. As the greatest master of the Florentine Quattrocento linear style, Botticelli was indifferent to *chiaroscuro* and perspective, preferring decorative surfaces that have the flatness of a tapestry. Even so, his *Portrait of a Young Man* shows an appreciation of Flemish realism, a sympathy shared by Ghirlandaio in his *Madonna*.

Primavera and *Birth of Venus*

Botticelli's *Primavera* and *Birth of Venus* are the best examples of beauty of human form fused with an intellectual idea, Neo-Platonism, itself a fusion of the spiritual and the secular – Christianity and pagan Greek philosophy. Botticelli's spell lies in melding old and new, placing the classical world in a Christian context, and combining humanism with the courtliness of medieval love poetry. In his refinement of ancient myths, he shows us the birth of love from the sea and the return of spring to the earth. He opens secular art to man's deepest emotions, in the belief that love purifies and leads mankind to truth.

Primavera, one of the most popular works in the Uffizi, is open to myriad interpretations which, to modern sensibilities, are secondary to the enchantment of spring. As Zephyr, the wind of spring, catches the nymph, Chloris, she is transformed into Flora, the herald of spring. Spring, as the season of love, sees a pregnant Venus accompanied by the dancing Three Graces, one of whom, touched by Cupid, is turning towards Mercury, the revealer of truth rather than merely a handsome youth.

The *Birth of Venus*, the other masterpiece and the most famous image in the gallery, depicts the pensive goddess posed on an upturned scallop shell, with winged zephyrs blowing her to shore. Botticelli's Venus has overtones of the Virgin, with the scallop shell symbolising the rising soul, and echoing the baptism of Christ. Yet the statuesque goddess also represents idealised beauty, the union of spiritual and sensual qualities. In addition, she embodies the Neo-Platonic virtue of *humanitas*, embracing Ciceronian culture as well as a deep humanity.

THE VASARI CORRIDOR

This famous and formerly private Renaissance corridor has only recently been opened to the public after 500 years of secrecy. A visit has to be booked well in advance – at least one month ahead *(tel: 055-2654321/238699; open: Tues–Sun at agreed times; closed in summer)* and places are limited. As preparation, or even as a substitute, the virtual visit available from any of the Palazzo Vecchio multimedia terminals *(see page 145)* provides a flavour of the experience, designed as a leisurely stroll along the corridor in the company of the architect, Giorgio Vasari.

Hailed as the first city walkway, a veritable Renaissance rooftop passage, the corridor runs from the Palazzo Vecchio and the Uffizi Gallery to the Palazzo Pitti and the Boboli Gardens on the far side of the Arno. The corridor was created during the reign of Cosimo de' Medici (1519–74) to connect the seat of government, the Palazzo Vecchio, with the court and residence at the Pitti Palace. The object was to enable the de facto city rulers to cross the city in safety, away from the prying eyes of lesser citizens, and to provide safe passage in times of flood or siege.

In 1565, Giorgio Vasari, court architect and master of public works for the Medici, was summoned to build the new walkway from the Uffizi, or public offices, along the quayside to the Ponte Vecchio, and from there over the medieval bridge and gold workshops to the Pitti Palace *(see page 62)*. The passageway even leads to the church of Santa Felicità in the Oltrarno (south side of the Arno) district, then the Palatine Chapel, in case a Medici should feel like slipping into a service unnoticed.

The Ponte Vecchio section is naturally the most intriguing, with a real sense of a secret walkway, and a reminder that this was the only bridge to escape Nazi bombing, when retreating German troops blew up the other bridges. Fortunately, the corridor has recovered from both the devastating 1966 floods and the Mafia bombing outrage in 1993.

A walk along the passage affords glimpses of the Duomo, tiled rooftops, arches and medieval alleys at every turn. The first stretch is lined by 17th- and 18th-century works, while the walkway over the bridge displays a remarkable collection of self-portraits, which is still being added to by contemporary artists.

The roll-call of artists includes Andrea del Sarto, Bernini, Bronzino, Canova, Corot, David, Ingres, Raphael, Rembrandt, Reynolds, Rubens, Vasari and Velázquez. Among the highlights are Guido Reni's rakishly decadent *David with the Head of Goliath* (c. 1605), set above the staircase leading down to the Vasari Corridor, and Eugène Delacroix's penetrating *Self-Portrait* (c. 1840), which lives in the Ponte Vecchio passageway.

The sea-born goddess, who lives in a gilded green world, looks wistful as she knows that natural human love is about to be transformed into love of the Christian kind.

Leonardo da Vinci

The Leonardo da Vinci and Perugino Room (15) pays tribute to the greatest genius of the age, the master of the High Renaissance style. As the quintessential Renaissance man, Leonardo da Vinci (1452–1519) filtered his studies of nature, botany and anatomy into his art. His feeling for atmosphere is reflected in his melting landscape and softly blurred outlines, an illusionistic *chiaroscuro* technique known as *sfumato*. Leonardo and his master Verrocchio both created the newly restored *Baptism of Christ*, with the soft background attributed to Leonardo. The smoky *sfumato* effect, the hallmark of a true Leonardo, is visible in the drapery of the angel on the left, and shows such prowess that Verrocchio supposedly abandoned painting forever.

Leonardo's newly restored *Annunciation*, a luminous masterpiece bathed in the dawn light, reveals a clearer grasp of perspective as well as a carpet of flowers in the foreground giving way to a misty seascape, partially obscured by the Tuscan countryside. His soft hues and sensibility find an echo with Pietro Perugino (c. 1450–1523), the Umbrian master to Raphael, celebrated for the poetic piety of his art. His *Pietà* is a study in soft colouring and diffuse light, matched by his *Madonna and Child with Saints*.

The Loggia of Maps (16), which is currently closed for re-organisation, displays geographical charts and maps of Tuscany in a room converted from a 16th-century loggia.

View of the first corridor, designed by Vasari and Bernardo Buontalenti, 1560–80.

The Tribune and the Medici Venus

Entered from the corridor, the Tribune (18) was the artistic showcase in Medici times, and has been preserved as it was, complete with an octagonal cupola encrusted with shells and lit from above. Designed in 1584, this temple to art represents the cosmos and the four elements in its design and houses High Renaissance and Mannerist masterpieces, as well as classical statuary that adorned the Villa Medici in Rome until 1677.

Given the popularity of the room, visitors follow a regimented circular route, making it difficult to admire the sculpture and art at the same time. If torn, select the sculpture and the lovely octagonal table, a masterpiece of inlaid marble. Sculpture includes the realistic *Wrestlers*, a classical copy of a bronze, and the magically engaging *Dancing Faun*. Equally impressive is the engrossing *Arrotino*, or Knife-grinder, probably a Scythian warrior, a classical copy of a 2nd-century BC work.

However, for centuries the most consistently praised work was the so-called *Medici Venus*. Discovered in Hadrian's Villa in Tivoli, the Medici Venus is a 1st-century BC copy of the Praxitelean Aphrodite of Cnidos. In Romantic times, the Venus, considered the perfection of female beauty, was a reason to visit Florence, and sent Byron into rhapsodic verse: "We gaze and turn away, and know not where/Dazzled and drunk with beauty, till the heart/Reels with fullness; there, forever there/Chained to the Chariot of triumphal Art/We stand as captives and would not depart."

Not to put too fine a point on it, Grand Tourists, predominantly male, were fascinated by her pert buttocks. In 1765, Smollett commented that "the back parts are executed so happily as to excite the admiration of the most indifferent spectator".

FOREIGN TASTES

Many visitors are surprised by the strength of the foreign collections within the Uffizi, particularly the presence of German, Flemish, French and Spanish works. Among the stars are Dürer, Holbein and Cranach, not to mention Breughel, Rubens and Rembrandt, or Goya and Velázquez. However, the cosmopolitan aspects of the collection are not so surprising, given the city state's powerful trading, diplomatic and dynastic connections, as well as the scale of patronage and sheer Medici acquisitiveness. In the case of Flemish works, artists such as Rubens and van Dyck were in demand all over Europe.

The Annunciation by Leonardo da Vinci, 1472–75.

Had tabloid journalism existed in 1765, *Venus* would undoubtedly have won an accolade for "rear of the year".

Courtly works

The courtly artworks studding the walls were the pride of the Medici collection, and hold up well for modern tastes. Rosso Fiorentino's *Musical Cherub* is a familiar charity Christmas card image brought to life in all its unfamiliar loveliness. Although Pontormo's *Portrait of Cosimo the Elder* remains a striking posthumous study, so, too, does the *Portrait of a Lady* by Andrea del Sarto, a masterly painter in the mould of Raphael.

This is not to underestimate Bronzino, whose lavish court portraits show a curiously modern sensibility. His *Portrait of Lucrezia Panciatichi* could be a contemporary society beauty, while the *Portrait of Eleanora of Toledo* is a decorative study of Cosimo de' Medici's wife wearing the same brocade dress

she took to her tomb. From the Tribune, one can glance into (but not visit) the curious Hermaphrodite room (17) which, amid a setting of frescoes and Roman statuettes, displays the *Sleeping Hermaphrodite*, a classical copy of the Greek original, which intrigues onlookers with its ambiguous sensuality.

Umbrian artists

The High Renaissance continues in the Perugino and Signorelli Room (19), devoted to Umbrian artists, a school which fused Flemish realism with spiritual awareness and a soft colouring often lacking in the Florentine tradition. On display are portraits by Perugino (*c.* 1450–1523), the Umbrian master who prefigures Raphael. Several works are being restored but Perugino's *Francesco delle Opere*, a penetrating portrait, embodies the best of Perugino.

In the same room is Luca Signorelli's *Holy Family*, a *tondo*, studded with classical references; and Piero di Cosimo's grotesque *Perseus Liberating Andromeda*, which depicts the death throes of a sea monster. The bizarre work was conceivably inspired by a Florentine carnival which saw the return of the Medici dynasty.

The Wrestlers, a classical copy of a Greek sculpture, 3rd century BC.

Breaking the thread

Rooms 20–24 cannot quite sustain the momentum of the collection, particularly when the Tuscan thread is broken. A brief diversion is provided by the Dürer and Cranach Room (20), a celebration of German artists that displays two sets of nudes interpreted differently. Dürer's *Adam and Eve* focuses on the fig leaf and rosy apple, while Cranach the Elder's version of *Original Sin* is more eye-catching, revealing a serpent arching over Eve's head.

Giambellino and Giorgione

The Giambellino and Giorgione Room (21) features a return to Italy, with art displayed beneath a Renaissance ceiling frescoed with exotic battles and grotesque myths. Tuscany has been transmuted into shimmering Venice in beguiling works by two subtle Venetian artists, Giambellino (*c.* 1433–1516) and Giorgione (*c.* 1478–1510).

Giambellino is often considered the founder of the Venetian school, one favouring a poetic, painterly sensibility at odds with the monumental, sculptural Florentine style. For Giambellino, light, colour and texture were more important than form.

His *Sacred Allegory* is an unfathomable yet intriguing work while the *Lamentation over the Dead Christ* is a darkly haunting work.

The unsettling mood is sustained by Giorgione, who has been called the first modern artist, thanks to the subjectivity of his vision. His *Judgement of Solomon* is a mysterious, brooding work while his *Warrior with a Sword* weaves a spellbinding atmosphere enhanced by *sfumato*, the soft gradations from light to dark.

Flemish and German realism

The Flemish and German Renaissance Room (22) is significant in its confirmation of the trailblazing realism of portraiture in Northern Europe. The Flemish had considerable influence on Italian Renaissance painters, prompting artists as diverse as Leonardo and Giambellino to reassess their approach to landscape and portraiture.

Although by no means the greatest Flemish artist, Hans Memling, represented here by several late 15th-century portraits, was influential. A number of works by Hans Holbein the Younger are also exhibited; he brought great realism and authority to the art of portraiture.

Warrior with Sword, by Giorgione, 1505–10.

Back to the Italian Renaissance

The Mantegna and Correggio Room (23) sweeps the story back to the Italian Renaissance, where Mantegna (1431–1506) was the undisputed innovator. Trained in Padua, this daringly influential painter is represented by several small, rigorous works created for the Mantuan court, where his masterpieces remain. Correggio (1489–1534), influenced by Mantegna in his compositions and by Leonardo in his sense of shading and mood, brings a poetic note in his *Virgin Adoring the Christ Child*.

Beyond, the Cabinet of Miniatures (24) displays 15th–18th century miniatures. Sadly, this ornate 18th-century room is cordoned off and can be admired only from the doorway.

Michelangelo's Holy Family

The Michelangelo Room (25) is the first of 11 rooms dedicated to the 16th century. Despite being the leading artistic figure of the Florentine Cinquecento, Michelangelo (1475–1564) considered sculpture the noblest art *(see page 50)*. However, in just one painting he demonstrates that he was as great as any of his peers working in paint. The *Holy Family*, considered the most enigmatic 16th-century masterpiece, betrays his sculptural bent, both in the depiction of the marble-like nudes in the background and in the polished, classical forms of the Holy Family. Also known as the *Doni*

Tondo, this sinuous, virulently coloured composition is both a prelude to Mannerism and a sign of an unquiet spirit in quest of formal perfection, which awaits in the Sistine Chapel.

Holy Family with St John (Doni Tondo), Michelangelo, 1504–5.

Florentine painting is also represented by the *Portrait of a Lady* by Ghirlandaio (1449–94), an accomplished draughtsman.

Raphael

The Raphael Room (26) is a showcase to a painter of sublime grace, grandeur and subtlety. Although influenced by Michelangelo and Leonardo da Vinci, Raphael (1483–1520) was a supreme classical painter and synthesising genius; only Titian, who greatly admired Raphael, has received greater accolades. Raphael is represented by several compelling portraits, even if his madonna is undergoing a lengthy restoration. Known as *The Madonna of the Goldfinch*, the work (replaced by a copy) reveals a lyrical sweetness in the soft modelling of the figures, and is more accomplished than his youthful and dreamy *Self-Portrait*. Far more powerful is the *Portrait of Pope Leo X*, a psychological study of this nepotistic and luxury-loving Medici, depicted with the two cousins whom he made cardinals.

As Henry James appreciated, Raphael was "strong in portraiture – easy, various, bountiful genius that he was." Andrea del Sarto (1486–1530), who painted in the *bella maniera* style of Raphael, strives after an idealised classicism yet strikes a slightly saccharine note in his *Madonna of the Harpies*, also on display here.

THE CONTINI BONACOSSI

The Contini Bonacossi collection, previously in a wing of the Pitti Palace, is now on display in the Uffizi. From Via Lambertesca, a temporary entrance leads to the first floor of the museum. This formerly private collection, set in attractively decorated 18th-century rooms, contains a choice selection of Florentine and Sienese Renaissance art as well as works from the Venetian school.

Apart from Spanish Old Masters, the collection holds ceramics, furniture and bronzes. The Sienese works include a Duccio *Madonna and Child* and an Early Renaissance *Madonna of the Snow* altarpiece by Sassetta (*c.* 1430), which records a miraculous August snowfall in Rome. The Venetian school is represented by a *Life of St Nicholas* by Paolo Veneziano, a *St Jerome* by Giambellino, and a number of Mannerist works by Tintoretto.

One of the Venetian highlights is Veronese's *Count Giuseppe da Porto with his Son* (*c.* 1553), an assured and intimate scene. Spain is also well-represented in the collection, with works by Velázquez, Goya and El Greco.

Venus of Urbino, by Titian, 1538.

Titian and the Venetians

After the Pontormo and Rosso Fiorentino Room (27), which reprises some of the Medici court painters honoured in the Tribune – such as Rosso Fiorentino (1494–1541), Pontormo (1494–1556) and Bronzino (1503–72) – the Tuscan thread becomes tenuous for the rest of the collection. The artistic baton passes to the virtuoso Venetian artists, from the classicising harmony of Titian to the theatrical Mannerism of Tintoretto, the rococo flourishes of Tiepolo and the watery picture-postcard realism of Canaletto.

The Titian Room (28) is dedicated to the polished master of the Venetian High Renaissance. Titian (*c.* 1485–1576) was the consummate classical artist, blessed with an ineffable technique and a range unsurpassed in Western art. He is represented by several of his most striking works, including the languidly erotic *Venus of Urbino*, one of the most influential nudes in the Western canon. Commissioned by the Duke of Urbino, the work was supposed to give his young bride an introduction to the erotic arts matched by a covert injunction to fidelity, symbolised by the loyal dog curled up on the bed.

The artist's equally celebrated *Flora* depicts a young bride with Titian-esque hair, and luxuriates in the artist's sensuous modelling, expressive style and luscious use of colour.

Moving south

The Dosso and Parmigianino Room (29–30) moves the story south to Emilia Romagna and the Mannerists, Dosso Dossi (1480–1542) and Parmigianino (1503–40), both of whom tend towards a Venetian use of paint. Parmigianino is the more beguiling, with his elongated, langorous figures.

Beyond is the Veronese Room (31), dedicated to the supreme colourist of the Venetian school. Veronese (1528–88) is concerned with pictorial effects and a striving for splendour, sensed in his *Annunciation* and *Holy Family*. The Tintoretto Room (32) celebrates the Venetian Mannerist artist in thrall to overwhelming contrasts and theatrical effects. *Leda and the Swan*, in particular, shows the bold style and passion for paint of Tintoretto (1518–94), a Venetian artist par excellence.

The later rooms

Dedicated to the 17th and 18th centuries, the later rooms, have finally been restored after the 1993 terrorist outrage; even so, several are sporadically closed or subject to re-hangs in the context of the revamped Uffizi. Rooms 33–35 are unexceptional, replete with minor Mannerist works as well as Lombard and Tuscan baroque art, but the collection comes alive again with Rubens (Room 41). The *Portrait of Isabella Brandt* catches the mischief and vivacity of Rubens' first wife, while the cosmopolitan court painter, van Dyck, Rubens' fellow citizen, is represented by several fine portraits. By contrast, Velázquez' *Philip IV of Spain on Horseback* conjures up a busy, swirling scene, evoking the style of the Spanish court.

Showcase for statuary

The Niobe Room (42) is a refreshing shift from art to sculpture, decorated as a vaulted showcase for classical statuary from the Villa Medici. These Roman copies of 4th-century BC Greek originals were found in a vineyard near Rome in 1583 and have been in Tuscany since 1770. Inspired by Greek myths, the statuary includes a slumbering Niobe, as well as a rearing horse and the impressive neo-Attic Medici vase.

Caravaggio to Rembrandt

The Caravaggio Room (43) contains several set-pieces by the theatrical master of *chiaroscuro*. Caravaggio (*c.* 1571–1610) is represented by the screaming, severed head of a *Medusa*, crowned by writhing serpents, as well as by his decadently sensual *Bacchus* and dramatic *Sacrifice of Isaac*. Whether Greek gods, priests or peasants, his gritty and often irreverent figures came from real-life dark alleys of art. By contrast, the Rembrandt Room (44) is a showcase of the Dutch Golden Age, symbolised by Rembrandt (1606–1745), and culminating in his knowing *Self-Portrait as a Young Man* (*c.* 1634) and its sorrowful companion, the *Self-Portrait as an Old Man*.

The Venetian Room (45) plays with the dying embers of Venetian art, the decadent 18th-century. The familiarity of Canaletto's *View of the Ducal Palace in Venice* is virtually a cliché, a limpid scene designed like an idealised stage set. Tiepolo's *Erection of a Statue to an Emperor* gives a flickering sense of the Venetian's illusionistic effects and decorative flair, typical of an artist celebrated for his sublime artifice and virtuosity. As Mary McCarthy claims, "each man strove, if he had genius, to stand alone." While this is true of Italian artists, foreign visitors will feel like collapsing in company, preferably in an art-free bar.

Sculpture gallery

The mesmerising effect of the glorious picture gallery means that the antique sculpture gallery is grossly under-appreciated, and relegated to a scenic thoroughfare. However, a stroll around the U-shaped corridors cannot fail to impress, with their solemn procession of Roman emperors, mythological figures and marble-featured Medici overlooked by portraits of European royalty and Medici Grand-dukes. When your eyes tire of the sculpture, there are beguiling views of the city at every turn.

Contemporary visitors will not be disturbed by the classical nudity that troubled generations past. Broad-minded novelist, E.M. Forster, was surprised at the Florentine equivalent of a fig-leaf, thought necessary to protect delicate Edwardian sensibilities: "How flagrantly indecent are the statues in the Uffizi with their little brown paper drawers. I almost feel that the permanent plaster article of the Catholic reaction is preferable; it did know its own mind."

As passionate patrons and collectors, the Medici amassed a stockpile of classical pieces, many of which were transferred here from the Villa Medici in Rome. However, provenance and dates of the sculpture are uncertain, particularly since many of the antique statues were repaired, or even remodelled, often by famous Renaissance or Neoclassical sculptors. Even so, some of the finest statues come from the core collection created by Cosimo I de' Medici (1519–74) and his sons, Francesco and Ferdinando. Officially founded by Cosimo's eldest son, Grand-duke Francesco de' Medici (1541–87), the sculpture gallery was designed as the companion

The Young Bacchus by Caravaggio, *c.* 1596.

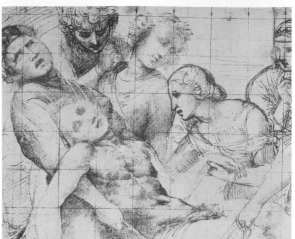

piece to the picture gallery. Fortunately, the present arrangement of the corridors of the Uffizi reflects the original 16th-century design, which remained in place until 1780.

Yet even the sculpture gallery is complemented by low-profile art, including historical and dynastic portraits created especially for the gallery. Ranged along the corridors are Classical statues and busts, displayed beneath a 16th-century ceiling frescoed with grotesque motifs. Masks, monsters and Medici emblems are interwoven with subtle symbols such as the emblem of Francesco's mistress, an oyster opening into the sunlight.

The East Corridor

Also known as the first corridor, the East Corridor begins beside the Vestibule and runs the length of the picture gallery, from rooms 1–24, where it joins the South Corridor and the West Corridor, which borders rooms 25–45. High on the walls, beneath vaulted ceilings, are portraits of ancient kings, emperors and popes, interspersed with dynastic portraits of the Medici and European rulers, from Charlemagne to Philip II of Spain and Elizabeth I of England. As for the statues and sculpture, there is no recognisable order, merely a traditional arrangement of these predominantly Hellenistic works.

THE PRINTS AND DRAWINGS COLLECTION

Known in Italian as the Gabinetto Disegni e Stampe, this world-class collection is currently housed on the first floor. The reorganisation of the Uffizi *(see page 79)* should see the revamping of the collection, but in the meantime, a rotating selection of prints is on display. Given that this is the finest collection of prints and drawings in Italy and the world's greatest collection of Renaissance and Mannerist works on paper, then the need for access is pressing.

The core collection was created by Cardinal Leopoldo de' Medici (1617–75), but, as a result of bequests and donations, the collection continues to expand. In a city that prides itself on the draughtsmanship of its artists, it is natural that these drawings should be superb. Some sketches and drawings date from the 14th century, but the finest are by Renaissance and Mannerist artists of the calibre of Leonardo, Michelangelo, Raphael, Andrea del Sarto and Pontormo. Among the most significant drawings are a fluid nude study by Raphael in charcoal, and a landscape of the Arno valley by Leonardo, a seminal work which is thought to be the first pure landscape drawing in Western art.

The busts in the corridor reflect the sequence of Roman emperors and face their equally stony-faced consorts on the window side of the corridor. Roman busts of Tiberius, Augustus and Agrippa surprise visitors with their contemporary-looking faces and are a testament to creative recycling: the heads may be Roman but the busts are of a later date. Originally, the Roman busts were displayed on walnut stands, of which four remain in the South Corridor; the rest are perched on marble columns.

Greek and Roman works

Next comes *Apollo* (or *Mercury*), a Roman copy of a Greek bronze, sculpted as a nude, curly-headed young god. The Greeks idealised physical beauty and were unabashed about enhancing nature in their male nudes. However, compared with the religious dimension of Tuscan Renaissance statuary, Greek grace is purely physical. Nearby is a statue of *Hercules and a Centaur*, a Roman copy of a Hellenistic original. Below are two world-weary faces of a *Married Couple*, funerary busts from the 1st century AD. On either side of the busts are statues of a *Seated Woman*, one representing Helen and the other Igea; the distinctly masculine portrayal acts as a reminder that Classical sculptors were more familiar with replicating the male body.

Above, the vaulted ceiling is enchanting, with frescoes of birds, battles, nudes and garlanded goddesses. Below, blank-eyed busts of *Julius Caesar, Cicero* and *Sappho* give way to *Sophocles, Demeter* and *Tiberius. Leda*, naturally depicted with a swan, is a powerful Roman work, with Leda's unconscious masculinity contrasted with the effeminate gaze of *Marcus Aurelius* facing her from across the corridor. *Hora*, beyond, is a Roman copy of a Greek original, but a more graceful, feminine portrayal.

The South Corridor

The short but significant South Corridor has lovely views stretching from San Miniato to the Duomo and embracing the Palazzo Vecchio, the River Arno, Santo Spirito and countless ochre-coloured palaces stacked up on the slopes. On display are key works, including a *Sleeping Cupid*; a statue of a mythical *Roman She-Wolf*, and a graceful *Seated Nymph*, which dates from the 2nd century BC. The romantic *Amore and Psyche* is a perennial favourite with visitors, while *Apollo* is an accomplished Hellenistic copy of an original by Praxiteles. Amid the stockpile of Classical pieces, another *Leda* proves the endless fascination with the ancient myth, a complex theme which inspired Michelangelo and other Renaissance artists.

The West Corridor

The adjoining West Corridor displays several statues favoured by Lorenzo the Magnificent; two represent *Marsyas* and are Roman copies of Hellenistic originals, with the red marble one restored by Mino da Fiesole. One of the star pieces is the statue of the *Wounded Warrior* that stands outside Room 42. This kneeling soldier is a rarity in being a Greek original, created in the 5th century BC, but now complete with a Classical head from a different work. Beside it is a seated *Apollo*, which faces *Ganymede*, both Roman copies of Hellenistic works. Other triumphs are a captivating cloven-hoofed *Pan and Daphne*, and a pleasing Hellenistic *Venus*, with a Roman body attached to a 17th-century face. Towards the end of the corridor awaits the most celebrated work, the huge-snouted *Wild Boar*, a first-century Roman copy of a Greek bronze. *Il Porcellino*, a bronze copy of this work, now sits in the Mercato Nuovo and acts as a Florentine lucky talisman.

*FOOD AND DRINK: The **Uffizi Caffeteria**, set beside the Loggia dei Lanzi terrace on the 2nd floor, is over-priced but has the appeal of a terrace and artless views over the rooftops. See also entries for Palazzo Vecchio, page 147, Casa di Dante, page 149 and Santa Croce, page 120.*

Roman bust of Marcus Tullius Cicero, 1st century BC.

Religious Buildings

Florentine churches are effectively galleries of divine art. This chapter covers both the art and architecture of the city's religious buildings from its magnificent cathedral and landmark churches to its cloisters, chapels and refectories

PIAZZA DEL DUOMO

The heart of Florence and home to its defining landmarks: the Cathedral, Baptistery and Campanile

Brunelleschi's dome (built 1420–36) – a poetic symbol of Renaissance grace.

The Piazza del Duomo is dominated by the world's fourth-largest cathedral (after St Peter's in Rome, St Paul's in London and the Duomo in Milan). The richly decorated monuments, clad in coloured marble, were designed to evoke the New Jerusalem, the visionary Paradise whose buildings are described in the Biblical Book of Revelations as "faced with all kinds of precious stones". So huge is the Cathedral that Leon Battista Alberti (1404–72), author of a famous treatise on Florentine art, claimed its shadow could cover every person in Tuscany.

Today, that shadow falls on the tour groups who pack the square, so expect to queue to see the major monuments – these are the Baptistery and Cathedral (Duomo), the remains of Santa Reparata church, the Belltower (Campanile), the Dome (Cupola), and the Cathedral Works' Museum (Museo dell'Opera del Duomo). Since the Baptistery doesn't open until noon, it is best to visit the square after lunch if you want to see everything in one go. To study key details such as the Baptistery doors, you should come before 10am or after 5pm, when you can look at leisure without being pushed aside by tour groups.

Battistero di San Giovanni

Map reference: page 42, E2
Piazza del Duomo. Tel: 055-2302885
Bus: 1, 6, 11, 14, 17, 22, 23
Open: Mon–Sat noon–7pm, Sun 8.30am–2pm;
closed public hols. Admission charge.

As was the practice in the early Christian church, the Baptistery is a separate building west of the Cathedral. Children were baptised as soon as possible after birth, mass baptisms taking place in a tank of swimming pool proportions (long since dismantled). Having been ceremonially plunged into its holy waters, children were regarded as doubly blessed – as both Christians, and as citizens of Florence.

Generations of Florentines were brought up to believe that the Baptistery was originally a Roman temple dedicated to Mars. Though it has not lost its status as the city's oldest building, excavations in the 1970s proved conclusively that there are no Roman foundations to the building at all – an inconvenient fact that modern Florentines prefer to ignore. The supposed link between their Baptistery and the city's Roman past was of immense symbolic significance to 15th-century Florentines. The Renaissance was rooted in the rediscovery of all things Classical, and this building represented a direct link between their golden age and that of Rome.

We now know that the Baptistery was built in the 6th century (the first documentary mention occurs in AD 897). Because it held such a special place in the affections of Florentines, they lavished money on its adornment. Bishop Goffredo of Florence celebrated being made Pope Nicholas II in 1057 by rebuilding it. The Baptistery was made to look more like a Roman building in the 12th century, when it was clad in white and green marble, formed into stripes, rectangles, pediments, pilasters and arcades. This work was completed in 1174 with the addition of the lantern that tops the pyramidal roof.

The south door

From the 14th century, the building was given its three renowned sets of bronze doors, important in marking the watershed between Gothic and Renaissance art. The south door, by Andrea Pisano, completed in 1330, is the oldest of the three. The top 20 uppermost panels depict *Scenes from the Life of St*

OPPOSITE:
The ornately decorated façade of the Cathedral and Giotto's graceful belltower.

THE BAPTISTERY GATES

South Door: *Left door:* 1. Annunciation of the birth of St John to Zachariah; 2. Zachariah is struck mute with disbelief; 3. The Visitation; 4. The Birth of St John; 5. The naming of St John; 6. St John entering the Wilderness; 7. St John preaches to the Pharisees; 8. St John announces the coming of Christ; 9. St John baptises his disciples; 10. St John baptises Jesus.
Right door: 11. St John reprimands Herod; 12. The imprisonment of St John; 13. The disciples visit John; 14. Jesus preaches and heals; 15. Salome's dance; 16. The beheading of St John; 17. The head is presented to Salome; 18. The presentation of St John's head; 19. St John's funeral; 20. His burial.
Bottom 8 panels (from left to right): Hope. Faith. Charity. Humility. Fortitude. Temperance. Justice. Prudence
North Door: *Left door:* 1. The journey to Calvary; 2. The Crucifixion; 3. The Agony in the Garden; 4. Jesus is arrested; 5. The Transfiguration; 6. Lazarus is raised from the dead; 7. The Baptism of Christ; 8. Temptation in the desert; 9. The Annunciation; 10. The Nativity.
Right door: 11. The Resurrection; 12. The Holy Spirit descends on the Apostles at Pentecost; 13. The Flagellation; 14. Jesus is brought before Pilate; 15. Jesus enters Jerusalem on Palm Sunday; 16. The Last Supper; 17. Expelling the money changers from the Temple; 18. Jesus walks on water; 19. The Adoration of the Magi; 20. The dispute in the temple.
Bottom 8 panels (from left to right): St John. St Matthew. St Luke. St Mark. St Ambrose. St Jerome. St Gregory. St Augustine.
Gates of Paradise: *From top to bottom, left to right:* The stories of: 1. Adam and Eve; 2. Cain and Abel; 3. Noah; 4. Abraham and Isaac; 5. Isaac and his sons, Jacob and Esau; 6. Joseph; 7. Moses; 8. Joshua; 9. David; 10. Solomon and the Queen of Sheba.

Esau and Jacob, one of the ten bronze panels that took Ghiberti 27 years to complete.

John the Baptist – the patron saint of Florence, and the saint to whom the Baptistery is appropriately dedicated. The eight lower panels depict Christian Virtues. These are magnificent reliefs by a man who learned his trade by studying the sculptures on Roman sarcophagi, and their Classicism prefigures the style of the Renaissance, though they are still essentially Gothic in their composition. The doors are surrounded by a delightful bronze frame (1462), decorated with nudes, birds and fruits, by Vittorio Ghiberti (son of the more famous Lorenzo – *see below*). Above the door is Vincenzo Danti's bronze group depicting the *Beheading of St John* (1571).

The north door

Next in date is the north door (1403–24), by Lorenzo Ghiberti. In order to win the commission to design these doors, Ghiberti had to compete against all the leading sculptors of his day in a public competition. Ghiberti's winning relief, and that of the runner up, Brunelleschi, can now be seen in the Bargello Museum *(see page 60)*. Together they have been hailed as revolutionary, imbued with the new aesthetic values that mark the start of the Renaissance *(see page 19)*. Despite this, Ghiberti did not actually use his winning panel in the final design. Instead he (and his many assistants in the project) fell back on a style that is late Gothic in essence, with 20 upper panels showing scenes from the New Testament above the Four Evangelists and the Four Fathers of the Church. Ghiberti also designed the frame and included a self-portrait (wearing a hat, on the left-hand side of the door). Above is a bronze group depicting *St John the Baptist with the Levite and the Pharisee* (1511), designed by Leonardo da Vinci but executed by Francesco Rustici.

The Gates of Paradise

For full-blown Renaissance reliefs, we need to turn to the east door, where realistic replicas now take the place of Ghiberti's original gilded bronze doors (the original relief panels are in the Museo dell'Opera del Duomo, *see page 101*). The 10 large panels depicting *Scenes from the Old Testament* (1425–52) took Ghiberti most of his life to execute, and when they were finally installed, Michelangelo hailed them as "fit to adorn the Gates of Paradise", hence the name by which they are now often known. Again the frame contains Ghiberti's self-portrait (fourth from the top on the left) among busts of the other artists who assisted him. The marble group above is a copy of Sansovino's *Christ and St John the Baptist* (1502).

Scenes from the *Last Judgement* on the Baptistery ceiling. The other mosaics, set in concentric circles, depict angelic choirs, stories from the Book of Genesis, stories about Joseph, the lives of Christ and the Virgin and the life of St John the Baptist.

The mosaics

Moving inside the Baptistery, we leave the Renaissance behind and return to the Middle Ages. The ceiling is covered in striking mosaics that depict the main events of the Old and New Testaments, from the story of Creation to the Last Judgement. Executed in sparkling gold, ruby and turquoise glass cubes, they are the work of various 13th-century artists. With binoculars you can pick out many humorous details. Having eaten the fruit of the Tree of Knowledge in the Garden of Eden, Adam ungallantly points the finger of blame at Eve, a ringlet-haired girl who puts her finger to her mouth in a cartoon gesture as if to say "What, me?" As Salome dances, King Herod claps his hands in time to the music and a dog lifts his head to howl.

Beneath the dome, there are the remains of the pavement of 1209, inlaid with signs of the Zodiac. To emphasise the antiquity of the building, two Roman sarcophagi have been reused as Christian tombs (left of the altar). Two genuine Roman columns have been incorporated into the graceful marble cladding to the right of the altar, where they flank the marble tomb of Pope John XXIII *(see page 13)*, who died on a visit to Florence in 1419, with a bronze effigy of the sleeping pope by Donatello (1425).

Santa Maria del Fiore

Piazza del Duomo
Bus: 1, 6, 11, 14, 17, 22, 23
The Duomo *(the Cathedral)*
Tel: 055-2302885
Open: Mon–Wed and Fri 10am–5pm, Thurs 10am–3.30pm, Sat 10am–4.45pm, Sun 1.30–4.45pm. Admission free.
Santa Reparata *(inside the Duomo)*
Tel: 055-230 2885
Open: daily 10am–5pm, closed public hols. Admission charge.
Cupola del Duomo *(the Cathedral Dome)*
Tel: 055-2302885
Open: Mon–Fri 8.30am–7pm, Sat 8.30am–5.40pm; closed Sun and public hols. Admission charge.
Campanile del Duomo *(Giotto's Belltower)*
Tel 055-2302885
Open: daily 8.30am–7.30pm, Sun 9am–1.40pm; closed public hols. Admission charge.

In the days when the Baptistery was still in use, newly baptised infants (neophytes) were carried in procession to the Domus Dei (Latin for "House of God", from which the modern Italian word *Duomo* – Cathedral – is derived). The Cathedral in

RIGHT: The inside of the dome, painted with scenes of The Last Judgement by Vasari, 1572–9.

FAR RIGHT: A vertiginous view from the top of the dome.

Florence was not only God's house, it was large enough to accommodate the entire population of 15th-century Florence – some 30,000 adults.

The project to build such a vast edifice was entrusted to Arnolfo di Cambio in 1294. Spurred on by rivalry with Pisa, whose magnificent white marble cathedral *(see page 207)* was nearing completion, the city council decided to go one better. Property around the square was compulsorily purchased and demolished, and di Cambio was instructed to build "with the greatest and most lavish magnificence possible, the finest work within the ability of man."

Giotto's Belltower (the Campanile)

Work proceeded rapidly, but was cut short by di Cambio's death in 1302. Various artists succeeded him as chief architect, including Giotto (1266–1337), whose contribution was to build the elegant Campanile (bell-tower) that stands to the south of the façade. Set into the south wall of the Cathedral, in the area between it and the Campanile, are two carved stones. One is an Annunciation scene from the di Cambio era, the other an inscription recording the start of work on the new building in 1296.

The Campanile itself is a graceful building, decorated with statues and reliefs (the originals are now in the Museo dell'Opera del Duomo, *see page 100*). Subsequent architects picked up decorative themes from the Campanile, so that the magnificent Gothic doorways and the green, red and white marble cladding on the north and south flanks of the Cathe-dral give the appearance of one harmonious building project, despite taking 170 years to complete. Even the neo-Gothic façade, added in 1876–87, manages to capture the spirit of the original work.

The crowning glory of the Cathedral is the swelling dome *(see next page)*, completed in 1436, the year in which the church was finally consecrated. As his reward for completing the world's tallest and widest dome, Brunelleschi was laid to rest in the cathedral in 1446, the only person ever to be honoured with burial within the Cathedral walls. His simple grave, with an epitaph comparing his gravity-defying achievement to that of Icarus, the mythical inventor of flight, can be seen by visiting the excavated remains of Santa Reparata church (entered down stairs in the nave, to the right as you enter the Cathedral).

Santa Reparata

The first cathedral on this site was Santa Reparata, and it remained standing for some time to allow worship to continue while the new one was built around it. Florentines continued to be buried within its walls – you can see the tomb of Giovanni de'Medici, for example, who died in 1351. At some stage the old Cathedral was demolished and forgotten until archaeologists rediscovered these remains in 1965–74. A model has been provided to help you interpret the tangle of remains, which include the fragments of successive churches on the site, dating back to the 8th century, as well as the walls and mosaic floors of late-Roman buildings.

The interior

After the magnificence of the exterior, the Cathedral's plain interior can seem an anti-climax. Such colour as there is comes from the stained-glass windows (mainly 15th-century) and from the frescoes that Vasari painted from 1572–79 on the underside of the enormous dome. Critics have questioned whether the quality of the work justified the US$6 million that has recently been spent on its restoration. Vasari intended these scenes of the Last Judgement to rival the work of Michelangelo in the Sistine Chapel in Rome, but the cartoon-like scenes of devils dragging their victims to hell by the testicles cannot match Michelangelo's more profound vision of eternal damnation.

To the left (north) of the main altar, the Sacristy is entered through magnificent bronze doors by Luca della Robbia, and is lined by cupboards decorated with pictures in inlaid wood. It was to this room that Lorenzo the Magnificent escaped after Mass on 26 April 1478, to avoid assassination by members of the Pazzi family while his brother, Giuliano, was being stabbed to death in another part of the cathedral.

Returning up the north aisle, the famous painting of *Dante and the Divine Comedy* by Domenico di Michelino hangs on the wall of the fourth bay. Though Dante was exiled from Florence by his contemporaries, later generations of Florentines worshipped him almost as a demi-god, and readings of his work that took place here in the Cathedral in the 15th century regularly filled the cathedral.

In the next two bays are two memorial frescoes commemorating Niccolò da Tolentino, painted in 1456 by Andrea del Castagno, and Sir John Hawkwood (known in Italian as Giovanni Acuto), painted by Uccello 20 years earlier. Both men were *condottieri*, mercenaries, under whom the Florentine army achieved numerous victories. Contemporaries derided the Florentines as mean-spirited for honouring their military heroes with mere frescoes, instead of magnificent equestrian statues. Perhaps they were right, but within the context of this very plain building, these frescoes stand out as distinguished and important monuments.

Turning to leave, you will see that even the cathedral clock (on the west wall) is a fresco, painted by Uccello in 1443. (The clock may puzzle you until you realise that the hand moves anti-clockwise and the 24 hours of the day start at sunset the previous day.)

Circulating round the Cathedral to the left as you leave, you will find the entrance to the dome on the southern side of the nave. Climbing the 96-metre (299-ft) dome is an adventure that allows you to study the construction and enjoy a wonderful view of the city and the surrounding hills. Be warned, though, that vertigo sufferers might find the catwalks and spiral staircases difficult to manage.

Brunelleschi's Cupola

With overweening confidence, the architects of Florence Cathedral planned to crown the structure with the highest and widest dome *(cupola)* ever built in the world, but they had no idea at all how to construct it. In 1418, they announced a competition and offered a prize of 200 gold florins to anyone who could show them how the dome could be built. With such a valuable prize on offer, hun-

Dante and the Divine Comedy, by Domenico da Michelino, 1465.

The Annunciation, detail depicting the Angel Gabriel from a stained glass window by Fra' Paolo di Mariotto da Gambassi, from a design by Ghirlandaio, 1508.

dreds of ingenious ideas were submitted. One suggested using lightweight pumice stone to build the dome. Another proposed supporting it with a huge mound of earth; if coins were buried in the soil, it was argued, street urchins would be motivated to remove the soil on completion in order to find the buried treasure.

One man emerged who had the skill and energy to undertake the work: Filippo Brunelleschi. He became obsessed with the challenge of the dome, and went to Rome to study the archetype of all domed buildings, the 2nd-century AD Roman Pantheon. He submitted a proposal to construct a self-supporting dome that could be built without the prodigious expenditure of timber for scaffolding. According to Vasari (in his *Lives of the Artists*), the judges dismissed him as "an ass and a babbler."

Brunelleschi bided his time. He won commissions to do building work elsewhere in the city, and his reputation for delivering sound structures began to grow. He continued to refine his ideas and lobby for their acceptance. In 1419, when the solution to the dome problem was still no nearer resolution, Brunelleschi was appointed one of three joint *capomaestri* (chief architects) to supervise the Cathedral's construction. By 1422 he had been given tentative permission to start work on the dome, and once he had proved that his ideas worked, nobody could quarrel with his method any more.

When the dome was finally completed in 1436, the ridicule that Florence had once heaped on his head turned to praise. Since then, as a mark of respect, no building in Florence has ever been constructed higher than this soaring dome. (For more detail on the construction of the Cupola and Brunelleschi's other work, see *The Brunelleschi Trail, pages 27–29*)

Museo dell'Opera del Duomo

Map reference: page 42, E2
Piazza del Duomo 9. Tel: 055-2302885
Bus: 1, 6, 11, 14, 17, 22, 23
Open: Mon–Sat 9am–7.30pm; closed public hols. Admission charge.

At the eastern end of the Piazza del Duomo you will find the Museo dell'Opera del Duomo, the Cathedral Works' Museum. This was set up by Brunelleschi in 1432 as the base from which the *capomaestri* supervised the construction and maintenance of the Cathedral. Today, it houses a number of outstanding works of sculpture from the Cathedral and the Campanile, many of them brought indoors as a conservation measure.

The museum opens with a display of Etruscan and Roman funerary urns from the excavation that took place in the area between the Cathedral and the Baptistery in 1971–72. While this failed to support the long-held Florentine belief that the Baptistery was a converted Roman temple, it did show that religious activity in the area dates back to the 5th century BC.

Saints, madonnas and stones

The next room has Gothic sculptures – including Tino di Camaino's marble figure of Christ raising his hand in blessing – which stood above the Baptistery doors before being replaced by the present Renaissance sculptures. In the next two rooms you will find sculptures that Arnolfo di Cambio and his assistants carved to adorn the façade and side walls of the Duomo. These statues formed part of the half-completed façade that was finally taken down in 1587, when the first in a series of competitions was held to find a new design.

Perhaps the most remarkable point about these weatherworn Gothic figures is that they are here at all: to assemble this collection of 14th-century saints and madonnas, the museum curators scoured private collections all over Europe and museums in Berlin and Rome. Some were found in Florentine gardens and others had long been hidden unrecognised in the Opera del Duomo stores.

Next comes the Lapidarium, an assemblage of carved and inlaid stones, some of which came from the huge Romanesque baptismal font that filled the centre of the Baptistery until it was dismantled in 1577. Dante mentions the font in his *Inferno*, where he sees the heretic Simon Magus and his followers standing in a series of fiery pits "seeming nor more nor less wide to mine eyes then those in my own beautiful St John made for the priests to stand in to baptise" (Canto XIX, 16–19).

Gates of Paradise

Next comes the courtyard – open to the skies until the glass roof was inserted as part of recent modernisation of the museum – which originally served as a masons' yard. It was here that Michelangelo carved his David, originally intended for display in front of the Cathedral. Now it is home to five of the original 10 panels from the Baptistery Gates of Paradise (the others are still being restored).

The original scheme was for 28 panels, to match the north and south doors, but one of Ghiberti's innovations was to combine the Biblical stories to create just 10 square panels, each of which contains several episodes from the same story. The various elements in the narrative are distributed fluidly over the space, leaving viewers to understand and supply the links. Episodes from the story of Cain and Abel, for example, are set in a hilly landscape, where the receding hills also help to give the panels that sense of distance and depth that was a key innovation of Renaissance sculpture, breaking free of the two-dimensionality of Gothic art.

Ghiberti was assisted by numerous artists in the creation of these panels, which perhaps explains the very different styles, from the formal patterning of the crowded battle scene in the story of David and Goliath, to the astonishingly realistic story of Jacob and Esau, in which the figures are sculpted in such bold relief that they literally stand clear of the background, like actors on a stage.

Michelangelo's *Deposition*

Climbing the stairs from the courtyard you come face to face with Michelangelo. The *Deposition* on the mezzanine floor is a pyramidal composition of three figures, which includes his self-portrait as Nicodemus, the hooded figure supporting the dead Christ, flanked by the Virgin and Mary Magdalene. Michelangelo was 80 years old when he carved this group, intended for his own funerary chapel in Santa Maria Maggiore in Rome. Vasari says, in *Lives of the Artists*, that Michelangelo stopped work because the imperfect marble shattered, leaving the statue mutilated. Another account says that Michelangelo wasn't happy with his own work – Christ's broken and tortured body successfully conveys a sense of the agony his limbs experienced on the cross but not of his essential divinity. One of Michelangelo's pupils, Tiberio Calcagni, attempted to complete the work and it was his hand that produced the rather stiff figure of Mary Magdalene.

A very different version of that work is found on the first floor, where Donatello's astonishingly expressive figure of Mary Magdalene is in a room to the right. This work, very modern in feel, is a dramatic portrait of the repentant Magdalene in old

The Deposition, by Michelangelo, *c.* 1550.

Zuccone" by irreverent Florentines because of the marrow-like shape of his head), and his very realistic Jeremiah.

Labours of Man

The adjacent room displays the original bas-reliefs made by Andrea Pisano for the Giotto Campanile, on the theme of the Labours of Man. The 28 panels are full of fascinating details showing how 14th-century builders, weavers, wood-carvers, and stonemasons went about their daily work.

That theme is picked up in the final section of the museum, which is concerned with Brunelleschi's achievement in building the dome – tools, brick moulds, pulleys and scaffolding are used to recreate the appearance of a 15th-century Florentine building – and with the competitions to design a lantern for the dome and a new façade for the Cathedral.

In the case of the lantern, the task was entrusted to Baccio Agnolo, but work stopped when Michelangelo passed unfavourable judgement, saying it looked as flimsy as a straw cage used by boys to capture crickets. Today, only the southern side remains complete. By contrast, after years of rivalry and contention, a design was finally chosen for the Cathedral façade – that of Emilio de Fabris – and this time it was completed in 1887, just 591 years after the Cathedral was begun.

Musical Angels, a relief from the Cantoria (choir gallery) by Luca della Robbia, c. 1435.

age, when sorrow and abstinence has hollowed her face to a skull, and her once luxuriant hair has become a penitential hair shirt.

Choir galleries

At the opposite end of the emotional spectrum, the main room on the first floor is devoted to the two wonderful choir galleries carved by Donatello and Luca della Robbia in 1348, covered with figures of children dancing and playing musical instruments to illustrate Psalm 150: "Praise him with the sound of the trumpet; praise him with the psaltery and harp." In the same room are statues of patriarchs, prophets, kings and sybils from Giotto's Campanile (the sybils were included because, though pagan, they are supposed to have prophesied the Coming of Christ). Some date from Giotto's time, some from a century later, such as Donatello's *Abakuk* (nicknamed "Il

The Drunkenness of Noah, a decorative marble relief tile from a series illustrating episodes from Genesis, c. 1334–48.

*FOOD AND DRINK: Immediately south of the Cathedral is **Sergio's Bar** (Piazza del Capitolo 1), a great place for enjoying coffee, cakes and a view of the cathedral, the dome, and the street artists who gather on this side of Piazza del Duomo. As the name indicates, **Le Botteghe di Donatello** (Piazza del Doumo 28r; tel: 055-216678; moderate) stands on the site of Donatello's workshop and serves anything from pizza to squid in garlic sauce or involtini di manzo (rolls of stuffed beef).*

***Buca San Giovanni** (Piazza San Giovanni 8; tel: 055-287612; moderate), to the west of the Baptistery, is a typical hole-in-the-wall Florentine restaurant with a menu of earthy basics, such as soup or salt cod and chickpeas, and more refined fish, truffle and asparagus dishes.*

Badia Fiorentina

Ancient Benedictine abbey with a landmark painting by Filippino Lippi and a peaceful cloister decorated with frescoes

Map reference: page 42, E3
Via della Condotta 4. Tel: 055-264402
Bus: A, 14 and 23
Open: Mon 3–6pm only (enter via side door on Via Dante Alighieri). The cloister is currently under restoration. Admission free.

The unusual six-sided *campanile* (belltower) of the Badia Fiorentina (also known as Santa Maria Assunta) is a distinctive component of the Florentine skyline. The abbey was founded in AD 978 by Willa, widow of Uberto, the Margrave of Tuscany, in memory of her husband. The Margraves had ruled northern Tuscany since the 6th century from their base in Lucca, but the focus of power was already shifting to Florence, and it was here that Willa's son, Ugo, chose to be buried, having lavished gifts on the abbey during his reign as Margrave. Originally, he was laid to rest in a Roman sarcophagus, but the monks honoured their benefactor with a new tomb, a fine marble shrine (decorated with angels carved by Mino da Fiesole in 1469–81) that stands in the left transept.

Before you get to the transept, your attention is likely to be grabbed by the radiantly colourful painting by Filippino Lippi showing St Bernard in a state of ecstasy as he holds a conversation with the Virgin, who has appeared to him in a vision. This wonderful work of 1486 is captivating because of the incidental details borrowed from everyday life that make this painting a landmark in the development of Renaissance realism – such as the crowd of angels who accompany the Virgin, listening to the conversation as they cluster around her skirts.

The appearance of the church has changed several times during its history. The present arrangement is due to the remodelling by Matteo Segaloni in 1627. He turned the orientation round by 90 degrees and added the sober baroque choir and coffered ceiling.

The cloister and the tower

The sacristy to the right of the choir leads to the delightful two-storeyed Chiostro degli Aranci, the Cloister of the Oranges, so called because of the sweetly scented citrus trees that the monks once cultivated here. The graceful cloister, designed by Bernardo Rossellino in 1435, is unusual in having two storeys, and the upper floor is decorated with scenes from the Life of St Bernard, founder of the Benedictine order. The frescoes are the work of a Portuguese artist, Giovanni di Consalvo, whose work bears similarities to the style of such Renaissance pioneers as Masaccio and Uccello.

The cloister (closed at time of writing for renovations) offers good views of the hexagonal belltower. This was built in 1330, on the circular base of its 1307 predecessor, a Romanesque structure that was demolished to punish the monks because, according to the chronicler, Villani, they refused to pay taxes and "closed the doors in the face of the official tax collector". Before Giotto's Campanile was built *(see page 98)*, this was the only belltower on the Florentine skyline. Dante mentions that the hourly ringing of its bell was heard by everyone in Florence, who used it as their timekeeper. The Badia Fiorentina is where Dante first set eyes on his revered Beatrice, the woman he idealises and idolises in the paradise of his *Divine Comedy*. Fittingly, the church was also the venue for the lectures that Boccaccio delivered on the great poet in the 1350s.

*FOOD AND DRINK: Just south of the Badia is a cluster of pavement cafés, including the hole-in-the-wall **Bar Nazionale** (Piazza San Firenze 7r), where there is just room to stand as you tuck into simple coffee, filled rolls or pastries. The **Bar-Pasticceria San Firenze** (Piazza San Firenze 2; tel 055-211 426; moderate; no cards) is a renowned pastry shop set inside the 15th-century Palazzo Gondi; you can either buy delicious savouries and fruit tarts to eat on the steps of the law courts, or you can sit down at the pavement tables and enjoy a light salad or a pasta dish.*

Detail of Filippino Lippi's *Virgin Appearing to St Bernard*, 1486.

Chiostro dello Scalzo

A little cloister built by Sangallo, frescoed with some of the most interesting murals in 16th-century Florence

Map reference: page 43, F1 (inset)
Via Camillo Cavour 6. Tel: 055-2388604
Bus: 1, 17 (or any bus to Piazza San Marco)
Open: Mon, Thurs and Sat 8.30am–2pm; closed public hols. Admission charge.

Sangallo's tiny and exquisite cloister consists of slender columns supporting just six arches, and was built for the religious confraternity of the Scalzi (Barefoot), known by that name because the cross-bearer in their annual Easter procession walked bare-footed. The walls of the cloister were painted in 1507 and 1526 by Andrea del Sarto (1486–1530) with *Scenes from the Life of St John the Baptist* (the patron saint of Florence), and the *Four Virtues* (Faith, Hope, Charity and Justice). In between those two dates, Andrea del Sarto was away working in Paris, leaving Franciabigio two scenes to paint: *The Baptist Taking Leave of his Parents* and *The Meeting of Christ and the Baptist*.

The paintings are executed in a technique known as *grisaille*, in which the artist uses just one neutral colour – in this case creamy brown – applied in contrasting shades to give the paintings the quality of a sculptural frieze. Resembling engravings or old sepia-tint photographs, the tragic story of St John is told through a series of memorable scenes that evoke the style of Raphael or Dürer: from the Angel Announcing the Conception of St John to the Elderly St Zacharias, to the Capture of St John, the Dance of Salome, and his final Beheading.

FOOD AND DRINK: see San Marco, page 113.

Fresco of *St Augustine in his Cell*, by Botticelli, *c.* 1480 (Ognissanti).

Ognissanti e Cenacolo

Works by Ghirlandaio and Botticelli in a monastic complex

Map reference: page 42, C2
Borgo Ognissanti 42. Tel: 055-2396802/055-2398700. Bus: 12.
Open: Church Mon–Sat 8am–noon, 4–7pm; Refectory Mon, Tues and Sat 9am–noon (entrance to monastery and refectory to left of church). Admission free.

Ognissanti, set back from the river, is graced by a newly restored baroque façade, a style that fails to find favour with purist Florentines. This, the monastic church of the Umiliati (Humiliated) was founded by a Benedictine order that worked in the woollen cloth industry, the mainstay of the Florentine economy in medieval times.

The interior is a blend of Renaissance and 17th-century styles, crowned by *trompe l'oeil* ceiling frescoes. Adorning the second altar on the right is Ghirlandaio's fresco of the *Madonna della Misericordia*, which depicts the Virgin protecting the Vespucci, whose family tomb lies nearby. These Florentine silk merchants and adventurers would probably have been forgotten were it not for the voyaging Amerigo Vespucci (1451–1512), a Medici agent who followed in the footsteps of the more trail-blazing Columbus and ended up giving his name to America. Between the third and fourth altars is a fresco of *St Augustine in his Study* by Botticelli, and, facing it, a matching *St Jerome in his Study* by Ghirlandaio.

The refectory (*cenacolo*)

The Cenacolo di Ognissanti, the refectory set in the monastic complex beside the church, has 15th-century cloisters. A large fresco cycle dedicated to the *Life of St Francis* bears witness to the fact that the monastery has been in Franciscan hands since 1561. The vaulted refectory contains the most significant art, dominated by Ghirlandaio's *Last Supper*, a work which probably inspired Leonardo da Vinci's *Last Supper* in Milan. This delightfully serene fresco feels far removed from the more poignant depictions in other Florentine refectories. The languid scene is dotted with decorative details, such as the flight of the quails or the lovely peacock and dove, all of which have religious symbolism *(see page 138)*. The Museum of Sacred Art and the sacristy, which contains a Giotto-esque Crucifix, are generally closed.

FOOD AND DRINK: *see entries for Santa Maria Novella, page 128, Museo Marino Marini, page 168, Palazzo Antinori, page 157.*

Orsanmichele

Renaissance statuary on the outside and inside of a Gothic grain hall, guildhall, and former medieval church

Map reference: page 42, E3
Via dell'Arte della Lana (museum entered via a footbridge from the Palazzo dell'Arte della Lana; entrance opposite church door)
Tel: 055-284944. Bus: line A
Open: Church Mon–Fri 9am–noon and 4–6pm in summer, Sat–Sun 9am–1pm; closed 1st and last Mon of month; Museum Mon–Fri guided visits at 9am, 10am and 11am; closed 1st and last Mon of month, Sat Sun at 9am and 1pm (entry after visiting church; see sacristan)
Admission free

O rsanmichele, one of the city's foremost medieval buildings, represents the intriguing meeting point between religious and secular architecture. As a result, the building demonstrates a curious marriage of spiritual and civic roles, with symbols of godly power in the form of patron saints, harnessed to bolster the temporal power of the guilds, who commissioned this unique place. After a Carolingian pilgrimage church was demol-

ished on the site, it was replaced by an open loggia in 1285 and used as a corn hall. However, miracles were still associated with the site long after the subsequent reincarnation of Orsanmichele as a covered grain market and merchants' court in 1337.

Even though the Gothic grain hall was converted into a church shortly after it was built, it still retains a mercantile medieval atmosphere. Indeed, Orsanmichele remained within the commercial centre of the city until the 1860s, when the medieval quarter was razed to make way for Piazza della Repubblica. But old commercial habits die hard: despite the disappearance of the main medieval market, Orsanmichele survives at the heart of the modern shopping district.

Resembling a truncated tower, the upper storey began as a granary but housed archives in the 16th century before eventually being converted into a museum for the statuary that graced the façade – the finest outdoor sculpture gallery in the city until conservationists won the day over nostalgic art-lovers. The original statues, which reflect the golden age of Florentine sculpture, have largely been moved inside, and are being replaced by copies on the façade. They are remarkable in running the gamut from Ghiberti and Donatello to Giambologna, representing the transition from the idealisation of late Gothic statuary to freer Renaissance forms.

RIGHT: Section of Orcagna's tabernacle showing the *Death and Assumption of the Virgin*, 1359.
ABOVE RIGHT: Niche statue of *St Mark* by Donatello, created for the Linen Drapers' Guild, 1413.

Andrea Orcagna's monumental tabernacle (1359) frames a *Madonna and Child* by Bernardo Daddi (1347).

Created in 1413–16 for a niche here, the work represents the first life-size bronze statue of the Renaissance, with the saint impressively cast in one piece. Next comes Verrocchio's *Incredulity of St Thomas*, a bronze replica commissioned by the merchants' guild and created from 1473–83 to replace an earlier work by Donatello. Beside it is Giambologna's *St Luke*, made for the judges and notaries guild in 1601.

On the Via Orsanmichele side, one's eye is drawn to the statue furthest away, a copy of Donatello's trail-blazing *St George* and his relief of *St George and the Dragon*, commissioned by the armourers' guild; the original is now on display in the Bargello *(see page 59)*. Historian Vincent Cronin comments on Donatello's debt to ancient Greek sculpture yet adds "Whereas Greek grace was purely formal and physical, here there is another, religious dimension." This chivalric saint also embodies the watchfulness and depth of character in stone for which Donatello was renowned.

Further along, on the Via de' Lamberti façade, the first statue that comes into view is a copy of Donatello's *St Mark*, created for the linen-drapers' guild. The penultimate work on this façade is Luca

Transformation

The transformation of Orsanmichele into a church in 1380 involved sealing the arcades and bricking up the façade, followed by the creation of new windows; even so, there are still signs of Gothic tracery on the façade. The lower walls have 14 canopied niches, each containing a statue of a patron saint of one of the city's major guilds. Known as the Arti Maggiori, the guilds commissioned sculptors of the stature of Donatello, Ghiberti, Verrocchio and Luca della Robbia to do the work. One-upmanship and ostentation might have been at the heart of the original enterprise, but the result is posterity's gain.

Before going inside Orsanmichele, walk around the building to admire the procession of saintly statues, even if most are now skilful copies. On the far left of the Via dei Calzaiuoli façade is the first statue, Ghiberti's revolutionary *St John the Baptist*.

THE GREATNESS OF THE GUILDS

Orsanmichele, built as a covered grain market, also served as a guildhall for the Arti Maggiori, or Greater Guilds, which provided the city with economic stability in times of political uncertainty, and represented the rising power of the bourgeoisie. This building, and the adjoining Palazzo della Lana *(see next page)* are also testaments to the wealth, cultural prominence and patronage of the medieval guilds who sponsored public buildings and commissioned great works of art to add to their prestige.

Foremost among the guilds was the Arte della Lana, which represented the wool-merchants and cloth-makers, and had its headquarters here. The building is a reminder that the wool and cloth trade fuelled the city's prosperity and growth in the 13th century, creating a vast trading empire which employed over a third of the population in medieval Florence. Without such wealth, the Renaissance would only have been an irrational whim on a Medici wish-list.

della Robbia's *Madonna Enthroned*, created by the inventor of the famous technique of enamelled terracotta *(see page 59)*.

The gloomy church (currently undergoing restoration) forms a rectangular hall, divided by two parallel naves and enlivened by frescoed vaults and Gothic stained-glass windows. A relic of the building's mercantile past survives in the grain chutes, still outlined against pillars, which once sent corn from the granary to the ground floor. The greatest art-work on view is the bejewelled Gothic tabernacle by Andrea Orcagna, intended as an act of thanksgiving after the city survived the Black Death. The work is also a jewel of Florentine craftsmanship, studded with cherubs and carved reliefs, and ornamented with vivid glass and marble. Amid the paintings, reliefs and devotional images of the Madonna is Bernardo Daddi's frame of carved angels for the *Madonna and Child*.

On to the museum

Orsanmichele stands beside the medieval Palazzo dell'Arte della Lana, which connects with the Orsanmichele Museum by means of an overhead passageway. Built for Cosimo I in 1569, the corridor gave the Grand-duke access to the contracts and wills archived in the upper storey. The Palazzo itself was built by the powerful wool-merchants' guild in 1308 but was clumsily restored in 1905.

The vaulted halls of the medieval granary and meeting room now house Orsanmichele Museum, which is essentially a showcase for the Renaissance statuary removed from the façade. The statues were commissioned by guilds ranging from butchers and tanners to silk-weavers and linen-drapers, judges and notaries, masons and carpenters.

The finest original statues on display are Ghiberti's *St John the Baptist*, Verrocchio's *Incredulity of St Thomas*, and Donatello's *St Mark* (copies of which have already been noted on the Orsanmichele façade). Ghiberti's *St Matthew* and *St Stephen* should be moved here after being restored. The floor above currently displays the smaller statues from the façade: 40 minor sculptures of saints and prophets linked to the guilds. However, while the restoration work is underway, the permanent arrangement of exhibits is open to doubt. Whatever the current state of the museum, compensations lie in the glorious views over the city, stretching from the Palazzo Vecchio to the Boboli Gardens.

FOOD AND DRINK: see Palazzo Vecchio, page 147.

San Lorenzo and the Medici Tombs

A remarkable Renaissance church, designed by Brunelleschi with pulpits by Donatello and Michelangelo's Medici tombs

Map reference: page 42, E2
Bus: 1, 17, 23
San Lorenzo Church
Piazza San Lorenzo
Tel: 055-216634
Open: Mon–Sat 10am–5pm; closed public hols.
Admission charge.
The Medici Tombs
Piazza Madonna degli Aldobrandini
Tel: 055-2388602
Open: Tues–Sun 8.15am–5pm, public hols 8.15am–1.50pm; closed Mon.
Bookshop. Admission charge.

Consecrated in AD 393 by St Ambrose, Bishop of Milan, San Lorenzo is the city's oldest church. At the same time it is the city's first modern church, for when the decision was taken to rebuild San Lorenzo, in 1418, with funds provided by Giovanni di Bicci de' Medici, Brunelleschi set out to produce a building that would embody Renaissance principles in stone. All the other great churches of

The Sagrestia Vecchia – the Medici family chapel designed by Brunelleschi (1419–28).

The Martyrdom of St Lawrence by Agnolo Bronzino, 1565–9.

Florence are Gothic, a northern style imported from Germany and France. This one marks a return to the Classical style that originated in Rome: it is the architectural equivalent of the rediscovery in art of realism and perspective, and in the humanities and sciences of the rediscovery of ancient Greek and Latin learning that fuelled the Renaissance.

Brunelleschi spent some years in Rome studying Classical buildings *(see page 27)*. He returned with precise ideas that took shape as he supervised the construction of San Lorenzo: the height of the columns in the nave in proportion to the height, width and depth of the building were all carefully planned; he didn't want tombs or frescoes violating the geometric perfection of his light-filled monochrome spaces.

Splashes of colour

He didn't quite get his way. There are some extraordinary splashes of colour among the sober tones of grey *pietra serena* sandstone. One is Rosso Fiorentino's *Marriage of the Virgin* in the second bay on the right, an inventive work in Mannerist style. Another is the huge fresco of the *Martyrdom of St Lawrence* in the opposite aisle, another piece of Mannerism by Agnolo Bronzino, full of naked human figures in a variety of contorted poses. In its own chapel to the left of this fresco is an unusual mid-20th-century work, showing *Christ in the Carpenter's Workshop*, by Pietro Annigoni (1910–88), the sky in the background symbolically streaked with the blood of Christ's sacrifice.

Two massive bronze pulpits, designed for the reading of the Scriptures during Holy Mass, stand nearby on top of marble columns. Executed in 1460, they are the mature work of Donatello (1386–1466), and are covered in crowded scenes depicting the Agony in the Garden, the Trial, Crucifixion, Deposition and Burial of Christ, on the northern side of the nave, and the Christ in Limbo, the Resurrection, Christ Appearing to the Apostles and Pentecost, to the south. Donatello himself is buried nearby, in the Martelli Chapel, the first chapel on the left in the northern transept. The same chapel contains an exquisite mid-15th-century *Annunciation* by Filippo Lippi, considered one of his finest early works.

Donatello was buried here at the request of Cosimo de' Medici (the Elder), who greatly admired the artist's work, and wanted his tomb to be close to his own. Cosimo, who died in 1474, is buried in a vault in front of the High Altar, under a memorial slab inscribed with the words: *Vixit Annos LXXV Menses III Dies 20 Pater Patriae* (Lived 75 years, 3 months and 20 days, Father of his Country).

Cosimo's father, Giovanni di Bicci de' Medici (died 1429), the wealthy banker who founded the Medici dynasty, is buried in the Sagrestia Vecchia (Old Sacristy), off the north transept, built by Brunelleschi as the Medici mausoleum.

The bronze entrance doors, with their animated figures of Apostles, Saints, Martyrs and Fathers of the Church, are by Donatello. His, too, are the circular *tondi* in the chapel walls depicting the Evangelists and the Life of St John the Evangelist in terracotta and plaster relief. Giovanni's sarcophagus in the centre of the chapel is by Buggiani, while his grandsons, Giovanni (died 1463) and Piero de' Medici (died 1469), are buried in the huge urn-like sarcophagi of porphyry and bronze set into the walls, designed by Verrocchio.

The failure of the Great Council

The dome over the altar is painted with the passage of the sun through the stars and constellations as they were on 4 July 1439. This was a date of great importance in the history of Florence and of the Christian church, for it was on this day that a document was signed in Florence Cathedral designed to unite the Roman Catholic and the Eastern Orthodox churches. The signing was the culmination of the Great Council, held in Florence to resolve differences over issues such as the nature of the Trinity and the authority of the Pope, aiming to reunite the two branches of the Catholic Church that had

been divided for six centuries. Agreement was greeted with ringing phrase: "Let the heavens rejoice, for the wall which divided the Western and Eastern Churches has fallen." Sadly, it was not to be: no sooner had the Eastern delegates returned to Constantinople than they abandoned the agreement.

Several more members of the Medici family are buried in Michelangelo's Sagrestia Nuova (New Sacristy), situated off the opposite transept, but this now has a separate entrance, which involves leaving the church and walking round the southern side to the eastern end, to the Cappelle Medicee.

The Medici Chapels

In the cold, dark mausoleum to the rear of San Lorenzo you will encounter the graves of Medici family members who once ruled great swathes of Europe, having married into the major ruling dynasties of Naples, France and Spain. You enter the mausoleum via the crypt, where floor slabs commemorate the lesser members of the family, including the very last of the line, Anna Maria

THE UNFINISHED FAÇADE

In 1516, Pope Leo X awarded Michelangelo the contract to design the façade for San Lorenzo. Michelangelo built a scale model (now displayed in the Casa Buonarotti Museum, *see page 148*), and visited Carrara to select marble for the work, but the Pope then changed his mind and asked Michelangelo to turn his attention to the Sagrestia Nuovo instead. Michelangelo got as far as completing the balcony and three doors that you can see on the interior of the western wall as you leave the church. The exterior consists simply of rough stone and brick, exactly as it was left in 1480.

San Lorenzo's unfinished façade.

Ludovica, whose death on 12 March 1743 marked the end of 350 years of Medici rule in Florence. Most are buried beneath simple slabs recording their names, titles and dates of birth and death.

For a select few, more elaborate arrangements were made: six Medici Grand-dukes are buried in the awesome splendour of the marble-lined Cappella dei Principi, above the crypt. Their massive marble coffins are surrounded by acres of coloured marble, a brilliant exemplar of the art of *pietra dura* (pictures made from inlaid stone), at which Florentine craftsmen of the 17th century excelled. Begun in 1589, the floor and walls are decorated with Florentine lilies and other floral symbols, as well as the coats of arms of the 16 bishoprics of Tuscany.

The Medici family members buried here – from Cosimo I (died 1574) to Cosimo III (died 1723) – may have been rulers of a small Italian state, but in their own minds they were near-divine monarchs, as the crowns surmounting their tombs, and the heroic statues of gilded bronze by Pietro and Fernandino Tacca (1626–42), indicate. In the octagonal dome, scenes by Pietro Benvenuti depict the story of Redemption from Adam and Eve to the Resurrection.

The female *Night*, by Michelangelo, reclines opposite a male *Day*, forming the statue pair that decorates the tomb of Giuliano de' Medici, 1533.

Significant achievements

Leading off this overblown chapel is a passage to the much simpler, but in every respect superior, Sagrestia Nuova, the work of Michelangelo from 1520–24 and 1530–33. Here, the chromatic interplay of grey sandstone and white marble walls was inspired by Brunelleschi's Sagrestia Vecchia, but the elemental marble tombs are entirely Michelangelo's own magnificent conception.

They are among the most significant achievements of the Renaissance, carved with the reclining figures of *Dawn* and *Dusk*, over the tomb of Lorenzo, Duke of Urbino (1492–1519), and of *Day* and *Night*, over the tomb of Giuliano, Duke of Nemours (1479–1516). These universal symbols of mortality and mutability – more pagan than Christian – express both the inevitability and tragedy of death.

Michelangelo's figures seem all the more expressive for being incomplete. He worked on these statues at a time of civil war in Florence, for a client (the Medici Pope, Leo X) whose totalitarian politics he detested. At one stage, he was forced to flee from the army of Pope Leo (see page 115). Hiding in this Sacristy, he made pencil and charcoal sketches of mouldings, cherubs, a male torso and a bearded head on the walls to either side of the altar and in the room to the left (distinguishing his sketches from those of his pupils and assistants isn't easy).

Michelangelo departed Florence for Rome in 1534, so the planned tombs of Lorenzo the Magnificent and his brother Giuliano were never begun. Instead, Lorenzo's remains were moved here in

Dawn and *Dusk* keep vigil over the tomb of Lorenzo de' Medici, *c.* 1525.

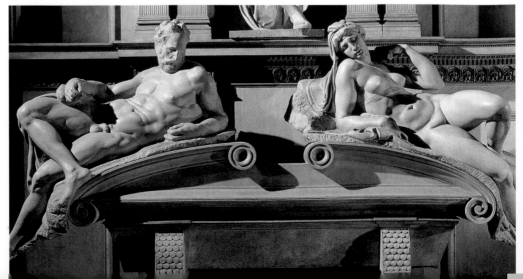

San Marco

The Convent of San Marco contains almost the entire artistic output of Fra' Angelico, who spent much of his life here

Map reference: page 42, F1
Chiesa di San Marco and Museo di San Marco
Piazza di San Marco 1. Tel: 055-2388608
Bus: 1, 6, 10, 11, 17
Open: Church daily 8.15am–1pm and 4–6pm.
Free; Museum Tues–Fri 8.15am–5pm, Sat
8.15am–6.50, Sun 8.15am–7pm, closed Mon
and public hols. Admission charge.

When Fra' Angelico entered the Dominican order at the age of 20, the convent was based in hilltop Fiesole *(see page 201)*. Cosimo de' Medici ("Il Vecchio"), however, invited the monks to move to Florence in 1436, and paid for the reconstruction of the existing medieval buildings, employing his favourite architect, Michelozzo, to create the present series of cloisters, cells, refectory and chapterhouse. Cosimo also donated a large and valuable collection of books and manuscripts, for which Michelozzo designed a beautiful library – the first public library in Europe in modern times.

The first prior of San Marco, the reforming Antonino Pierozzi, was made archbishop of Florence in 1446 and canonised as Saint Antoninus in 1523. He was laid to rest in the Chapel of St Antoninus on the north side of the church, decorated with bronze reliefs by Giambologna. His name was also given to the beautiful Cloister of St Antoninus (1440), which stands to the south of the church, shaded by a huge old cedar. The tranquil cloister is a masterpiece of understated simplicity – appropriate for a monastery that eschews the inessentials of life. The cloister also epitomises Cosimo Il Vecchio's political philosophy. The Florentine magnate deliberately cultivated the image of being a plain, simple man of deep faith, and didn't like ostentation (which attracted only envy in politically turbulent Florence).

Fra' Angelico's gruesome vision of Hell, from his *Last Judgement* fresco, 1432–5, in San Marco.

1559 and three statues were placed above his tomb: Michelangelo's beautiful long-necked *Virgin and Child*, flanked by *Saints Cosmos* and *Damian* (by Montorsoli and Rafaello da Montelupo), medical saints chosen by the Medici as their patrons because of their supposed descent from apothecaries.

*FOOD AND DRINK: escape the bustle of the San Lorenzo market for a coffee in the **Bar Ginori** (Via de'Ginori 11r), opposite the garden entrance to the Palazzo Medici-Riccardi; serves delicious hot chocolate as well as coffee, pastries and light lunches. The area is packed with cheap eateries. One of the most convenient is **Hydra** (Via del Canto de'Nelli 38r; tel: 055-218922), opposite the entrance to the Cappelle Medicee, a pizzeria with a short menu of Tuscan specials, such as ribollita soup and steak Florentine. Typically Florentine is the stall opposite the entrance to the Mercato Centrale selling trippa (tripe) or lampredotto (pig's intestines) in spicy tomato and garlic sauce. Follow that with the home-made ice cream sold at the **Siena Gelateria** (Via dell'Ariento 29r), to the left of the tripe stall.*

The Ospizio and Refectory

On the south of the cloister, the Ospizio (Hospice or Guest House) holds numerous works by Fra' Angelico, gathered together here from churches and collections all over the city. Many of these paintings are characteristic of the transition from the late-Gothic style to the Renaissance. The *Deposition*

The Annunciation
(detail), by Fra'
Angelico, *c.* 1450.

(also known as the *Pala di Santa Trinità*) is a force-ful work that combines Renaissance realism and concern for perspective with a spiritual, dream-like quality that is often missing from Renaissance work. The "Holy Conversation" paintings show various saints standing beside the seated Virgin and Child, apparently discussing spiritual matters. Again, the Renaissance concern to portray real people is mixed with a Gothic delight in gorgeously patterned back-grounds of embossed gold. The saints wear vest-ments of rare and costly colours and tread on the finest of Oriental carpets: heaven is a place of courtly splendour, where it is always springtime.

Moving round the cloister anti-clockwise, you enter the Refectory, with its fresco by Sogliani of *St Dominic and his Brethren fed by Angels*, and the Lavabo, with a *Last Judgement* fresco by Fra' Bartolomeo (1475–1517). Here, too, also by Fra' Bartolomeo, is a haunting portrait of Savonarola, who led a short-lived rebellion against Medici rule, and died at the stake for his pains. Clad all in black, with only the side of his face visible, the firebrand preacher is portrayed with a beak-like nose, thick, sensuous lips and the glimmer of a complacent smile.

The north side

The Chapter House on the north side of the cloister contains an entrancing *Crucifixion* (1441–42) by Fra' Angelico. Once again we are in the realm of the deeply spiritual – there is little sense of the agonising pain that Christ suffered on the Cross; instead, he is presented for our veneration, with a group of saints, monks and evangelists in resplen-dent vestments and halos. The huge convent bell displayed in the Chapter House was rung to warn Florentines that their leader, Savonarola, had been arrested and was being taken to the Palazzo Vecchio for imprisonment, trial and, ultimately, execution.

In the far northeastern corner of the cloister there is another serene work by Fra' Angelico, showing *St Dominic at the Foot of the Cross*. From the centre of the north cloister a passage leads to the foot of the stairs to the Dormitory. At the top is one of Fra' Angelico's most famous works, his *Annunciation*, famous from countless reproduc-tions, and as fresh as the morning when the angel arrived to greet the young Virgin with the good news. It reflects the particular reverence the Dominicans had for the Mother of God.

The monastic cells

The *Annunciation* fresco sits on the side wall of one of the dormitory's 44 monastic cells. Each of these has its own vaulted ceiling, while a second timber roof covers the whole complex. This extraordinary structure was designed to replicate the appearance of the primitive caves in which the first Christian monks led their solitary lives, hermit-like but still part of an organised community. Each cell has a small devotional painting by Fra' Angelico or one of his assistants. Some of these paintings depict recognisable subjects – the Annunciation, or the Nativity, for example – but others are almost surrealistic in their depiction of a ladder, nails, a crown of thorns, a disembodied hand wielding a scourge – symbols of Christ's Passion.

These mystical symbols, designed for intimate contemplation, seem far removed from the enlightened project Cosimo de' Medici embarked upon when he donated the antique manuscripts that form the core of San Marco's public library. This long narrow arcaded hall, designed by Michelozzo, now displays mainly illuminated Antiphonies, huge books containing music to be sung at various feasts of the church. Cosimo's original collection included many of the newly discovered antique (that is, pagan) works that set the intellectual pulse of Florence racing with their revelation of ancient philosophies in the early years of the Renaissance. Perhaps by lodging them here, Cosimo was signalling that pagan ideas had to be filtered through the superior teachings of the Church.

Certainly, Cosimo was in the habit of retreating to the convent, where Cells 38 and 39 (the very last cells on the right as you leave the library) were reserved for his use. The wall of Cell 39 is decorated with the exotic figures of the Three Kings and their retinue visiting the Nativity, in a scene painted

by the young Benozzo Gozzoli. The same artist was later commissioned to paint a larger version of the same subject on the wall of the Medici private chapel in the Palazzo Medici Riccardi *(see page 160)*.

On the opposite side of the building is a group of cells (12–14) occupied by Savonarola when he was prior of San Marco. Today, they are used to display a chair that he is said to have used and fragments of clothing, a hair shirt and a rosary. You can also see two late 15th-century paintings of Savonarola being burned at the stake in Piazza della Signoria, his short-lived Republican revolt ending in ignominy when he was abandoned by his former supporters and executed as a heretic.

Returning downstairs from the Dormitory, the shop on the right of the staircase occupies a small Refectory, painted with a fine *Last Supper* by Ghirlandaio. The last part of the museum, known as the Museo di Firenze Antica, consists of a collection of carved medieval and Renaissance stonework from the Mercato Vecchio and part of the Ghetto demolished at the end of the 19th century and replaced by the Piazza della Repubblica. These are displayed in the rooms and cloisters that once formed the Foresteria (Guest Quarters) of the convent.

Portrait of fanatical reformist, Savonarola, by Fra' Bartolomeo, c. 1498.

*FOOD AND DRINK: For coffee and sandwiches, choose between the **Café S** (Piazza di San Marco 4r) and its near neighbour, **Dini Caffè** (No. 6r), which also sells home-made ice cream. The cool and calm **Accademia** (No. /r; tel. 055-217343) serves a choice of salads, and a special lunch menu featuring seasonal produce. On the corner of the square, the **Gran Caffè San Marco** (tel: 055-284235) is a cake shop that also sells a huge range of pizzas by the slice, as well as pasta dishes and roast. There's a garden terrace at the rear, entered round the corner, at 122r, Via Camillo Cavour .*

Storiated initial "S" depicting the Virgin sheltering supplicants under her cloak, from an illuminated missal by Fra' Angelico.

San Miniato al Monte

A graceful Romanesque church with white marble façade set in a delightfully rural environment of cypress trees and olive groves

Map reference: page 43, G6
Via delle Porte Sante 34
Tel: 055-2342731
Bus: 12, 13 (from the main station)
Open: Church and crypt Mon–Sat 8am–noon, 2–6pm, Sun 8am–noon, 3–7.30pm, but often open over lunch as well, especially on Sun in summer. Cemetery Oct–Mar Thurs–Tues 8am–noon, 2–5pm, Wed 8am–12.30pm; Apr–Sept Thurs–Tues, 8am–noon, 3–6pm, Wed 8am–12.30pm.
Admission Free.

Set in the hills to the south of the city, San Miniato is one of Tuscany's best-preserved Romanesque churches. A chapel stood on the site in the 4th century, marking the spot where St Minias, beheaded in AD 250 in the city's amphitheatre, is said to have expired. According to legend, he got here by picking up his severed head and walking from Florence until he reached this spot, where his followers buried him in a secret cave until it was safe to build a more permanent memorial. Bishop Hildebrand (later Pope Gregory VII) ordered the construction of the present church in 1050.

The earliest part of San Miniato is the crypt (1062), followed by the main body of the church (1070). Last to be completed (in 1207) was the graceful façade, built in white Carrara marble, with columns, arcades and geometric panels in contrasting green *verde di prato* stone. Above the central portal, the Byzantine-style mosaic shows Christ, the Virgin and St Minias (1260), and high above that is the eagle symbol of the Arte di Calimala, the Cloth Merchants' Guild, who funded the maintenance of the church from the 15th century.

The building is a masterpiece of Romanesque design, which still looks back to the Roman basilica (or law court) for its inspiration. The altar is raised high on a dais (where the magistrate's chair was placed in a Roman basilica). The apse is decorated with a huge, 13th-century mosaic of Christ in Majesty –

ABOVE RIGHT: San Miniato's Romanesque facade.

RIGHT: Enthroned Christ between Mary and St Minias, mosaic in the choir apse, 1297.

again with the Virgin and St Minias, but also with the symbols of the Four Evangelists.

Marble covers every surface. The carpet-like decorations of the floor feature dragons, lions and plant motifs derived from Islamic art absorbed through trade contacts with Africa and the East, and from illuminated manuscripts. Right in the centre of the nave is a Wheel of Fortune, with the signs of the Zodiac set within the spokes.

The walls above the arches of the nave are decorated with Christian symbols: the indivisible trinity represented by an endless knot, resurrection by a peacock, self-sacrifice by the pelican, and purity by candles and flowers.

Chapel and crypt

At the focal point of the nave is the little Cappella del Crocifisso (Chapel of the Crucifix). This classically inspired tabernacle was commissioned by Piero de' Medici (Il Gottoso – the Gouty) from

Vault frescoes in the Sacristy depicting the Four Evangelists, by Aretino Luca Spinello, 1387.

Rossellino in 1448. The cupboard at the rear was made to house a miraculous 13th-century crucifix (now in Santa Trinità church), venerated because the painted figure of Christ was seen, allegedly, to nod in approval when John Gualberto agreed to pardon his brother's murderer. The two central figures on the cupboard doors were painted by Agnolo Gaddi in 1394. One represents St Minias, the other John Gualberto, who became a monk, joined the Benedictines of San Miniato, later founded the two great Tuscan monasteries at Camaldoli and Vallombrosa and was made a saint shortly after his death in 1073.

Steps from here lead down into the vaulted crypt, with its forest of reused Roman columns and capitals, sheltering the body of St Minias. The upper choir gives access to the Sacristy, with its frescoes on the *Life of St Benedict*, by Aretino Spinello

(1387). Bearing a strong resemblance to Giotto's *Life of St Francis* in Assisi, this is one of the first depictions of St Benedict's life, and it was to influence greatly those that came after. Among the scenes is one on the south wall, in which Totila the Goth, who invaded Italy in the mid-6th century, tries to trick St Benedict by dressing up one of his guards in purple robes to impersonate him. Though he had never met Totila before, St Benedict instantly recognises the fraud and picks out from the crowd the real Totila, who, in a scene on the east wall, then kneels at the saint's feet.

Among many other 13th- and 14th-century frescoes of saints in the nave walls, the Chapel of the Cardinal of Portugal stands out on the northern side as being a later Renaissance work. The Cardinal died in Florence in 1459, and his uncle commissioned some of the leading artists of the day to create this fine monument. Antonio Rossellino carved the marble figure of the sleeping Cardinal, and Luca della Robbia made the ceiling medallions depicting the Cardinal Virtues.

The cemetery

As you emerge from the church, to the left lies the former bishop's palace, dating from 1295 and used as the summer residence of the Bishops of Florence. Straight ahead is a terrace with sumptuous city views and, to the right, a shop selling toiletries and honey produced by the monks of San Miniato and the mother monastery at Monte Oliveto Maggiore, south of Siena.

Beyond the shop, through an arch, is the Cimitero Mounumentale delle Porte Sante, a cemetery created in 1864 on the site of the demolished fortifications that once surrounded the church. Among hundreds of elaborate tombs here are those of Carlo Lorenzini (the real name of Carlo Collodi, author of *The Adventures of Pinocchio*, who died in 1890), the artist, Pietro Annigoni (died 1988), and former Italian statesman, Giovanni Spadolini (died 1994).

*FOOD AND DRINK: walk down to Piazzale Michelangelo to numerous stands selling cold drinks, or the **Bar Michelangelo**, offering a terrace table with views across olive groves and the city walls. If money is no object, escape the crowds at the **Bar Ristorante La Loggia** (tel: 055-234832), in a 19th-century stone pavilion in gardens to the south of the square. Depending on your mood and the time of day, you can indulge in ice cream, sorbet, fresh fruit, coffee, cakes and sparkling wine, or classic Tuscan cuisine, in elegant surroundings with impeccable service.*

MICHELANGELO UNDER SIEGE

To the north of the church is the damaged stone campanile that Michelangelo incorporated into the city defences to protect Republican Florence against attack in 1530 by an alliance of Charles V of Spain and Cardinal Giovanni de' Medici (later Pope Leo X). In preparation for the expected siege, Michelangelo had extended the walls to encircle the church and tower. He then mounted cannon on the tower, which he wrapped in mattresses to absorb the impact of enemy fire. When battle began in earnest, Michelangelo did not wait to see if his works were effective; he lost his nerve and fled. His fellow Florentines blamed his cowardice on his artistic temperament.

Sant'Ambrogio

Surrounded by the tripe stalls and bustle of the Sant' Ambrogio market, this church is a fascinating building, often overlooked because it is off the beaten tourist track

Map reference: page 43, G3
Piazza Sant'Ambrogio
Bus: line C. Open: usually 8am–1pm, 4–6pm.
Admission free.

Sant'Ambrogio is one of those small, unassuming parish churches that Florence has in abundance, full of fascinating detail, but eclipsed by bigger attractions. Built in the 7th century, it stands on the spot where St Ambrose stayed while visiting the Roman city in AD 393. The church was rebuilt in the 10th century and retains its early-Christian basilican form, behind a 19th-century neo-Gothic façade.

The walls are covered in frescoes and paintings that amount to a mini art gallery. To the right is Niccolò Gerini's late 14th-century *Deposition*, and close by is the slab marking the grave of the architect Cronaca (died 1508), the architect who designed a number of fine palaces in the city as well as the unfinished balcony round the Cathedral dome that Michelangelo so much disliked. In the Baptistery to the right of the altar is an exquisite 14th-century Gothic triptych of the *Virgin and Saints* by Lorenzo di Bicci.

Detail of Cosimo Rosselli's Procession with a Chalice fresco, showing three of the artist's contemporaries, 1486.

Chapel of the Miracle

To the left of the Sanctuary is the Cappella del Miracolo, which once attracted pilgrims in their thousands. The miracle occurred in 1230 when Frate Uguccione, the parish priest, did not dry the chalice properly after Mass. The next day, he returned to find droplets of blood in it instead of wine. Mino da Fiesole designed the marble tabernacle that was built to house the chalice, with its bas-relief depicting the miraculous event. Mino da Fiesole, who died in 1484, chose to be buried at the entrance to the chapel. He is one of several artists depicted in the procession that forms the subject of the chapel's delightful fresco by Cosimo Rosselli, who was clearly influenced by the painting of the *Journey of the Magi* in the Palazzo Medici Chapel *(see pages 4–5 and 160)* by his teacher, Benozzo Gozzoli.

Coming back on the left side of the church, you will walk over the slab that marks the grave of the great sculptor, Verrocchio (died 1488). Works of art worth lingering over include a 16th-century wooden statue of St Sebastian by Leone Tasso, and an unusual mid-15th-century *Nativity* by Alessio Baldovinetti, showing the manger surrounded by angels and saints, rather than the usual shepherds and Magi.

FOOD AND DRINK: *One of the city's top Tuscan restaurants, **Cibreo**, is alongside in Via de'Macci. It is really three eateries in one: a trattoria at 124r, a restaurant that shares the same kitchen just around the corner (Via Andrea del Verrocchio) and a café at No. 124r. The wine bar serves salads and light meals (plates of prosciutto or salami, smoked salmon or cheese), with a long list of wines and cocktails.*

Santa Croce e Museo dell' Opera di Santa Croce

The city's greatest Gothic church, with chapels frescoed by Giotto, and a Renaissance chapel built by Brunelleschi

Map reference: page 43, G4
Piazza di Santa Croce 16. Tel: 055-244619 (church and museum); 055-244533 (leather school). Bus: 14, 23, lines A and C
Open: Church Mon–Sat 8am–5.45pm, Sun 8am–1pm for worship, 3–5.45pm for visits; Museum summer, Thurs–Tues 10am–6pm, winter, 10am–5pm. Bookshop. Leather school with hand-tooled leather goods on sale.

Seen from the far end of the dramatic square, Santa Croce's neo-Gothic façade (1857) makes an immediate impact, with its bold palette of pink, green and white Tuscan marble. This pleasing pastiche, inspired by Orcagna's tabernacle in Orsanmichele *(see page 107)*, has its admirers, who balance its lack of authenticity against the fact that at least it seems finished, unlike numerous other Florentine façades. Supposedly founded by St Francis himself, the Franciscan church was a rival to the Dominicans' Santa Maria Novella.

Despite their love of luxury and splendour, the Florentines were curiously drawn to the asceticism of the Franciscans. The church was built beyond the city walls in a poor quarter populated by tanners, dyers and leather-workers. As the most animated square in the eastern part of Florence, Santa Croce retains its characteristic raffishness and craft workshops; the church even shelters an historic leather school founded by the Franciscans.

Civic pride

Commissioned in a flurry of civic pride in 1294, the majestic church, with the main plans attributed to Arnolfo di Cambio (the Duomo's original architect), was designed to replace an earlier chapel on the site. Santa Croce was finally consecrated in the 14th century and frescoed with a kaleidoscope of early Renaissance painting. Ever since, it has been a place of pilgrimage, in the past attracting everyone from the Romantics to literary Grand Tourists such as Stendhal and E.M. Forster.

Although many were awe-struck by the church, the heroine of Forster's *Room with a View* was at first left unmoved, "unwilling to be enthusiastic over

monuments of uncertain authorship or date". But then she succumbs to "the pernicious charm of Italy…and instead of acquiring information, she began to be happy." The graceful Gothic interior still dazzles, despite the officiousness of ushers who drape gauzy white shawls over tourists who enter the church with exposed arms.

Santa Croce's sense of space, austerity and purity of line are in keeping with Franciscan values. Despite the cavalcade of statuary, the stained-glass windows and the fresco-filled end chapels, the tone is austere, dictated by the barn-like interior and open timber roof. The view from the main doorway spans a satisfying sweep, stretching to the shimmering sanctuary and jewel-coloured windows at the end, and offers a more uplifting experience than the Duomo.

The interior was remodelled by Vasari, a fine art critic but often a poor judge of fine art in the flesh. He destroyed Andrea Orcagna's fresco cycle that once covered the nave, and replaced it with mediocre side altars. On the floor of the apse is an array of realistic or abstract marble tombstones as impressive as the funerary monuments in the nave or the artworks in the lavishly decorated chapels.

The Florentine Pantheon

Dubbed the Florentine Pantheon because of the tombs and funerary monuments to legendary citizens, Santa Croce is a shrine to such luminaries as Dante and Galileo, Michelangelo and Ghiberti, and Marconi, honoured as "the inventor of the radio". Funerary monuments line the long aisles and marble tombstones pattern the floor. In Renaissance tombs, the influence of humanism emphasised the

The coloured marble façade of Santa Croce was re-clad in 1863, financed by an English benefactor, Francis Sloane.

RIGHT: Detail from the *Coronation of the Virgin* altarpiece showing angels, saints and apostles, by Giotto.

BELOW: *The Tree of the Cross* by Taddeo Gaddi, 1360.

exaltation of the dead person's achievements on earth rather than their God-given grace.

The roll call of honour begins in the south aisle, on the left side of the entrance: Michelangelo's tomb (1570), designed by Vasari, is a vacuous work, which cannot hold a candle to the *Pietà* Michelangelo sculpted for his tomb, and which is now in the Museo dell'Opera del Duomo *(see page 101)*. Beside it is Dante's ostentatious funerary monument (1829), with a depressed-looking Dante on top, implying that his exiled spirit prefers to lie at rest in Ravenna rather than linger in the home city that caused him so much suffering *(see page 149)*.

Facing the nave is the fine Renaissance pulpit by Benedetto da Maiano, currently shrouded in scaffolding, as are several chapels. Beside it is Canova's accomplished Neoclassical tribute to the poet, Alfieri, complete with grieving woman at the foot of the monument, modelled on his mistress, the Countess of Albany. By comparison, Machiavelli is ill-served by a vapid 18th-century monument catching nothing of his subtle mind.

Next-door is Donatello's *Annunciation*, a high relief in gilded limestone, and a work of genius. The figures are given exaggeratedly large heads since the head was considered the repository of the soul. Beside it is Rossellino's influential Renaissance tomb for Leonardo Bruni (1447), depicting an effigy of the supine humanist supported by eagles, and completed by an inscription borne by lions. The tomb was the first funerary monument in which a human rather than religious figure predominates. Across the nave is the equally significant monument to another humanist, Carlo Marsuppini, sculpted by Desiderio da Settignano.

Frescoes by Giotto

Just beyond the monument to Bruni and a mediocre memorial to Rossini is the Castellani Chapel, the first of the frescoed spaces painted by Giotto and his school. Although ill-lit and in poor condition, the chapel contains impressive Giotto-esque frescoes attributed to Agnolo Gaddi and his workshop. In the pinkish-green background, the Florentine medieval cityscape unfolds; nearby is a newly restored painted cross attributed to Gerini, set against a traditional gold background.

The adjoining Baroncelli Chapel displays the *Coronation of the Virgin*, a large gilded altarpiece attributed to Giotto (1267–1337), the greatest early Renaissance artist. The work stands in front of frescoes painted by Taddeo Gaddi (1332–38), Agnolo's father and Giotto's most faithful pupil. The gloriously coloured frescoes include serene, harmonious visions of the Virgin and haloed saints, matched by fine stained-glass windows. In the same chapel is a fresco of an angel announcing the birth of Christ to shepherds; executed in 1338, this is one of the earliest depictions of night scenes in fresco painting.

Masterpieces of Santa Croce

The Peruzzi and de Bardi chapels, set on the right of the chancel, represent the artistic masterpieces of Santa Croce. Ill-advised frescoed on dry rather than wet plaster, Giotto's vision miraculously survives, all the more surprising given that the frescoes were whitewashed over in the 18th century, clumsily retouched in the 19th century, and only correctly restored in the 1950s. Framed by stained-glass windows, the Peruzzi Chapel is frescoed with scenes from the lives of *John the Baptist* and *St John the Evangelist*, and graced with a bold altarpiece of the *Madonna and Saints* by Taddeo Gaddi. The de Bardi chapel contains Giotto's poignant fresco cycle devoted to the *Life of St Francis* and evokes a mood of great pathos, with the grieving mourners at the funeral of St Francis echoing the lamentation over the crucified Christ. Giotto's mastery of detail and realism are clear in the scene showing the Ordeal by Fire, while the fresco of *St Francis Receiving the Stigmata* is suffused with spiritual power. On the vaulted section are depictions of the Franciscan vows of poverty, chastity and obedience.

The second de Bardi Chapel in the left transept displays Donatello's *Crucifix* in front of a stained-glass window. Vasari recounts the tale of how Brunelleschi dismissed his friend's attempt at pathos as a "peasant on a cross" and then secretly constructed his superior work *(see page 21)*, which demoralised Donatello enough for him to renounce any future attempts.

Before calling in at the leather school or the museum, visit the sacristy and glance at the neighbouring Medici chapel, reserved for Mass. The chapel is the work of Michelozzo and is graced with a della Robbia altarpiece, while the sacristy, adorned with Taddeo Gaddi's frescoed *Crucifixion*, ends in the inevitable shop – and the corridor connecting to the leather school, set in the former monastic cells.

Secret garden

South of the church lies a secret garden and cloisters designed by Brunelleschi, as well as the worthwhile monastic museum. The Museo dell'Opera di Santa

Croce, reached through the first cloister, occupies the entire former monastery, including the cloisters, refectory and chapels. The serene gardens lead to the somewhat austere Pazzi Chapel, built as a challenge to international Gothic, the prevailing style, for the Medicis' arch-rivals; the Pazzi family met an untimely end, assassinated by Lorenzo de' Medici in an act of revenge.

Yet the deathless chapel could not feel less macabre: it is classic Brunelleschi in its geometry and simplicity of decoration. Although Brunelleschi longed to design fully circular buildings, he was thwarted by ecclesiastical objections. Even so, the chapel, commissioned as a chapterhouse, took the form of a squared circle, considered conducive to

Glazed terracotta altarpiece of *Madonna and Child with Six Saints* from the workshop of Andrea della Robbia, 1490–1500.

contemplation. Set in front of the neo-Gothic bell-tower, the chapel is framed by a colonnaded portico surmounted by a frieze of cherubs and an *Agnus Dei* based on designs by Brunelleschi's friend, Donatello.

The pared-down interior is adorned by terracotta *tondi* of the apostles by Luca della Robbia and by roundels of the Evangelists, by Donatello. In keeping with Brunelleschi's usual practice, grey *pietra serena* highlights the architectural features, with the rest left plain white.

The Pazzi Chapel leads to the second cloister, a restful space also designed by Brunelleschi, but completed in 1453, seven years after his death.

View of the
church and
convent of
Santa Croce
in 1718
(fresco).

Museum of sculpture and art

The rest of the monastic buildings house a museum of sculpture and religious art, focusing on works rescued from the devastating flood of 1966 and the earlier devastations inflicted on Santa Croce by Vasari. The Pazzi Chapel even contains a plaque indicating the floodwater level, which reached a height of 6 metres (18 ft) here *(see page 36)*.

The Gothic refectory is the centrepiece of the museum, containing the symbolic Cimabue *Crucifix*, which was virtually destroyed during the flood. It has been only partially restored, but this was intentional so that the work remains a poignant reminder of the city in peril.

At the end of the hall is a beguiling *Tree of the Cross* by Taddeo Gaddi *(see page 118)* and, in keeping with the traditions of refectory art, an admirable *Last Supper* (1333). Also attributed to Gaddi and set on a lower level, the detached fresco represents the earliest surviving *Last Supper* in

Florence *(see also pages 138–9)*. Nearby are faded frescoes by Orcagna salvaged from the nave of Santa Croce.

The adjoining rooms display fragments of frescoes, friezes and 14th-century stained-glass, as well as enamelled terracottas by the della Robbia workshop. Among the finest of these idealised works by Andrea della Robbia is a lovely *Resurrection* framed by luscious avocados, oranges and pine cones.

FOOD AND DRINK: Vivoli (Via Isola delle Stinche 7, tel: 055-292334, closed Mon) is a bar and gelateria serving the best ice cream in the city. Osteria del Caffè Italiano (Via Isola delle Stinche 11/13r, tel: 055-289368; midday to midnight, closed Mon) offers a light lunch in a lovely palazzo. Boccadama (Piazza Santa Croce 25r, tel: 055-243640; closed Mon) is a wine bar serving light meals, accompanied by fine wines. Il Francescano (Largo Bargellini 16/Piazza Santa Croce, tel: 055-241605) is a convenient, if touristy trattoria for rustic Tuscan food and international cuisine. Santa Croce (Piazza Santa Croce 11r, tel: 055-2479896; closed Nov–Jan) is a touristy but fine pizza and pasta place.

*FOOD AND DRINK: There are two restaurants outside: **Celestino** (Piazza Santa Felicità 4r; tel. 055-2396574) and **BIBO** (No. 6r; tel. 055-2398564). Both offer fresh-air dining, typical Tuscan food, and a good-value fixed price menu. There are also numerous sandwich and pizza bars.*

Deposition, by Pontormo, 1528 (Santa Felicità).

Santa Margherita dei Cerchi

Known as "Dante's Church", because of its associations with the poet, this simple building hosts concerts of baroque music

Map reference: page 42, E3
Via Santa Margherita. Bus: A, 14 and 23
Open: Mon–Sat 10am–2pm, 3–6.30pm, Sun 10.30–11.30am. Organ recitals every Sat at 6pm, and chamber concerts most evenings in summer (see noticeboard outside church). Admission free

Santa Felicità

Late-Roman church, reworked in the 18th century with frescoes by Pontormo, the great exponent of early Mannerism

Map reference: page 42, D4
Piazza Santa Felicità. Bus: line C
Open: usually 8am–1pm, 4–6pm. Admission free.

The graceful portico of Santa Felicità is surmounted by the Vasari Corridor *(see page 85)*. Behind the portico, the present church dates principally from Ruggieri's baroque rebuilding of 1736–39. Sadly, this 18th-century restoration destroyed the fine proportions of the stunning Capponi Chapel, to the right of the entrance, originally designed by Brunelleschi in 1420–5. Even its reduced proportions cannot detract, however, from the weighty emotional punch of Pontormo's *Deposition* painting on the altar and his fresco of the *Annunciation*.

The Mannerist school, to which Pontormo (1494–1556) belongs, is much maligned by people who forget that the arch Mannerist was Michelangelo himself. Mannerists used exaggeration to artistic ends – to heighten the drama of their scenes and to make viewers look at them afresh. Sometimes they altered the proportions of the human body or painted people in exaggerated poses – sometimes they used unnatural colours, as here. Mary McCarthy, the author of *The Stones of Florence*, disliked these works because of Pontormo's homosexuality, and dismissed them as decadent, but she nevertheless described very accurately the extraordinary colours: "peppermint green and boudoir pink, orchid, gold-apricot, pomegranate and iridescent salmon".

Dedicated to St Margaret of Antioch, this tiny dark church is probably late-Roman in origin, although there is no mention of it in records until 1032. From 1353, it was maintained by the Cerchi family, but it became associated with the much more famous names of Dante and Beatrice in the 13th century. Dante (1265–1321) first set eyes on his beloved Beatrice Portinari (1265–91) in May 1274, when she was attending Mass at the Badia Fiorentina *(see page 103)*. He was only nine years old at the time and she was eight. Thereafter, he saw her regularly at this parish, always chaperoned by her nurse, as depicted in the romantic painting (1991) by Mario d'Elia that hangs on the left-hand wall of the nave. The painting on the opposite side shows the *Marriage of Beatrice Portinari* (1928) by R. Sarbi – but the marriage was not to Dante, although he became obsessed with "the glorious Lady of my mind".

Beatrice was married off at the age of 17 to Simone de' Bardi, the son of a wealthy banker, but she died only seven years later. Beatrice and her nurse are buried on the left side of the nave, in the Portinari family vault, where the 14th-century tomb slab carved with the figure of an elderly woman is always marked by a bunch of fresh flowers. Dante married Gemma Donati, but this did not prevent him from portraying Beatrice, the subject of his boyhood passion, as the embodiment of perfection in his various poetic works.

*FOOD AND DRINK: Round the corner from the church, the **Cucciolo Bar** (Corso, No. 25r) does a swift morning trade in bobbolini – doughnuts filled with creamy custard, chocolate sauce or jam – plus focaccia sandwiches or pizza.*

Santa Maria del Carmine

Within this late-baroque church is one of the most influential works in Western art: the fresco cycle on the Life of St Peter

Map reference: page 42, B4
Piazza del Carmine. Tel: 055-2382195.
Bus: 6, line D
Open: Mon and Wed–Sat 10am–5pm, Sun 1–5pm; closed Tues and public hols.
Admission charge

The Temptation of Adam and Eve, by Masolino, c. 1427.

The Carmelite church of Santa Maria del Carmine was built in 1268. Fire destroyed most of the original in 1771, but it spared the Brancacci Chapel in the south transept, and the adjacent Sacristy of 1394, with its frescoed *Scenes from the Life of St Cecilia* by Lippo d'Andrea.

The body of the church was rebuilt by Giuseppe Ruggiere in 1775–82. The style is late baroque, with *trompe l'oeil* circular "windows" through which we glimpse the heavens above. In its way, this rich decoration is very accomplished, and the chapel in the north transept is considered one of the finest works of the Florentine baroque. Designed by Pier Francesco Silvani, with a ceiling fresco by Luca Giordano, it marks the burial place of Andrea Corsini, Bishop of Fiesole, who died in 1373 and was made a saint by Pope Urban VIII in 1629.

Brancacci Chapel

But it is the relatively simple Brancacci Chapel, opposite, that steals the show. Restored in the 1980s, its astonishingly fresh and vibrant frescoes are well worth queuing to see: only 30 people are allowed into the chapel at a time, and theoretically you are allowed to stay only 15 minutes, but if you come towards the end of the day, you can usually stay as long as you wish.

Felice Brancacci, a rich Florentine, commissioned Masolino (1383–1440) to paint the chapel with *Scenes from the Life of St Peter*, but it was his young pupil and collaborator, Masaccio (1401–28), who changed the course of Western art with his innovative and emotionally charged work. Having worked together on the cycle during 1427 and 1428, both artists left for Rome (where Masaccio died tragically young at the age of 27) leaving the cycle unfinished.

Masaccio's contribution can best be appreciated by comparing the two scenes that face each other across the entrance arch. On the right, Masolino's *Temptation of Adam and Eve* shows the graceful, naked couple in the Garden of Paradise. The style is typically late Gothic: Adam and Eve are otherworldly icons of innocence and beauty, sharply delineated but unreal figures representing the peace and harmony with nature that existed until the moment they chose to disobey their Creator.

Masaccio's *Adam and Eve Expelled from Earthly Paradise* on the opposite side are very different. Symbolising the misery of human existence after the Fall, they are among the most powerfully emotive figures ever painted in Western art. Companions no more, each is caught up in lonely despair. No longer beautiful, but gauche, huddled and lumpy, these are very real people. To create these rounded figures, Masaccio pioneered a new and very direct style of painting *(chiaroscuro)*, in

bold gestures, sculptural figure groups and expressive faces (note, for example, the contrast between the head of Christ, painted by Masolino, and the stormy features of St Peter).

The story of the Tribute Money was of particular contemporary relevance, referring to the new tax system – the *catasto* – levied by the Florentine city council to help pay for the maintenance of its army. Until the 1420s, the main source of tax revenue was the *gabella*, levied on sales of food and wine and on goods passing through the city gates.

The new tax was based on an estimate of the citizen's wealth, and was therefore strongly opposed by the city's richest merchants. Brancacci was instrumental in setting up the new tax, but this did not prevent him from being sent into exile in 1436; it was at this time that all the portraits of the Brancacci family were eliminated from the scene on the far left (lower tier) of *St Peter Raising Theophilus from the Dead*. This was one of the paintings that Filippino Lippi worked on in 1481–82, when he skilfully completed the cycle, adapting his style to blend with the earlier work.

Adam and Eve Expelled from Earthly Paradise, by Masaccio, *c. 1427*.

*FOOD AND DRINK: In the square in front of the church, the chic, modern **Dolce Vita** (Piazza del Carmine 6r; tel: 055-28495) is a great place for coffee during the day (closed Sunday). The polar opposite is old-fashioned **Trattoria del Carmine** (No. 17; tel. 055-218601), with a basic but tasty menu of crostini, arista al forno (roast pork), salads and beans. West of the square, **Il Brindellone** (Piazza Piatellina 10r) is one of the city's few vegetarian cafés, serving big salads and meat-free pasta sauces (it also serves generous platefuls of carpaccio, prosciutto and smoked swordfish).*

which only one colour is deployed, in boldly contrasting shades of light and dark.

Similar contrasts in style can be seen in two of the main scenes. On the right, in the upper tier, Masolino's painting of *St Peter, Accompanied by St John, Brings Tabitha to Life and Heals a Lame Man* is full of decorative detail, including the gorgeous clothing worn by the onlookers – a reference to the trade of their patron, Felipe Brancacci, who was a silk merchant.

The Tribute Money

Opposite, Masaccio's *The Tribute Money* is a forceful and direct telling of the story in which Christ instructs St Peter to pay the tax demanded by Caesar; to the left, St Peter discovers the necessary coins in the mouth of a fish. The drama of the scene is heightened by the lack of the decorative effects so loved by Gothic artists. Instead, Masaccio concentrates on conveying the essence of the story through

KEY TO THE FRESCOES

Upper Tier, right to left: Temptation of Adam and Eve (Masolino); St Peter, Accompanied by St John, Brings Tabitha to Life and Heals a Lame Man (Masolino); St Peter Baptising (Masaccio); St Peter Preaching (Masolino); The Tribute Money (Masaccio); The Expulsion from Paradise (Masaccio).

Lower Tier, left to right: St Paul Visits St Peter in Prison (Lippi); St Peter Brings the Emperor's Nephew, Theophilus, to Life (all three artists); St Peter heals the Sick with his Shadow (Masaccio); St Peter and St John Distributing Alms (Masaccio); Saints Peter and Paul Sentenced to Death by the Proconsul and the Crucifixion of St Peter (Lippi, who includes his own self-portrait in the scene – he is the second man on the right of the Crucifixion, looking out of the picture); St Peter Released from Prison by an Angel (Lippi).

Santa Maria Maddalena dei Pazzi

This church played an influential role in the Counter-Reformation of the 17th century, and its crypt contains a luminescent 15th-century *Crucifixion* by Perugino

Map reference: page 43, G2
Borgo Pinti. Bus: 6, line C
Open: Mon–Sat 9–11.50am, 5–5.20pm,
6.10–6.50pm, Sun 9–10.45am, 5–6.50pm;
closed public hols. Donation for lighting the
Perugino fresco

Section from Perugino's *Crucifixion* fresco, showing the Virgin Mary and St Bernard, *c.* 1493.

The Church of Saint Mary Magdalene "of the Penitents" was founded in 1257. It was rebuilt in 1481–1500 by Florentine architect Sangallo, who devised the innovative porticoed cloister that fronts the church, a work of serene beauty and mathematical precision. Instead of the usual arches, this has flat architraves, supported by columns with unusual ionic capitals. This rectilinear structure is interrupted over the chapel entrance by a perfect hemisphere.

Inside, we leap suddenly from the simplicity of Sangallo's classicism to the rampant religiosity of the Counter-Reformation. The church underwent another rebuilding in 1677, to form a theatrical mausoleum for the body of a Florentine nun, also named Maria Maddalena, who was canonised by Pope Urban VIII in 1669. Santa Maria Maddalena was held up as a model of virtue by the Carmelite nuns who built a convent round the church, sponsored by Grand-duke Cosimo III, and dedicated themselves to converting the city's fallen women.

The nuns moved on to Careggi in 1888, leaving behind them the saint's huge mausoleum, covered in coloured marble and gilded bronze, as well as the fervent baroque ceiling paintings of the *Glory of Santa Maria Maddalena dei Pazzi* by Jacopo Chiavistelli, and *Scenes from Her Life*, high up on the walls by Cosimo Ulivelli.

A door to the right of the altar leads to stairs and passages that pass beneath the church and into the old Chapterhouse where Perugino's beautiful fresco of the *Crucifixion* can be seen. This serene and mystical painting occupies three panels, united by a single landscape, as if we were looking through a window onto the scene. The misty dawn landscape, with flowing waters and fresh leaves on the trees, symbolises the Resurrection, even though it is the Crucifixion we see in the central panel, with Mary Magdalene at the foot of the Cross, the Madonna and St Bernard on the left and St John the Evangelist and St Benedict on the right.

*FOOD AND DRINK: The nearest bar is the **Caffè Mingo** (Borgo Pinti 62r; turn left out of the church entrance). It serves good-value sandwiches, pastries and pizza.*

Santa Maria Maggiore

Another of the many churches in central Florence that were founded in the late-Roman era but rebuilt in the Middle Ages

Map reference: page 42, D2
Via de' Vecchietti. Bus: 1, 6, 11, 14, 17, 22, 23
Open: daily 8am–1pm, 4–6pm.
Admission free.

Santa Maria Maggiore, which lies just off the cathedral square, is known to Florentines for the late-Roman female head known as Bertha, located high up on the northern face of the Romanesque belltower. Local legend has it that it is the petrified head of a woman who mocked a prisoner on his way to the gallows: his curse turned her to stone. The tower is all that survives of an earlier 8th-century church on the site. The rebuilt 13th-century nave is a simple Gothic structure; its chief work of art is Jacopo di Cione's late 14th-century *Massacre of the Innocents*, by the high altar. In the chapel to the left of the altar is a pillar marking the tomb of Bruno Latini (died 1294), Dante's teacher, man of letters and Chancellor of Florence. The nearby tomb slab carved with an effigy of an old man is that of Bruno Beccuti (died 1272).

FOOD AND DRINK: see Piazza del Duomo, page 102.

Santa Maria Novella

Richly decorated with Renaissance frescoes, this may be the most rewarding and beautiful church in Florence

Map reference: page 42, C2
Piazza Santa Maria Novella.
Bus: 6, 11, 12, line A
Santa Maria Novella Church
Tel: 055-215918. Open: Mon–Thurs, Sat 9.30am–5pm, Fri and Sun 1–5pm, closed public hols.
Santa Maria Novella Museum
Tel: 055-282187. Open: Sat–Thurs 9am–2pm; closed public hols. Admission charge

Detail from the façade of Santa Maria Novella, designed by Leon Battista Alberti from 1458–70.

FRESCOES IN SANTA MARIA NOVELLA

Ghirlandaio's frescoes (Cappella Tornabuoni)
Left wall from top to bottom: Death and Ascension of the Virgin; Adoration of the Magi; Massacre of the Innocents; Presentation at the Temple; Betrothal of Mary; St Joachim's Expulsion from the Temple; the Birth of the Virgin.
End wall: Coronation of the Virgin; Miracle of St Dominic; Death of St Peter; The Annunciation; St John in the Wilderness; kneeling figures of Giovanni Tornabuoni and his wife.
Right wall: Feast of Herod; John the Baptist Preaching; Baptism of Christ; Naming of St John; Birth of John the Baptist; The Visitation; The Annunciation to Zachariah.
Filippino Lippi's frescoes (Cappella di Filippo Strozzi)
Right wall: Crucifixion of St Philip; St Philip performs a Miracle in front of the Temple of Mars.
Left wall: Martyrdom of St John the Evangelist; the Raising of Drusiana.
Vault: the Four Patriarchs – Adam, Noah, Abraham and Jacob.

Dominican monks built Santa Maria Novella from 1246, on former vineyards on the western fringes of the city. The area remained undeveloped until the railway arrived in the mid-19th century and the elongated square in front of the church, now a popular meeting place for members of the city's immigrant community, was used for horse and chariot races in the 16th and 17th centuries. Giambologna's marble obelisks at each end of the square, supported on the backs of bronze turtles, mark the turning points on the track.

Standing in the square you can see the handsome marble façade (1458–70) of Santa Maria Novella, which was almost the last part of the church to be completed. The lower part of the façade is mid-14th century, the work of Fra' Jacopo Talenti, the architect who built the main body of the church. The upper part is a masterpiece of design by one of the great architects of the Renaissance, Leon Battista Alberti. His achievement here was to blend the old and the new. The proportions of the façade, and the use of green and white marble, respect the traditions of the Tuscan Romanesque style, and the whole façade is reminiscent of the Baptistery, or San Miniato al Monte. But the beautiful flower motifs, the scrolls, volutes and wheels are motifs firmly rooted in the Renaissance, as is the classical pediment with its blazing sun – the symbol of the Dominicans.

The inscription on the façade makes it clear who paid for this glorious work: the wealthy cloth merchant, Giovanni Rucellai. The Rucellai family emblem – the billowing sail of the ship of good fortune is worked into the façade, as is the ring and ostrich feather symbol of the Medici family, to whom the Rucellai were related by marriage.

Behind and to the left of the church you can see the spire-topped Romanesque campanile, also built by Talenti, on the site of an ancient watchtower.

ABOVE: Main
section of *The
Birth of St
John the
Baptist* from
Ghirlandaio's
fresco cycle in
the Cappella
Tornabuoni.

RIGHT: *Woman
Carrying Fruit*
(detail from
above).

Entering the church

The church is now entered through the cemetery to the right of the church. A graceful wall of green and white marble surrounds the cypress-shaded burial ground, and the wall arcade is carved with the coats of arms of the bankers, merchants and clothiers whose family members are buried here. Built in the 14th century, the cemetery is a reminder that the city was then in the grips of the Black Death, and that Boccaccio used the setting of this church as the springboard for his rambling *Decameron (see box)*.

The interior of the church is a breathtaking masterpiece of Gothic design, the soaring arches of the nave emphasised by being formed in zebra stripes of alternating white and grey stone. Hanging in the nave is Giotto's huge and emblematic Crucifix, back in its original position after restoration.

Among the many minor works that decorate the aisle chapels, do not miss Masaccio's masterpiece, the *Holy Trinity* which is in the north aisle, almost opposite the door through which you enter the church. Masaccio's fresco, painted when he was 27, shortly before his tragically early death, was the first to deploy Brunelleschi's recently articulated principles of linear perspective, which he had worked out mathematically by studying antique Roman architecture (indeed, it is thought that Brunelleschi helped Masaccio design the work). There are two different perspective points in the work. The painted tomb with its cadaver, and the two praying donors, members of the Lenzi family, kneeling either side of the niche, are painted in one perspective. As if to mark the separation of the earthly and spiritual worlds, the figures of the Virgin, St John, and the Trinity, occupy a different space. Despite the odd discontinuity that results, the painting revolutionised artistic practice and painters became obsessed with achieving the illusion of spatial depth in their work, often helped by the inclusion of architectural elements, as here.

Delightful frescoes

The richest decoration is found in the transepts and sanctuary, starting with chapels on the left, as you face the altar. The frescoes here date mainly from the Gothic era: the Strozzi di Mantova Chapel, in the north transept, preserves its mid-14th-century appearance, with Nardo di Cione's *Last Judgement* frescoes of 1357 showing a vision of Heaven and Hell clearly influenced by Dante's writing. In the Gondi Chapel, to the right of this one, is a *Crucifixion* that Brunelleschi is said to have carved as a riposte to Donatello, whose own version in Santa Croce Brunelleschi dismissed as too coarse ("just like a peasant"), and insufficiently expressive of Christ's nobility and divinity *(see page 21)*.

The walls either side of the main altar are decorated with some of the most delightful frescoes to be seen in Florence – though it isn't at all easy to see them (binoculars help) because visitors are kept out of the Sanctuary area. These scenes by Domenico Ghirlandaio were commissioned by Giovanni Tornabuoni in 1485 to celebrate the marriage of his sister to Piero de' Cosimo, a dynastic alliance of great importance. Showing scenes from the *Lives of the Virgin* and *St John the Baptist*, they are full of incidental details (and portraits of real people) from upper-class Florentine society. Ghirlandaio also designed the stained-glass windows, and the *Four Evangelists* in the vault.

Quite different in style, but equally arresting, are the frescoes and stained glass by Filippino Lippi in the Filippo Strozzi Chapel, to the right. Lippi's love of the bizarre and his theatrical style are well displayed in these scenes from the *Lives of St Philip and St John the Evangelist*, which form the monumental setting for Benedetto da Maiano's tomb (1486) for the wealthy banker, Filippo Strozzi. Lippi's audacious pictures build on the exotic nature of his subject matter – people being raised from the dead, dragons being slain – bringing back the element of strangeness and surprise that is missing from so many matter-of-fact religious paintings.

Also at this end of the church there are three fine Gothic tombs and a chapel enclosed by medieval ironwork. The lower of the three tombs is that of Joseph, patriarch of Constantinople, who died here in 1440. His presence is a reminder that this church and convent was the setting, in 1439, for the great Council of Florence, called by Pope Eugenius IV in 1439 in an attempt to reconcile the divided Greek and Latin churches.

The meetings of the Great Council were held in the Dominican Convent next to the church, now the Museo di Santa Maria Novella, entered from the northwestern corner of Piazza di Santa Maria Novella. Parts of the conventual buildings now house a police training college, but you can visit the Green Cloister, the Chapter House and Refectory.

Cloister and Chapter House

The Green Cloister (Chiostro Verde) is so named from the predominant colour of the frescoes by Uccello on the cloister walls, telling the story of Noah. These pleasing narrative scenes show none of the artist's obsession with the mathematics of spatial perspective, which, according to Vasari, eventually drove Uccello mad. Damaged by the 1966 floods, the

frescoes have been leached of much of their colour, but they still remain powerful, and surprisingly modern in concept. Noah's Ark, for example, is not the traditional stumpy boat, but a vast futuristic ship, not unlike a space station in a science-fiction comic. As the winds and rains blast the earth, Uccello paints a powerful vision of the reality of the Flood, with fish swimming among drowned babies, and people clinging to branches and the last remaining pieces of dry land.

The Chapterhouse is also known as the Spanish Chapel because several Spanish consuls, nobles and merchants are buried here, followers of Eleanora di Toledo, the Spanish-born wife of Grand-duke Cosimo de' Medici.

Members of Eleanora's entourage worshipped here beneath the frescoes of Andrea di Firenze showing *Scenes of the Passion and Crucifixion*, the

The Triumph of St Thomas Aquinus from the Chapterhouse, Andrea di Bonaiuto, c. 1365.

Harrowing of Hell, the *Church Militant and Triumphant*, and the *Triumph of St Thomas Aquinas*.

The lively Gothic frescoes include a depiction of the Apostles sailing in a ship that represents the Church, and young people renouncing such earthly pleasures as dancing and climbing trees to steal fruit and being shown the stairway to heaven as a reward. On the right-hand side, the civil and religious authorities are guarded by spotted dogs tearing the throats of wolves who represent heretics. This is a pun on the name of the Dominican order – *Domini Canes* being Latin for the Lord's Dogs.

Last of all comes the refectory, now used to display Bernardo Daddi's lovely Gothic altarpiece of *The Madonna Enthroned with Evangelists* (1344). On the wall above is a fresco on a similar theme by Agnolo Gadi (third quarter of the 14th century). Other frescoes by Alessandro Allori (1597) depict scenes appropriate to a refectory: the Jews in the desert drinking water from the rocks struck by Moses, and eating manna as it falls from heaven.

Giotto's Crucifix, *c.* 1292, in Santa Maria Novella.

*FOOD AND DRINK: The left-hand side of the square (as you emerge from the church) is one long run of cheap cafés and restaurants, including the good-value **Città Imperiale** Chinese restaurant. For something more up-market, the **Croce al Trebbio** (Via delle Belle Donne 47r; tel: 055-287089) lies down a narrow lane a few steps from the Chinese restaurant, and serves excellent Tuscan dishes·*

Santa Trinità

Home to two gems by Ghirlandaio: his *Life of St Francis* fresco sequence and his *Adoration of the Shepherds*

Map reference: page 42, D3
Piazza Santa Trinità. Tel: 055-216 912
Bus: 6, 11
Open: Mon–Sat 8am–noon, 4–6pm, Sun 4–6pm.
Admission free

Santa Trinità was founded in the 11th century and, although the present façade is baroque, having been remodelled by Buontalenti in 1593–94, the interior face was left alone and retains its original Romanesque appearance. Further evidence of the original church is to be found in Ghirlandaio's marvellously plastic but crisply delineated frescoes in the Sassetti Chapel, to the right of the main altar. Commissioned by Francesco Sassetti, one-time manager of the Medici bank, these *Scenes from the Life of St Francis* are not set in the saint's native Assisi, but in the streets of Florence.

The scene depicting the *Miracle of the Child Being Raised from the Dead* is set in Piazza Santa Trinità, thus documenting the original Romanesque façade and showing the old Santa Trinità bridge. Another scene, in which *Pope Honorius Approves the New Franciscan Order*, is set in Piazza della Signoria, and depicts various contemprary Florentines, including Sassetti himself (front right) with his son, his patron, Lorenzo de' Medici, and Antonio Pucci. On the stairs are Piero, Giovanni and Giuliano de' Medici (the sons of Lorenzo).

The altarpiece in the same chapel is a glowing and beautiful painting by Ghirlandaio, the *Adoration of the Shepherds*, flanked by the kneeling figures of Sassetti and his wife. The Roman sarcophagus which serves as Jesus's crib, along with numerous references to antiquity (Sassetti's own black porphyry tomb, for example, and the vault paintings of the Sybils who prophesied the coming of Christ to Emperor Augustus) reflect the contemporary interest in Classical literature, and the continuity between Classical and Christian learning.

Treasure hunt

Elsewhere, the church is dotted with treasures. The first chapel on the right (north) contains the venerated Crucifix from San Miniato al Monte (*see page 115*) that is said to have bowed to signal approval

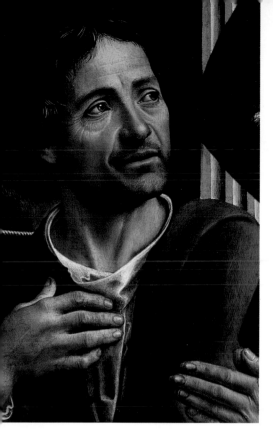

Santi Apostoli

This simple Romanesque church is one of the few in Florence unaltered since its construction in the 11th century

Map reference: page 42, D4
Piazza del Limbo 1. Tel: 055-290642. Bus: A
Rarely open except for services: try Sat 6–7pm, and Sun 8am–1pm. Admission free

A plaque to the right of the door says that Santi Apostoli was founded in 805 by Charlemagne, the first Holy Roman Emperor. In reality, it probably dates from the 11th century, but it looks much older because of the Roman-style columns and Corinthian capitals of green marble incorporated into the nave. Lit only by the golden light that filters through the tiny windows, the simple basilican church is used to store what are said to be the flints from Christ's tomb that play an important part in the city's Easter ceremonies.

These fragments of stone, taken from the Holy Sepulchre in Jerusalem by the Crusader, Godfrey of Bouillon, were given in 1096 to fellow Crusader and Florentine nobleman, Pazzino de' Pazzi. At the first Mass of Easter morning, they are used to strike the first symbolic flame that represents the Risen Christ. The flame is used to light a piece of charcoal that is then carried in procession from here to the Cathedral. Here, it is used to ignite the *columbina*, the dove-shaped rocket that shoots along a wire from the Cathedral high altar straight into the heart of a cartload of fireworks placed outside the Cathedral west door. The explosive result (the *Scoppio del Carro* or Explosion of the Cart) symbolises spring, fertility and the start of the new Christian year, and it has long been believed that the bigger the explosion, the better the Tuscan harvest will be that year.

The flints and bird-shaped brazier are stored in the tabernacle of the chapel on the left as you enter, which also features a *sinopia*, or under-drawing, sketched in wet plaster, for a lost fresco of an early 15th-century *Madonna and Child* by Paolo Schiavo. The other feature of note is the early 16th-century glazed terracotta, to the left of the main altar, by Giovanni della Robbia.

Self-portrait of Ghirlandaio; detail from the Santa Trinità altarpiece.

when St John Gualberto pardoned his brother's murderer. The fourth chapel on the right has its original decorative scheme, with late Gothic frescoes on the *Life of the Virgin* by Lorenzo Monaco and a beautiful wrought-iron screen of linked quatrefoils. To the left of the main altar, the tomb of Benozzo Frederighi, bishop of Fiesole (died 1450), is an unusual work by Luca della Robbia, sensitively carved in marble with a delightful frame of fruits and flowers in majolica mosaic.

Heading back west, the fifth chapel in the south aisle contains a powerful painted wooden statue of *Mary Magdalene*, carved by Desiderio da Settignano and completed by Benedetto da Maiano in 1455, which closely resembles Donatello's own statue in the Museo dell'Opera del Duomo *(see page 101)*. The third chapel contains the tomb (1444) of Giuliano Davanzati, carved by Bernardo Rossellino and placed on top of a 3rd-century Roman sarcophagus depicting the Good Shepherd.

FOOD AND DRINK: *turn right and walk towards Ponte Santa Trinità, then turn right onto Lungarno Corsini embankment and to* **Capocaccia** *(No 12r; tel: 055-210 751), a sandwich bar with a difference, noted for its great range of panini – meat, fish and vegetarian – and its generous salads. There are also wonderful views of the Arno, particularly at sunset when swifts wheel overhead.*

FOOD AND DRINK: *there are no bars in the immediate vicinity, but there are a couple of notable food shops where you can shop for picnic ingredients – ham, cheese, bread, fruit and olives. One is* **Gastronomia di G Tassini** *(Borgo Santi Apostoli 24r), to the right as you leave the square on the side furthest from the river.*

Santissima Annunziata

Santissima Annunziata closes off the northern side of one of the city's most beautiful squares. Mass is said here almost continuously in front of a much-venerated image of the Virgin

Map reference: page 43, F1 (see map inset)
Piazza Santissima Annunziata
Tel: 055-2398034. Bus: 31, 32
Open: 7.30am–12.30pm, and 4–6.30pm. Free

The seven-bay portico fronting Santissima Annunziata (The Most Holy Annunciation) deliberately echoes the design of the Spedale degli Innocenti *(see page 136)* on the eastern side of the square. It gives access to an unusual glass-roofed cloister (1447) at the western end of the church. Called the Chiostrino dei Voti, this used to be crammed with votive offerings – pictures, wax statues, armour and battle trophies – left by pilgrims who came to pray for miracles or give thanks for favours in front of the image of the Virgin. Today, it is famous for its frescoes on the *Life of the Virgin*, dating from the second decade of the 16th century and painted by some of the most promising young artists of their day. Rosso Fiorentino painted the *Assumption*, Pontormo the *Visitation*, Franciabigio the *Betrothal of the Virgin*, and Andrea del Sarto the *Nativity* and the *Visitation of the Magi*. In these works by the leading lights of the emerging Mannerist school of painting, you can already detect the use of a varied and unusual palette.

Inside the church, you will immediately note the unusual layout, for the high altar at the eastern end is almost ignored in favour of the oratory at the western end, which is the focus of almost continuous devotion. The temple-like structure, surrounded by candles and votive lamps, was designed by Michelozzo in 1448 to house a 14th-century painting of the *Annunciation* by the artist Fra' Bartolomeo. Devout worshippers believe that the friar fell asleep, exhausted by his attempts to capture the spiritual beauty of the Virgin, and he awoke to find that the image had been completed for him, by angelic hands.

Design by Michelozzo

The rest of the church was designed by Michelozzo, but his characteristically stripped back Classicism is now difficult to detect as the church was clad in coloured marble and given a baroque gilded ceiling, with a fresco of the *Assumption*, in the 17th and 18th centuries. Numerous baroque chapels radiate from the aisles and tribune, and among notable works are Andrea del Castagno's *Holy Trinity with St Jerome*, in the second chapel on the left, and the ornate organ (dating from 1509) opposite, which is the oldest in Florence and the second oldest to have survived in Italy.

A door (often locked – you have to ask the sacristan to open it on those rare occasions when there is no service on in the church) from the left aisle leads into the adjacent Chiostro dei Morti (Cloister of the Dead), so called because of its numerous graves and memorials. On the cloister side of the door you will find Andrea del Sarto's celebrated fresco, the *Madonna del Sacco*, so named from the sack that Joseph leans on.

The remaining frescoes (much damaged) tell the story of the founders of the Servite order (also known as the Servants of St Mary). Also off the cloister is the Chapel of the Company of St Luke, where the Confraternity of Painters had its headquarters in the 16th century – hence the many artists who are buried here, including Cellini and Pontormo. On the altar is a self-portrait by Vasari, a founder member of the Confraternity, who painted himself as *St Luke Painting the Madonna*.

FOOD AND DRINK: there is nowhere to eat in Piazza della Santissima Annunziata, but if you are gasping, there is a little unnamed hole-in-the-wall bar immediately to the left of the church façade selling ice cream and cold drinks. See San Marco, page 113, and Galleria dell'Accademia, page 54.

Santo Spirito

Major Renaissance church designed by Brunelleschi, studded with 15th-century paintings, as well as Michelangelo's newly displayed Crucifix

Map reference: page 42, C4
Piazza di Santo Spirito
Tel: 055-210030 (church), Tel: 055-287043 (refectory)
Bus: 6, 37, line D
Church: Thurs–Tues. 8.30am–noon, 4–6pm (Michelangelo's Crucifix visible only 4–6pm)
Refectory: Tues–Sun 9am–2pm

Piazza Santo Spirito is a lively market square, the medieval heart of the most appealing neighbourhood in Florence. Set in the Oltrarno district, the unpretentious piazza is home to a diverse mix of craftsmen, students and bohemian residents who share the arty bars, genuine inns and morning market with enthusiastic visitors. The welcoming bustle makes a contrast to the cooler, monumental quarters on the smarter side of the river.

Apart from the relaxed atmosphere, the square's chief asset is one of the city's finest churches. Brunelleschi *(see page 27)* originally designed his last Renaissance church to adjoin a new square

The simple elegance of Santo Spirito.

overlooking the Arno, but the scheme was foiled by aristocrats who were reluctant to see their land expropriated and their property demolished. Nor was the intended Renaissance façade for Santo Spirito ever built – a familiar Florentine refrain.

Although the palette for Florentine Gothic façades was generally white marble from Carrara, pink from Maremma, and dark green from Prato, Brunelleschi espoused simplicity and lack of adornment. Critics also suspect that the architect was perplexed by the lack of a definitive Classical model as far as façades were concerned. As it stands, the unpromising 18th-century façade is no indicator of the treasures that lie within.

Brunelleschi's swansong

Set on the site of a 13th-century Augustinian foundation, Santo Spirito represents Brunelleschi's swansong and his greatest church. Although the design was completed by 1434, work started only a few years before the architect's death. Brunelleschi may have witnessed the erection of only one column but, his design for the solemn interior was followed slavishly by later architects.

Santo Spirito cloisters.

The plan is a Latin cross with a dome over the crossing, complemented by a chain of 38 chapels around the walls and a colonnade of 35 columns running around the nave, transept and chapels. As historian Vincent Cronin points out, Santo Spirito is a model of proportion, even more so than San Lorenzo. "The nave is twice as high as it is wide, the ground floor and clerestory are of equal height, the aisles have square bays, again half as wide as they are high. The result is of such harmony and apparent simplicity that henceforth Gothic came to be looked on as impossibly fussy."

Noble commissions

Inside, the pale grey *pietra serena* and the sobriety of the space make an austerely satisfying backdrop for displaying the artworks. Some of the city's noblest families, from the Frescobaldi downwards, commissioned works of art to embellish their family chapels. Since several chapels are being restored and many paintings are darkened with age, the overall mood of Santo Spirito makes more impact than any particular works of art. Nonetheless, certain works catch the eye, particularly in the transepts. In

a chapel off the south transept is Filippino Lippi's so-called Nerli altarpiece, which, despite the murky patina of age, is a captivating work depicting the Nerli donors amid the saints. In the background is a pleasing view of the Borgo San Jacopo and San Frediano districts of Florence.

Four chapels further on is Maso Bianco's *Madonna and Saints*, a 14th-century panel-painting with the familiar gold background and static postures associated with the Byzantine style.

At the eastern end, two chapels further on, await the Pitti and Frescobaldi chapels, with the former dis-

playing an Allori altarpiece and a predella featuring the Palazzo Pitti with its original owner, Luca Pitti.

Michelangelo's Crucifix

Michelangelo's Crucifix, discovered in the church in 1963 and recently restored, is now on display in the sacristy and is an influential work, showing Christ in an anguished *contrapposto* (lit. opposite, referring to the head and legs falling in opposite directions) position. The octagonal sacristy and barrel-vaulted vestibule were designed by Giuliano da Sangallo (1489) but inspired by Brunelleschi. The only jarring

ABOVE: *Madonna and Child with the young St John the Baptist, St Martin and St Catherine*, from the Nerli altarpiece by Filippino Lippi, 1494.

LEFT: Activity around the San Frediano gate (detail from above).

note in Santo Spirito is the late 16th-century high altar, surmounted by a baroque baldachin.

Unlike Gothic churches, which presumed that the penumbra was mystical and more conducive to prayer, Brunelleschi's churches were not afraid of clarity. Like a true Renaissance man, the enlightened architect sought to bring citizens to God through symmetry, harmony and reason. Since Santo Spirito is a place of deep repose, he has succeeded beyond measure. Even so, critics of the church would like to have even more light: on dark winters' days, it is difficult see well enough to appreciate some of the art.

Traditional refectory

Beside Santo Spirito stands the refectory, or *cenacolo (see pages 138–9)*, the only section of the medieval monastery to survive. As a traditional Florentine refectory, it has high windows on one side and a *Last Supper* on the main wall, with a pulpit in the place where the abbot's chair generally stood. The severely damaged *Last Supper* was frescoed by Orcagna and his school in subtle shades of blues and browns, but the lower section was largely effaced after the insertion of a large door in the wall in 1866.

Even so, the fresco above, which depicts Christ on the Cross surrounded by swirling angels and set against dramatic lowering skies, is in better condition; it also has the merit of being the only scene definitively attributed to Orcagna. Apart from this Crucifixion, the refectory's magpie collection, founded by a Neapolitan antiquarian, contains minor sculpture and carvings from Venice, Verona, Piedmont and, of course, the collector's native Campania. A baptismal font, medieval terracottas, friezes and capitals are mixed with distinctive pieces of Romanesque sculpture, including a gruesome griffin and a couple of marine monsters from Campania.

FOOD AND DRINK: Borgo Antico (Piazza Santo Spirito 6r; (tel: 055-210437) is a deservedly popular trattoria serving Tuscan dishes. Caffè Ricchi (tel: 055-215864; closed Sun), next door at No. 9r, is the ideal place for a light lunch of pasta or salad, best taken on the terrace. Cinghiale Bianco (Borgo San Jacopo 43r; tel: 055-215706; closed Wed) is a trusty, rustic-style inn serving good-value Tuscan dishes. Il Cantinone (Via di Santo Spirito 6r; tel: 055-218898; closed Mon) is a candle-lit wine cellar serving good country cooking, from rabbit to wild boar. Cecco Beppe (Via Santo Spirito 64r; tel: 055-290076) is a cheap and cheerful trattoria open until late. Dolce Vita (Piazza del Carmine 6r; tel: 055-284595) is a trendy café for light meals and people-watching.

Santo Stefano al Ponte

Santo Stefano is worth a visit for the theatrical design, and the adjacent Diocesan Museum

Map reference: page 42, E4
Piazza Santo Stefano. Bus: line B
Open: Fri only, 3.30–6.30pm in winter, 6–7pm in summer; closed Aug. Admission Free.

Santo Stefano al Ponte (St Stephen of the Bridge – a reference to the nearby Ponte Vecchio) is a highly theatrical, baroque church whose acoustics make it an excellent venue for the baroque concerts that are regularly held here (see posters outside for details). The elegant marble staircase leading to the raised high altar is by Buontalenti (1531–1608) and was moved here from Santa Trinità in 1895.

Hidden behind the high altar is the choir, with fine 17th-century choir stalls carved with the heads of angels, all tilted to the sky and singing as forcefully as they can. Follow their gaze upwards and you will see a deeply coved ceiling carved with floral motifs. In the left-hand (northern) aisle the unusual bronze relief of the *Stoning of St Stepehen* is by Ferdinando Tacca, and above it is a lovely, mid-15th-century Carrara marble relief of the *Virgin and Child* by Mino da Fiesole.

On the opposite side of the nave, a door leads to the Museo Diocesano, which is packed with works of art from various redundant churches in Florence. This is a mixed bag of works ranging from Giotto's heavily restored *Madonna Enthroned with Two Angels* and Masolino's *St Julian*, to embroidered vestments, Byzantine icons, and some delightful wooden crib figures.

On your way out, don't miss the tombstones mounted on the walls of the courtyard, including the handsome armoured figure with flowing locks, carved in relief in memory of Wolfgang von Trutschler of Stein und Liebnitz, in Germany.

FOOD AND DRINK: You are a short step from several good-value tavola calda (self-service) restaurants on Via Por Santa Maria. Enjoy large bowls of fresh salad or pasta, or pizza by the slice at the Queen Victoria (No. 32r) or the un-named café at No. 26r. If you are here for a pre-concert supper, try the Antico Fattore (Via Lambertesca 1r; tel: 055-288975), where the Uffizi bomb went off in 1993. As venerable as ever, it has a menu of Tuscan specialities, including wild boar, pigeon, and spicy sausages with beans.

The Florentine
Synagogue.

Sinagogo e Museo Ebraico di Firenze

The Florentine Synagogue (also known as the Tempio Maggiore Israelitico) is an architectural masterpiece with a small Jewish museum of ritual objects

Map reference: page 43, G2
Via L C Farini 4. Tel: 055-245252
Bus: 6, line C
Open: Sun–Thurs 10am–5pm, Fri 10am–2pm.
Admission charge.

When you look down on Florence from any of the surrounding hills, two domes catch your eye: the first is the tile-clad dome of the Cathedral, the second is the green copper-clad dome of the Synagogue, rising above the rooftops of the city's eastern suburbs. The great copper dome, and the four corner towers topped by smaller domes, are the work of Marco Treves, whose design for this striking Moorish/Byzantine building was executed in 1874–82, with funds bequeathed by David Levi, President of the Hebrew University, who died in 1868.

The Oriental ambience continues inside, where golden light filters through the windows lighting an interior made splendid by the red and blue arabesques decorating the underside of the dome. There are women's galleries to left and right separated by wrought-iron railings. Framed by a baldachino and surmounted by the Tablets of the Law is the Holy Ark, whose doors still bear the scars inflicted by Nazi bayonets during the World War II occupation of Florence.

On the first floor is a tiny, one-room museum displaying vestments and ceremonial objects dating mostly from the 19th century. There are lamps and lecterns, mantles for wrapping the Torah Scroll and pointers of silver and coral to protect the text from damage. One small display details the history of Judaism in Florence. Jews were welcomed to the city and offered protection by Lorenzo de' Medici in 1568, at a time when they were being persecuted elsewhere by the forces of the Inquisition and the Counter-Reformation. Some very old photographs show prayer rooms and synagogues in the ancient ghetto, in the now-demolished Mercato Vecchio district (occupied today by the Piazza della Repubblica).

*FOOD AND DRINK· Next door is **Ruth's** (Via L C Farini 2a; tel: 055-2480888; daily noon–11pm, closed Fri from 2.30pm and Sat till 7.30pm), a bright modern café serving kosher food. Daytime snacks include brik (cheese-filled filo pastry parcels) and imam bayildi (stuffed aubergines). The evening menu features grilled vegetables, fish couscous and Ruth's Platter – a selection of Middle Eastern specialities.*

Spedale degli Innocenti

Renaissance art gallery in a foundling hospital designed by Brunelleschi

Map reference: page 43, F1 (see inset)
Piazza Santissima Annunziata 12
Tel: 055-2491708
Bus: 31, 32
Open: Thurs–Tues 8.30am–2pm
Istituto degli Innocenti (Unicef foundation), tel: 055-2477951; Biblioteca Innocenti (Unicef research library), tel: 055-2037363
www.biblioteca.istitutodeglinnocenti.it

TOP:
Terracotta
roundel of an
orphan in
swaddling
clothes, by
Luca della
Robbia.

Prompted by the concerns of the merchant classes and guilds, the enlightened Republic of Florence took radical measures to put an end to the habit of abandoning children. In 1419, the city created a foundation and charged the Arte della Seta, a prosperous guild of silk and textile merchants, with building a foundling hospital where children could be provided with shelter and support. As a prominent architect and member of the guild, Brunelleschi (1377–1446) was appointed to oversee the project, which was finished after his death, but in accordance with his plans *(see page 28)*.

Part hospital, part orphanage, the Ospedale has acted as a refuge for children ever since. The UNICEF foundation housed here claims to be a continuation of the 15th-century foundling hospital and children's social centre, making it, in effect, the oldest children's centre in the world. Also on the ground floor is the new UNICEF library, which deals with all issues affecting children and young people, from children's rights to the exploitation of minors.

Rebirth of beauty

To see the ground-breaking Hospital of the Innocents in the context of this perfect 15th-century square is to sense the rebirth of the laws of ideal beauty in architecture, the Classical perfection that was at the heart of the Renaissance. The hospital represents the quintessential Renaissance building, the first to be modelled on Classical lines, and proved influential for generations of architects to come. In particular, the porticoed façade was the prototype for what became the most emblematic feature of Florentine Renaissance architecture. Although, at first sight, the portico simply seems an extension of a medieval loggia, the harmonious division of space made it revolutionary. The loggia is supported by slender Corinthian columns, reminiscent of those in the Baptistery *(see page 95)*, and rise to semi-circular rather than pointed arches. Widely spaced pedimented windows are set above the centre of each arch. The width between the columns is exactly the same as the height of the columns and is identical to the diameter of each arch, while the nine arches are matched by nine rectangular windows above.

Decorative devices

The classical simplicity of the original building is embellished by Luca della Robbia's decorative devices – the sculptures in the spandrels, set between the arches. Luca della Robbia *(see page 59)*, who invented enamelled terracotta, designed these blue and white glazed terracotta plaques to represent "the innocents", the babes in swaddling clothes. From 1605 to 1612, further decorations were added, including busts of the Medici, discreet murals, frescoes and lunettes and the vaulting above the entrance.

PIAZZA SANTISSIMA ANNUNZIATA

Piazza Santissima Annunziata, universally acknowledged as the loveliest square in the city, is the setting for the landmark secular building of the Renaissance. The recent pedestrianisation of the square adds to its serene atmosphere, a spell not broken by the concerts which now take place on hot summer evenings in front of the Spedale degli Innocenti. In the middle of the cloistered square stands a statue of Grand-duke Ferdinand. According to the poet Robert Browning, Ferdinand ordered the statue to be placed here so that his proxy could gaze for all eternity at the della Robbia bust of the woman he had loved in vain. Sadly, the bust has disappeared but Browning's poem remains a tribute, as do other della Robbia images on the façade of the foundling hospital. To most modern visitors, it is the della Robbia depictions of children that are the most touching, partly because they echo the purpose of this charitable institution, and partly because they are children, rather than the more familiar Florentine male nudes. This change of subject matter was also an innovation in Renaissance art: in medieval Florentine art there are few depictions of children, except of the Baby Jesus.

Under the portico is a plaque attesting to the revolving wheel, known as the rota, upon which the abandoned babies were placed. This was finally sealed up in 1875, but much else survives from the erstwhile orphanage. Set around a quadrangle, the complex embraces two sets of cloisters, segregated for the sexes, as well as the former refectory, kitchens, dormitories, and a sick-bay.

The Chiostro degli Uomini, the main cloisters, and the centrepiece of the boys' quarters, are adorned with a lunette containing an *Annunciation* by Andrea della Robbia. The smaller Chiostro delle Donne, once the heart of the girls' quarters, still contains a children's health centre in one section, as well as a UNESCO library. At the end of the 18th century, these cloisters were altered by the Grand-dukes of Lorraine and, more recently, most of the premises have been occupied by UNICEF offices.

The museum collection

Fortunately, the small museum, set in Brunelleschi's portico, in the former boys' dormitory, remains open to the public and displays the hospital's original art collection, enriched by donations. Although the collection was diminished by an ill-advised sale in the 19th century, a significant number of panel-paintings survive, mainly from the 15th–17th century. The restrained Renaissance setting makes a suitably austere backdrop for an intimate collection of 15th-century chests and paintings. The foundling theme is echoed in most of the art-works, which rather poignantly stress maternal love and the ultimate protection of the Virgin Mary, images which doubtless consoled more stoical foundlings. Pontormo's *Madonna Protecting the Innocents* is in this vein, even if the plump cherubs look in little need of protection from a smug-faced Madonna.

One of the highlights, dominating the far wall, is the *Adoration of the Magi* by Ghirlandaio, commissioned for the high altar of the church. The artist places himself in the work, along with the foundling hospital and scenes of a suffering Christ and the Massacre of the Innocents; despite the gloom, the prevailing mood is of the tender care and consolation provided by the Madonna. The paintings gain further significance because we know that they were created for the hospital.

Luca della Robbia's serene *Madonna and Child* adorned the women's church until the 19th century while Botticelli's *Madonna and Child*, a youthful work, was designed for the church sacristy, where it was displayed until 1890. Piero di Cosimo's *Madonna Enthroned* includes a depiction of St Catherine of Alexandria, patron saint of unwed women, a moral theme close to the foundling hospital's heart.

FOOD AND DRINK: see entries for the Opificio, Accademia and San Marco.

Adoration of the Magi, by Ghirlandaio, 1488.

Florentine Cenacoli

The *Last Supper (Cenacolo)* was a familiar feature of Gothic and Renaissance refectories (*cenacolo,* by extension, also means refectory) but only Florence is fortunate enough to possess a cluster of masterpieces frescoed by Renaissance artists. Set in a rectangular refectory with high windows on one side, the main wall was frescoed with the traditional theme of the *Last Supper*, typically with Judas at one end of the table and the Apostles at the other. These narrative paintings play on two aspects of the Christian story: Jesus's revelation to his Apostles that one of them will betray him; and the institution of the sacrament of the Eucharist with the communion of the Apostles.

However, individual artists were equally interested in displaying their mastery of colour, form, mood and technique, including the revolutionary use of perspective in early Renaissance art. Curiously, since some of the convents were closed orders, certain *Last Supper* frescoes came to light only in the 19th or 20th century, an inaccessibility which also helped to conserve these masterpieces.

First Renaissance refectory

The Cenacolo di Sant'Apollonia was the first Renaissance refectory in Florence, set in a Benedictine convent now occupied by the University of Florence. On the main wall is a *Last Supper* by Andrea del Castagno, a work first attributed to Uccello because of its early use of perspective. The scene is full of dramatic intensity, with the livid colours signifying betrayal. Judas is isolated in the foreground and shown in profile with the face of a satyr (the lustful creature of Greek mythology, usually depicted as a human figure with some bestial aspect) a familiar representation of evil in Renaissance art. Until the suppression of the order in 1860,

the nuns successfully avoided the public attention that the discovery of the frescoes would bring.

The same was true of another closed order, the Romanesque Vallombrosian abbey, which houses the Cenacolo di San Salvi and Andrea del Sarto's celebrated *Last Supper*, one of the most accomplished in existence. Framed by an arch, this animated scene is lit by warm-hued tones, accentuating the individuality of each Apostle. Also on display in the adjoining gallery are theatrical Cinquecento works by Ghirlandaio, Pontormo and Vasari, as well as images representing the saints associated with the order.

An earlier masterpiece is celebrated in the Cenacolo di Foligno, set in a former convent of the same name. Here, a *Last Supper* by Perugino conveys the luminosity and grace associated with Umbrian art. The masterpiece, originally attributed to Raphael, came to light only with the suppression of the order.

Even more delightful is the Cenacolo di Ognissanti *(see page 104)*, which displays Ghirlandaio's graceful pastoral scene masquerading as a *Last Supper*. As a complete contrast to these Renaissance works, the damaged Cenacolo di Santo Spirito *(see page 134)* still retains Orcagna's dramatic High Gothic *Crucifixion*.

The main refectories

The main Florentine refectories are:
Cenacolo di Foligno, Via Faenza 42, tel: 055-286982; open daily 9am–noon; ring the bell; Cenacolo di Ognissanti (or del Ghirlandaio, *see page 104*); Cenacolo di San Salvi, Via di San Salvi 16; tel: 055-2388603; open Tues–Sun 8.15am–1.50pm; Cenacolo di Sant'Apollonia, Via XXVII Aprile 1, tel: 055-2388607; open Tues–Sat 8.15am–1.50pm and 2nd and 4th Sun of month, and 1st, 3rd and 5th Mon of month; and Cenacolo di Santo Spirito *(see page 134)*.

The Last Supper by Andrea Castagno in the Cenacolo di Sant' Apollonia, *c.* 1447.

Public Palaces and Private Homes

Much of Florence's appeal lies in its well-preserved *palazzi*. Most are now museums, from the Palazzo Vecchio and other Medici strongholds, to great collectors' homes and dynastic palaces linked to such luminaries as Dante and Michelangelo

Palazzo Vecchio

Historic seat of government and the original residence of the ruling Medici family. The sumptuously decorated palace contains works by Michelangelo, Donatello, Vasari and Verrocchio and overlooks a square that is in itself an outdoor museum of sculpture

Map reference: page 42, E4
Piazza della Signoria
Tel: 055-2768465 (general information); 055-2768224/2768558 or www.museoragazzi.it (to book "Secret Routes" – guided tours visiting normally closed sections of the palace – and children's workshops run by the Museo dei Ragazzi)
Bus: 14 or line A
Open: summer, Tues, Wed, Sat 9am–7pm, Mon and Fri 9am–11pm, Thurs and Sun 9am–2pm winter, Mon–Wed, Sat 9am–7pm, Thurs and Sun 9am–2pm
Café. Bookshop. Audio-guide. Free virtual guide. Multimedia room. Wheelchair access. Admission charge.

The Palazzo Vecchio, with its bold swallow-tail crenellations and asymmetrical bell tower, is the most evocative of city symbols. The palace has been the emblem of Florentine power since the 14th century. Based on designs by Arnolfo di Cambio, the leading master-builder of the day, it was built between 1299 and 1314. Given that Florence is so concretely visual, even the shape of a building is a reminder of a political lesson. In the interminable Guelf–Ghibelline battles for supremacy, the Guelfs were ultimately victorious and demolished palaces belonging to the defeated faction, in this case the Ghibelline Uberti clan. An edict to prevent the Uberti ever recovering their ground declared that no rebuilding could take place on the same site, hence the strange trapezoidal shape of the Palazzo Vecchio, forbidden from occupying tainted Uberti Ghibelline soil.

The palace is faithful to the principles of medieval architecture, with a tower, a porticoed courtyard, a vaulted hall on the ground floor, and a ceremonial hall on the floor above. The architect also incorporated military devices, from the battlemented crenellations to the windowless fortified tower. However, it is better proportioned than its predecessor, the Bargello. Inside are the luxurious trappings of a refined Renaissance court, at odds with the sober exterior and its official role as a political seat.

Opposite: *The Goldsmith's Workshop*, from the series of paintings produced under Giorgio Vasari for Francesco I's study in the Palazzo Vecchio, *c.* 1570–5.

Left: 19th-century French engraving of the Palazzo Vecchio.

Historical transition

The Palazzo Vecchio has symbolised civic authority throughout its myriad incarnations, from Signoria (city government) and Grand-ducal power-base to seat of the national parliament during the city's brief spell as capital of Italy. It also marks the historical transition from war to peace, from fortress to pleasure palace, from feudalism to oligarchy and eventually democracy. Apart from being a treasure house of art and history, the palace houses the offices of the mayor, city council and administration. Yet, as Machiavelli reminds us, the building's role shifted with the tides: the great political theorist was aware that Florence was fundamentally an oligarchical society in which democracy occasionally broke out.

Built on behalf of the guilds, the arbiters of city life, the palace originally symbolised the burgeoning power of the bourgeoisie. The Signoria, the city government, ruled from the palace. To ensure its independence, the Signoria decreed that governing magistrates, elected for a period of two months, were virtual prisoners, living communally in the Palazzo Vecchio and forbidden from going out alone, even to see their families. Under the Medici, however, when the palazzo doubled as a Ducal palace, the republican institutions were hollow shells with key roles filled by Medici place-men. All caution was thrown to the wind under Cosimo I, when the dynasty abandoned the pretence of distancing itself from public office and ostentatious displays. In 1540, Cosimo's move to the Palazzo Vecchio signalled a programme of embellishments to reflect the palace's dual role as

ABOVE: Cosimo de' Medici surrounded by artists of his time, in the Sala del Duca Cosimo I, by Giorgio Vasari, *c.* 1537.

ABOVE RIGHT: The inner courtyard designed by Michelozzo, 1454; the *Putto with Dolphin* on the central fountain is a copy of the original bronze by Verrocchio, *c.* 1470.

seat of government and home to the Ducal family. Cosimo was newly married to Eleonora di Toledo but the birth of 10 children eventually prompted the move to the more spacious Pitti Palace *(see page 62)*. However, as a celebration of ancestor worship, Palazzo Vecchio has no equal: the Pitti Palace may display greater treasures but the family links are more tangible here. The highlight of a visit remains the sumptuous monumental apartments and the private quarters of the Medici family.

Vasari, court architect

As court architect to the Medici, Vasari was entrusted with embellishing the palace to reflect its new role. Apart from extending the palace at the back while ensuring that the façade remained the same, he also transformed the interior, with further remodelling by Buontalenti in 1588. Arnolfo di Cambio's medieval staircase was replaced by a monumental affair, while painters such as Ghirlandaio transformed the outdated fortress into frescoed apartments. Under Vasari's guidance, elaborate new ceilings were added to the second floor salons, simply placed on top of existing medieval ones.

Subjects depicted on ceilings and walls were selected by the court sage, the person who could best match the chequered Medici history with mythological glories. It was then the duty of the court painters, guided by Vasari, to present these scenes with the right blend of artistry and sycophancy. As master of ceremonies, he also succeeded in combining the works of different artists into a cohesive whole, with the finest works taking the form of fresco cycles or of panel paintings on deeply recessed ceilings.

The porticoed inner courtyard was renovated by Michelozzo in 1453, but the frescoed vaulting and stucco-work were added to the columns by Vasari in the following century. The courtyard was redecorated in honour of the marriage of Francesco I de' Medici to Joanna of Austria in 1565, a doomed union which nonetheless propelled the status-seeking Medici into the ranks of European royalty. In honour of the event, Vasari frescoed the courtyard with views of Austro-Hungarian cities interspersed with grotesque scenes. The medieval well was replaced with Vasari's fountain, surmounted by Verrocchio's winged spirit, originally designed for the Villa Medici in Careggi *(see page 194)*. A copy of this delightful *Cherub with a Dolphin* (*c.* 1470), depicting a winged child clutching an equally chubby dolphin, stands here still, with the original upstairs, on Juno's Terrace. Beside the courtyard is the former guards-room, an exhibition space which has kept its medieval dimensions.

Hall of the Five Hundred

Vasari's monumental staircase leads to the Salone dei Cinquecento, the Hall of the Five Hundred, where members of the Great Council held their meetings. The room was planned by Simone del Pollaiuolo (known as Il Cronaca) in 1495 and designed to hold 500 representatives of the 1,500-strong Signoria, who ruled in three rotating groups. It was the largest room in Italy, graced with a coffered ceiling.

Michelangelo and Leonardo da Vinci were commissioned to fresco Florentine military victories on the walls, with Leonardo assigned the Battle of Anghiari, depicting the trouncing of the Milanese. However, this mural faded to such an extent that Vasari felt justified in covering the walls with mediocre frescoes by himself and his peers. Michelangelo was commissioned to depict the Battle of Cascina, a Florentine victory over the Pisans, but had barely started before being summoned to Rome.

In any case, the return to power of Cosimo I in 1537 meant that the function of the chamber changed from democratic forum to showcase of Medici might, symbolised by the depiction of Cosimo on the ceiling. In keeping with this vainglorious conception, a stage was created from which courtiers, ambassadors and honoured guests could view the splendid new decorations.

Vasari was entrusted with embellishing the room, including raising the ceiling by 7 metres (22 ft), a considerable engineering feat. The redecorated walls depict Cosimo's military victories against the city's bitter rivals, Siena and Pisa, covered at great length in the excellent audio-visual commentary *(see box on page 145)*. Below the Pisan scenes is Michelangelo's *Genius of Victory*, a muscular but unmemorable sculpture intended for the tomb of Pope Julius II. At the end of the room, the *udienza* or dais is adorned with vacuous statues by Bandinelli and Caccini.

Secret rooms

Exploring other rooms on the first floor and interconnecting mezzanine level can be more problematic. The mysterious studies of Cosimo I and his son, Francesco I, can be seen only on a "secret routes" visit *(see page 145)*, while other rooms are subject to periodic reorganisation or closure, depending on demands made by the city council. The Salone dei Duecento, the Hall of the Two Hundred, is the oldest and finest room in the palace but generally closed to the public. Created as the seat of the ancient Florentine Grand Council, it is still the meeting place for the city council. Set in the heart of

the medieval palace, the hall retains its late 15th-century appearance, with a lovely coffered ceiling complemented by Flemish Renaissance tapestries.

On the same floor, the more accessible Quartiere di Leo X celebrates a different Medici in every room, with the most authentic apartment dedicated to Leo X, the Medici Pope. Redecorated (1556–62) by Vasari, the chamber has ornate stucco-work framing equally bold paintings depicting the Papal progress. The room opens onto the (often closed) Lorenzo the Magnificent Chamber, which displays portraits of Lorenzo and his son, Leo X. The apartment of Cosimo I is the most sumptuous of all, complete with paintings of all the cities conquered by the Medici ruler. However, as proof that desire for the trappings of power is eternal, the main Medici rooms are the preserve of the mayor of Florence.

The second floor

By comparison, the second floor is both accessible and beguiling, with the grandeur of several monumental halls matched by the intimacy of the apartments created for Cosimo I's consort. The Quartiere degli Elementi, reached via a staircase from the apartment of Leo X (or from a lift outside the Salone dei Cinquecento), is inspired by allegories of the four elements and classical divinities. Decorated by Vasari in the 1550s, the main room is centred on a mythological ceiling fresco evoking the castration of the sky by the classical divinity of time. Next-door is the frescoed Saturn Terrace, with a view of the Oltrarno and even San Miniato on the hillside.

In the next room, a lovely view of Florence opens up from the Juno Terrace, an enclosed loggia, with a

The vast Salone dei Cinquecento was designed by Il Cronaca to hold the 500 members of the Great Council and is decorated with artworks glorifying the Medici.

ceiling displaying Juno's chariot pulled by peacocks. Also on display is the original of Verrocchio's playful bronze *Cherub with a Dolphin*. Rooms dedicated to a quartet of deities follow before the circuit ends where it started. The Sala di Opi depicts the goddess of fertility (Jupiter's wife) in a lion-drawn chariot, while the Sala di Ceres shows the Roman goddess in a chariot pulled by snakes, hunting for her daughter, Proserpine, the goddess of the Underworld.

The next suite, the Quartiere di Eleonora, was created for the newly married Eleonora di Toledo, in 1561–62. Under Vasari's guidance, the former dormitories of the city leaders were recast as private quarters. The vaulted green bedchamber was decorated by Ghirlandaio and interweaves marine monsters, birds and floral motifs into a playful spring scene. From here, a sculpted portal leads to a tiny private chapel decorated by Mannerist artist, Bronzino (1503–72). The following rooms depict a sequence of edifying scenes for a young wife, essentially variations on the theme of fidelity. In swift succession, rooms evoke the ill-fated Sabine Women, and the virtuous Esther and Penelope, with one scene showing the faithful Penelope spinning until the safe return of her husband, Odysseus. Lest Eleonora needed further wifely advice, the final room is dedicated to Gualdrada, an obscure Florentine heroine who chose death rather than submit to a mere kiss by Emperor Otto IV.

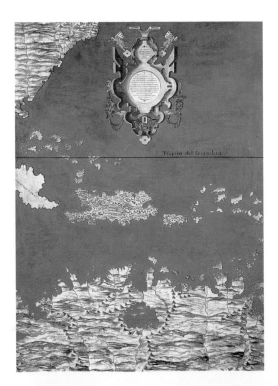

Map of the West Indies as charted by Ignazio Danti 1563–75, from a series of maps and sea charts displayed in Cosimo I's map room.

Florentine monumentality

The final suite was carved out of the medieval heart of the palace. In 1472, Lorenzo the Magnificent converted the hall on the second floor into the Lily Chamber and the Audience Chamber, adorning both with lavish coffered ceilings. The Sala d'Udienza, the recently restored Audience Chamber, was where Medici justice was meted out, hence the statue of justice crowning the doorway. The superb 15th-century gilded ceiling is complemented by well-restored Mannerist murals by Salviati.

The adjoining Sala dei Gigli, named after the Florentine lily motif on the gilded blue walls, served as a reception and banqueting room. Decorated from 1472–81, the chamber has another coffered ceiling and sculpted door, as well as fine views over the Duomo and Bargello. Donatello's gruesome statue of *Judith and Holofernes*, an allegory of virtue, stands on a high pedestal here; it has been replaced by a copy in the Loggia dei Lanzi on Piazza della Signoria *(see page 147)*. A door connects with the Chancellery, which served as Machiavelli's office between 1498 and 1512, when he worked as a diplomat for the city-state. He is commemorated by a bust and portrait, which might have amused him since he was often reviled in his own time.

The map room

An intriguing chamber created for Cosimo I, the Sala delle Carte Geografiche served as a treasure house and dressing room. Walls covered by 57 maps conceal walnut cupboards where Cosimo stored his prize possessions, from court finery and precious documents to jewels and *objets d'art*. The effect is a fascinating, almost virtual reality overview of the known world in the 16th century, including a map depicting "England, Scotland and Hibernia". The room also plays on the linguistic associations between Cosimo and Cosmos. A secret door behind a map of Armenia connects with the rooms covered on the "secret routes" tour, including the studies of Cosimo and Francesco and spaces dedicated to costumes, children and theatrical workshops.

Secret Medici study

Of the newly created "secret routes", the best is the guided visit to Francesco I de' Medici's study. Known as the Studiolo, it acted as a retreat from court life for Cosimo I's melancholic and reclusive son. Created by Vasari in 1570, it is a Mannerist gem, studded with enigmatic symbolism inspired by alchemy, Francesco's ruling passion. Shaped like the inside of a jewel box, this claustrophobic chamber was where the heir apparent gazed on his treasures, meditated on Bianca Cappello, his married lover and eventual wife, and conducted experiments in alchemy. According to a court confidant, it was here that Cosimo's heir kept his "precious medicines, jewels, unicorns' horns, poisons and antidotes".

Cardinal Ferdinando, Francesco's brother and successor, supposedly poisoned Bianca and Francesco in 1587, but a more innocent death by malaria cannot be ruled out. However, credence is lent to the poisoning theory by the fact that Ferdinando had Bianca buried in a pauper's grave and removed any trace of her presence in the palace. After the end of Medici rule, this windowless chamber served as a coal-store and was rediscovered only in modern times, culminating in its complete restoration in 1910. The original paintings and sculpture that once adorned the study were retrieved from the Bargello and the eight marble niches were again filled with bronze Mannerist statuettes of sea goddesses.

Representing the elements

The vaulted ceiling depicts Prometheus, who invented fire, encircled by allegories of the four elements, air, fire, earth and water. If fire is represented by Vulcan's forge, air is more obscure, symbolised by gold and diamond mining since these precious minerals were considered products created by combustion. Facing one another are School of Bronzino portraits of Francesco's parents, including an idealised image of his mother. Exceptionally for a Medici marriage, this was a happy relationship, not mirrored in the romantic misfortunes of their sons.

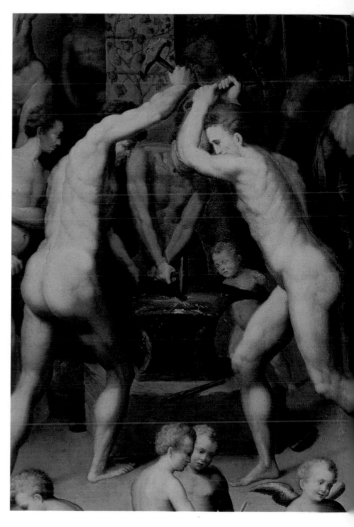

Detail from *The Vulcan's Forge*, one of the allegorical paintings that decorate the secret study (Studiolo), designed for the reclusive Francesco de Medici, 16th century.

MULTIMEDIA COMES TO THE PALACE

The Palazzo Vecchio is the only museum in Florence to have moved into the 21st century in terms of presentation. The controversial experiment with multimedia and a children's perspective on great artworks has proved a resounding success. Multimedia, a radical approach for such a conservative city, offers different stories and approaches to the palace, from historical background to insights into Medici court life. Visitors can access screens offering virtual visits to the palace in different periods. The commentaries, presented in different languages and accompanied by period music, include descriptions of the palace treasures. Since young children are ill-served by most Florentine museums, this approach, coupled with the creation of a "children's museum", is a welcome step. The name is a misnomer, since there are no exhibits on permanent display, but the space is devoted to educational activities, theatre workshops and dressing-up sessions. Visitors are entertained by actors assuming Renaissance dress and roles who guide their audience through themes as diverse as Medici protocol, court costumes, the discoveries of Galileo or the artistic overview of Vasari and his peers. To make the transformation of the Palazzo Vecchio complete, all that is needed is for the mayor and his administration to vacate the most splendid Medici apartments, allowing the public to appreciate the trappings of Medici power first-hand.

Another popular development is the creation of "secret routes", which take small groups of individuals to explore sections of the palace otherwise closed to the public. Guided visits include: the Duke of Athens' staircase, named after a 14th-century tyrant; a rooftop visit to see Vasari's ingenious ceilings; and the genuinely secret visit dedicated to Cosimo's introverted son, Francesco I, with visits to Cosimo and Francesco's secret studies.

Piazza della Signoria

An open-air museum of sculpture starring a copy of Michelangelo's *David*.

More than any other square, the Piazza della Signoria evokes the ancient world and the overweening pride of the Renaissance city. Colossal statues stand in serried ranks under the Loggia dei Lanzi; a fountain spurts over the muscular statue of Neptune and his attendant nymphs. Although the square is not a place for private epiphanies or the solitary contemplation of great art, by night it regains a semblance of composure, with ghostly statues dominating the glorious Palazzo Vecchio.

This harmonious square has been the civic heart of Florence since the Middle Ages, and the centre of power for Republican and oligarchical institutions alike. Grace and symbolism aside, the square offers the perfect introduction to Florentine sculpture before a visit to the Bargello. In the 16th century, the square assumed its present appearance, with statuary no longer intended to be an expression of Republican freedom but an ostentatious display of Florentine grandeur. Before then, in the Quattrocento, heroic statuary was synonymous with good citizenship. The statues acted as lessons in civics, with civic duty often tantamount to obedience to a dictator. As an art form, sculpture has always spelt durability and permanence, echoing the aspirations of the megalomaniac regime that commissioned it. The fact that the sculptures on display range from Roman and Hellenistic to Renaissance and Man-

nerist does not detract from the harmony of the scene, nor negate the implicit political messages.

Loggia dei Lanzi

Beside the Palazzo Vecchio stands the imposing Loggia dei Lanzi (1376–82), graced by curiously un-Gothic round arches. Although designed to shelter dignitaries watching civic ceremonies, the severe loggia became a brutal symbol of power. The portico is named after Cosimo I's intimidating Swiss lancers *(lanzi)*, who stood guard here after being brought in to support the Medici return to power in 1527. To contemporary visitors, the loggia's main claim to fame is as a showcase for a superb collec-

---

DAVID AL FRESCO

In front of the Palazzo Vecchio looms a copy of Michelangelo's David, execrated for its size and proportions yet lauded for its supreme depiction of youthful masculinity. This David may be an imposter but at least he is seen in his rightful context, embodying Republican triumph and symbolising his valiant city. According to Vasari, "There has never been seen a pose so fluent, or a gracefulness equal to his, or feet, hands and head so well-related to each other with quality, skill and design." The novelist D.H. Lawrence appreciated the powerful impact of seeing David in his rightful place, and not confined in a gallery: "He may be ugly, too naturalistic, too big but...in the position chosen for him, there standing forward stripped and exposed and eternally half-shrinking, half-wishing to expose himself, he is the genius of Florence... Here men had been at their intensest, most naked pitch, here, at the end of the old world and the beginning of the new."

A copy of Michelangelo's heroic *David* – embodiment of Republican triumph – has pride of place in front of the Palazzo Vecchio.

tion of statuary, even if many newly restored works have been replaced by copies in recent years.

Under the portico stands an array of monumental statuary encompassing Renaissance masterpieces, prosaic Roman works and vacuous Neoclassicism. Most are united in battle, strife and discord, with the female victims symbolising the price of political tyranny. Giambologna's *Rape of the Sabine Women*, an essay in three-dimensional Mannerism, is grouped with a Neoclassical work, the *Rape of Polixena* by Fedi, and *Germany Conquered*, represented by a Roman female. Rare examples of sculptures not dying on their pedestals include a line of matronly Romans, and a pair of lions.

Donatello and Giambologna

Donatello's *Judith and Holofernes* was moved from Palazzo Medici Riccardi and set up here as a symbol of freedom from Medici oppression. However, this emblematic sculpture was only partly intended as an heroic act of the people rising against their oppressors; it is also a meditation on the pain and delusion of history. Judith's troubled face is at odds with the usual scenes of exultation shown in contemporary portrayals of the scene. In Vasari's estimation, Donatello's grace and sense of composition emulated the achievements of classical sculptors more closely than any of his contemporaries. After a recent restoration, the work is now in the Palazzo Vecchio, with a copy on display here.

Yet every emblem of freedom is matched by a weighty symbol of enslavement. When Cosimo I installed himself as a dictator, he commissioned a statue to celebrate the restoration of despotism. Cellini's *Perseus*, his bronze masterpiece, shows a helmeted figure flaunting the severed head of a Medusa, symbolising the death of democracy. The newly restored statue is currently on display here but will probably be replaced by a copy.

Giambologna (1529–1608) had a gift for theatrical Mannerism and created several set-pieces for the Piazza della Signoria. His masterpiece, *The Rape of the Sabine Women*, inspired by Michelangelo, is a sublime work, with three entwined figures bound in an upwards spiral. For 16th-century Florentines, there was a fascination with *terribilità*, a mood of voluptuous horror conjured up by sensationalist mythological themes involving massacre, rape and decapitation.

The Neptune Fountain

Beyond Donatello's *Marzocco*, the heraldic lion on the Loggia dei Lanzi, stands the Neptune Fountain, a Mannerist composition intended to celebrate Cosimo's naval victories. Ammannati's bloated *Neptune* is less impressive than the bronze group of nude nymphs, satyrs and marine-horses clustered around the basin, and credited to Giambologna and Ammannati. However, with the end of the heroic age of Florentine sculpture, the noble nudity of public sculpture became an embarrassing burden. In a fit of prudery, Ammannati attacked Michelangelo's *David* and publicly regretted the nudity of his own *Neptune*, known as *Il Biancone*, "the great white one". Yet citizens have a sneaking affection for this cumbersome work, even if superstitious souls believe that the mighty river god was petrified into a marble statue as a punishment for forsaking the love of women. Legend has it that if a full moon falls directly on the statue, it springs to life and strolls around the square.

*FOOD AND DRINK: Rivoire (tel: 055-214412; closed Tues), opposite the Palazzo Vecchio, is the best spot in the city centre for good hot chocolate and aperitifs. **Giubbe Rosse** (Piazza della Repubblica) lacks Rivoire's views but is full of literary and artistic associations. **Il Bargello** (Piazza della Signoria 4/r; tel: 055-214071; closed Mon) is an expensive restaurant with a view, serving Tuscan and international dishes.*

LEFT: *Fireworks in Piazza della Signoria, c. 1560 (from a fresco in the Palazzo Vecchio).*

BELOW: *Rape of the Sabine Women, by Giambologna, 1579–82.*

Portrait of a turbaned Michelangelo, by Giuliano Bugiardini, 1522.

Casa Buonarroti

A celebration of Michelangelo's life in his 17th-century descendants' home

Map reference: page 43, G3
Via Ghibellina 70
Tel: 055-241752. www.casadibuonarroti
Bus 14, line A. Open: Wed–Mon 9.30am–2pm
Bookshop. Research library. Admission charge.

Michelangelo Buonarroti (1475–1564), the quintessential Renaissance man, is not fully represented in this museum, either in spirit or in sculpture – his masterpieces are displayed in the Accademia *(pages 49–52)*, the Bargello *(page 57)*, the Uffizi *(page 89)* and the Medici Chapels *(page 109)*. However, thanks to his descendants, this handsome townhouse conveys the atmosphere of a family home and remains a touching tribute to the great sculptor, painter, architect and poet. Although Michelangelo bought the property, it was his nephew, Leonardo, who transformed it. In turn, his great-nephew, Michelangelo the Younger, finished the decoration in 1612, turning it into a virtual shrine to his namesake. As a cultivated Florentine art collector and playwright, he tended to gild the lily in his eagerness to honour his ances-

try. Given its lavish frescoes and friezes of illustrious Tuscans, the house risks overshadowing the somewhat meagre Michelangelo artefacts. Yet this is acceptable in the context of proud descendants basking in the glory of their greatest son.

The museum traces Michelangelo's life through models, sketches and working diagrams. Some of the memorabilia has been collected by his direct descendants while much is borrowed from the state collections. Set around a courtyard, the ground floor displays a small archaeological collection. On the same floor are works by Michelangelo's near contemporaries. Authentic works by Michelangelo await on the first floor, even if they simply provide visual footnotes to the sculptor's masterpieces in the Accademia.

Jostling for attention are virile models in wax, terracotta and marble, notably the wrestlers in combat, a muscular torso of a river god, and the *Slaves (see page 50)*. A painted crucifix of a nude Christ can be attributed only to the audacious virtuoso. Equally memorable is the *Battle of the Centaurs*, a writhing heap of bodies. This expressive marble bas-relief is matched by the precocious skill displayed in the *Madonna of the Steps*, made by the 16-year-old master sculptor. Michelangelo's sheer inventiveness is clear in tantalising glimpses of unfulfilled projects, such as a wooden model for the façade of San Lorenzo.

In the first-floor gallery, illustrious 16th- and 17th-century artists have created a sumptuous display covering every surface. The eclectic collection built up by Michelangelo's great-nephew includes della Robbia glazed terracottas and *putti*. The collection comes to a close with a Titianesque painting by Rosina Vendramin, wife of Cosimo Buonarroti (1790–1858), Michelangelo's last direct descendant. As in the Dante museum *(see page 149)*, the essence of the man eludes the bricks and mortar, but here, at least, it is an honourable failure.

*FOOD AND DRINK: Try **Alle Murate** (Via Ghibellina 52–54r; tel: 055-240618; Tues–Sun) for pricey Florentine dishes in formal surroundings; **Enoteca Pinchiorri** (Via Ghibellina 87; tel: 055-242777; Tues–Sat; closed Aug) for a gastronomic feast in the city's most prestigious (and expensive) restaurant; **Caffè Cibreo** (Via Andrea del Verrocchio 5r; tel: 055-2345853; Tues–Sat) for pastries and snacks; **Cibreo** (Via de' Macci 118r; tel: 055-2341100; Tues–Sat; closed Aug) for creative peasant cuisine at aristocratic prices; **Osteria del Caffè Italiano** (Via Isole delle Stinche 11–13r; tel: 055-289368; Tues–Sun) for Tuscan dishes at reasonable prices in a medieval palazzo; **Bar Vivoli Gelateria** (Via Isole delle Stinche 7r; tel: 055-292334; Tues–Sun, closed Sun at 1pm) for the best ice cream in Florence.*

Casa di Dante

Portraits, maps and documentation celebrating the life of Italy's greatest poet

Map reference: page 42, E3
Via Santa Margherita 1. Tel: 055-219416
Bus: 14, 23, line A
Open: Wed–Sat 10am–4pm (6pm in summer),
Sun 10am–2pm
Bookshop. Guided group visits if booked.
Admission charge.

The museum, set in the medieval heart of Florence, occupies a heavily remodelled 13th-century tower-house. Reputedly the birthplace of Dante Alighieri (1265–1321), this contentious pastiche is home to an ill-conceived collection. While it is more challenging to create an engaging literary collection than a captivating picture gallery, this mothballed museum languishes in Dante-esque purgatory. Scholars might find solace here but the general public, especially non-Italian speakers, will feel rather at sea.

At its best, the museum is a re-evocation of Dante's Florence rather than an attempt to come to terms with the poet's genius. As a citizen in the medieval city, Dante's horizons embraced the Bargello, the Baptistery, the Badia Fiorentina and Palazzo Spini-Feroni, as well as a forest of tower-houses which have since been demolished or subsumed into other palaces. Illustrations of the medieval city feature Dante's parish church and an evocative fresco of Florence in 1342, which represents one of the first views of the city. Copies of The *Divine Comedy*, the epic poem which established the Tuscan dialect as the model for Italian literature, are on display, including one dating from 1372. Amid the plethora of Dante portraits is a copy of Henry Holliday's famous Pre-Raphaelite painting, *The Meeting of Dante and Beatrice*, alluding to the doomed non-relationship that inspired much of Dante's poetry.

The museum presents an incoherent view of the Guelf–Ghibelline political struggles in medieval Florence, including family crests and battle maps. Unjustly cast into exile after factional disputes within the Guelf party, Dante declared himself "a Florentine by birth but not by character". The exiled poet sought refuge in Verona, Rome, Bologna and Poppi castle before eventually settling in Ravenna, where he died. His native city belatedly redeemed itself with a Dante memorial in Santa Croce *(see page 118)*.

*FOOD AND DRINK: **Cantinetta dei Verrazzano** (Via dei Tavolini 18–20r; tel: 055-268590; Mon–Sat 8am–8pm) is the place for genuine Florentine snacks and wines, either from the bench or in the café. See also Badia Fiorentina, page 103 and the Bargello, page 61.*

The Meeting of Dante and Beatrice by Henry Holliday, 1883.

Casa Guidi

Home to two great English Victorian poets, Elizabeth and Robert Barrett-Browning

Map reference: page 42, C5
Piazza San Felice 8
Tel: 055-354457
Open: Mon, Wed, Fri 3–6pm Apr–Nov
Informal tours in English, French and Italian.
Admission charge
Apartment rental: about £300 per night for min 3 nights; sleeps 6; guests must allow public access to reception rooms during opening times. Book through the Landmark Trust in the UK: (tel: 01628-825925) or in the US (tel: 802-264-6868); or visit www.landmarktrust.co.uk

Casa Guidi manages to be both a literary shrine to two legendary English poets and a distillation of Victorian expatriate life. After a stifling stay in Pisa, the Barrett-Brownings settled in Florence in 1847, and found happiness in Casa Guidi until Elizabeth's death. Set virtually opposite the Pitti Palace, the apartment occupies the *piano nobile* of a 15th-century palazzo. The cluttered yet appealing suite of rooms are in Victorian style and include Robert's study, the dining room and the overstuffed drawing room. These are decorated in green and pink, Elizabeth's favourite colours, and contain a few pieces of the couple's original furniture, from the rococo mirror to portraits and busts of the poets. Apart from writing in the room, the credulous Elizabeth also held seances there; spiritualism was much in vogue in the Anglo-Florentine community.

Happiness and creativity

The most celebrated female poet of her time, Elizabeth (1806–61) declared her love for her adoptive city: "Florence is my chimney corner, where I can skulk and be happy." Although believing that "being too happy doesn't agree with literary activity", Elizabeth was creative in the city, and the view from Casa Guidi windows slipped neatly from reality into her most famous poem. Since the semi-invalid was largely confined to home, her verandah was central to her happiness. There, her son kept rabbits, and, among the citrus trees, Elizabeth, an ardent Republican, saw the Austrians invade the cowed city, and later awaited the Unification of Italy.

Robert Browning (1812–89) was equally at home in Florence and wrote prodigiously, producing two notable poems, *Andrea del Sarto* and *Fra Lippo Lippi*, as well as channelling his erudition into theology, psychology and botany. All this was in addition to sculpting, organising literary salons and looking after his sickly "lyric love", whom he called "a soul of fire in a shell of pearl". Pen, their delicate and ethereal son, was born in the bedroom that is now on offer to guests.

Wallowing in happiness in Casa Guidi, Elizabeth never tired of praising Italy at the expense of her

The Drawing Room at Casa Guidi, by George Mignaty, 1861.

Elizabeth Barrett Browning

On Elizabeth's death, Robert commissioned a painting of the drawing room by George Mignaty, the model for its painstaking recreation by ardent Barrett-Browning fans. Given that this was also Pen's greatest wish, there is a pleasing symmetry to the story, especially now that visitors can stay here. The Browning Institute of New York began the restoration, with the baton passing to the Landmark Trust, a British charity that rescues historic buildings and makes them available for holidays. Eton College, the English public school, then stepped in, largely because of its significant Browning connections. As a result, the apartments still give pleasure, both to public schoolboys and visiting professors. *(For more about the Brownings and Florence's 19th-century expat community, see pages 30–32).*

Elizabeth Barrett Browning in 1859, just two years before her death.

FOOD AND DRINK: Caffè Pitti (Piazza Pitti 5r; tel: 055-2396241; daily 11am–1am) is an attractive if touristy bar. See also Palazzo Pitti, page 70.

homeland: "Our poor English want educating into gladness. They want refining not in the fire but in the sunshine." Virginia Woolf put it more astutely, aware that the poet's spirits were also raised by the wine Robert used to wean his wife off laudanum: "So Mrs Browning, every day, as she tossed off her Chianti and broke another orange off the branch, praised Italy and lamented poor, dull, damp, sullen, joyless, expensive, conventional England."

Robert shared his wife's contentment, writing in 1847: "We are as happy as two owls in a hole, two toads under a tree-stump; or any other two queer poking creatures that we let live after the fashion of their black hearts." After Elizabeth's death, Robert left Florence, died in Venice, and is now buried in London's Westminster Abbey. On his departure, the poet glanced around the drawing room and declared: "the cycle is complete: here we came 15 years ago; here Pen was born; here Ba wrote her poems for Italy". The grateful city responded in kind, burying Elizabeth in the English Cemetery, and describing her poetry as "a ring of gold joining England and Italy".

RENEWED INTEREST

Owing to the popularity of the film, *Tea with Mussolini*, set in Florence, the cypress-covered cemetery has been re-opened to burials. There has also been increased interest in Casa Guidi since the publication of Margaret Forster's book, *Lady's Maid*, based on Wilson, Elizabeth's devoted maid, who moved out after her marriage.

Casa Museo Siviero

Small art collection in the former home of a wartime Tuscan art investigator

Map reference: page 43, G5
Lungarno Serristori 1/3 (garden entrance at side)
Tel: 055-2345219
Bus: lines C and D
Open: Mon 9.30am–12.30pm, Sat 3.30–6.30pm
Bookshop. Admission charge

This relatively modest house overlooking the river was the home of Rodolfo Siviero (1911–83), a controversial figure responsible for recovering major works of art stolen from Italy during and after World War II *(see pages 33–4)*. If Siviero has never been accorded his rightful recognition in the preservation of Florentine heritage, it is largely because of the murkiness of wartime events and the borderline activities Siviero was involved in. As an ardent patriot, art historian and keen collector, he used his art detective's eye to trace stolen works. Given the nature of the times, however, the pursuit involved espionage, and a double game played with the Italian Fascist authorities and the occupying German forces. Whatever the compromises, Siviero's dedication resulted in the saving of thousands of Renaissance masterpieces for major Italian museums.

Compared with the great treasure houses of art, Siviero's private collection is distinctly slight, but takes on greater significance when seen in the context of his extraordinary life and times. The collection is currently on the ground floor of Palazzina Poggi, an elegant 19th-century house, but should expand to the top floor in the next few years. (The recent death of Siviero's sister means that space has become available for exhibitions and a research library.) It is now run by a charity, the Amici dei Musei Fiorentini (Friends of Florentine Museums), which is also setting up a World War II study centre.

The collection includes Capodimonte porcelain, minor Tuscan Renaissance works and Etruscan pieces, as well as a small arms collection, and dignified antiques from the 16th century onwards.

Siviero was a mass of contradictions: this worldly, cosmopolitan art-lover slept in a spartan bed in a monastic cell, albeit one hung with minor Tuscan treasures. The austerity is underlined by a severe 16th-century statue of San Rocco, the saint of plague victims, restored after the 1966 flood which struck this riverside palazzo. In keeping with the art investigator's wartime exploits, and his role as a double-agent, Siviero's bedroom has a secret passage leading out to an alley. The adjoining guest-bedroom, with its canopied bed and period furniture, is far more inviting.

As for mementoes of Siviero's secret past, the Giorgio de Chirico painting in the sitting room is a fitting reminder that this James Bond of the art world saved de Chirico's works from being spirited off to Nazi Germany or destroyed as subversive *(see page 34)*.

The art investigator Rodolfo Siviero, who recovered hundreds of artworks stolen in World War II, pictured here in 1968.

FOOD AND DRINK: Beccofino (Piazza degli Scarlatti 1r, off Lungarno Guicciardini; tel: 055-290076; closed Mon night) is a Scottish-run upmarket wine bar/restaurant serving reasonably priced contemporary Italian cuisine. Bordino (Via Stracciatella 9r; tel: 055-213048; closed Sun) is a simple place for a good lunch a few minutes' walk uphill from the Ponte Vecchio. See also Museo Horne, page 155.

Museo Bardini

An eclectic collection of art and salvaged architectural elements occupying several medieval palaces

Map reference: page 43, G5
Piazza de Mozzi 1. Tel: 055-2342427
Bus: line C
Currently closed for restoration, but due to re-open by 2003. New facilities expected.

Museo Bardini enjoys an enviable location in the sleepy side of the Oltrarno, on the far side of the Ponte alla Grazia bridge. Like many of Florence's major palaces, it owes much to the dedication of an inspired antique dealer and collector *(see page 33)*. Stefano Bardini (1836–1922) claimed to be aghast at the demolition of an ancient quarter razed to make way for Piazza della Repubblica, the glossy symbol of 19th-century Italian unity. This wanton destruction prompted Bardini to salvage architectural elements from the wreckage, although the less charitable interpretation is that he quietly encouraged the demolition to serve his own magpie instincts. Either way, he rescued fine pieces from the ruins and the core collection in the Bardini Museum is an eclectic assemblage of Roman sarcophagi, Romanesque capitals, Renaissance chimney pieces, medieval architraves and doors, all salvaged from demolished churches and houses.

The palace itself is a partial reconstruction, carried out in the 1880s. Along with several adjoining medieval palaces, this one was left to the city by Bardini's son. When restoration is complete, the collection is expected to overflow into the connecting palaces and gardens, allowing space for an exhibition and research centre.

As well as such bizarre touches as a drawing room paved with tombstones, the core collection includes a number of fine della Robbia ceramics, period carpets, tapestries, arms and musical instruments. Frescoed ceilings provide an atmospheric setting for 15th- and 16th-century Tuscan and Venetian religious statuary. There are also several significant Tuscan Renaissance works of art, including paintings by Pollaiuolo and sculptures attributed to Donatello.

FOOD AND DRINK: Le Volpi e L'Uva (Piazza dei Rossi 1r, off Piazza di Santa Felicità, just across the Ponte Vecchio; tel: 055-2398132). This enoteca (wine bar) has a contemporary feel and serves fine wines and tasty Tuscan snacks, such as crostini.

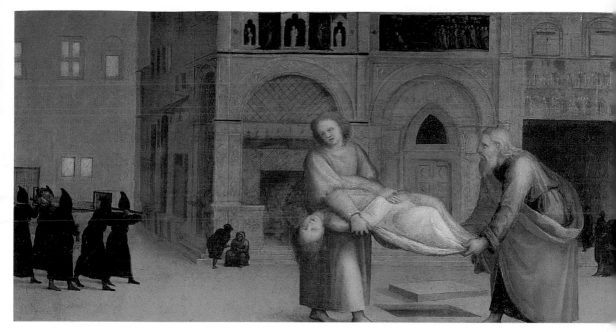

Loggia e Museo del Bigallo

Opposite the Baptistery, this pretty chapel and loggia is a superb example of a Confraternity Chapel, of which only a handful are open to the public

Map reference: page 42, E3
Corner of Piazza di San Giovanni and Via dei Calzaiuoli. Tel: 055-2302885
Bus: 1, 6, 11, 14, 17, 22, 23
Open: Mon 8.30am–noon, Thurs 4–6pm
Admission charge

Medieval Florence had numerous lay confraternities, charitable organisations set up by pious citizens to do good works, each with its own chapel and meeting room. One such confraternity that has survived into the 21st century – still performing the role for which it was established – is the Arciconfraternità della Misericordia (Brotherhood of Mercy), founded in 1244 to carry the sick to hospital and to bury plague victims. They now run the ambulance service in Florence (and in many other Tuscan cities), still operating from their original premises immediately opposite the Bigallo.

The Compagnia del Bigallo itself was founded in 1245 to look after abandoned children and orphans. Its premises consists of a beautiful open loggia (1352–58) decorated with marble reliefs and medieval ironwork. In this exquisite setting, lost or abandoned children were exhibited for three days, and if not claimed by any relation were found foster homes. The beautiful hemispherical arches of the loggia anticipate the Renaissance, while the windows are pure late Gothic. Three 14th-century niches and statues set in the wall facing the Baptistery come from the Bigallo's former premises, and the *Madonna and Child* above the entrance dates from 1361.

The door below leads into the confraternity chapel and meeting rooms, decorated with works of art donated by well-wishers, most of which depict the Virgin and Child, or the symbolic figure of Charity giving succour to lost children.

Among the exhibits is the earliest known view of Florence (1342), forming part of a fresco by a follower of Bernardo Daddi. The multi-towered city of Florence (with the Baptistery clearly visible in the foreground, and the unfinished façade of the Cathedral) is depicted at the base of the fresco, protected by the skirts of the Virgin. Her robes are decorated with scenes illustrating the charitable works of the Bigallo. At her feet are various worshippers – possibly members and patrons of the confraternity. In the same room is a fine fresco of 1386 depicting members of the confraternity handing children over to new foster mothers.

Tobias buries the dead in Nineveh, by Ghirlandaio, 1515 (Museo del Bigallo).

FOOD AND DRINK: *see Piazza del Duomo, page 102.*

Giotto's rare painting of St Stephen (13th century) is the highlight of the Horne collection.

Museo Horne

A Victorian English aesthete's recreation of an authentic Renaissance home

Map reference: page 43, F4
Via de' Benci 6
Tel: 055-244661
Bus: lines A and B (until 8pm)
Open: Mon–Sat 9am–1pm; Mon till 11pm in summer; Oct–Dec Sun am only
Themed tours; tiny bookshop

Close to the river in the Santa Croce district stands a severe 14th-century merchant's palace, known as the Palagetto. Inside is a Renaissance world in miniature, justifying the passion of its Victorian creator. Herbert Percy Horne (1864–1916), an English architect and art historian, sold his collection of English watercolours to purchase the palace, the most authentic he could find. Here, submerged in nostalgia for a lost era, he devoted himself to restoring the galleried loggia, leaded windows, monumental fireplaces and sculpted portals. As a merchant's house, here public and private worlds coexisted, with the quieter north-facing wing reserved for the family and the south-facing wing used as workshops and studios.

Horne respected this layout – rooms still fan out from an inner courtyard – and slowly accumulated a collection of Renaissance art to transform his dream into reality *(see page 31).*

The compact courtyard, framed by a loggia and a frieze, contains the medieval workshops and studios. Horne used the most authentic room on the ground floor as a showcase for his coins, seals, ceramics and devotional works. This collection remains essentially as he left it, along with a display of priceless 16th–18th-century drawings in adjoining rooms.

Drawings and prints by Poussin, Raphael, Rubens and Guardi, which were removed after the 1966 flood, have been returned recently. These represent the most valuable items in the collection. Given their quantity and quality, they are on display on a rotational basis.

Sanctified panels

Above, overlooking the courtyard, is the banqueting room with the master bedrooms leading off. The room presents a harmonious whole, with shuttered, bottle-glass windows, terracotta tiled floors, and 15th-century wedding chests, known as *cassoni (see box)*. On the walls are works from the 14th century onwards, especially small, sanctified panels: Signorelli's *St Catherine*; Masaccio's *St Julien*; and Pietro Lorenzetti's *St Catherine and Saints*. Here, too, is Giambologna's terracotta model for the *Kneeling Venus*, a favourite of Horne's, and a restored *Deposition* by Benozzo Gozzoli. Tucked into a corner is a fascinating *Exorcism of a Woman Possessed by Devils*.

The adjoining Saletta (the wife's bedroom in Renaissance times) is adorned with wedding chests and Giotto's serene *St Stephen*, the most precious painting in the museum. The master bedroom, opening onto the inner courtyard, is impressive, with a gilded panelled ceiling, a sculpted Pisan fireplace and 15th-century furniture. Beccafumi's elaborately framed *Holy Family tondo* presides over Florentine paintings and *cassoni* panels.

The floor above, intended for the children and favoured servants, also contains a reconstructed Renaissance kitchen and dining room. On display are Renaissance knick-knacks including knives decorated with ivory-headed handles or encrusted with semi-precious stones. The bedrooms have authentic inlaid doors, recycled from Umbrian palaces, and furniture salvaged from churches. Among the Renaissance art, two pieces stand out: a Filippino Lippi *Pietà* and a *cassone* panel by the same artist, based on Botticelli designs. The strangest object is

the *lettuccio*, a 15th-century day-bed, the equivalent of a sofa, but distinctly less comfortable. Equally uncompromising are the tall Strozzi stools, actually high-backed, three-legged chairs designed to compensate for uneven 15th-century floors.

FOOD AND DRINK: Il Francescano (Largo Bargellini 16, adjoining Piazza Santa Croce; tel: 055-241605; closed Tues, Oct–May) is a rustic trattoria serving Tuscan dishes. Boccadama (Piazza Santa Croce 25–26r; tel: 055-243640; open late) is a wine bar serving light meals. Il Tirabuscio (Via de' Benci 34r; tel: 055-2476225/667317; closed Wed, Thur) serves steaks, with lighter lunch options. See also Museo Siviero, page 152.

WEDDING CHESTS

Wedding chests *(cassoni)* are often considered the symbol of patrician social life in Renaissance Florence. These marriage gifts not only served to display status and wealth in 14th–16th-century society but were an essential part of everyday life: the chests held and represented riches while serving as seats or day-beds when placed side by side; or, when mounted on mules, were used to transport furniture. While simpler chests are adorned only with the family crest, many can be considered works of art in their own right, with individual panels displayed as paintings in the Uffizi, Horne Museum and many other galleries. Intended as a side panel, the gorgeous Filippino Lippi painting in the Horne collection is a superb example of the art form. Generally, the outside panels of the chests were decorated with scenes depicting a public blessing of the union, based on Petrarch's *Triumph of Love*, or, less cheerfully, *The Rape of the Sabine Women*, intended as a propitiatory theme. The inside of the chest lid often contained a private message, commonly a symbol of fertility, in the form of an entwined nude couple.

Painted *cassone*, or wedding chest, depicting the *Triumph of David*, 15th century.

The Story of
Antonio
Rinaldeschi, a
Florentine
gambler. In a
fit of rage
after heavy
losses at the
gaming table,
he threw dung
at a statue of
the Virgin –
an offence
which cost
him his life.

Museo Stibbert

An Anglo-Florentine collector's rural villa, now a museum crammed with arms and artworks

Map reference: page 42, E1
Via F. Stibbert 26
Tel: 055-475520
Bus: 4 from Piazza Unità d'Italia; 20-minute journey to Via Fabroni (3rd stop on the street; ask the driver) and a 5-minute walk uphill
Open: Fri–Sun 10am–6pm, Mon–Wed 10am–2pm
Café. Small bookshop. Accompanied visit (in Italian). Admission charge.

Set in an attractive residential area with rural views, this Gothic Revival museum encapsulates the passions of Frederick Stibbert (1838–1906), a wealthy Anglo-Florentine aesthete, dandy and collector *(see page 32)*. This is a curiously alluring collection. As a young man, Stibbert inherited a fortune and an early 16th-century villa, which he connected to an adjoining 19th-century country house to create a rambling 64-room mansion, both museum and residence. Stibbert's life-work impressed Queen Victoria and was bequeathed to the British government, who gave it to the city of Florence.

The cluttered villa still evokes the concerns of a 19th-century gentleman: a map room, billiards room, ballroom and library lead to an Empire-style music room and a tiled smoking room influenced

by the English Arts and Crafts movement. Yet William Morris florals and Pre-Raphaelite stained-glass windows effortlessly flow into rococo furnishings and exotic chinoiserie, as every room reveals another facet of Stibbert's eclectic taste. The décor embraces Oriental porcelain, malachite fireplaces, Murano chandeliers and Flemish tapestries.

Although Botticelli and Lorenzetti are represented, for once Tuscan art plays second fiddle to Flemish portraits and Dutch still lifes, Gothic armour, Oriental porcelain and historical costumes, including the dress uniform Napoleon wore when crowned king of Italy. As a self-confessed dandy, Stibbert could not resist displaying models of himself dressed as a Scottish highlander, Egyptian god or medieval knight. Most of the arms and armour are authentic, but Stibbert had no qualms about recreating missing pieces to enhance the effect. The *pièce de resistance* is the cavalcade of knights in the medieval Great Hall, a phalanx of costumed models presented like a freeze-frame of a grave battle scene. Given the personal nature of the museum, every scene is designed to create an impact, to bedazzle rather than to instruct.

Designed to dazzle

In the superb arms collection, nothing is presented systematically: among historical gems are Roman and Etruscan helmets, with Islamic scimitars alongside bayonets from the French Revolution. Most pieces are from 15th–17th- century Western Europe but Stibbert enriched the collection with Persian and Ottoman weaponry and Indian arms inherited from his grandfather, a governor of Bengal. As for the antique Japanese armour, swords and saddles, the finest collection outside the Far East, the cumulative effect is of a boy playing with a medieval train set. Stibbert's compelling game continues in the Victorian-style garden, which is slowly being

restored, from the Gothic terrace and Tuscan orangery to the Egyptian folly guarded by a sphinx. A small lake sits snugly amid a pine grove dotted with cypresses, cedars of Lebanon, lime trees and conifers, a reminder that even in landscaping, Stibbert was nothing if not eclectic.

FOOD AND DRINK: The Stibbert Museum is in a residential area, so for a proper meal you will need to go back to the city centre. The on-site café is pleasant and friendly and serves hot and old drinks and light snacks.

St Dominic, by Carlo Crivelli, 15th century (Museo Stibbert).

Palazzo Antinori

A model 15th-century palace and the ancestral home of the Antinori family

Map reference: page 42, D2
Piazzetta Antinori, Via de' Tornabuoni 3
Access only to Cantinetta Antinori
Tel: 055-292234

Palazzo Antinori is set on a small square adjoining the city's most aristocratic street, and faces the only baroque church in the city. As the smartest part of town, Via de' Tornabuoni is lined with gracious palaces, a testament to the wealth and refinement of Florentine nobles from Renaissance times onwards.

The 15th-century palazzo is a model of its kind, the perfect Florentine Renaissance palazzo. The restrained façade is of characteristic austere elegance. The attention to detail can be seen in the geometric patterns, the traditional overhanging roof and the sober, well-proportioned windows.

The palace once hosted literary salons and even housed the British Institute and Consulate. Today, the second floor contains sumptuous reception rooms, but access to society events is restricted to privileged guests. Like many Florentine aristocratic familes, the Antinori, the dynastic owners, began as noted merchants, city dignitaries, humanists and scientists, but are now successful entrepreneurs in the food and wine business. Their Chianti vineyards are the source of some of Tuscany's most prestigious wines, which can be tasted in the family's fashionable restaurant on the ground floor. Unfortunately, this is the only accessible part of the palace.

FOOD AND DRINK: Cantinetta Antinori (see above) is the place for authentic Tuscan cuisine and fine wines. I Latini (Via dei Palchetti 6r, off Via della Spada; tel: 055-210916; Tues–Sun) is a lively popular Tuscan trattoria.

Palazzo Corsini

A fine collection of Florentine art in a baroque riverside palace

Map reference: page 42, D3
Lungarno Corsini (main entrance Via del Parione 11). Tel: 055-218944 (bookings); 055-282283/282635 and www.mostraantiquariato.it (for art and antiques fair information – see page 174)
Bus: line B.
Open: Gallery and palace by appointment only (tel as above); Gallery morning only (groups of 5 or more preferred); Palace visits more flexible (but groups preferred). Book on Mon, Wed or Fri and ask for Donna Giorgione Corsini. Admission charge.

Built in grandiose Roman baroque style, this huge waterfront palace is at odds with the austere monumentality of earlier Florentine mansions. Palazzo Corsini is a palace in all senses of the word, but its alien baroque style bewildered Florentines at first, even if the city has come to prize this striking cuckoo in its midst. With its baroque wings overlooking the Arno, the stately U-shaped façade is stunning, enhanced by statuary and a terrace overlooking the river. Still inhabited by the aristocratic Corsini family, this palace represents their ancestral seat, but is complemented by their country seat, a magnificent villa on the city outskirts, the gardens of which can also be visited *(see page 197)*.

The Corsini family bought the palace from the Medici Grand-duke Ferdinand II in 1640 and promptly set about remodelling it. The pastoral mood of the previous palace was swept away amid the lavish renovations, completed in 1735. A delightfully intimate private gallery of masterpieces was founded in the 17th century. Lorenzo Corsini, better known as Pope Clement XII, established a glittering court at the palace, and the festivities continued under Napoleonic rule. In 1870, Victor Emmanuel II, the new king of Savoy, chose the palace for his official receptions. After triumphing over war damage in 1944 and flood damage in 1966, the palace is again the setting for sumptuous events, including the annual art and antiques fair *(see page 174)*.

A monumental staircase leads to the *piano nobile* and the Sala del Trono, the late 17th-century throne room. The ornate cornices, columns and chandeliers

Palazzo Davanzati/Museo della Casa Fiorentina Antica

The Wrestling Match, from a wedding chest painted by Lo Scheggia, 1440 (Palazzo Davanzati).

Museum of Medieval and Renaissance life in one of the city's best-preserved period palaces

Map reference: page 42, D3
Via Porta Rossa 13
Tel: 055-2388610
Bus: 6, 11, 36 and line A
Open: Tues–Sat 8.15am–1.45pm, plus 1st, 3rd and 5th Sun of month and 2nd and 4th Mon of month.
Closed for renovation until 2003.

T his beguiling museum has been closed for restoration since 1994 but is due to re-open by 2003. In the meantime, you can see an exhibition on the ground floor portraying the domestic life of Florentine noblemen and merchants in times past.

The 14th-century palace was acquired in 1578 by wealthy banker, wool-merchant and humanist, Bernardo Davanzati, and stayed in the family until 1838 when Elia Volpi, an antique dealer and passionate medievalist, restored it. Unfortunately, the cost of the restoration proved Volpi's undoing, and he was forced to sell the magnificent period furnishings, antiques and artworks at auction. Since the state acquired the palace in the 1950s, suitable furnishings and antiques have been purchased, including a medieval bed.

In architectural terms, the highlights are the majestic façade that extends from the former 15th-century wool workshops on the ground floor to the graceful loggia that crowns the palace.

Inside the palazzo, striking aspects include the vaulted entrance hall and the staircase supported by flying buttresses. In terms of decoration, the great Gothic halls on the second and third floors are the most unusual spaces. The walls and cupboards are decorated with frescoes to give the semblance of fabrics and drapery. In style and décor, the lofty, galleried palace bridges the medieval and Renaissance eras, making Palazzo Davanzati the most authentic surviving example of a patrician dwelling from the period.

*FOOD AND DRINK: **Caffè Gilli** (Piazza della Repubblica 36–39r; tel: 055-213896; Wed–Mon 8am–midnight). Atmospheric café with lovely belle époque interior and terrace. Serves hot chocolate, coffee and drinks.*

are overshadowed by allegorical frescoes depicting the vainglorious Apotheosis of the Corsini, a riotous scene of gilded chariots, cherubs and angels. The frescoed ballroom, adorned with stucco-work and a marine scene of cavorting sea nymphs, contains the finest fresco in the palace. The frescoed Aurora gallery is equally grand but the scene is softened by a view of hills on the far side of the Arno. Other highlights include a grotto on the ground floor and a cunning 17th-century spiral staircase.

The gallery, in the east wing, is arguably the finest in private hands in Florence, and presents a sweeping survey of 16th- and 17th-century art, created in the glory days of the palace. Occupying a series of frescoed 17th-century rooms, the private gallery has Renaissance and Mannerist works by major artists, including early works by Filippino Lippi. Ghirlandaio's *Portrait of a Man* is matched by a cartoon of Raphael's *Portrait of Julius II*, Pontormo's *Madonna and Child*, and a Giovanni Bellini crucifix. Other highlights include a *tondo* of the *Madonna* by Luca Signorelli, and a similar work by Botticelli or his workshop. Interspersed with paintings by the great Tuscan masters are family busts and portraits, including a Bouchardon bust of Clement XII, the sole Corsini Pope. In many cases, the glittering original frames are almost as impressive as the artworks. Given the ostentation of the palace, the predilection for style over content is an apt summation of this Florentine showcase.

*FOOD AND DRINK: **Uvafragola** (Piazza di Santa Maria Novella 9; tel: 055-215387; Thurs–Tues until late) serves classic pizza and pasta.*

Byzantine emperor, John VII Palaeologus, as one of the Three Kings, from the *Procession of the Magi* cycle by Gozzoli, *c.* 1460.

Palazzo Medici Riccardi

The first Medici seat, containing a frescoed chapel, state rooms and library

Map reference: page 42, E2
Bus: line A, 6, 11 and 17
***Palazzo**: Via Cavour 3.*
Tel: 055-2760340 (pre-booking possible)
Open: Thurs–Tues 9am–7pm (numbers to Cappella dei Magi restricted to 15 at a time)
***Biblioteca Riccardiana**: 10 Via Ginori/corner of Piazza San Lorenzo. Tel: 055-212586*
Open: Mon–Fri 9am–1pm (same ticket as for palace; also valid the following day)
Bookshop. Admission charge

When the art historian and aesthete John Ruskin, visiting Florence in the 1840s, scorned the "Newgate-like palaces", he had grim places like this one in mind. Although not so prison-like as Palazzo Strozzi *(see page 163)*, its severe rusticated façade is daunting rather than uplifting, impressive rather than inspiring. In fact, this was exactly the effect sought by Cosimo Il Vecchio, who commissioned it. Cosimo rejected Brunelleschi's plan as being "too great and too sumptuous". Flamboyance and the flaunting of wealth were political suicide in republican-minded Florence, as Cosimo realised: "envy is a plant one should never water" was the shrewd ruler's watchword. Instead, he entrusted

the project to Michelozzo, requesting a restrained palace "which would be the austere reflection of [our] economic and political power". Even so, the location was a statement in itself: set on the widest street in Renaissance Florence, the dynastic seat was close to both the Duomo and San Lorenzo. The Medici lived there from 1452 until 1540, when they moved to the politically symbolic Palazzo Vecchio. The former family seat was passed down to minor members of the clan until the 17th-century, when Carlo de' Medici rashly exchanged it for a casino in Venice.

While much of the palace is swathed in institutional gloom, parts are open to the public, including the ground floor, which is now given over to temporary exhibitions. In its heyday, Cosimo lived in the ground floor apartments, surrounded by his collection of classical sculpture and artwork. One room on the ground floor contains a permanent display of newly restored classical sculptures, notably busts of emperors, philosophers and poets.

Cosimo's eldest son, Piero di Cosimo (1416–69) and grandson, Lorenzo the Magnificent (1449–82) expanded the collection; while Piero collected jewellery, silverware and illuminated Bibles, Lorenzo preferred Oriental vases. When the Medici were expelled in 1494, the palace was plundered, though some objects eventually found their way into the Uffizi and Pitti collections. Donatello's bronze *Judith* was moved from the palace and set in front of the Palazzo Vecchio, symbolising the regaining of liberty by the republic. When the Medici, in the form of the future

Pope Leo X, returned to the palace in 1512, changes were made to increase their sense of security, notably the sealing up of the loggia.

Riccardi make-over

The Riccardi marquesses, who bought the palace in 1659, were the wealthiest family in Florence until the early 18th century, and enlarged the family seat in keeping with their ambitions but still in accordance with Michelozzo's designs.

The family commissioned a grand staircase, a library and a gallery painted by Neapolitan artist, Luca Giordano, in 1685. Set on the first floor, the baroque mirrored gallery has white and gold stucco friezes surmounted by Giordano's graceful frescoes. The formal theme, the Apotheosis of the Medici, pays tribute to the princely dynasty while floating into a sugary, illusionistic allegory on the gaining of wisdom, by way of carnal love, sacred love, virtuous marriage and fortitude.

Under these frothy scenes, surrounded by painted mirrors and cabinets of curios, Florence's provincial administration conducts equally illusionistic debates. In an ante-room there is a sweetly demure *Madonna and Child* painted by Fra' Filippo Lippi (c. 1406–69), the most lascivious of artist-friars.

People's palace

After the departure of the despotic Medici and the hapless Riccardi, the mansion became a "people's palace", housing local government offices. This transfer of power could be seen as the city-state's ultimate triumph over tyranny; yet most of the palace remains closed to the public, and citizens rightfully feel aggrieved. The fitting finale would be the departure of officialdom and the complete opening of the palace. Until then, the prefect's frescoed study is as inaccessible as the former Medici apartments. Only the Italian President is allowed to stay, a reminder that the palace continues to play political power games.

One of the grandest events staged here was the marriage of Lorenzo the Magnificent to Clarice Orsini, allowing the Medici to marry into the Roman papal nobility. In celebration, Lorenzo's first-floor bedroom was adorned with Paolo Uccello's famous *Battle of San Romano*, but the panels are now divided between the Uffizi *(see page 82)*, the Louvre and London's National Gallery, a sign of the wealth the city has unwittingly shared with the world.

Michelozzo's inner courtyard makes a major impact, enhanced by walls adorned with fragments of Roman masonry *(see page 174)*. However, the palace's masterpiece is the Cappella dei Magi, the delightful chapel frescoed by Benozzo Gozzoli (1420–97), tucked away on the first floor. The tiny chapel presents a coherent decorative whole, down to the carved Gothic choir-seats designed by Sangallo. The coffered ceiling echoes the patterns of the inlaid floor of red porphyry and green serpentine

---

RICCARDI LIBRARY

The Biblioteca Riccardiana, founded by Marchese Riccardo Riccardi, is set in the 17th-century extension to the palace. The Medici were passionate collectors of rare books, from humanist works to Bibles and Classical texts illuminated by 15th-century miniaturists. Fortunately, while the art collections have been dispersed, the library remains intact. The Medici works aside, the core collection came from the Riccardi family's early 17th-century home and was transferred here at the behest of the enlightened Grand-duke Cosimo III "because it enhances the public decorum and glory of the city for the items to be more easily seen." The Riccardi created a new library for the collection and it has been open to the public since 1718. On the ceiling is Luca Giordano's allegory of divine wisdom, described by his biographer as "Intellect released by Knowledge from the bonds of Ignorance." Alas, ignorance was rife when the treasures of the Riccardi museum were dispersed in 1808: although the library was saved, the Napoleonic government in Florence refused to purchase the Roman and Renaissance contents of the palace, which left the city forever.

The formal palace gardens.

marble, all designed by Michelozzo. The *Procession of the Magi* (1459–60), the frescoes' ostensible subject, fuses worldliness and piety in a gorgeous cavalcade that recalls the Compagnia de Magi, the city's most patrician confraternity, and features flattering portraits of the Medici.

Cosimo the Elder chose Gozzoli as the painter most capable of producing a celebratory fresco cycle in the naturalistic yet highly decorative style that the Medici admired. Despite greater works on display in the city, many visitors share the dynasty's tastes, citing this as their favourite Florentine work. The lively narrative, the richly coloured costumes, the pageantry, the white chargers and exotic beasts, the idealised Tuscan landscape: everything conspires to charm, even the eagle nonchalantly putting its talons into a rabbit. Piero's son, Lorenzo, is depicted as a golden boy on horseback, while Piero is portrayed as a statesmanlike prince on a white charger, beside a black bow-man.

Angel feeding a peacock, detail from the Procession of the Magi *cycle in the chapel, c. 1460.*

With his wise child's eye, the artist presents his patrons riding with the cream of Florentine society and mingling with emperors and eastern prelates on equal terms. Gozzoli even slips in his own self-portrait: a knowing scarlet-capped courtier looking out at us. The artist's influences include his master, Fra' Angelico, as well as Piero della Francesca, Donatello, and even Flemish tapestries. But the lavish result, a sweeping portrait of princely Florence, belongs to Benozzo Gozzoli alone.

FOOD AND DRINK: ***Trattoria La Burrasca*** *(Via Panicale 6r; tel: 055-215827; closed Thurs) is a cosy, family-run trattoria serving classic Tuscan dishes at low prices.* **La Fiaschetteria** *(Via degli Alfani 70r/corner of Via de' Servi) is a long-established rustic wine bar for lunches based on pasta or bruschetta.* **Za-Za** *(Piazza del Mercato Centrale 26r; tel: 055-215411; closed Sun) is a celebrated Tuscan trattoria; its cheerful atmosphere and low prices draw the crowds. And there's* **Gelateria Yogurteria** *(Via Guelfa 10r/corner of Via Cavour) for home-made ices.*

Palazzo Strozzi

**A model 15th-century palace housing
libraries, cultural and exhibition centres**

Map reference: page 42, D3
Via de' Tornabuoni. Tel: 055-2398563/287728
Bus: line A and 22
*Biblioteca Centro Romantico (library, ground
floor): Mon–Fri 9am–1pm, 3–6pm*
*Centro Culturale Vieusseux (library and cultur-
al centre, 2nd floor): Mon–Fri 9am–1pm*
*Istituto Nazionale di Studi del Rinascimento
(Renaissance studies centre, 2nd floor library)
and Firenze Mostra (Florence-centred exhibi-
tions, mezzanine floor): Mon–Fri 9am–1pm*

This grandiose building is a testament to the overweening pride of the powerful merchant and banker, Filippo Strozzi, who dared to build a bigger palace than the Medici's *(see Palazzo Medici Riccardi)*. As the closest rivals to the Medici, the princely Strozzi family were banished from the city by Cosimo the Elder, but they returned the richer, having established a banking dynasty in Lyon. Filippo Strozzi then spent 16 years acquiring parcels of land to create his massive palace in the most prestigious part of the city. The palace was intended to overshadow the splendid residences built by the rival Pitti, Medici and Rucellai dynasties. It achieved its goal, given that each floor of this fortress is as high as a normal palace.

Several architects came and went, including Giuliano da Sangallo, whose wooden model for the palace became a treasured artefact in its own right (now in the Bargello). Eventually, Strozzi settled on Simone di Pollaiuolo (Il Cronaca), who shared his patron's vision of an exceptionally high building composed of sheer, seemingly unsupported storeys and a courtyard that soared upwards.

By 1491, after three years' work had been done on the palace, Strozzi died, leaving it to his sons on condition that they finished the building. By 1502, the massive cornice was in place, with the great endeavour culminating in the successful remodelling of Piazza Strozzi in 1534.

The quintessential palace

As the quintessential 15th-century Florentine princely palace, Palazzo Strozzi was a highly influential model for centuries to come. Crowned by an ornate cornice, the façade achieves a certain symmetry and majesty despite the dense patterning of the rustication. The cube-shaped structure is lit by elegant twin-light mullioned windows which offset the weightiness of the façade, while the windows are decorated with lunar motifs, copies of the moons on the Strozzi family crest. The magnificent torch-holders, which once illuminated the palace during festivals, were a privilege only permitted to noble families.

The monumental nature of the façade is echoed by the inner courtyard, which was partly inspired by the ruling dynasty's Palazzo Riccardi Medici. Even so, the grandeur and magnificence of the Strozzi loggia counteracted the prevailing Florentine ethos for feigned modesty in private palaces: the display of excessive ambition and ostentatious wealth were considered to be in poor taste in Renaissance Florence. In 1864, the façade was restored for Prince Ferdinando Strozzi, with the interior stripped down in 1938, returning the building to its pure Renaissance form.

Contemporary uses

The palace remained in the family until 1937 but is now state-owned and used by diverse exhibition and cultural centres. After a recent restoration, the rusticated blocks look more imposing then ever.

As home to the Institute for Renaissance Studies, the palace holds regular conferences and events linked to Renaissance themes. In addition, under the banner of Firenze Mostra, the city stages its own events in the palace.

Another important centre in the palace is the Gabinetto G.P. Vieusseux, founded by the Swiss bibliophile, Gian Pietro Vieusseux (1779–1863). Commonly known as the Libreria Vieusseux, the lending library and cultural association was a familiar meeting place for Florentines and Victorian expatriates, and was transferred from the neighbouring Palazzo Buondelmonti to Palazzo Strozzi in 1940. This library once welcomed virtually every visiting writer, from Longfellow, Thackeray and Ruskin to Stendhal, Zola and Tolstoy. Remarkably, Dostoevsky completed *The Idiot* against a backdrop of chatter from the library's expatriate community and went on to plan *The Brothers Karamazov* here. As for Robert Browning, the grieving poet continued to visit the library even after he had abandoned the city for Venice *(see page 151)*.

FOOD AND DRINK: See entries for Palazzo Antinori, page 157, Museo Marino Marini, page 168 and Museo Salvatore Ferragamo, page 171.

Modern Arts and Ancient Crafts

This Chapter brings to light the post-Renaissance art and artists of Florence so often ignored, pinpointing where to discover the Tuscan Post-Impressionists and the Futurists as well as contemporary artists and sculptors

Galleria d'Arte Moderna

Panorama of Italian 19th- and 20th-century art in state apartments remodelled by the houses of Lorraine and Savoy

Map reference: page 42, D5
Palazzo Pitti, Piazza Pitti
Tel: 055-294883. This is the state museums' reservation line. You can avoid queues by getting a fixed-entry time slot for a small fee.
Bus: line D, 37
Open: Tues–Sat 8.15am–1.50pm plus 1st, 3rd and 5th Sun of month, 2nd and 4th Mon of month; last entry 45 mins before closing Bookshop. Café. Compulsory cloakrooms for large bags (all facilities just outside ground-floor entrance to museum). Admission charge.

Set on the floor above the Palatine Gallery, this collection presents an overview of Italian art from Neoclassicism to the early 20th century. The picture gallery was created by the enlightened Grand-duke Pietro Leopoldo (1765–90), who proved a popular and progressive ruler. Later Grand-dukes added to the collection, which has been enriched by private bequests. The span covers Neoclassical, Romantic and historical art, with the thoughtful Tuscan Impressionist works, known as Macchiaioli, representing the highlight of a visit. As far as an historical sweep is concerned, the collection takes up where the Palatine Gallery *(see page 63)* leaves off, and paves the way for the more modern perspective of the Raccolta Alberto della Ragione *(see page 171)*. This, in turn, prepares one for the utterly contemporary collection at the Pecci Museum in Prato *(see page 213)*. However, while the Pitti collection currently ends in 1923, there are plans to bring the exhibits up to 1945.

Unlike the Palatine Gallery, which respects the original rulers' arrangements and tastes, the Modern Art Gallery has been subject to a recent re-hang. However, this is quite acceptable in that the current presentation is more coherent and, unlike the more historical collection in the picture gallery, is a chronological display unconditioned by Medici tastes. Nor are these the grandest state apartments: the museum's main rooms once housed the Medici library, with the side rooms reserved for the children. Even so, the decoration, particularly of the rooms on the second floor, has been respected, allowing for a sense of how the Grand-dukes of Lorraine lived. As cousins to the Austrian Habsburgs, the Lorraine dynasty did not stint on ostentatious china or sumptuous brocade in questionable taste.

The early rooms, designed in cool Neoclassical style, afford lovely views of the Boboli Gardens *(see page 75)*, stretching from courtyards and fountains to the Forte di Belvedere silhouetted against the skyline. The excavation of Pompeii provoked a revival of interest in the ancient world throughout Europe, and prompted a return to eternal classical values in art. Pietro Tenerani (1789–1869) is typical of the Neoclassical sculptors favoured by the Grand-ducal court and is represented by his softly expressive *Psyche*, a work commissioned by Carlotta Lenzoni Medici. The literary-minded duchess, who held gracious salons attended by Byron, Rossini and Leopardi, shared her peers' taste in portentous sculpture which wallowed in themes of love and death.

French influence

The next section pays tribute to the French influence in Florence after the Napoleonic occupation of the city. The French brought an avant-garde note to Tuscan art, as well as indispensable supplies of Sèvres porcelain vases, which adorn these restored rooms. Elegant portraits of ladies in high-waisted Empire-style dresses do honour to Napoleon's sister, Elisa Baciocchi, promptly installed as ruler of the Grand-duchy of Tuscany. At the same time, Paolina, Napoleon's worldly favourite sister, was installed in Palazzo Borghese, and was set on turning the palace

OPPOSITE:
One of the Crowd, by Marino Marini, 1952.

BELOW: *At the Piano*, by Zandomeneghi (Pitti Palace).

Self-portrait, by Antonio Mancini, *c.* 1878 (Galleria d'Arte Moderna).

into Versailles-in-miniature. The finest work in this section is the bust of the muse *Caliope*, probably an idealised likeness of Elisa, by Canova (1757–1822), the pet sculptor at the French imperial court.

Romanticism

Just as Neoclassicism swept away the cobwebs of baroque, so Romanticism was a reaction to the chilling soullessness of much of Neoclassical art. The movement ushered in a passion for historical paintings and a nostalgia for heroes of the medieval and Renaissance eras. Giuseppe Bezzuoli's *Charles VIII Entering Florence* is emblematic of the desire to evoke another era and portray strong passions: Savonarola and Machiavelli are depicted as citizens in a jeering crowd. Among the statuary, the bronzes of *Cain* and *Dying Abel* by Giovanni Dupre (1817–82) stand out. Nonetheless, unlike French Romanticism, which had an epic quality, in Italy the movement was more sentimental and on a smaller scale, with paintings resorting to atmospheric effects bordering on the melodramatic.

Poetic realism

Devotees of the Tuscan Impressionists, known as the Macchiaioli (literally "spot-makers"), will find

much to enchant them in this collection *(see box on page 167),* even if lovers of French Impressionism may be less impressed. The school portrayed fleeting images of everyday life with a poetic realism that revels in human intimacy and savours the slow pace of rural life. Two of the main exponents were Giovanni Fattori (1825–1908), known for his highly impressionistic soldiers on horseback, and Silvestro Lega (1826–95), who created intimate portraits and pastoral scenes. Fattori is represented by historical scenes, especially cavalry charges, including his *Battle of Magenta*, which depicts the French and Piedmontese forces defeating the Austrians in 1859.

However, in more reflective mood, Fattori, like most of the Macchiaioli, is capable of producing pastoral scenes of oxen in the fields or atmospheric seascapes such as *Libecciata*, which depicts a wind-blown tamarisk tree set against a stormy sea. By contrast, Lega's *Portrait of a Peasant Girl* is clichéd but his justly famous *Singing a Stornello* is a small masterpiece, a conversation piece depicting three women singing at the piano. From the intimate scene in the villa to the open window overlooking the soft Tuscan hills, the mood conspires to evoke the discreet charm of the bourgeoisie.

Galleria Rinaldo Carnielo

THE MACCHIAIOLI: TUSCAN IMPRESSIONISTS

The Tuscan Impressionists represent the most innovative movement in 19th-century Italian art. The school was dubbed Macchiaioli, "spot-makers" or "splatterers", a term describing their impressionistic way with paint.

As a closely knit group, the Macchiaioli generally studied and socialised together, congregating in the Caffè Michelangelo, the artists' haunt of its day. The key figures in the Macchiaioli movement were Signorini, Fattori, Lega and Boldini. Signorini, the arch-theorist, declared that his avowed aim was to capture immediacy in the form of impressions or perceptions of reality.

Under the influence of the French Impressionists, notably the Barbizon school, the Tuscans soon took to painting from nature, producing idyllic sun-baked scenes, distinctive portraits and even historical battle scenes. Yet compared with the superior passion and technique of the French masters, the Tuscan painters seem prisoners of the genre rather than trail-blazing protagonists. The paintings remain more restrained and figurative than their French equivalents and never achieve the sensuality of a Renoir or the freedom of a Monet. Trapped in provincialism, the works still show a certain sensibility, albeit one which rarely rises above bourgeois portraiture and sun-dappled pastoral scenes.

Galleria Rinaldo Carnielo

Eclectic 19th-century sculptures by a Veneto artist

Map reference: page 43, G1
Piazza Savonarola 3
Tel: 055-2625961
Bus: 10, 11, 13, 17, 10
Open: Sat 9am–1pm only (upon re-opening)
Wheelchair access
Currently closed. Due to re-open 2002/3

Set just south of the arcaded Piazza della Libertà, this handsome Art Nouveau house contains a collection of sculptures by Rinaldo Carnielo (1853–1910). The small collection, which occupies the sculptor's former studio on the ground floor, was bequeathed to the city by Carnielo's son. The sculptures attest to the influence of Florentine Renaissance art on the sculptor, which is particularly marked in the more classically inspired bas-reliefs. However, other works are much more eclectic, in keeping with the spirit of the artist, and the whimsical furnishings on display.

Singing a Stornello, by Silvestro Lega, 1867 (Galleria d'Arte Moderna).

Giovanni Boldini (1842–1931) also painted distinctive and introspective portraits of the bourgeoisie, including the coy *Signorina in White*, depicting the daughter of a family friend he had fallen in love with.

His contemporary, the Florentine-born Telemaco Signorini (1835–1901), had a wider vision and was admired by Degas, rare recognition indeed from a French master. His favourite subjects were the city and the countryside, from the rolling Tuscan hills to Florentine squares peopled with market-traders and solid citizens. *End of August* captures the hot, dustiness of Tuscany, echoing the bucolic mood of Fattori's *Oxen in the Fields*. Signorini has also left us a visual record of a rural and medieval Florence that was fast disappearing, from ancient city walls to the countryside itself.

Piagentina, depicting a tiny child standing in front of a Tuscan farmhouse, is a typical work, with its soft focus, its impressionistic use of paint and sense of a sun-dappled world tinged with nostalgia. The title has particular poignancy in that it refers to a stretch of countryside that has since been swallowed up by the city.

FOOD AND DRINK: See Palazzo Pitti, page 70

Museo Marino Marini

**Sculptures and etchings dedicated to
a notable modern Tuscan sculptor**

*Map reference: page 42, D3
San Pancrazio, Piazza di San Pancrazio
Tel: 055-219432. Bus: line D
Open: Mon–Sat 10am–5pm, Sun 10am–1pm;
closed Tues
Small bookshop. Wheelchair access. Guided visits
for groups if booked. Admission charge.*

Set in the deconsecrated church of San Pancrazio (one of the oldest in Florence), the museum is a homage to Marino Marini (1901–80), the Pistoia-born artist, and one of the country's greatest modern sculptors. The pleasure of this compact, coherent museum lies in the harmonious interplay between sculptures and surroundings. Minimalist walkways, exposed vaulting, terracotta, slate and wooden floors allow for novel perspectives over huge, semi-abstract horses, sculpted beasts bursting with energy. When the stark interior of this early Christian basilica is suffused with light, the statues take on a new vitality.

Illuminated by natural daylight flooding into the apse, the ground floor is dominated by a huge equestrian group. Often referred to as *The Hague Group*, these powerful, angular, semi-abstract compositions have an atavistic energy. Equally fine works on the same floor include a bronze warrior and the *Gentleman on Horseback*.

On display are almost 200 works featuring classically inspired sculptures in bronze, terracotta, plaster of Paris, cement or wood. Like many Italian sculptors of his generation, Marini felt more comfortable using "poor" materials such as terracotta, rather than the dazzling marble preferred by his German contemporaries. As a Tuscan, Marini was also heavily influenced by Etruscan art, to the extent that terracotta figurines were second nature. As for the spirit of the work, echoes of Etruscan inscrutability can be felt in the faces of certain humanoid sculptures, even if his later portraits are distinctly Expressionistic.

Although theoretically arranged according to subject-matter, the collection consists of variations on the theme of self-realisation through strife. The figures include dancers and swimmers, jugglers and thinkers, but it is the vigorous riders and warriors who hold the greatest iconic significance. The contrast is between Marini's pure, introspective bronze nudes, which feel rooted to the spot, and his euphoric or enraged riders and horses striving for release. Leaden though the thick-thighed female nudes may be, they convey the dignity and monumentality of all Marini's work.

The titles of sculptures are not translated and there is an absence of background information, but the works are powerful enough to command attention.

*FOOD AND DRINK: **Caffè Amerini** (Via della Vigna Nuova 63r; tel: 055-284941; Mon–Sat 8.30am–8.30pm) is a contemporary-style café, good for substantial snacks. **Belle Donne** (Via delle Belle Donne 16r; tel: 055-2382609 Mon–Fri noon–2.30pm, 7.30–9.30pm, Sat noon–2.30pm, closed Aug) is a tiny, cheap inn serving rustic dishes.*

ABOVE RIGHT:
Rider, 1947.
The horse and
rider was one
of Marini's
pet themes.

RIGHT: *The
Expectation*,
1926.

Museo dell'Opificio delle Pietre Dure

Florentine mosaics and inlaid marble objets d'art from the Medici period

Map reference: page 43, F1 (see map inset)
Via degli Alfani 78 (around the corner from the Accademia)
Tel: 055-265111
Open: Mon–Sat 8.15am–2pm, Thurs till 7pm (check for variations), plus 2nd Sun of month Bookshop. Wheelchair access. Group visits on request. Admission charge.

Pietra dura (literally "hard stone") is the art of inlaying gems or semi-precious stones in mosaics, a fashion which swept 16th-century Florence and lasted for several centuries. Originally housed in the Uffizi, the Opificio, or workshop, was founded in 1588 by Grand-duke Ferdinand I who wanted a centre for craftsmen working on the family mausoleum, the Cappella dei Principi, the bombastic memorial to Medici glory *(see page 110)*.

The Opificio remains the most prestigious national institute for the teaching of this ancient art, and passes on the skills of marble restoration to Italian and international students. Although the institute is out of bounds for security reasons, visitors can catch glimpses of precious objects being delivered to the workshop or stacked up in the courtyard.

As for the adjoining museum, although technically minor, this is a coherent, largely chronological collection which puts flesh and bones onto the more obvious set-pieces of Florentine artistry. The Opificio also con-

veys a sense of the sophisticated skills that still underpin the city's artistic output today.

The treasure-trove on display ranges from cameos to cabinets by way of sculpture, vases, inlaid marble table-tops and paintings; there are even portraits of the Grand-dukes studded with semi-precious stones. Sumptuously inlaid *objets d'art* are rightly referred to as "paintings in stone". However, to modern eyes at least, the striking table-tops represent the best marriage between materials and design, with the monumental marble offset by graceful details picked out in contrasting precious stones. The classic design is black marble inlaid with images inspired by the wonders of the natural world, especially exotic song-birds, flowers and shells.

The first room contains a red porphyry head of a dying giant, a copy of a Hellenistic model, and proof of how prized ancient marble was by the Medici. Since porphyry evoked the splendours of ancient Greece and Rome, Cosimo de' Medici was not alone in seeing it as a noble stone, conferring glory by association. The next room is dedicated to work on the Chapel of the Princes, including plans for an elaborate altar that was never realised. Here, and in adjoining rooms, marble and mother of pearl are complemented by lapis lazuli, Bohemian jasper, ebony and bronze. In the section dedicated to the last of the Medici, lavish table-tops are inlaid with ivory, tortoiseshell and semi-precious stones, a tribute to the tradition of artistic cross-fertilisation between stone-masons and sculptors, goldsmiths, painters and cabinet-makers.

The section dedicated to the Lorraine period shows that although decadent 18th-century taste affected the decorative styles in the Grand-duchy, vapid genre scenes were still interspersed with classic still lifes. Here and in the adjoining room are objects produced in a poor

A fashionably lavish cabinet decorated with *pietra dura* scenes and semi-precious stones.

Sunflower tile in *pietra dura*, late 17th century.

Museo Salvatore Ferragamo

Shoe museum in an historic palace owned by the Ferragamo fashion dynasty

Map reference: page 42, D3
Palazzo Spini-Feroni, Via de' Tornabuoni 2
Tel: 055-3360456. www.museo.ferragamo.it;
www.salvatoreferragamo.it
Bus A. Open: Mon–Fri 9am–1pm, 2–6pm
(booking essential)
Ferragamo shop on ground floor

Built in a dominant defensive position over-looking the Arno and the Ponte Trinità bridge, the fortress-like Palazzo Spini-Feroni is a familiar landmark on chic Via de' Tornabuoni. Somewhat incongruously, this 13th-century tower-house is reduced to defending designer boutiques rather than guarding against fearsome enemies as it did during the Guelf–Ghibelline factional feuds that were rife in medieval Florence. The Spini, the original owners, were bankers to the Pope and commissioned this stern building, both as a symbol of prestige and as a practical necessity to shore up their power. The crenellations on this square, stone fortress speak of the family's Guelf sympathies.

The interior, adorned with frescoed vaults, stucco-work and tapestries, displays a splendid della Robbia fresco in the entrance, and a private chapel frescoed in the early 17th century. After the Spini line died out in 1651, the palace passed to Marchese Feroni and, in the 1840s, housed the city administration during Florence's brief period of glory as capital of Italy. Since then, the magnificent palace has been in private hands, notably owned by the Ferragamo fashion house, whose flagship store is surmounted by the Spini and Feroni coats of arms.

The family fortune is founded on a rags-to-riches tale of an impoverished Neapolitan cobbler who became shoemaker to the stars. Salvatore Ferragamo (1898–1960) founded his first shop at the age of 14, and emigrated to America at 16 before settling in Florence in 1927. Only Florence had the craft traditions and skilled labour pool he required to create a factory producing hand-made shoes. Salvatore's genius lay in his reverence for feet, his enthusiasm for innovation, and for his early understanding of the seduction of retail therapy. His sense of innovation, prompted by the lack of fine leather during World War II, is clear in his invention of wedge heels, made from Sardinian cork, and in his

man's version of *pietra dura*. Known as *scagliola*, this less costly and time-consuming technique uses plaster and paint, and rabbit glue as a sealant. Although an elaborate fake, Florentine *scagliola* is often convincing, and reached its peak in terms of artistry and skill in the 16th and 17th centuries.

On the mezzanine floor is a workshop with an array of exotic stones, marble, quartz and agate, as well as tools and work-benches. To the satisfaction of the Opificio's skilled marble-workers, semi-precious stones and traditional techniques are still used in the institute's pioneering restoration work.

FOOD AND DRINK: Fiaschetteria (Via degli Alfani 70r, corner of Via dei Servi; Mon–Sat 9am–7pm) is a rough and ready wine bar for pasta, Tuscan snacks and local wines. See also San Marco, page 113.

myriad creations made of fabrics as diverse as lace, silk, raffia, real gold, and even fish scales.

Expanding the empire

Although Ferragamo was founded on footwear, the family fashion empire now embraces leatherware, accessories and prêt-à-porter collections. This is in addition to the Ferragamo property portfolio, which embraces some of the best Tuscan hotels, including the stylish new Museum Art Hotel.

Salvatore Ferragamo manufactured shoes with consummate craftsmanship and claimed to be able to "read" feet to discover his clients' personality and health. Whether cobblers or not, it was excellent public relations and made for wonderfully cosy relationships with the stars, who cheerfully drowned their sorrows in 18-carat gold sandals. At the height of his fame, Salvatore once had four monarchs in his salon waiting for hand-made shoes. When Claretta Petacci was killed with her lover, Mussolini, she left behind 40 newly made pairs of shoes at the Palazzo Feroni.

The museum is awash with shoes, evocative film stills and photographs of celebrities trying on Ferragamo shoes with the master himself. Salvatore's quest for the perfect fit led him to focus on lasts (the wooden forms used to mould the leather on shoes), so hundreds of models are on display, including those made for movie stars.

Surreal and literally toe-curling Roman sandals were produced for Cecil B. De Mille's 1923 film of *The Ten Commandments*. Every pair of shoes says something about the wearer: there are gamine, velvet ankle boots for starlet Brigitte Bardot; sexy sandals for a voluptuous Sophia Loren; masculine shoes for Greta Garbo; bejewelled sandals for an Indian Maharani; vulgar two-toned summer shoes for the Duchess of Windsor; and two trunks of high-heeled shoes for ballerina Alicia Markova. As for Marilyn Monroe, the ultra-feminine star insisted on narrow-toed court shoes or stilettos with an 11-cm (4¼-inch) heel. Not that anything similar is currently on sale: the Ferragamo flagship store in Palazzo Feroni has, sadly, abandoned bejewelled vulgarity for quiet good taste.

FOOD AND DRINK: **Cantinetta Antinori** *(see Palazzo Antinori, page 157) for an aristocratic Tuscan lunch.* **Giubbe Rosse** *(Piazza della Repubblica 13r) is an historic café with a terrace overlooking the square.* **Rose's** *(Via del Parione 26r; tel: 055-287090; open late) is good for pasta and creative salads.* **Mariano** *(Via del Parione 19; tel: 055-214067; open till 7.30pm) is a pleasant sandwich bar/café.*

Raccolta di Arte Moderna Alberto della Ragione

Varied and accessible overview of Italian 20th-century art with major Tuscan works

Map reference: page 42, E3
Piazza della Signoria 5. Tel: 055-283078
Bus: A or Bus 14
Open: Wed–Fri 9am–1.30pm, Sat–Sun 8am–1pm. Admission charge.
Due to move to an undisclosed location in 2002–3

S hamefully, this showpiece site has been sold to an insurance company, so this fine collection is currently awaiting a new home. However, it should at least gain space, good lighting and clear labelling in a more suitable site. In the meantime,

Salvatore Ferragamo, shoemaker to the stars.

Les Bains Mystérieux, Giorgio de Chirico, 1934.

A sound introduction

The museum is a sound introduction to some of the major movements and Italian artists from the turn of the 20th century to the post-war period. On show are metaphysical works by de Chirico, a few bronzes by Marino Marini *(see page 168)*, Futurist art by Severini, Expressionist works by Guttuso and Scipione, and still lifes by Morandi and de Pisis. Giorgio Morandi (1890–1964) is represented by his familiar yet unsettling compositions of bottles; his contemporary, Filippo de Pisis (1896–1956), a cosmopolitan artist from Ferrara, mixed landscape, classical figures, fish and vegetables in surreal yet melancholic compositions. Both artists portrayed universal themes, even if one chose a narrow canvas and the other selected a profusion of shifting surfaces.

In the late 1920s and early 1930s, French artistic innovation in the fields of Surrealism, Art Deco and the École de Paris-influenced Italian artists working in Paris. Most protagonists had a poetic or metaphysical bent, including Giorgio de Chirico (1880–1978), Filippo de Pisis and the Futurist, Gino Severini (1883–1966), all represented in this collection. Many of these artists share close Tuscan ties. Gino Severini was drawn to Paris, where he formed friendships with Picasso and Braque, but still felt rooted in his Tuscan homeland. Florentine Massimo Campigli (1895–1971) dabbled in Futurism and Cubism but his Etruscan-inspired figures clearly show his Tuscan soul. De Pisis and Morandi, both major artists from Emilia Romagna, had close links with Tuscany, and exhibited in Florence.

The inter-war years

In the inter-war years, Italian art focused on seascapes and cityscapes, often tinged with a mysticism that sought to portray the landscape of the soul. De Pisis, Mario Mafai (1902–65) and Carlo Carra (1881–1966) were all painters in this vein. Roman-born Mafai was a rigorous yet emotional artist who preferred to work in Florence.

As for Carra, he transcended his Futurist and Metaphysical labels to such an extent that art historians see something of Giotto in his simplified yet universal scenes, reduced to their essence. Seascapes by both Carra and de Pisis are timeless scenes that hark back to the eternal truths of Classicism and the Renaissance.

However, the shadow of Fascism hangs over many works in the collection, including the Expressionist art by Renato Guttuso (1912–87), Sicily's

the gallery in the Piazza della Signoria remains the showcase for a wide-ranging display of art which starts where the Pitti Modern Art Gallery *(see page 165)* tails off.

The collection was amassed by a naval officer who became a significant patron of the arts, collecting works by the finest 20th-century Italian artists, from Modigliani to Rosai. Portraits, landscapes and still lifes are at the heart of the collection but are as diverse as the artists themselves. Just as the portraits can be either poetic or Expressionistic, so the still lifes can be nostalgic or suffused with symbolism. As for the landscapes, seascapes and cityscapes, nature is alternately seen as a symbol of solitude, nostalgia or unbridled power.

Alberto della Ragione collected work from the period between the wars, influenced more by intuition than by school or style. In 1938, his passion for art overcame his desire for property: he decided to buy a Modigliani rather than an apartment. He had two guiding principles: ever-nationalistic, he was uninterested in foreign artists; and had no fondness for abstract art. His collection was left to Florence in 1969, partly out of respect for a city that had recently survived a flood, and partly to "restore the city's role as a living art capital". The core collection has since been enriched by other donations.

greatest modern painter. His works from the 1930s to 1940s are characterised by primeval forces and garish colours, reflecting the heat and passion of the south, as well as veiled political references.

Painters such as Guttuso, Mafai and Marini, who had fallen foul of Fascism, owe a great debt to Alberto della Ragione, who helped support black-listed artists through his gallery in Milan. Afterwards, as a reaction to the sense of loss produced by the war, Italian art became more inward-looking, abandoning avant-garde movements for portraits, landscapes, still lifes and domestic scenes, a response reflected in the collection. This domesticity is seen in the private world conjured up by the cocooning of family, loved ones and everyday objects. Even so, these traditional values are tinged with a new informality, coupled with a deep uncertainty in all artistic and intellectual fields.

Ottone Rosai

Ottone Rosai (1895–1957) is one of the greatest and best-loved modern Tuscan painters, and the one who best immortalises his city. His Florentine paintings strike a deep chord with his fellow-citizens, from his expressive portraits of illustrious men to his soulful cityscapes. Captured for posterity, between the 1920s to the 1950s, is the circle that gathered around Rosai in the Giubbe Rosse café in Piazza della Repubblica. Rosai's *Via di San Leonardo by Day* and *Via di San Leonardo by Night* depict his home street, the city's loveliest transition from town to country via a winding road leading up to the observatory. These canvases, in Monet-like shades of deep mauves and greens, evoke a mysterious Post-Impressionist mood.

However, the ominous tone conveyed by *Omino della Strada*, a mysterious shadow in a sombre street, represents the veiled threat of Fascism. As if in compensation, softer paintings depict an enchanted world of feathery-white jasmine and ancient walls enclosing olive groves or a lone villa. Nearby are large impressionistic canvases of Florence Cathedral, and the churches of Santa Maria Novella and the Carmine. Despite the paintings' geometric forms and highly charged colour combinations, modern critics sense a harmony that recalls 15th-century Renaissance art.

*Food and Drink: **Rivoire** (tel: 055-214412; closed Tues), next-door to the gallery, is the best spot in the city centre for good hot chocolate and aperitifs. **Giubbe Rosse** (Piazza della Repubblica) lacks Rivoire's views but is full of literary and artistic associations. **Il Bargello** (Piazza della Signoria 4/r; tel: 055-214071; closed Mon) is an expensive restaurant with a view, serving Tuscan and international dishes.*

Basket with Flasks, by Renato Guttuso, 1941.

Exhibition Centres

To follow Florence's fast-moving arts scene, buy *Firenze Spettacolo*, the monthly listings magazine, and check the tourist office's monthly calendar of events (available from the APT, Via Cavour 1). Also have a look at the regional culture website: *www.culturatoscana.it*. Bear in mind that most of the major museums stage temporary exhibitions on a regular basis, from the Accademia and Bargello to the Pitti Palace, while the so-called minor museums, such as the Palazzo Medici-Riccardi, often hold exhibitions of national or international importance.

Certain centres, such as the Fortezza da Basso, the Palazzo Corsini and the Palazzo Pitti, are associated with specific exhibitions, including art, fashion and crafts fairs. In addition, the city's prestigious foreign institutes and historic libraries often hold free public lectures and exhibitions. At the other end of the scale, more cutting-edge artistic exhibitions and events are held in such iconic conversions as the Manifattura Tabacchi, a former tobacco factory, and Stazione Leopolda, an erstwhile train station.

Forte di Belvedere

Map reference: page 42, D5
Via di San Leonardo
Tel: 055-2342425
Closed for restoration; due to re-open late 2002
Designed by Buontalenti in the form of a six-pointed star, the fortress offers glorious views over the city. The bulwark, built under Grand-duke Ferdinand I in 1590, is a resonant symbol of the city. The centre of the fortress is occupied by the galleried Palazzina di Belvedere, which is due to re-open as an exhibition centre in 2003.

Fortezza da Basso

Map reference: page 42, C1
Via Filippo Strozzi (just north of Santa Maria Novella station, outside map area)
This fearsome 16th-century fortress, which served as a prison and barracks, was the most hated symbol of Medici tyranny. Since 1967, it has been transformed into an exhibition centre, acquiring ugly pavilions in the process.

The Pitti fashion shows organised by Pitti Immagine are a regular fixture on the international fashion calendar (*Website for all shows: www.pittimmagine.com*). However, in addition to high-profile fashion shows, the Fortezza stages countless exhibitions and conventions, including the recent UNESCO world summit on culture and sustainable development.

Less worthy-minded antique-lovers may prefer to browse in the regular antiques markets held around the fountain of the fortress: here, small dealers and collectors from all over Italy sell their wares, usually at weekends (*tel: 0338-2280044*).

Palazzo Borghese

Map reference: page 43, F3
Via Ghibellina 110
Tel: 055-2396293/2382041
Bar and cafeteria. Centro Guide Turismo (Florence Association of Guides). Private club.
Virtually opposite the Bargello, this grand palace is a rare example of Neoclassical architecture in the city. Prince Camillo Borghese, who was married to Napoleon's sister, Paolina Bonaparte, had the palace built in under a year for a party to celebrate the marriage of Ferdinando III in 1821. The tone is set by the gilded hall of mirrors, and the vast chandeliered ballroom, adorned with frescoes, statuary and stucco-work.

Like Palazzo Strozzi, Palazzo Borghese shelters numerous cultural institutions. Since 1844, the palace has been home to the Florentine press club and the Circolo Borghese, an exclusive private club. Fashion shows, exhibitions and events are regularly staged in these endearingly faded reception rooms. The Centro Guide Turismo, the Florentine guides' association, is also based here (*see page 216*).

Palazzo Corsini

Map reference: page 42, D3
Via del Parione 11
Tel: 055-282635
www.mostraantiquariato.it
The baroque palace has a fine gallery (*see page 159*) but, to collectors, it is best-known for the Biennale, the International Antiques Fair, which is held over a fortnight in September or October. On sale are fully authenticated period furniture, paintings, sculpture, jewellery, silverware, ceramics, *objets d'art* and Oriental rugs. The fair is also a cultural event, supported by public lectures on art history and restoration.

The palace also hosts an autumn antiquarian book fair, known as the Mostra Mercato del Libro Antico; and Cartantica, an antiquarian prints and drawings fair. In addition, there is a May crafts fair in the Corsini palace gardens: on sale here are works by contemporary book-binders, basket-weavers, bronze-casters, paper-makers, jewellers, embroiderers, perfumiers, costumiers and fabric-designers.

Palazzo Medici Riccardi

Map reference: page 42, E2
Via Cavour 3
Tel: 055-2760340
Open: Thurs–Tues 9am–7pm
Ongoing restoration and the gradual transfer of public offices to other buildings means that the

palace is increasingly becoming available for international exhibitions, which are held on the ground floor. These often have Renaissance themes, such as music and entertainment at the Grand-ducal court. While there are plans to turn the whole palace into a Medici museum, the political will may be lacking *(see main entry, page 160)*.

Palazzo Pitti (Pitti Palace)

Map reference: page 42, D5
Piazza Pitti (Tel: see individual Pitti museums, page 62)
Pitti Immagine Fashion shows:
Tel: 055-36931
www.pittimmagine.com
Temporary exhibitions tend to be linked to the museum contents; for instance, the Museum of Grand Ducal Treasures recently hosted an exhibition on 20th-century jewellery design. In general, however, the main cultural and artistic exhibitions are held in the gilded Sala Bianca, which forms part of the Royal Apartments.

A recent exhibition covered poets and artists in Renaissance Florence, although prestigious fashion shows, linked to the launch of the main collections, also take place in the Sala Bianca. More challenging exhibitions, including ones on contemporary photography, are held in the Pitti's Andito degli Angiolini.

Alternative Centres

Manifattura Tabacchi

Map reference: page 42, A2
Via delle Cascine 16 (by the Cascine park, just outside map area). Tel: 055-361121
Set in an old tobacco factory, this venue has acquired a reputation for innovative or alternative exhibitions, particularly in the fields of contemporary art and photography. Some are cross-cultural events, combining performance art, design and multimedia.

Stazione Leopolda

Map reference: page 42, A1
Viale Fratelli Rosselli 5
Tel: 055-3693407
Set in a converted station, this new venue presents modishly challenging exhibitions of contemporary art, photography and fashion. Given Florence's role as a key fashion centre, recent exhibitions include one on the power of fashion accessories.

Foreign Institutes

While all the foreign universities run cultural programmes, including exhibitions, they are often restricted to students and staff at the relevant institutions.

The British Institute

Map reference: page 42, D3
Piazza Strozzi 2
Tel: 055-26778200
www.britishinstitute.it
Harold Acton Library: Palazzo Lanfredini, Lungarno Guiccardini 9 (map page 42, C4); tel: 055-284032; open: weekdays, 9.45–1pm, 3.30–6.30pm
Set in the Renaissance Palazzo Strozzini, facing the imposing Palazzo Strozzi *(see page 163)*. Founded by Anglo-Florentines in 1917, "Il British" is arguably the most prestigious of the historic foreign institutes in Italy. Since Evelyn Waugh's day, the institute has been promoting British culture and running Italian and history of art courses, which now attract a broader cross-section than in its *Room with a View* incarnation. The courses on offer have also expanded to include Tuscan food and wine appreciation, opera, Dante, drawing and watercolours, as well as exhibitions and lectures on art and history, which are open to the public. The Institute also has Italy's largest lending library of books in English, which is housed in Palazzo Lanfredini, on the other side of the river. Since one of the founders of the Institute was Sir Arthur Acton, it was fitting that his son, the writer and aesthete, Sir Harold Acton, left the library and premises to the Institute on his death in 1991. This charmingly fusty lending library is still a popular haunt for English-speaking residents in Florence, and attracts the general public to its Wednesday public lectures.

Deutsches Institut Florenz (Istituto Tedesco)

Map reference: page 43, H2
Via Giuseppe Giusti 4
Tel: 055-2491123
Founded in 1897, the German Institute occupies a 16th-century artist's studio and is an international research centre for history of art studies. Although the library is only open to research students, the institute's art history lectures and exhibitions are sometimes open to the public. (There is another German Institute at *Via degli Orti Oricellari 10*.)

L'Institut Français de Florence (Istituto Francese)

Map reference: page 42, C3
Piazza Ognissanti 2
Tel: 055-214757/287521
The French Institute pioneers cultural and language courses as well as exchanges between France and Italy. In addition, the institute stages French-related exhibitions on art and literature, musical and theatrical events, and runs a French film festival, all of which are open to the public.

Often overlooked, the city's handful of historical museums
are worth seeking out. The outstanding collections of
Egyptian and Etruscan artefacts, paintings and engravings
present a vivid picture of Florence through the ages

Biblioteca Medicea Laurenziana

This Medici-Laurentian Library, a fascinating example of the architectural genius of Michelangelo, hosts regularly changing exhibitions of great interest to bibliophiles

Map reference: page 42, E2
Piazza San Lorenzo. Tel: 055-210760
Bus: 1, 17, 23. Open: daily 8.30am–1.30pm.
Admission charge

The Medici-Laurentian Library occupies the western side of a delightful two-storey cloister attached to the south side of San Lorenzo church *(see page 107)*. The cloister (which you can enter free of charge) offers unusual views of the nearby Cathedral dome and of Giotto's campanile, thrusting up above the rooftops of Florence. The library itself is a masterpiece of inspired design by Michelangelo, who was commissioned by Pope Clement VII (otherwise known as Giulio de' Medici) to build a new home for the huge collection of rare manuscripts collected by his uncle, Lorenzo de' Medici (Il Magnifico), and his great-grandfather, Cosimo de' Medici (Il Vecchio). Michelangelo is thought to have designed the building in around 1524. He was not involved in its construction, however, which was delayed for many years due to lack of money, and eventually undertaken by Vasari and Ammannati in 1559–71.

The library is entered through a vestibule that could have been a simple functional space, but Michelangelo turned it into a *tour de force* of imaginative architecture, with columns, volutes, pilasters and blind niches as elaborate as the façade of any baroque palace. In the middle, he placed a wonderful triple staircase, whose parabolic central flight of steps is carved from soft-grey *pietra serena* sandstone. The whole effect is sculptural and monumental – as you would expect from Michelangelo.

A space for scholars

From the very tall vestibule, you enter the long, narrow library, with its ranks of wooden reading desks (which Michelangelo also designed). The bench-ends list the precious folios that were once displayed on these desks for scholars to consult. If these desks are medieval in style, the rest of the library is typically Mannerist, with grotesque animals decorating every inch of the wooden ceiling, and

CICERO, PLATO AND THE RENAISSANCE

Why lavish so much creativity on a library and why hire the leading artists of the day to design it? It was, surely, because the contents of this library were central to the Renaissance, which we think of primarily in terms of painting, architecture and sculpture. In reality, the Renaissance was all about ideas – ideas stimulated by the rediscovery of the literary heritage of the ancient Romans and Greeks.

The Medici were avid collectors of the philosophical, ethical and scientific works of Marcus Aurelius, Aristotle, Seneca and Cicero. Plato's theories of the *summum bonum* – the archetype or ideal that lies behind the shadowy material world – kept them talking late into the night. Virgil's *Georgics* inspired aristocrats to take up farming and become experts on beekeeping, viticulture and livestock breeding.

Their excitement at the rediscovery of the Classics spilled over into a taste for humanistic, pagan and secular art – so that, while the artists of Siena, Lucca and Pisa went on turning out sweet-faced Virgins throughout the 15th and 16th centuries, Florentine patrons wanted to decorate their rooms with pictures and sculptures from mythology – Venus, Mars, Cupid, Mercury, Neptune, Hercules and all their retinue.

The Medici-Laurentian Library is a repository of all that knowledge, paralleled only by the Vatican Library for the importance of its transcriptions of the classics. For that reason it was well worthy of Michelangelo's attention – the giant of his age designing a home for the ideas of the giants of the past.

OPPOSITE: Tablet depicting four scribes at work, *c.* 1400 BC (Museo Archeologico).

LEFT: Manuscript illumination portraying the grain trade, 14th century (Biblioteca Laurenziana).

tiled floor, and stained-glass windows between more of Michelangelo's pillars and blind niches.

There are no books displayed in the library any more. Instead, temporary exhibitions on bibliographical themes are mounted in the four rooms that lie beyond the library – drawing on the 15,000 or so books in the collection, which include a 5th-century manuscript of the works of Virgil, and 6th-century copy of the Gospels.

*FOOD AND DRINK: The **Bar Ginori** (Via de' Ginori 11r), opposite the garden entrance to the Palazzo Medici Riccardi, serves delicious hot chocolate as well as coffee, pastries and light lunches. The San Lorenzo area is packed with cheap places to eat. One of the most convenient is **Hydra** (Via del Canto de' Nelli 38r; tel: 055 218922), opposite the entrance to the Medici Chapels, a pizzeria with a short menu of Tuscan specialities, such as ribollita soup and steak Florentine. Don't miss the home-made ice cream sold at the **Siena Gelateria** (Via dell'Ariento 29r). See also Palazzo Medici Riccardi, page 162.*

Museo Archeologico Nazionale

The museum contains a treasure trove of Egyptian and Etruscan artefacts

Map reference: page 43, F1 (see map inset)
Via della Colonna 38. Tel: 055-23575
Bus: 31, 32
Open: Mon 2–7pm, Tues and Thurs 8.30am–7pm, Wed, Fri, Sat–Sun 8.30am–2pm. Admission charge

The Archaeological Museum in Florence is a mixed bag, consisting of an outstanding Egyptian Collection, a small collection of Etruscan bronzes and stone-carved tombs, an internationally renowned collection of Attic vases, and a new display of ancient jewellery.

As you inspect the museum's treasures, you will also be able to see the immaculately tended gardens. Admiring them through the windows is all you are allowed to do, however, unless you can arrange to make a special appointment to visit them (ask at the ticket office).

As well as being extremely beautiful, the gardens contain numerous subterranean tombs – in some cases they are copies of Etruscan tombs from all over Tuscany, while others are the actual tombs themselves, moved here stone by stone and carefully rebuilt.

Both the ornate Reading Room (right) and the triple staircase leading to the library (above) were created by Michelangelo.

The Egyptian collection

Climbing the stairs from the entrance hall to the first floor you will come to a splendid oil painting showing the members of the Franco-Tuscan expedition of 1828–29, dressed in Arabic garb. Led by Ippolito Rosellini, and funded by Charles X of France and Grand-duke Leopold II of Tuscany, the expedition collected numerous ancient Egyptian treasures that were shared between France and Tuscany. The Tuscan share is on display in the 13 rooms that start to the left of the painting

The objects are displayed chronologically, from the Palaeolithic era (15,000 BC) to the Coptic period (3rd–7th century AD). Among the familiar stelae, statues and pots there are some remarkable finds made from organic materials – wood, cloth, rope and papyrus – conserved by the extremely dry Egyptian desert climate. Room III, for example, has finds from the Tomb of Queen Hatscepsut, in the Valley of the Kings, dating from the XVIIIth Dynasty (1552–1306 BC). Among the items are miniature votive models of everyday objects, such as knives, hoes, chairs, boxes, baskets and foot-rests, made from wood, rope and woven reed. One case displays musical instruments – among them a flute and a lyre. Most remarkable of all is the near-complete wooden war chariot, a unique find, similar to those depicted on the walls of the tomb of Tutankhamun (1347–38 BC).

Religion, death and domesticity

Rooms IV and V are concerned with religious belief and death. One fascinating exhibit is a pyramidion – a miniature pyramid, not much more than 75 cm (30 inches) in height – carved of red sandstone. This was someone's private version of the great pyramids built for the Pharaohs, designed to sit on top of a funerary shrine, the pyramidal shape suggesting the rays of the sun descending on the tomb, and symbolising the protection of the sun god, Ra.

Room VIII is again packed with ordinary household objects of diverse date – from the 8th-century BC to the 4th-century AD – illustrating the continuity of design over this 1,200-year period: there are leather sandals, net bags, polished bronze mirrors, bone combs, window shutters, topes, and even a basket full of desiccated fruits.

Room XI has an intersecting fragment of limestone relief from a tomb, known as the "Relief of the Arts and Trades" because it depicts craftsmen at work, making and painting various objects. There are metal workers, vase painters, sandal makers, and even one man making a chariot like the one in Room III.

The Coptic era

Room XIII is dedicated to the Coptic era and contains one of the biggest collections in the world of Coptic textiles, displayed in chests with pull-out drawers. These beautiful and vividly coloured fragments of woven cloth are the product of Egyptian Christians whose culture was influenced equally by their Egyptian heritage, by Roman art and by Christian iconography. The result is a fascinating mixture of tunic decorations that include centaurs, heroes and deities from classical mythology, images of Christian saints, peacocks and phoenixes symbolising the resurrection, dancing *putti* and assorted animals. One case has several near-complete garments: caps, hair nets, children's tunics, stockings and a delicate silk cape.

Etruscan bronzes

Forming a bridge to the other parts of the museum is Room XIV, a narrow corridor filled with Etruscan bronzes. The three stars of the collection *(see box on page 180)* are often absent – either on loan to other museums or special exhibitions, or undergoing conservation. The remaining cases are filled with votive statues, mirrors and household objects, such as bowls, basins and pitchers.

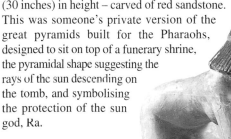

Painted clay statuette of a woman grinding corn, Old Kingdom, 5th dynasty, 2450–2290 BC.

Ancient jewellery

A new wing of the museum, entered from the Etruscan bronze corridor, has been created from the long, narrow corridor skirting the northern side of the museum gardens. Not always open in its entirety, the corridor houses temporary exhibitions on the ground floor, and cases full of antique jewellery on the floor above, mostly from the collections made by Grand-duke Pietro Leopoldo di Lorena in the 18th century, but enhanced by various bequests and purchases.

Of the latter, there is the small but choice selection donated by the English collector, William Currie (died 1863), consisting of exquisite Etruscan goldwork, but also some early medieval pieces, and some forgeries made to imitate Hellenistic jewellery and intended to deceive collectors and souvenir hunters.

The Etruscan Chimera: part lion, part goat and part snake, 4th century BC.

Attic vases and ancient bronzes

Back at the Etruscan bronze corridor, stairs take you to the 11 rooms on the upper floor that are devoted to a comprehensive overview of ancient Greek black- and red-figure vases. Collected by the Medici Grand-dukes, these represent some of the finest and most complete products of the ancient Greek ceramic industry. The exhibits are well labelled with panels explaining the evolving styles and political background to the scenes depicted on the vases – mainly battles, both historic and mythological. Light relief is provided half way round by the Dionysian diversions depicted on the vases in Room VI.

Two other rooms on this floor are used to exhibit the museum's collection of Graeco-Roman bronzes, which include several treasures from the Medici Collections. One is a mid-4th-century BC head of a horse, which Lorenzo de' Medici greatly treasured. Another is the 5th-century *Livorno Torso* – depicting a warrior or athlete – dredged from the sea bed in 1860. The last is the 1st-century AD *Idolino of Pesaro*, found in 1530 and depicting a naked young man, once thought to be Bacchus but now considered to be a decorative figure designed to stand on a banqueting table: his outstretched hand was intended to carry a lamp.

ETRUSCAN TREASURES

The ancient Etruscans were accomplished bronze workers, who migrated to Tuscany from somewhere in Asia Minor (their exact origins have never been discovered) in the 10th century BC to exploit the region's rich mineral deposits. Two of the three star exhibits of the Archaeological Museum – the *Chimera* and the *Orator* – are Etruscan works of the highest quality. Their discovery in the 16th century caused astonishment among Florentine sculptors such as Benvenuto Cellini, who recognised that even the greatest sculptors of the Renaissance would be challenged to produce work as good.

Dating from the early 4th century BC, the *Chimera* was ploughed up by a farmer near Arezzo in 1553, and depicts a mythical creature with a lion's body and three heads – those of a lion, goat and serpent. It is possible that the statue represents only part of a votive group: the rest of the sculpture would have featured the hero Bellerophon, mounted on Pegasus, the mythical winged horse, about to slay the *Chimera*, who is depicted wounded and in agony.

The *Orator* is a more recent work, found in 1566 at Sanguineto, the town on the northern shores of Lake Trasimeno where Hannibal defeated the Roman army under Flaminius in 217 BC. The statue itself dates from around 80 BC and is a portrait of the middle-aged Aule Meteli, a member of a powerful Etruscan family that had adopted Roman ways – as confirmed by his tunic, toga and boots, and his gesture – calling for silence so that he might speak before an assembly.

The third of the museum's bronze treasures is the statue of *Minerva* (Athena, to the Greeks, goddess of wisdom), found in the church of San Lorenzo in Arezzo in 1541, where it was worshipped as a saint. This statue is probably a 1st-century AD Roman copy of a 4th-century BC statue by the ancient Greek sculptor, Praxiteles.

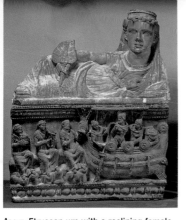

ABOVE: Etruscan urn with a reclining female figure on the lid. On the urn is a relief of Odysseus and the Sirens, 2nd century BC.

BELOW: The Sarcophagus of Larthia Seianti, 2nd century BC.

Etruscan stone sculpture

The last section of the museum consists of two rooms stacked from floor to ceiling with Etruscan funerary monuments. Some are carved to resemble houses, while others feature idealised portraits of the deceased, shown reclining at a heavenly banquet. Obesity symbolised wealth and prosperity to these ancient pre-Roman peoples, so the figures have ample bellies – as in the lifesize reclining figure in Room X.

Most of the Etruscan tombs are carved from limestone or sandstone, but there are some rare alabaster tombs in Room IX and an even rarer painted terracotta version, depicting a high-born lady in tunic, girdle and veil, holding a mirror. The original epigraph names her as Larthia Seianthi, but this inscription has been overpainted by a second one, suggesting that the coffin was later re-used for a different individual.

FOOD AND DRINK: There are vending machine selling snacks and cold drinks on the staircase landing between the Etruscan bronze corridor and the new wing, but there are no cafés or restaurants in the area around the museum – the nearest are in Piazza di San Marco. For example, the Café S (Piazza di San Marco 4r) and its near neighbour, Dini Caffè (No. 6r), which both sell coffee and sandwiches. The cool and calm Accademia (No. 7r; tel: 055-217343) serves a choice of salads, and a special lunch menu featuring seasonal produce. On the corner of the square, the Gran Caffè San Marco (tel: 055-284235) is a cake shop that also sells a huge range of pizzas by the slice, as well as pasta dishes and roasts.

Greek red-figure vase depicting the battle between the Centaurs and the Lapiths.

Museo Fiorentino di Preistoria

Florence's Prehistory Museum documents the earliest traces of humanity in Tuscany

Map reference: page 43, F2
Via Sant'Egidio 21. Tel: 055-295159
Bus: 14, 23
Open: Mon–Sat, 9.30am–12.30pm.
Admission charge

This small, specialist museum is concerned with the very earliest evidence of human activity in Tuscany, and further afield. The collections consist largely of fragments of bone, flint and ceramic, as well as copper, bronze and iron grave goods. There are also reproductions of cave paintings and rock art, while the upper rooms provide an overview of hominid development and the evolution of complex human societies, with material gathered from Africa, Europe, Asia and North America.

Prehistory is a fast-changing subject, with new discoveries being made every year that shift our understanding of the origins of homo sapiens. Therefore, inevitably, the material on display doesn't always give an up-to-date picture; it does, however, provide a good introduction to the major typologies that anthropologists and archaeologists have worked out over the last 150 or so years.

*FOOD AND DRINK: Turn left out of the museum and a short way down the street on the left you will find the **Pasticceria Zani** (Via Maurizio Bufalini 5r), a mirrored café/bar with Art Nouveau details. Next door is the **Pizzeria Pomodoro** (No 9r, no telephone), great for inexpensive pizzas and salad.*

Museo Storico-topografico 'Firenze Com'era'

The Historical-Topographical Museum – "Florence as it was" – is best seen once you have got Florence under your skin, so that you can recognise the buildings depicted in the collection

Map reference: page 43, F3
Via dell'Oriuolo 24. Tel: 055-2616545
Bus: 14, 23
Open: Fri–Wed 9am–2pm. Admission charge

Housed in the peaceful cloisters of a former convent, the "Florence as it was" museum is packed with paintings and engravings of the city at various stages in its evolution. The earliest exhibit is an exact copy (made in 1887) of Francesco Rosselli's view of Florence, painted in 1470 (the original is in the Kupfesrtickkabinett, in Berlin). This shows the city in lively detail, with fishermen wading in the Arno, workers driving piles into the river bed to repair a timber weir, pack horses laden with bales of cloth, and crows picking over the bones of a dead horse on wasteland outside the city. Many of the buildings in the historic centre are recognisable, as is hilltop Fiesole in the upper left-hand corner of the painting.

The next room contains a famous series of lunettes (semi-circular paintings) of the various villas around Florence owned by members of the Medici clan. Painted in 1599 by the Flemish artist, Giuosto Utens, they document in pleasing and precise detail every tree, fountain, and plant pot. This is an invaluable source of documentary evidence showing, for example, what the Pitti Palace and

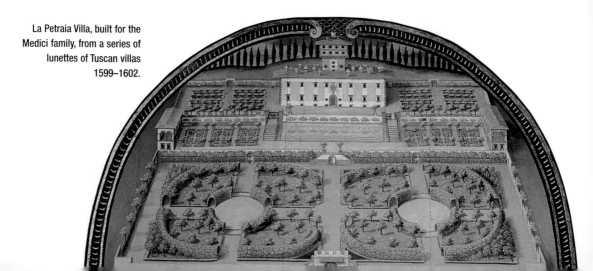

La Petraia Villa, built for the Medici family, from a series of lunettes of Tuscan villas 1599–1602.

Boboli Gardens looked like before the side wings were built and the gardens re-landscaped by Duke Cosimo's heirs.

In the same room, you will find some highly romantic oil paintings and engravings of the city as it was experienced by Grand Tourists, such as Dickens, Trollope, Twain and Goethe, in the 18th and 19th centuries. This is not the tourist-crowded city of today, but a city of street hawkers and idlers, of military men and clerics, scurrying about streets dominated by monumental and decaying buildings and statues.

Thwarted plans

In the next room, the word "demolition" hangs unspoken over the exhibits, as all the pieces gathered together here illustrate various 19th-century schemes for remodelling the city to create vistas and wide open spaces - the antithesis of the narrow alleyways and dark passages of medieval Florence.

An international outcry put paid to these plans, but not before the planners had succeeded in demolishing the Jewish Quarter and Mercato Vecchio, to make way for the triumphal arch that now stands in the Piazza della Repubblica.

The atmosphere of the Mercato Vecchio district is captured in the endearing series of drawings by R. della Gatta, showing peeling buildings, hens picking over piles of rubbish, street sweepers, and women seated at their needlework. A model in the centre of the room shows what this area was like – including the little Loggia del Pesce, a covered market designed by Vasari in 1568 for the sale of fish, which was rescued and moved to its present position in the Piazza dei Ciompi, in the Santa Croce district of Florence.

Archaeological finds

A separate wing of the museum is devoted to the results of archaeological excavations carried out in Florence over the past five decades. The exhibits set Florence in its geographical context with maps and terrain models, then looks at the pre-Roman evidence for settlement here, using mainly ancient Etruscan funerary urns. The main exhibit is a large-scale model of the city as it was in Roman Imperial times, onto which the Cathedral and the Palazzo Vecchio have been superimposed to provide a sense of scale.

FOOD AND DRINK: there are no recommended places for refreshment in the immediate vicinity of the museum. Your best bet is to head for the Piazza del Duomo, which offers plenty of choice. There you could try, for example, **Sergio's bar** *(Piazza del Capitolo 1), a great place for enjoying coffee, cakes and a view of the cathedral, the dome and the street artists who gather on this side of Piazza del Duomo. There is also* **Le Botteghe di Donatello** *(Piazza del Duomo 28r; tel: 055-216678; moderate), which stands on the site of Donatello's workshop and serves anything from pizza to squid in garlic sauce or involtini di manzo (rolls of stuffed beef).* **Buca San Giovanni** *(Piazza San Giovanni 8; tel: 055-287612; moderate), to the west of the Baptistery, is a typical hole-in-the-wall Florentine restaurant with a menu of earthy basics, such as soup or salt cod and chickpeas, and more refined fish, truffle and asparagus dishes.*

A 19th-century copy of a woodcut of Florence made in 1470.

In the 17th and 18th centuries Florence was as important a centre for astronomy, navigation and medical research as it had been for art in the previous two centuries. These fine museums dedicated to science are worth exploring

Museo Nazionale di Antropologia e Etnologia

A pleasingly old-fashioned museum, documenting a bygone world

Map reference: page 43, F3
Via del Proconsolo 12
Tel: 055-2396449. Bus: 14, 23
Open: daily except Sun and Tues
9am–12.30pm. Admission charge

The huge, rambling, old-fashioned National Museum of Anthropolgy and Ethnology is stuffed with relics from all the remote and fascinating corners of the globe that have captured the attention of anthropologists over the past 150 years. The museum is set in the Palazzo Nonfinito (The Unfinished Palace), begun by Buontalenti in 1593 but, as the name indicates, never completed.

Climbing the stone staircase to the first floor you are greeted by a giant of a man, 2.5 metres (nearly 10 ft) tall. This lifesize sculpture, carved in wood in the late 18th century, depicts a Patagonian man that a Captain Byron met, sketched and measured on his voyage round Cape Horn in 1767. More such curiosities and wonders fill the museum's 35 rooms. The old-fashioned display cases are packed with (mostly unlabelled) objects, organised by continents. They include scarlet and emerald felt clothing from Siberia, light, windproof sealskin parkas (and fur underwear) from the Arctic, desiccated Peruvian mummies, fearsome head-hunting knives and spears from Borneo, and radiant feather headdresses from the Amazon.

From Captain James Cook's 1776–79 voyage to Hawaii (where he met his death), there are costumes of fish-skin, feathers and mother or pearl, body armour of woven string, and daggers of wood set with razor-sharp shark's teeth.

You are likely to be alone in the museum, and it will be as silent as a morgue, poignantly emphasising that it is a memorial to long-gone ways of life.

*FOOD AND DRINK: Turn left out of the museum to **Bar 16** (corner of Via del Proconsolo and the Corso). It serves delicious pastries and sandwiches. See also Museo di Firenze Com'era, page 183.*

Museo di Storia Naturale

Three scientific museums that will both inform and amaze curious visitors

Map reference: page 43, F1
Via G La Pira 4. Bus: 14, 23
Museo Botanico
Tel: 055-275462
(by appointment only)
Museo di Mineralogia
Tel: 055-2757537
Open: Sun–Fri 9am–1pm.
Museo de Geologia e Paleontologia
Tel: 055-2757536. Open: Tues–Sun 9am–1pm. Admission charge

These three museums all lie within the same university complex. The Botanical Museum, containing some 4 million dried plant specimens, wood specimens, seeds, plant fossils and wax models of plants made in the late 18th and early 19th centuries, is open only by prior appointment.

Mineral magic

The Mineralogy Museum is so packed with cases full of specimens that there is scarcely room for visitors. This is a very technical museum (with labelling in Italian). To appreciate the exhibits it helps to have considerable knowledge of the subject – or you can just wander, admiring the astonishing colours and forms of the mineral world. The collection is huge, and includes some exquisite 16th-century cups, boxes and chalices made from rare minerals.

The latter part of the museum is devoted to an account of the incredibly complex geology of the island of Elba and of the province of Tuscany – reminding us that it was for its mineral wealth that the ancient Etruscans first settled and exploited this region back in the 10th century BC.

Geology and Palaeontology

The Geology and Palaeontology Museum is the most rewarding for non-specialists (though all the labelling is in Italian). It opens with an account of the various theories about the origins of life on earth – did the first organisms arrive in dirty snowballs

OPPOSITE:
Galileo instruments (Museo di Storia della Scienza).

LEFT: Warrior from the Indonesian island of Nias in battledress (Museo di Antropologia).

Archidiskon meridionalis – an ancestor of the elephant. This complete skeleton found in Tuscany is about 1.5 million years old.

from outer space or did they evolve in the hot mineral-rich soup of underwater volcano fumeroles? A diorama shows the life-forms known to us from fossil records, from the earliest primitive cuttlefish and ammonites of the Silurian era (440 million years ago) to the first land mammals of the Carboniferous (360 million years ago).

Similar displays follow the evolution of primates, showing how far humans have evolved from the first shrew-like mammals that were our ancestors back in the Cretaceous era.

Next comes an area devoted to fossil skeletons from the Florence region. The size and mass of some of them suggest that you would not have wanted to meet them in the flesh. One room has an almost complete *Archidiskodon meridionalis*, the ancestor of the elephant, as big as a juggernaut.

Finally, there is a display of the building stones of Florence: the *pietra forte* sandstone used for palace exteriors and paving, the fine-grained, grey sandstone called *pietra serena* used for architectural detailing, and the greeny-grey serpentine from quarries near Prato, called *ofiolito*, used for decorating numerous church façades, including the Baptistery, Santa Maria Novella and San Miniato.

FOOD AND DRINK: *There are no refreshment places in the immediate vicinity of the museums. Your best bet is to head for the Piazza di San Marco (see page 113).*

BOTANICAL GARDEN (GIARDINO DEI SEMPLICI)

Anyone looking for acres of colour or classical Italian garden design would do better to visit one of the villas around Florence *(see pages 190–197)*, because the Orto Botanico, or Botanical Garden *(Via P Micheli , tel: 055-2757402, open daily except Sat 9am–1pm; admission charge)* is a research-based facility that makes few concessions to the interests of the non-specialist. The gardens (the third-oldest in the world) were established in 1545 for the cultivation and study of medicinal plants, or "simples" as they were known – hence the garden's alternative name. Some beds on the western boundary of the 2-hectare (5-acre) garden remain planted with herbs and Tuscan flora, but much of the site is neglected and covered in grass and weeds. The gardens specialise in the unspectacular-looking (though often very long-lived) plants of the tropical Cycad family. These are grown in glass houses running along the northern boundary of the garden – most of which are closed to the public. There is nowhere to stop for refreshments in the immediate vicinity of the gardens. Your best bet is to head for the Piazza di San Marco *(see page 113)*.

Museo di Storia della Scienza

Galileo is the star of this museum but there is much else of interest here

Map reference: page 42, E4
Piazza dei Giudici 1
Tel: 055-2398876. www.imss.fi.it
Bus: 23. Open: Mon, Wed–Fri 9.30am–5pm,
Tues and Sat 9.30am–1pm
Admission charge

The History of Science Museum is housed in the 14th-century Palazzo Castellani, and consists largely of scientific instruments from the Medici collections, especially those commissioned by Grand-duke Cosimo II (1590–1620). Obsessed by the similarity of his name to that of the cosmos, he announced an ambitious programme to "extend Medici dominion over the cosmos". His aspirations were achieved in part when Galileo, using one of the first-ever telescopes, discovered the moons of Jupiter and named them after Medici princlings.

Cosimo gathered some of Europe's leading scientists to his court, including Sir Robert Dudley (1573–1649), son of the Earl of Leicester, the favourite of the English Queen Elizabeth I. Dudley was employed to build ships for the Tuscan fleet, based at Livorno, and he bequeathed to his patron the beautiful instruments displayed in Room 2, along with his book, the *Arcano del Mar (Mysteries of the Sea)*, detailing the construction of naval instruments, and containing the first atlas of the seas.

Galileo, court mathematician

Greatest of all Cosimo's protégés was Galileo, who became the Grand-duke's court mathematician and spent the last years of his life under Medici protection. The esteem in which Galileo was held can be judged by the exhibits in Room IV, where the middle finger of his right hand is displayed like a relic of a Christian saint. There are also two of his telescopes on display.

In 1608, Dutch glassmakers had patented the first telescope, with the power to magnify objects by three. Galileo improved the design and created a telescope capable of 30 times magnification. With this he made a series of fundamental discoveries: that the moon is covered in craters, mountains and valleys; that the Milky Way consists of countless stars; and, most controversially, that planetary motion can be satisfactorily explained only if the sun, and not the earth, is placed at the centre of the solar system.

Galileo's discoveries shattered the views represented in Room VII, where elaborate celestial globes set the earth at the centre of the universe, with a region at the outer

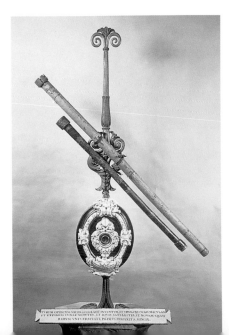

The museum's prized collection of Galileo's instruments includes an astrolabe *(above)* and telescope *(left)*.

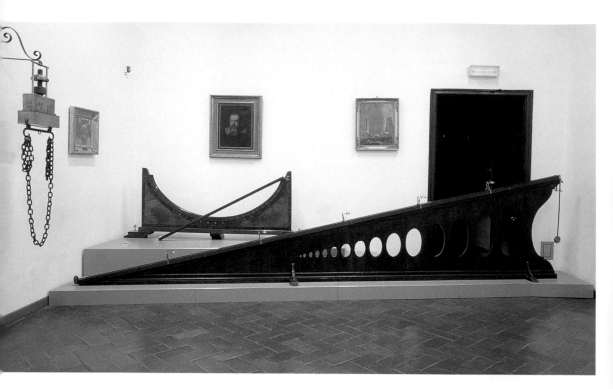

The Galileo Room with the inclined plane – a large apparatus used to confirm the "law of falling bodies".

edge called the *Primum Mobile* – the Prime Mover – envisaged as a heavenly engine driving the motion of the stars.

The rest of the museum is packed with microscopes and barometers, thermometers, clocks and surgical instruments. There are waxwork models designed to teach human anatomy to trainee surgeons, and several examples of science harnessed to the desire for amusement.

*FOOD AND DRINK: **Bar Giudici** is in the Piazza dei Giudici, just to the left as you come out of the Science Museum. Next door is **Roberto** (Via dei Castellani 4; tel: 055-2670082), a good, traditional trattoria strong on fish (try zuppa di cozze e vongole, for example – clam and mussel soup). In the same street, the **Uffizi** (22r; tel: 055-219520) does a good-value menù del giorno (daily menu) which doesn't skimp on quality – truffle risotto, grilled prawns and porcini have all been known to feature in their season·*

GALILEO: SHOWMAN AND REFUGEE

Pisa-born mathematician Galileo Galilei (1564–1642) is now celebrated as the father of empirical science – science based on observation and experiment. In his time he was considered arrogant, a sarcastic and fiery-tempered know-all whose teachers at Pisa voted against him when he was proposed for a university professorship. Instead, he went to teach at Padua, until Cosimo de' Medici invited him to Florence, where the flamboyant scientist specialised in mounting dramatic demonstrations of his theories of motion. Famously remembered for dropping dead bodies of different weight from the top of the Leaning Tower of Pisa, to prove that gravity acts equally on bodies of different mass, he also created the various models – like giant executive toys – that are displayed in the Science Museum. One consists of an inclined plane with bells set at proportionately greater distances from each other; despite being further apart, the bells sound at exactly equal

intervals when struck by a ball rolling down the slope, showing that bodies in free flight accelerate at a constant rate.

Galileo's fame also rests on his tangle with Jesuit astronomers and mathematicians, who did not approve of his advocacy of the Copernican, sun-centred model of the solar system. They knew well enough that the earth-centred model didn't work, but preferred an intermediate model proposed by Swedish astronomer Tycho Brahe (1546–1601), later shown to be based on arithmetical errors. Pope Urban VIII played an ambivalent role – first encouraging Galileo's innovative ideas, then subjecting him to the rigours of the Inquisition, which forced him to abjure his "heresy" in 1633. Galileo lived the rest of his life under the protection of Grand-duke Ferdinando II, residing in a villa in the village of Pian de' Giullari, just south of Florence (still under restoration after more than a decade of work, but eventually to open to the public).

Museo Zoologico "La Specola"

From limpets to human organs, the Zoological Museum is full of surprises

Map reference: page 42, C5
Via Roman 17
Tel: 055-2288251. www.specola.unifi.it
Bus: line D, 37. Open: Thurs–Tues 9am–1pm.
Admission charge

Be warned – there are some disturbing images in this apparently innocent Zoological Museum (known as La Specola – the Observatory – after an astronomical laboratory set up on the rooftop in the 18th century). You will be lulled into a false sense of security by the early exhibits, of simple seaweeds and shells. A mild frisson of distaste is engendered by the snail collection, which includes some large and unattractive slugs. Other potentially chilling exhibits include the displays of bugs – with horned beetles as big as your hand – and what looks like a doll's house, but which turns out to be a visual catalogue of all the creepy crawlies that live in your house – sucking your blood when you are asleep, grazing on the detritus of your home.

Crabs, worms, limpets, lobsters, starfish and tapeworms follow, so it is with some relief that you leave these creatures behind to explore case after old-fashioned case full of stuffed mammals. Every mammal under the sun is represented here, and in case you were wondering about the human species, there is a mirror strategically placed among the displays of monkeys, so that you can take your proper place among the primates.

As you work your way through the museum, through the birds and their nests, the safely stuffed reptiles, crocodiles, tortoises and snakes, the shock awaits you. Just around the corner from the fish, be prepared to come face to face with all the bits of your body – muscles, bones, internal organs, the circulatory system – all modelled in absolutely realistic detail and in full colour. Normally, such sights are reserved for the abattoir, the operating theatre, the dissecting room or the morgue. Now regarded as works of art, these waxwork models were made between 1775 and 1814, many by the master wax modeller, Clemente Susini, and used as teaching aids for trainee doctors and surgeons right up to the 20th century.

Once you are over the surprise of seeing human body parts displayed like meat in a butcher's shop, you begin to admire the astonishing complexity of something we take for granted – the way blood circulates to all parts of the body, for example. The collection is relentless – no part of the body is left unrevealed: a whole room is devoted to the mechanics of reproduction, with models of flayed penises, and a clear and detailed explanation of the nerves connected to the clitoris (giving the lie to the idea that this was a late 20th-century discovery).

After human anatomy, other members of the animal kingdom are given the same treatment. There are also some truly gruesome wax tableaux by the 17th-century wax modeller, Giulio Gaetano Zumbo, depicting such topics as "The Plague" and "The Corruption of the Flesh", revelling in the colours and details of putrefaction. One tableaux not on display (ostensibly because of flood damage) is entitled "The Gallic Disease" – the mind boggles at the thought of how the topic is depicted.

*FOOD AND DRINK: If you still have an appetite for food, turn left out of the museum for the **Trattoria Boboli** (Via Romana 45r; tel: 055-2336401), where you can sample numerous spaghetti dishes with traditional Florentine sauces. There are hole-in-the-wall snack bars at Nos 54r and 33r, and you can buy picnic ingredients (perhaps to be enjoyed in the nearby Boboli Gardens - see page 75) from the Alimentari Cuntina Bensi at No 21r.*

"Lymphatic Man" – a wax specimen, *c.* 1775.

Villas and Gardens

The Florentine hills are dotted with patrician villas, built as bucolic retreats for Tuscan aristocrats. All within easy reach of the city, they are worth visiting as much for their glorious gardens as for the grand villas themselves

CASTELLO

The Medici villas have long ranked among the glories of Florence, even if these days the encroaching nature of the suburbs means that several have lost much of their original allure. Yet visiting the Renaissance villas isn't always straightforward. A number of the most evocative places remain firmly closed: from Villa La Colombaia in Bellosguardo, where Florence Nightingale was born

in 1820, and which is now a convent school, to the neighbouring Villa Brichieri-Colombi, where Henry James wrote *The Aspern Papers* (1888).

In certain cases, the garden is open but the villa closed, or vice versa; in other cases, the villas are privately owned and subject to whimsical opening times. Moreover, the proliferation of American and European university campuses and conference centres has reduced the choice further still, particularly since certain foundations have commandeered some of the best villas.

In any case, it is wise to call the site in advance: of all Florence's attractions, the villas are the least reliable in terms of opening hours, especially as many are closed for restoration at short notice. The villas described here are either on the city outskirts, in the gentle hills around Fiesole or Settignano, or are easily accessible from Florence.

A celebration of life

Under the Medici, villa building became a form of self-exaltation and self-indulgence, allied to bucolic pleasures and property speculation. The 15th century brought peace and political stability to Florence and the surrounding countryside, prompting the transformation of the fortified feudal estate into a celebration of gracious country living. Perched on a scenic hill, the patrician villa became not just a rural estate and glorified hunting lodge but a place for feasting and festivities, and an escape from the summer heat.

Philosophically, the Renaissance villa represented a celebration of life, nature and art in a harmonious whole. In keeping with such humanistic ideals, the Medici villas received philosophers, scholars and artists, notably in the Platonic Academy at Villa di Careggi. Architecturally, the Tuscan villa was centred around an inner courtyard and graced with porticoes on the ground floor and a loggia above. A legacy of the feudal age was the watchtower, which became a decorative component of the villa. However, the Florentine virtues of proportion, symmetry and space soon came into play in villa design, creating a model that still has great resonance today.

Harmonious link

Yet no matter how lovely the villa, the centrepiece was the garden, which provided a harmonious link with the wild countryside beyond the walls. The enclosed medieval garden, the *giardino segreto*, survived at first, with kitchen, vegetable and herb gardens planted near the villa. However, Renaissance landscape gardeners embellished the concept of enclosure so that, in keeping with humanistic ideals, it became the symbol of tamed nature.

In a humanistic framework, the villa and garden were considered as an organic whole, linked by loggias, porticoes and new perspectives. The emphasis was placed on geometrical rigour, with symmetrical parterres framed by box hedges providing a natural extension to the villa. The laws of perspective were used to create terraced gardens with straight avenues lined by cypresses or lemon trees in tubs; semi-circular ponds, adorned with striking sculpture, closed the line of vision. Roman and Classically-inspired statuary was displayed in the grounds, complemented by topiary bowers or flowering trees garlanded with roses. The Mannerist era witnessed a profusion of allegorical fountains and grotesque sculpture. The main players were Buontalenti, who brought architectural rigour to garden design, and Il Tribolo, a pupil of Michelangelo and the landscape gardener responsible for the Boboli Gardens and numerous Medici villas.

OPPOSITE: The 15th-century Villa Medicea di Castello, by Giusto Utens, c. 1599.

BELOW: Poggio a Caiano (1480–85) was Lorenzo Il Magnifico's favourite retreat.

RIGHT: The large cloister of La Certosa del Galluzzo.

BELOW: Soldier Guarding Christ's Tomb, from the Passion frescoes by Pontormo, 1523–26.

La Certosa del Galluzzo

Medieval charterhouse and monastic art collection

Map reference: page 44, H11
Via Cassia, Località Galluzzo, Galluzzo
Tel: 055-2049226
Open: summer Tues–Sun 9am–noon, 3–6pm;
winter 3–5pm
Bus: 37 from SM Novella station; a 30-min ride
to the Certosa request stop, just past Galluzzo
village, 6 km (4 miles) from the city centre.
Bookshop. Guided tours. Admission charge

Set in the hills off the Siena road, south of the city, this tranquil charterhouse is inhabited by a dwindling population of monks. Founded in 1342 as a Carthusian monastery and centre of learning, the Certosa came under Cistercian rule in 1958, signalling the first return of the order after its expulsion by the Grand-duke of Tuscany in the 18th century. Niccolò Acciaioli, a powerful 14th-century banker and founder of the charterhouse, is commemorated in a Gothic monument in the monastic church. The peaceful atmosphere is enhanced by lovely cloisters and by a vicarious sense of participation in the daily life of the foundation. The monks allow visits to one of their unspartan cells – frescoed

three-roomed apartments, each with its own loggia and garden. The tiny hatch in each cell is a reminder that the brothers ate in solitude except on feast days.

A guided visit focuses on the picture gallery, the Gothic Palazzo degli Studi, a showcase of Mannerist art. On display are impressive fragments from frescoes by Pontormo which were detached from the great cloister. These works, depicting the Passion, were created during the painter's monastic retreat from the Plague, which was raging in Florence in 1522. As well as the original works, there are fine copies of Pontormo's lunettes and works by Ghirlandaio and Orcagna. The visit also takes in the 16th-century courtyard, small cloister and partially vaulted church, as well as the frescoed chapterhouse. The Renaissance-style great cloister is decorated with glazed terracotta *tondi* by Andrea and Giovanni della Robbia *(see page 59)*. In keeping with Cistercian brewing traditions, a visit ends with a tasting of liqueurs brewed by the monks.

Villa Demidoff & Parco di Pratolino

Mannerist gardens and statuary

Map reference: page 44, H10
Pratolino, Vaglia
Tel: 055-409427
Open: Mar Mon–Sat 10am–6pm; Apr–Sept
Thurs–Sun 10am–8pm; Oct Mon–Sat
10am 7pm
Bus: 25 from SM Novella Station (east side)
Café-restaurant in the carriage-house.
Bookshop. Guided tours. Wheelchair access.
Admission charge.

Villa Demidoff was created by Francesco de' Medici as a love nest for himself and his second wife, Bianca Cappello in 1569 *(see page 145)*. He envisaged the villa and gardens as a surreal water-world set in enchanted woods. Under the 18th-century Grand-dukes, the villa fell into ruin and the waterworks were neglected. The grounds were transformed into romantic English-style gardens in the 1820s, submerging the underlying Mannerist design.

After most of the villa itself was demolished in 1824, Prince Demidoff, a wealthy industrialist, created a new residence for himself in a service wing that had once housed the court pages and jesters. Demidoff also tried to reverse centuries of neglect by salvaging the garden's most remarkable Mannerist features. Fortunately, a few elements such as Buontalenti's domed chapel (1580) survive, as do the grottoes by Giambologna and Buontalenti. The *pièce de resistance* is Giambologna's extraordinary sculpture of the *Apennine Colossus*, which appears to rise from the lake, tricking the eye as to where water and mossy bank begin and where the jagged sculpture ends. The grounds are gradually being restored to reveal Buontalenti's original Mannerist design.

Little remains of the fabulous residence built by Buontalenti for Francesco de' Medici. Today, Villa Demidoff is better known for the beautifully landscaped Parco di Pratolino

Villa Gamberaia

A distinctive Classical garden

Map reference: page 44, H11
Via Rossellino 72, Settignano
Tel 055-697205
Open: Mon–Sat 9am–5pm, till 6pm in summer
(call in advance to check opening times)
Bus: 10 from SM Novella station for a 30-minute journey east of the city
Bookshop. Guided tours. Admission charge.

Set off Via San Romano, the main street in the village of Settignano, Villa Gamberaia conceals a compact but enchanting garden, behind a cypress-lined drive. The early 17th-century villa has had a chequered history, but owes much to the Capponi family, who lived here until the 19th century. One of the most characteristic Tuscan gardens, La Gamberaia displays regimented greenery, grottoes and pots of citrus trees on the terrace. The highlight of this magical garden is the topiary, including parterre gardens with perfectly formed yew and box hedges. The original flower-beds were replaced by romantic pools by the Russian princess who owned the villa in the early 1900s; perfectly pruned topiary and sombre statues of animals are reflected in the water. From every angle there are views of cypress and olive groves in the middle distance.

ABOVE: An 18th-century engraving of the Villa Careggi, after Giuseppe Zocchi.

RIGHT: Villa di Castello.

Villa Medicea di Careggi

Historically important villa and gardens

Map reference: page 44, H10
Viale Pieraccini 17
Tel: 055-4279755
Open: Mon–Fri 8am–6pm, Sat 8am–noon (by appointment only)
Bus: 14c from SM Novella station to Villa di Careggi request stop, 5 km (3 miles) northwest of city centre, then 10 mins' walk

Northwest of the city, in the direction of industrial Sesto Fiorentino, Careggi suffers from a combination of urban blight and benign neglect. The air of faded glory is confirmed by the villa's location, amid hospital buildings (it currently serves as hospital administrative offices). This was once the most famous Medici villa, and the favourite retreat for several generations of the ruling family. It was here that Cosimo, his son Piero and grandson Lorenzo the Magnificent all came to die. It was also the seat of the Platonic Academy, the gathering of artists and intellectuals that promoted humanism.

In 1434, Cosimo Il Vecchio commissioned Michelozzo to create a villa on the site of a fortified farmhouse. Given the absence of a Renaissance model, he built conservatively, modelling the villa on a medieval castle. The result is a ponderous, low-slung façade and a greater sense of enclosure than in later villas. When the Medici were forced into exile in 1494, the villa was ransacked, although restored by Cosimi I, then by Sir Francis Sloane in the 1850s. The villa is historically important but aesthetically disappointing. Donatello, Michelangelo and Verrocchio all made works for the villa but these are now in the major museums. The truncated gardens and woodland show the heavy hand of Sloane, who planted conifers, from fir trees to cedars of Lebanon.

Villa Medicea di Castello

Authentic Medici garden open for visits

Map reference: page 44, H10
Via di Castello 44
Tel: 055-454791
Open: daily 9am–dusk; joint ticket with Medici Villa della Petraia
Bus: 28 from SM Novella station, 7 km (4 miles) northwest of city centre (request "last Castello" stop)
Wheelchair access. Admission charge

The insensitively restored villa, sacked during the Siege of Florence in 1530, is the seat of the Accademia della Crusca, a fusty research institute which preserves the purity of the Italian language; it is not open to the public. Fortunately, it is the authentic 16th-century garden that appeals most. Begun in 1537 by Cosimo I de' Medici and attributed to Il Tribolo and Vasari, the garden was

Villa Medicea della Petraia

Medici villa designed by Buontalenti for Ferdinando de' Medici

Map reference: page 44, H11
Via della Petraia 40, Località Castello
Tel: 055-451208
Open: daily 9am–dusk, except 2nd and 3rd
Mon of month; ring bell for entry to the villa
Bus: ideally take a taxi; or bus 28 from SM
Novella station to Via Reginaldo Giuliani and
walk; ask the bus driver where to get off.
Cafeteria (or bring a picnic). Guided tours.
Admission charge (joint ticket with Medici Villa
di Castello).

Set on a steeply sloping hill, this gracious villa comes as a relief after a dismal journey through industrial suburbs. The villa was remodelled on the site of a castle belonging to the Brunelleschi family, whose medieval tower was incorporated into the villa. In 1575, Ferdinando de' Medici commissioned Buontalenti to transform the site into an elegant villa suitable for sumptuous entertaining. Although the garden has survived reasonably well, the interior is marred by the pretentious taste of the House of Savoy: in 1865, Victor Emmanuel II chose it as his summer residence and glorified hunting lodge. Inside the villa, the most eye-catching space is the central hallway, frescoed by Volterrano (1636–48) to glorify the Medici dynasty. Not to be outdone, the Savoy dynasty covered the courtyard with a glass roof so that it could serve as a ballroom.

Erase the memory of the soulless Neoclassical apartments by strolling in the far more appealing grounds. An Italianate garden, designed by Il Tribolo *(see page 191)*, has three tiers of terraces, box hedges and geometric parterres descending from the moat in front of the villa. The upper terrace has a fountain crowned by a copy of Giambologna's allegorical bronze statue of *Venus* (1572); the sculpture is now displayed in the first-floor study. The formal, geometric Classical garden is in direct contrast to the so-called "English garden" that stretches beyond, linking La Petraia with its companion, Villa Medicea di Castello *(see above).*

The extensive woodland embraces pine groves and plane trees, holm oaks and cedars and is part of the juxtaposition of formality and mysterious woodland that is a familiar device in Florentine garden landscaping.

famous for its audacious water effects, of which little trace remains. But as the supreme example of Florentine Renaissance gardening, Castello offers a compendium of familiar devices, from the measured formality of geometric parterres to the surprise of mysterious grottoes and grotesque statuary.

The compact garden, which is laid out over three terraces, is particularly appealing in spring, when the bluebells and daffodils are in bloom. The terracotta pots of citrus trees still perform a practical function since strange hybrids of oranges and lemons are produced here.

Two Etruscan columns mark the entrance to the pebble and shell-encrusted Grotta degli Animali, the centrepiece of the garden. The grotto was conceived as a showcase for a grotesque menagerie of fantastic creatures created by Giambologna (a number of the original bronze birds and beasts are now on display in the Bargello). The upper terrace displays another set-piece, Ammannati's bronze figure of *The Apennine* (1563), which depicts a shivering old man rising from a pool.

Villa Medicea di Poggio a Caiano

Sangallo's Classical masterpiece

Map reference: page 44, G10
Poggio a Caiano
Tel: 055-877012
Open: Garden Mon–Sat 9am–sunset, Sun 9am–noon; Villa Mon–Sat 9am–1.30pm, Sun 9am–noon; guided visits obligatory for the villa. Bus: frequent Copit buses from SM Novella station (north side, in front of McDonalds); 18 km (10 miles) west of Florence, off the Pistoia road

Right: The Villa Medici and gardens (1458–61) in Fiesole, designed by Michelozzo for Giovanni de' Medici.

Below: A section of Poggio a Caiano's portico, highlighting the fine grotesque decoration.

Poggio a Caiano, Lorenzo the Magnificent's favourite retreat, is often dubbed the perfect Tuscan villa, even if its Classical design differs greatly from its peers. Certainly, it is the best-preserved of Florentine rural retreats. In 1480, Lorenzo the Magnificent commissioned Giuliano da Sangallo to create a villa on the slope of wooded hills. The innovative result, a façade modelled on a Greek temple, owes more to Lorenzo's taste for mythology than to the architect's vision. The Classical façade, graced with portico, pediment and frieze, prefigures Palladio's work in the Veneto. The pediment also unifies the design and gives it a grandeur lacking in many Tuscan villas. The horseshoe staircase was added in 1802 but does nothing to detract from the harmonious whole.

The interior was designed as a sumptuous setting for receptions attended by ambassadors, painters and humanist philosophers. Nonetheless, the airy, two-storey Salone is an exercise in Medici self-glorification, depicting the dynasty dressed as Romans in historical epics that paralleled their own lives. Pope Leo X, Lorenzo's son, commissioned Mannerist artists of the stature of Pontormo and Andrea del Sarto to decorate the villa. It was here that Francesco I and his wife, Bianca Cappello, died in mysterious circumstances *(see page 145)*. The pleasant gardens were landscaped in accordance with 19th-century "English" tastes.

Villa Medici, Fiesole

Built by Michelozzo for Cosimo Il Vecchio

Map reference: page 202, B2
Via Vecchia Fiesolana, Fiesole
Tel: 055-2398994
Open: Mon–Fri 9am–3pm, Sat 9am–noon (call in advance).
Bus: 7 from SM Novella station (east side) for Fiesole; a 30-minute journey

This rural retreat was built by Michelozzo for Cosimo Il Vecchio in the 1450s, so belongs to the first wave of Medici villas. Given that the house was remodelled in the 17th and 18th centuries, the Renaissance gardens are of greater interest. Laid out on two terraces, the gardens include an orangery, grottoes, and a geometric garden, as well as lemon trees in pots, box hedges and superb views.

Villa La Pietra

Renaissance art in a 15th-century villa, the Florentine campus of New York University

Map reference: page 44, H11
Via Bolognese 120
Tel: 055-474448; fax 055-472725
Closed for restoration, but the garden is usually open on Mon, by written request (use fax no)
Bus: 25 from SM Novella station (east side); request stop for La Pietra

T he 15th-century villa is set on the outskirts of Florence, on the old Roman road to Bologna. It belonged to Sir Harold Acton *(see page 34)*, doyen of expatriate writers in Florence; on his death it was bequeathed to New York University, allegedly after Acton had been snubbed by Oxford. The villa contains a fine collection of Renaissance art amassed by his family. The rigorously structured Tuscan garden, inspired by Renaissance models, contains a series of 17th-century allegorical statues.

Villa I Tatti

Harvard University's Centre for Renaissance Studies

Map reference: page 44, H11
Via Vincigliata 26, Ponte a Mensola
Tel: 055-603251
Open: Tues and Wed pm; on request to scholars.
Bus: 10 from SM Novella station; a 30-minute journey east of Florence

T his historic villa is set in the Florentine hills, close to Settignano, an attractive semi-rural location that retains its appeal as a prestigious residential area. The former home of the distinguished art critic and collector, Bernard Berenson *(see page 32)* now houses Renaissance scholars from Harvard University. Inside lies the predominantly Renaissance collection that Berenson (1865–1969) bequeathed to Harvard. As well as works by Lorenzo Lotto, Luca Signorelli, Domenico Veneziano and Cima da Concgliano, there is a small collection of Oriental art and Berenson's library and photographic collection.

In keeping with his passion for the period, Berenson had the grounds landscaped to resemble a Renaissance garden, with box hedges, pebble-mosaic paths, symmetrical parterres, and lines of miniature lemon trees in terracotta pots. The steeply terraced gardens, framed by cypresses, culminate in a small wood of holm oaks.

The cypress avenue leading to Villa La Pietra.

THE BEST OF THE REST

A number of villas set amid cypresses and olive groves in the Fiesole hills open their gardens at certain times of year, including **Villa Le Balze**, the campus of Georgetown University *(for details: freephone 800-414240 or Fiesole tourist office, tel: 055-5978373)*. Just south of the centre of Fiesole is the **Badia Fiesolana**, a former monastery now housing the Universitario Europeo *(see page 203)*. The monastic Brunelleschi-inspired church, which was Fiesole cathedral in Romanesque times, can be visited. **Villa San Michele** *(Via Doccia 4; tel: 055-5678200)* is a former Franciscan monastery transformed into a splendid hotel and restaurant. Grafted onto the hillside and set under low-pitched terracotta tiles, the hotel has a lobby which was once a chapel and a refectory which is now a library.

Back in Florence, **Giardino Corsini al Prato** *(Via il Prato 58; tel: 055-218994)* is the Florentine family villa of the noble Corsini family *(see page 158)*. Although the 16th-century villa is closed to the public, the Renaissance gardens can be seen on request, including the contrasting, romantic "English" gardens.

Towards the Bellosguardo area, and within walking distance of the Oltrarno district, is **Villa Strozzi** on Via Pisana, in Monteoliveto. The pleasant gardens *(open 9am–dusk)* are owned by the city and are used for summer concerts and exhibitions, while the villa is a school of design. Bellosguardo has always been loved by foreign residents, including Violet Trefusis, who lived in Galileo's former home, the **Villa dell'Ombrellino**, now a conference centre whose gardens can sometimes be visited. Next door is the splendid **Torre di Bellosguardo** *(tel: 055-2298145)*, the ultimate small villa hotel, with a 14th-century tower, gorgeous gardens and sweeping views over the city.

The Best of Cultural Tuscany

This chapter presents an overview of the best of Tuscan art and architecture to be found outside Florence, focusing on the selected museums, galleries and churches of Tuscany's most picturesque towns, all within easy reach of Florence

There is scarcely a town, village or city in Tuscany that doesn't have a church and a museum worth stopping to see – in fact, the sheer choice can be overwhelming. Here, we present an overview of the very best and most representative of Tuscan art in all its variety – from ancient Etruscan tombs to modern art, by way of Renaissance villas and gardens – even a theme park devoted to the world's best-known wooden puppet, Pinocchio.

Some of these museums are accessible by public transport from Florence: in particular, Fiesole, Pisa, Lucca and Siena are easily reached by bus or train, and make for a full and rewarding day out. Many others are best reached by hiring a car and exploring Tuscany at leisure. This way you will also encounter the astonishingly beautiful Tuscan countryside, in all its natural beauty, enhanced over the centuries by the planting of a cypress avenue, the placing of a church, or the crowning of a hilltop with a walled city of stone and terracotta roofs.

Arezzo

From a Piero della Francesca fresco cycle to a Roman amphitheatre, Arezzo has much to offer. *(Map: page 45, E5)*

Arezzo is rich in buildings, monuments and works of art of all eras. The old hilly part of the city is the most picturesque, with its massive main square, the Piazza Grande, so far from being level that its numerous slopes and steps present a severe test even to the sober. This square is the venue for Tuscany's biggest antiques market (held on the first Sunday in every month), and many shops around the square also sell antiques.

Rising from the southern side of the square, and sitting on the city's main shopping street, is the Romanesque **Pieve di Santa Maria** *(Corso Italia 7; open daily)*, with its "tower of a hundred holes", so-named because of the filigree pattern of arches piercing the belfry. Two blocks west you will find **San Francesco** *(Piazza San Francesco; open daily)*, renowned for its restored cycle of paintings by Piero della Francesca, depicting the *Story of the True Cross* (1452–66).

Spiritual and other-worldly, this masterful fresco cycle weaves together a complex story in which the wood of the Tree of Knowledge (from which Adam and Eve ate the apple) becomes the wood of the Cross on which Christ died, and which was later discovered by the Empress Helena, mother of the Emperor Constantine the Great, who converted to Christianity and made it the state religion of the Roman Empire in AD 313.

Medieval monuments

Medieval monuments cluster together in the northern part of the city, where you will find the **Duomo** *(Piazza del Duomo; open daily)* sheltered by the

encircling walls of Grand-duke Cosimo's 16th-century Fortezza, now a public park with fine views. Further west is the **Casa del Vasari** *(Via XX Settembre 55; open daily)*, the attractive house that Giorgio Vasari – painter, architect and author of *The Lives of the Artists* (1550) – built for himself and decorated with frescoes of the artists he most admired. Close by is the **Museo d'Arte Medievale e Moderna** *(Via di San Lorentino 8; open daily)*, with more paintings by Vasari, and modern works by Italian Impressionists.

Last but not least, in the flat southern part of the city, you will find the **Anfiteatro Romano** (Roman Amphitheatre), against whose walls is built the excellent **Museo Archeologico** *(Via Margaritone 10; open daily)*. This contains many examples of the local Aretine ware, high-quality Roman pottery that once competed with the more famous Samian ware as the crockery of choice on aristocratic Roman dinner tables.

OPPOSITE: *Effects of Good Government in the Country,* by Lorenzetti, 1338–40 (Palazzo Pubblico, Siena).

ABOVE: From the *Story of the True Cross* fresco cycle by Piero della Francesca, 1452–59, (church of San Francesco, Arezzo).

Chiusi

Etruscan tombs are the highlight of a visit to Chiusi, but the splendid Roman mosaics in the Cathedral are worth seeking out *(Map: page 45, F6)*

A visit to Chiusi is greatly enhanced if you can secure a guided tour of one of the ancient Etruscan tombs to be found in the immediate environs of the town, some with intact 3rd- and 2nd-century BC wall paintings. Tours depend on the availability of staff, and you need to enquire at the **Museo Nazionale Etrusco** *(Via Porsenna 93, tel: 0578 177; open daily)*. If you are out of luck, you can at least look at the exhibits in the museum, which include numerous carved sarcophagi, carvings, black burnished vases and a fragment of tomb fresco. Be warned, though, that the displays are rather old-fashioned and academic, and the best of the material from local tombs has been taken to museums in Rome and Florence.

Chiusi is not a big city, and the other main sights are all close to the museum. The best is the **Duomo**, opposite *(Piazza del Duomo; open daily)*, a wonderful building with Roman mosaics beneath the High Altar and *trompe l'oeil* mosaics in the nave. These enjoyable scenes were painted in 1887 by Arturo Viligradi.

The Etruscans were not the only ones to dig burial chambers into the soft rock of Chiusi. Early Christian catacombs underlie the city, and you may be able to secure a visit to one of these if you visit the **Museo della Cattedrale** *(Piazza del Duomo; open daily)*, next door to the cathedral. Here, too, you can see good exhibits of Roman, Lombardic and medieval sculpture from local churches and tombs.

The Annunciation, from a predella by Fra' Angelico (Museo Diocesano, Cortona).

Collodi

The two main sights here are the Pinocchio Park and Villa Garzoni, former home of the puppet's creator *(Map: page 44, C3)*

If you were entranced as a child by the adventures of a wooden puppet with a remarkable nose, you may recognise the name of this town as being that of the author of *The Adventures of Pinocchio* (1881). Carlo Lorenzini adopted Collodi as his pen name because he had fond memories of staying here as a child. The town now has a **children's park** *(open daily)* devoted to Pinocchio, consisting of mosaics, mazes and statues based on scenes from the story.

Contemporary children, accustomed to virtual reality and snazzy theme parks, may find it rather tame, but there are plans to revamp the park, and to enhance the attractions at the nearby **Villa Garzoni**, a glorious baroque garden full of mythical monsters modelled in terracotta, fountains and topiaried animals. The steep terraces of the 17th-century garden lead to some memorable viewing points.

Cortona

Cortona is one of several Tuscan hill towns rich in attractions out of all proportion to their tiny size *(Map: page 45, F5)*

Cortona is one of the oldest settlements in Tuscany. It was founded by the Etruscans and, by the medieval period, it had become a major centre of power. The main attraction of this enchanting walled town lies in the steepness of its streets. Getting about involves climbing up and down the stone staircases that link one street to the next.

It is entered from the relatively flat Piazza Garibaldi and Via Nazionale, which lead to Piazza Signorelli, with its 13th-century Palazzo Comunale (Town Hall) and the **Museo dell'Accademia Etrusca** *(closed Mon)*, which has two star exhibits: the lovely fresco of *Polymnia*, generally considered to be a fine Roman painting of the *Muse of Song* until recent research proved it to be an 18th-century forgery; and a genuine Etruscan chandelier dating from 300 BC, consisting of 16 bronze oil lamps set around a wheel.

West of the piazza is the 16th-century cathedral and its companion, the **Museo Diocesano** *(closed Mon)*, which contains some rare masterpieces by Fra' Angelico, Lorenzetti and Luca Signorelli.

Returning to the town centre, it is worth seeking out Via Janelli for its row of brick buildings, with overhanging upper storeys – some of Tuscany's oldest surviving medieval houses.

Fiesole

Sitting on a ridge of hills north of Florence, just a 30-minute bus ride away, tranquil Fiesole makes a perfect day out *(Maps: area – page 44, D4; town – page 202)*

Everything you will want to see in Fiesole lies a short distance from the Piazza Mino da Fiesole, the main square, where the bus from Florence *(No. 7 from Santa Maria Novella station or Piazza San Marco)* will drop you. On the south side of the square, the Caffè Aurora offers coffee and cakes on a bougainvillaea-shaded terrace with stunning views over Florence. The square slopes steeply upwards to the town hall, fronted by a bronze statue of Garibaldi and Victor Emmanuel II, the main protagonists in the struggle to create a united Italy in the 1870s.

East of the square, geraniums spill from the upper-storey balcony of the **medieval town hall**, whose walls are covered in *stemmae* (stone-carved coats-of-arms) of Fiesole worthies. Next door is the simple medieval church of Santa Maria Primerana, with a baroque *sgraffito*-decorated façade. To the right of the church, a lane (Via Giuseppe Verdi) leads uphill to another viewpoint, from where the Arno valley spreads out below your feet.

Roman theatre

Back on the square, a lane leads north to the Teatro Romano, where you can buy tickets for all the museums in Fiesole. The first of these is the **Area Archeologica** *(map: C1; open 9.30am–7pm, Nov–*

Mar closed Tues), entered from the ticket office and comprising the city's 1st-century BC Roman theatre, public baths of the same era, and an Etruscan temple, built in the 4th-century BC and dedicated to Minerva, goddess of wisdom and healing.

View from the Teatro Romano, Fiesole.

The theatre is in a remarkable state of repair, and is still used for dances and shows during the summer festival season. It is built into a hillside which falls steeply away to the north, so that the events on stage take place against the stunning backdrop of the Mugnone valley, a patchwork of green fields, villa-farms, woodland and olive groves.

Save the much-extended **Museo Archeologico** *(map: C1)* until last, perhaps enjoying coffee first in the pleasant garden café just inside the entrance to the site. The oldest part of the museum, built in the style of a Roman temple, is packed with finds from excavations in Fiesole. These bronze votive figures, ceramics and pieces of carved marble are displayed on the ground floor, while the upper storey displays treasures from the Collezione Constantini, consisting of beautiful antique vases from all over the ancient world (the musuem's own guide warns, however, that some are "of very doubtful authenticity", which might explain why some of them look just a little too perfect).

The new part of the museum exhibits finds from a later period in the site's use, when the area around the Roman theatre was used as a cemetery by Lombardic migrants who invaded Italy in AD 568, conquering Rome itself two years later. Here, they settled until driven out of Italy with the help of Charlemagne in 800. The Lombardic burials in Fiesole were discovered as recently as 1988, and

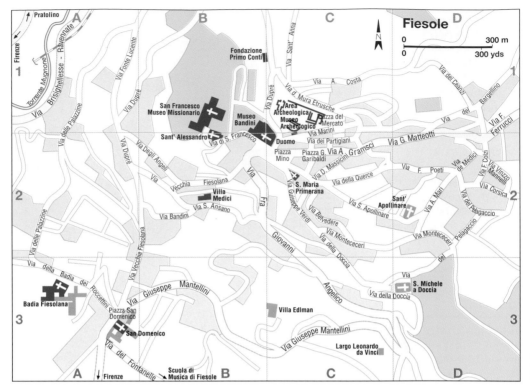

the grave of a warrior, aged between 50 and 60 and dated to about AD 650, has been reconstructed in the museum, complete with his war axe, and blue Rhenish wine glass.

Other finds include silver spoons, a gold pendant shaped like a tankard, and lots of broken glass from bowls and tankards, suggesting perhaps where the Lombards' priorities lay.

The museum exit takes you through the well-stocked shop, from where you turn right, back towards the cathedral, to reach the **Museo Bandini** *(map: C1; open 10am–7pm, closed first Tues of the month)*. Here, the collection consists of a small number of 14th- and 15th-century religious paintings, all of the highest quality, plus one secular group of four allegorical scenes, *The Triumph of Love, Chastity, Time and Piety*, painted on a *cassone*, a wedding chest in which wealthy Florentine women traditionally stored the linen that formed part of their dowry *(see page 155)*.

From the museum exit, you can turn left to walk downhill to the **Fondazione Primo Conti** *(map: C1; Via Giovanni Duprè 18, tel: 055-597095, open Tues–Sat 9am–1pm; admission charge)*, a private collection of avant-garde works by Primo Conti, dating from the first half of the 20th century.

The Cathedral and beyond

Alternatively, turn right to return to the main square to explore the **Cattedrale di San Romolo** *(map: C2; open daily 9am–7pm)*. The huge basilica of bare sandstone is almost completely unadorned except for four frescoes, which include a serene portrait of *St Sebastian* by Perugino (early 16th century), and later 16th-century apsidal frescoes by Nicodemus Ferrucci of the *Life of St Romolo*. The Cathedral's jewel is the marble funerary monument to Bishop Leonardo Salutati, by Mino da Fiesole (1429–84), with a realistic portrait bust of the smiling bishop.

Emerging from the Cathedral, you face the bishop's palace, to the left of which is a narrow lane that leads uphill to the **Cappella di San Iacopo** *(open 9.30am–7pm)*, with five cases displaying ecclesiastical treasures and a fresco of the *Coronation of the Virgin* by Bicci di Lorenzo (1373–1452).

Continuing slowly uphill, you will come to a public garden set around a World War II war memorial, with sweeping views over Florence; on the way up you will pass a moderately priced little restaurant called La Reggia dell'Etrusca, where you can enjoy a plate of pasta, a glass of wine and, if you're lucky enough to get a table on the small terrace, an unforgettable view.

Just above the garden is a small Franciscan monastic complex, sited where the acropolis, or main temple, of the ancient Etruscan city once stood. The first church on the right is **Sant'Alessandro** *(map: B2)* an important 10th-century building constructed from recycled Roman masonry, but rarely open except for occasional exhibitions.

Further up is a simple church of **San Francesco** *(map: B1)*, packed with artistic treasures, including Jacopo del Sellaio's radiant *Adoration of the Magi* (late 15th century). A lavender-scented cloister to the left of the church leads to the **Museo Missionario** *(open 9.30am–12.30pm and 3–7pm)*, a rambling junk shop of a museum packed with dusty and unlabelled Chinese ceramics of questionable aesthetic value, collected by Franciscan missionaries in the 19th century. More interesting is the fact that the museum is built right up against an exposed section of the 3rd-century BC Etruscan city wall.

Before you leave the complex, see if the door to the north of the church is open: this leads into another delightful cloister where you can visit some of the monastery's simple cells. Albert Camus (1913–60), the French writer and philosopher, came here on retreat in the 1930s, describing his time at San Francesco as a valuable escape from *la vie effrenée*.

Return journey

For your own escape from the frenetic world, you could walk part way back to Florence, by returning to Fiesole's main square, and then taking the right-hand exit (the main road to Florence) but keeping straight on when the road bears left after 50 metres/yards. From here, you follow the winding Via Vecchia Fiesolana all the way downhill to San Domenico, a 15-minute walk, past numerous high-walled villas, offering tantalising glimpses of beautiful gardens.

This peaceful and shady walk will bring you to the church of **San Domenico** *(map: A3)*, rarely open, but worth seeing if you can for early frescoes by Fra' Angelico. Opposite the church is the bus stop for the return to Florence. If you have time, take the short walk down the lane opposite the church, which takes you to the **Badia Fiesolana** *(map: A3)*, once a monastery and now home to the European University. The unfinished brick and stone façade of the huge church (dull inside, so don't worry if it is closed) incorporates the lovely green and white Romanesque façade of an earlier and smaller church. From the terrace in front of the church there are views down the Mugnone river valley back to Florence.

Lucca

Several trains a day depart from Santa Maria Novella station in Florence, and take around 90 minutes to get to this delightful and often overlooked city
(Maps: area – page 44, B4; town – page 204)

The lovely walled city of Lucca is full of lanes too narrow for cars, so people get about by bicycle. This, combined with Lucca's reputation for culture and intellectual pursuits, has earned the city the nickname of "Cambridge in Tuscany".

If you arrive by train, cross the main road from the station plaza and head straight for the city's formidable bank of red-brick walls – a small underpass takes you through them. They were built after 1500 to keep Lucca's enemies at bay. In 1817, the massive ramparts were planted with a double row of plane trees, which now shade the broad avenue running along the top of the walls, used by Lucca's citizens as a playground, a jogging and cycle track and a promenade.

Inside the city walls

A path from the walls takes you to the front of the **Duomo di San Martino** *(map: C3; open daily 7am–6.30pm, holidays till 5.45pm; free)*. The Cathedral's striking façade is decorated with a sculpture of St Martin dividing his cloak (the original sculpture is now just inside the church) and with the inlaid marble designs that typify the Tuscan Romanesque style: hunting scenes figure large, with dogs, boars, and huntsmen on horseback, some carrying hawks, some with spears. Flanking the central portal are scenes of the Labours of the Months, and the Miracles of St Martin.

The splendid Romanesque façade of San Michele in Foro, *c.* 1143, (Lucca).

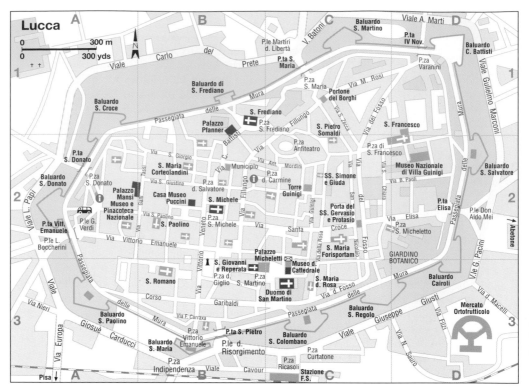

Inside is the domed *tempietto* that contains the larger-than-life Crucifixion in carved and painted wood. Known as the *Volto Santo* (Holy Face), the Romanesque carving was once believed to be a true and accurate portrait of Christ, carved by Nicodemus, who witnessed the Crucifixion.

Off the south aisle is the Sacristy *(open Mon–Fri 9.30am–5.45pm, Sat till 6.45pm, Sun 9–9.50am, 11.20–11.50am, 1–6.15pm; a combined ticket gives admission to the Sacristy, Museo della Cattedrale and the church of Santi Giovanni e Reperata)*. This contains another celebrated image: the tomb of Ilaria del Carretto, who died in 1405, a masterpiece of realistic carving by Jacopo della Quercia. Ilaria was the wife of the then ruler of Lucca, Paolo Guinigi; she died two years after their marriage, at the age of 24, following the birth of their second child.

Immediately north of the cathedral is the **Museo della Cattedrale** *(map: C3; open daily 10am–6pm; combined admission fee)*, where you will be given a free audio-guide providing background information on the exhibits. These range from some very rare ivory and wax writing tablets from the 6th century, to the festive costumes and jewellery that are used to adorn the *Volto Santo* when it is carried in procession round Lucca on 13 September every year.

Coming out of the museum, turn right and walk straight across the Cathedral square to the church of **Santi Giovanni e Reperata** *(map: B3; open daily 10am–6pm; combined admission fee)*. The now-redundant church has been comprehensively excavated, and beneath the modern floor there is a wealth of Roman and medieval structures. The earliest is a 1st-century BC mosaic floor, part of a house that was superseded by a 2nd-century AD Roman bath house, which itself gave way to a 5th-century baptistery, later joined by a series of churches, culminating in the present 12th-century building.

Piazzas and alleyways

Leave the church and take the left-hand exit on the opposite side of the square (Via del Duomo), which leads to Piazza del Giglio, home to the city's theatre and opera house, the Teatro Comunale del Giglio. Adjoining the square to the right is the far larger Piazza Napoleone, where you'll find a choice of outdoor restaurants, shaded by tall plane trees.

Heading north out of the square takes you to Piazza San Michele, ringed by Renaissance arcades. At the centre of the square, the church of **San Michele in Foro** *(map: B2; closed)* has a façade to rival that of the Cathedral, featuring hunting scenes in green and white marble, with animals both exotic (bears, dragons and elephants) and domestic (a rabbit, a duck and a crow eating grapes).

Turning your back on the façade, take the alley called Via di Poggio, which leads past the **Casa Museo Puccini** *(map: B2; Corte San Lorenzo 9; open daily 10am–6pm; admission charge)*, the birthplace of Lucca's celebrated operatic composer, Giacomo Puccini (1858–1924). Continue down Via di Poggio, then right into Piazza del Palazzo Dipinto and left down Via del Toro. If you have navigated successfully through Lucca's maze of medieval alleys you will now be at the Palazzo Mansi, in Via Galli Tassi, which houses the **Museo e Pinacoteca Nazionale** *(map: A2; open Tues–Sat 8.30am–7.30pm, Sun and holidays 8.30am–1.30pm; admission charge)*.

Deities and allegorical figures romp across the ceilings of the splendidly furnished 17th-century home of Cardinal Spada (1659–1724). Upstairs, at the end of a sequence of rooms decorated around the theme of the Four Elements is a sumptuous bedchamber dedicated to Fire. This fire is not a destructive one, but the flame that burns when Eros strikes with his arrow. The room features a gorgeous double bed, its lovely hangings decorated with birds and flowers.

Contrasting attractions

Turn left out of the museum, back onto Via Galli Tassi, and then take the first right into Via San Giustina, and head all the way down past fine palaces to Piazza del Salvatore, with its graceful fountain and 12th-century church. Continue for two more blocks and you will reach Via Fillungo, the city's main shopping street. You join the street at Piazza dei Mercanti, where the covered market is now a stylish café, the Loggia dei Mercanti (No 42). The street has many fine shop fronts dating from the turn of the 20th century. One of them – the Perfumeria Venus – is opposite the café (No 65), its Art Nouveau façade decorated with an ecstatic dancing Venus, carved in marble.

With your back to this shop, go straight down Via Sant'Andrea, heading for the **Torre Guinigi** *(map: C2; open daily 9am–7.30pm; admission charge)*, the red-brick tower at the end of the lane with trees growing from its top. Dating from the 14th century, this is a rare example of the kind of defensive tower that was once commonplace in medieval Tuscany, built as a status symbol and as a place of retreat in times of trouble. If you climb the tower you will see, as well as views of the nearby countryside, the outline of Lucca's Roman amphitheatre (Anfiteatro), perfectly preserved in the buildings that were constructed up against it in the Middle Ages.

For a closer look at what is now a remarkable egg-shaped piazza, turn right out of the tower, and first right in Via delle Chiavi d'Oro. Passing the Art Deco public baths (now a cultural centre), keep going until you reach the curving wall of the amphitheatre. Ringed by pavement cafés, restaurants and souvenir shops, the amphitheatre is an atmospheric place to put your feet up and enjoy a bowl of fresh fruit or home-made ice cream, or even linger on for dinner.

The medieval houses lining the Piazza del Mercato were built against the walls of an ancient Roman amphitheatre, hence its arena-like shape.

Romanesque font in the church of San Frediano, carved with scenes from the *Story of Moses* (Lucca).

Exit through the opposite archway, and follow the curve of the amphitheatre to the left. You will return to Via Fillungo, close to **San Frediano church** *(map: B1)* with its huge gold and blue façade mosaic of Christ in Majesty. The treasure of this church is its Romanesque font, as big as a fountain and carved with scenes showing Moses and his entourage of camels, leading his people (dressed in medieval armour) through the divided Red Sea.

To the rear and left of the church is the **Palazzo Pfanner** *(map: B1; Via degli Asili 33; open daily 10am–6pm; admission charge)*, a delightful 17th-century residence used as the location for the filming of *A Portrait of a Lady*. Without paying, you can get a sneak view of the wonderful garden and exterior staircase at the rear of the palace by climbing onto the city walls at the rear of San Frediano church and walking left for a short distance. Back at San Frediano, turn right down Via Fillungo and keep straight on all the way back to the city walls and the station.

Pienza

Pius II created everything that is historically and artistically worthwhile in Pienza and the town is a tribute to his vision *(Map: page 45, E6)*

Piazza Pio II, centre of Pienza, a model Renaissance town.

Pienza's fame and all of its monuments stem back to one man: the enlightened, humanistic scholar and philosopher pope, Pius II. Born Aeneas Sylvius Piccolomini in Pienza in 1405, he was elected pope in 1458. Two years later he embarked on an ambitious plan to turn his native village into an ideal Renaissance city. After spending a fortune, and with only a handful of the planned buildings completed, Pius II had to acknowledge that he had been too trusting and naïve: his architect, not to mention everyone else involved, had been embezzling funds for years. With good grace and humour, the pope forgave everyone, because he was so enamoured of those few buildings that had been completed. They are grouped around two squares at the centre of the town, and consist principally of the **Duomo**, and the **Palazzo Piccolomino** *(both in Piazza Pio II and both open daily)*.

Art historians see the two buildings as greatly symbolic of the intellectual atmosphere of the time. The huge windows of the airy Duomo were ordered by the pope himself, who said that he wanted a *domus vitrea* (house of glass) to stand as a metaphor for enlightenment and rationality, in contrast to the medieval mysticism of the past. Another window, this time in the palace, frames spectacular views of the surrounding countryside, and of the cone-shaped volcanic peak of Monte Amiata. Needless to say, this has also been the subject of much speculation by seekers of symbolism: the window is seen as a frame to a beautiful "landscape painting", and the pope who so loved this view has been presented as if he were one of the first intellectuals to value nature for its own sake.

If you want to experience the dark demons of the medieval world and see what the pope was reacting against, you should visit nearby **Corsignano.** The little *pieve* (parish church), where Pius II was baptised, has vivid Romanesque carvings of mermaids and sea monsters.

Pisa

Pisa is synonymous with the Leaning Tower, but the city's Square of Miracles could keep a curious visitor busy all day *(Maps: area – page 44, B4; town – page 208)*

hile Florence was still a relatively minor town from the 11th–13th century, Pisa was a major maritime power. Trade with Muslim Spain, North Africa and the Lebanon proved a rich source of money and ideas. Arabic numerals were introduced to Europe through Pisa, and the city's major architectural monuments – the Leaning Tower, the Duomo and Baptistery – show the clear influence of Islamic architecture.

These crowd-pulling monuments are all found on the well-named **Campo dei Miracoli** (Square of Miracles), a green swathe of manicured grass in the northwestern corner of the city walls; from the railway station, walk in a straight line for about 1 km (⅔ mile), crossing the River Arno, and following the main shopping street until signs direct you to the left.

The cathedral museum

Buy your combined ticket *(see box)* and start your day with a visit to the **Museo dell'Opera del Duomo** *(map: B2)*, which is the best way to put the monuments in context. Room 1 contains casts of the foundation stones of each of the buildings and a chronology, which begins in 1064 with the start of work on the Cathedral, followed by the Baptistery in

1154, the Campanile in 1173, and the Campo Santo a century later, in 1277. This short burst of fireworks was followed by swift decline as the city's harbour silted up. (Recent excavations have revealed Roman and medieval boats, complete with cargoes, preserved in the waterlogged silt, which will be exhibited in the city's Arsenal once conservation work is complete.) By 1406, the city had been conquered by Florence and was about to be eclipsed culturally by that city's determination to build even bigger and bolder monuments.

The museum is packed with 12th–15th-century sculptures and paintings: Giovanni Pisano's ivory *Virgin and Child* (1299) is one of the highlights, using the natural shape of the ivory tusk to give the Virgin her naturalistic stance. There are models to show the construction techniques used to build the domed Baptistery, and to explain the marble inlay technique used to give all the buildings their intricate exterior decoration. Best of all, the rooms of the museum open out onto a quiet shady cloister, with a spectacular view of the Leaning Tower and the cathedral.

The famous tower

Emerging from the museum, the **Leaning Tower** *(map: B1)*, or Campanile, is next in sequence. The tower really does lean to a frightening degree, but work to stabilise the tilt has been pronounced a success, and the tower is once again visible, after 10 years of being enshrouded in scaffolding. Detractors have often accused Pisa of deliberately building the tower on a slant to attract attention. In reality, the unstable subsoil that underlies the Piazza dei Miracoli has caused all the buildings to tilt and subside, to dizzying effect.

Just to the right of the tower's entrance is a date stone inscribed ANDMI CLXXIII (Anno Domini 1173), the year in which construction started. Work stopped at the third stage because the building was already collapsing. A century later, three more stages were added, deliberately constructed to tilt in the opposite direction, so the tower has a decided kink to it as well as a tilt.

The recently stabilised Leaning Tower of Pisa.

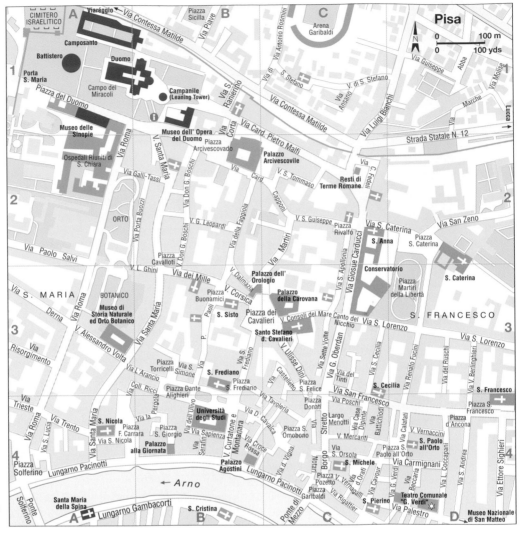

Nicola Pisano's marble pulpit in the Baptistery, carved with scenes from the *Life of Christ*, 1260.

The Duomo

To the left of the tower is the beautiful **Duomo** (*map: A1; open Mon–Sat 10am–7.40pm, Sun 1–7.40pm*), entered through the Porta di San Ranieri, the east door in the south transept. In your eagerness to explore the church, don't rush straight in, but stop to look at the great bronze entrance doors. The work of Bonanno Pisano, dating from 1180, they are decorated with 24 New Testament vignettes, including such delightful scenes as shepherds in their conical caps playing their pipes to soothe the newborn child, and the figures of the Apostles under swaying palm trees.

The rich complexity of the Cathedral interior is created by the forest of pillars rising to arches of

banded white and grey stone, and the colourful mix of altar paintings and Cimabue's apsidal mosaic, from 1302. The beautiful marble pulpit by Giovanni Pisano (1301–11) is a masterpiece. Supported by figures representing prophets, sibyls and allegorical figures, its crowded and dramatic marble panels depict scenes from the *Life of Christ*.

Hanging from the westernmost arch of the great dome is Galileo's Lamp, so called because its pendulum movement is said to have inspired Galileo to discover the rotation of the earth (in reality, the lamp wasn't here in Galileo's time).

You leave the Cathedral through the eastern doors. Looking back, you will see the astonishingly rich façade, with the tomb of the first architect, Buscheto, set above eye level to the left, above the foundation stone dating the cathedral to 1064. The 16th-century bronze doors are surrounded by frames enlivened by animals: look for the unicorn, the squirrels and the armour-plated rhinoceros.

The Baptistery

Opposite is the **Battistero** *(map: A1)*, with its richly decorated exterior niches and statues of saints. The interior is far plainer, but it has one great treasure: Nicola Pisano's pulpit of 1260, carved with scenes from the *Life of Christ*, clearly influenced by ancient Roman art (the source for which we shall see next, in the Campo Santo). Mary, for example, has the long neck, veil and ringlets typical of middle-aged matrons in Roman portraiture.

You may be lucky enough during your visit to hear one of the attendants demonstrate the Baptistery's remarkable acoustics – they tend to do it when groups of visitors are present. As four or more individual notes are sung, the long echo allows them to build up to a complete chord that rings eerily round the dome.

Campo Santo

North of the Baptistery is the **Campo Santo** *(map: A1)*, one of the world's most beautiful cemeteries. The graceful white marble cloister is paved with the grave slabs of medieval Pisans, carved with coats of arms or tools of their trade. Roman sarcophagi, imported from the Holy Land and re-used as coffins for wealthy Pisans, line the walls, carved with the mythological scenes that inspired the pulpits of Nicola and Giovanni Pisano. Frescoes damaged by incendiary bombs during World War II have been restored to their original positions. They include a grim series of frescoes (1360–80) inspired by the Black Death, on the themes of the *Last Judgement* and the *Triumph of Death*.

View of the cathedral façade from the Baptistery.

On the opposite side of the Piazza dei Miracoli is the **Museo delle Sinopie** *(map: A2)*, where you can learn more about the Campo Santo frescoes, and how they were created by laying down a sketch on the plaster undercoat using red paint (called *sinopia* because the pigment came from Sinope on the Black Sea). When the final thin layer of white plaster was applied, the *sinopia* sketch showed through and guided the artists as they completed the fresco in full colour.

Just one more church

Pisa is packed with other churches and monuments, as well as characterful squares and street markets. You would need more than a day to see them all, but try to make time for one more church and one more museum. **Santa Maria della Spina** church *(map: A5; open daily 10am–1.30pm, 2.30–5pm; free)* is on the southern bank of the Arno, near the Ponte Solferino. Don't worry if it is closed when you visit: it is the vivacious exterior that is the most important feature, a *tour de force* of Gothic pinnacles and niches, crowded with statues of saints carved by members of the Pisano family from 1230.

The statues are copies of the originals now displayed in the **Museo di San Matteo** *(map: D6; open Tues–Sun 9am–7pm; admission charge)*, located on the north bank of the Arno, on Lungarno Mediceo. Set in rooms around the cloister of a medieval church, the museum contains such treasures as Masaccio's *St Paul* (1426), a contemplative man with a high brow, hooked nose and patriarchal beard; Donatello's bust reliquary for San Rossore; and a whole room of glowing Renaissance paintings by such artists as Gozzoli and Ghirlandaio.

Statue in the Campo Santo.

San Gimignano

The town gets very crowded in high summer, so try to come for an overnight stay, to enjoy crowd-free churches and monuments in the early and late part of the day *(Map: page 45, C5)*

San Gimignano's fame as a visitor attraction is well justified and, thanks to the tourists, there are numerous good hotels, restaurants and shops. Medieval and Renaissance music of the highest quality echoes around palace courtyards and cloisters all over the city, performed by buskers, many of whom are music students.

San Gimignano is famous for the sculptural quality of its skyline. It is now a cliché to call it a "New York in stone", but the multiple towers (built both for defence and as a symbol of status and wealth) thrusting up from the medieval hilltop city do resemble miniature skyscrapers. This view is best appreciated from the approach roads to the town. Once you are there, it is the completely unspoiled townscape that bowls you over: almost nothing seems to have changed since the 16th century.

Among the many buildings worth exploring, the **Collegiata** *(Piazza del Duomo; open daily)* will detain you longest, as you study the fresco-covered walls. The left aisle has Bartolo di Fredi's appealing and dramatic scenes from the Old Testament (1367), while the opposite aisle has Lippo Memmi's *Life of Christ* (1333–41) and the nave the *Last Judgement* by Taddeo di Bartolo (1393–96). Contrast these Gothic-style narrative paintings with Ghirlandaio's Renaissance frescoes (1475) on the life of a local young woman, Santa Fina.

ABOVE: The unmistakable San Gimignano skyline.

BELOW: St Augustine teaching Philosophy and Rhetoric in Rome, from the St Augustine fresco cycle by Benozzo Gozzoli, 1465.

Next to the church is the delightful cloister that houses the **Museo dell'Arte Sacra**, with its Etruscan and medieval art treasures. Alongside is the **Museo Civico**, housed in the forbidding fortress that served as the town hall. Completed in 1311, its tower is the tallest in the town (54 metres/175 ft) and you can climb to the top. Among the museum's many good paintings is a set of early 14th-century frescoes by Memmo di Filippucci – rare in that they depict secular rather than religious scenes. Known as the *Wedding Frescoes*, they show a young bride and groom sharing a bath and climbing into their nuptial bed – an intimate glimpse into the private life of medieval Italy.

Every church in San Gimignano offers some reward, but perhaps the best is **Sant'Agostino** *(Piazza Sant'Agostino)*. Here, in Benozzo Gozzoli's frescoes on the *Life of St Augustine* (1465), you will find the same love of colour, rich clothing and exact portraiture as in Gozzoli's other frescoes, such as the *Journey of the Magi* in the Palazzo Medici Riccardo in Florence *(see page 161)*.

Siena

Siena is full of pleasant surprises, but the glorious main square, the Piazza del Campo, alone would make it worth a visit *(Map: page 45, D5)*

Siena's golden age ended with the Black Death of 1348, and this city of wealthy bankers and merchants seems never to have fully recovered. Florence, on the other hand, went into the ascendancy, conquered Siena and then deliberately repressed its neighbour and rival to the extent that relations between these two great Tuscan cities remain strained to this day. The result is a city that is medieval in feel, but with plenty of surprises that make you look again just when you think you have got to know the place.

The biggest surprise is the main square, the **Piazza del Campo**, whose spacious airiness contrasts so markedly with the tunnel-like warren of the surrounding streets. The fan-shaped piazza is a memorial to the city's brave early experiments in democracy, its surface divided into nine segments by coloured paving stones, symbolising the Council of Nine, whose members governed the city in its medieval heyday.

The rooms where the council met can be visited: they form part of the **Museo Civico** *(open daily)*, housed in the Palazzo Pubblico on the eastern side of the great square. Almost every room in the museum has important frescoes, furnishings and paintings, but most pertinent are the famous scenes in the Sala del Pace (Room of Peace). Created by Ambrogio Lorenzetti in 1338, they form an *Allegory of Good and Bad Government* – a constant visual reminder to the Council of the potential consequences of their decisions.

Viewing the rooftops

If you have the stamina, you can climb the huge **Torre del Mangia**, the second-highest tower in Italy at 102 metres (330 ft), which stands to one side of the square. An easier way to view the city's terracotta rooftops, however, is to climb to the roof of Siena's Cathedral, which lies east of the main square. The huge building was intended to be bigger still: today's church was extended on the southern side, but the Black Death interrupted the work, and the building now houses the **Museo dell'Opera del Duomo** *(open daily)*. Most people visit this museum for the *Maestá* (Majesty), showing the Virgin enthroned, painted in 1308–11 for the Cathedral's high altar. However, an unexpected bonus of a visit to the museum is the chance to climb through a warren of medieval staircases and passageways that lead up to the Cathedral rooftop for an unexpected vista across the city to the surrounding hills.

From the museum, you can visit the completed part of the **Duomo** *(open daily)*, a magnificent Gothic structure of banded black and white stone, with a superb floor of inlaid marble depicting themes not only from the Bible but also from pagan myth and magic. The Cathedral's **Piccolomini Library** *(open daily)* has colourful frescoes on the life of the man who became Pope Pius II – Aeneas Sylvius Piccolomini. They include a scene in which the future pope acted as marriage broker, which led to the betrothal of the Emperor Frederick III to Eleanora of Portugal – a marriage of true love, judging by the tender glances they exchange.

The Siena School

To anyone used to the variety of subjects tackled by Florentine Renaissance artists, the endless proces-

The figure of Peace, from the *Allegory of Good Government*, by Lorenzetti, 1338–40.

BELOW: an Etruscan vase and the emblematic bronze known as *Ombra della Sera* (Evening Shadow), two of the ancient treasures displayed in Volterra's Guarnacci Museum.

Siena's spectacular Gothic Cathedral (1136–1382).

sion of madonnas painted by the artists of the Siena School might seem monotonous. Yet there is no doubting the technical accomplishment of these works, which can be fully appreciated in the outstanding collection displayed in the **Pinacoteca Nazionale** *(Via San Pietro 29; open daily)*, located in the 14th-century Palazzo Buonsignori, to the south of the Cathedral. Some welcome variation is provided by Il Sodoma's colourful and dramatic *Deposition* (1502), and Lorenzetti's *Two Views*, which is an early example of pure landscape painting.

Volterra

Perched on a windy plateau overlooking the Sienese hills, Volterra has some of the best Etruscan art to be found outside Rome *(Map: page 45, C5)*

The modern city of Volterra sits within the walls of its much larger Etruscan predecessor, and wherever archaeologists dig in the city, they turn up new treasures. Sometimes they do not even need to dig, since parts of the city, built on soft tufa and undermined by subterranean springs, have been slipping slowly down the hillside for centuries, revealing the remains of an extensive necropolis.

The best of the city's ancient treasures are displayed in the **Museo Etrusco Guarnacci** *(Via Don Minzoni 15; open daily)*. Here you will see fine alabaster and marble funerary urns, not greatly different, though of finer quality, than those you can see in museums all over Tuscany. One exhibit is unique, however: the elongated bronze figure appropriately dubbed the *Ombra della Sera* (Evening Shadow). This was the name given to the sculpture by writer Gabriele d'Annunzio (1863–1938) when it was finally recognised as a masterpiece of Etruscan art, after it had been ploughed up by a local farmer in 1879, and used as a fireside poker for several years. The mysterious, naked 3rd-century figure does indeed resemble the shadow of a human being thrown by the low beams of the setting sun.

In the nearby **Duomo** *(Piazza San Giovanni; open daily)*, the sculpture of the *Deposition* over the main altar is an extremely rare and unusual Romanesque wood carving, simple in execution but full of dramatic pathos. Rosso Fiorentino chose the same subject – Christ being taken down from the Cross – for the Mannerist painting (1521) that is the highlight of the **Pinacoteca e Museo Civico** *(Via dei Sarti 1; open daily)*.

The tradition of fine carving still continues in Volterra today, and the main square is ringed by workshops selling alabaster figures.

SHORT EXCURSIONS

Within the immediate environs of Florence there are some fine buildings containing Renaissance and medieval works, as well as numerous museums, some dedicated to eminent native sons, some to local skills.

The towering genius of Leonardo da Vinci is celebrated in his birthplace, the tiny hill town of **Vinci** *(map: page 44, C4)* , located in the rolling green countryside between Florence and Pisa. Here, the 13th-century castle in the centre of the town houses the **Museo Leonardiano**, where you can discover how Leonardo's fertile mind came up with such inventions as the bicycle, the helicopter, the parachute, the submarine, tank and machine gun.

A short way south, **Empoli** *(map: page 44, C4)* is an industrial town that few people visit as they pass through on the train from Florence to Pisa. If you have time to spare, it is worth stopping off here to explore the old town, whose Romanesque Collegiata church has a fine green and white marble façade dating from 1093. In the **Museo della Collegiata** picture gallery *(closed Monday)*, there is a rare masterpiece, a *Pietà*, by Masolino (1424–25).

The two industrial towns of Prato and Pistoia on the parallel rail line that links Florence to Pisa via Lucca, are both worth half a day. Amid the industrial estates of a city proud to be called the "Manchester of Italy", **Prato** *(map: page 44, D4)* has a compact medieval centre, with a delightful green and white marble Duomo. The Cathedral façade has an external pulpit decorated with dancing cherubs, sculpted by Donatello (these are copies, the originals are in the Museo dell'Opera del Duomo, to the left). The pulpit is used to display the *Virgin's Holy Girdle*, a precious relic that came to Prato in the 12th century.

Inside the church are Filippo Lippi's frescoes on the *Martyrdom of St John the Baptist* (1452–66). South of the square lies the Palazzo Pretorio, where the Galleria Comunale contains paintings by Bernardo Daddi and Filippo Lippi. Here, too, is the new Museo del Tessuto, dedicated to the fine textiles that made Prato's fortune. Gorgeous masterpieces of antique cloth are on display, and the skills that led to their production are not lost – as the section on contemporary textiles clearly demonstrates.

To the west of the city is the **Museo Pecci** *(Viale della Repubblica 277; tel: 0574 5317, permanent collection by appointment)*, a contemporary arts and exhibition centre.

The artistic masterpieces of **Pistoia** *(map: page 44, C3)* span the centuries, from Romanesque churches to the bold figurative bronzes of locally born sculptor, Marino Marini (1901–80; *see page 168*).

Three of the city's churches have outstanding pulpits that testify to the astonishing skills of local sculptors in the 13th century: San Giovanni Fuorcivitas has New Testament scenes by Guglielmo da Pisa (1270); Sant'Andrea has Giovanni Pisano's masterful *Scenes from the Life of Christ* (1301); and San Bartolomeo has a damaged pulpit by Guido da Como (1250). In the main square, the Duomo contains an extraordinary silver altar covered in miniature saints, on which silversmiths laboured for over 200 years, starting in 1287.

Alongside is the Gothic Palazzo del Comune, whose courtyard and ground floor rooms make the perfect setting for a collection of medieval and Renaissance art, while the Palazzo del Tau, in the south of the city, is the new home for a collection of Marini's rugged bronze sculptures.

Pride in the local ceramic industry has resulted in the **Museo Archeologico e della Ceramica** *(closed Monday)*, in **Montelupo** *(map: page 44, D4)*. Here exhibits range from prehistoric pottery production in the Arno Valley to the fine-glazed wares invented in the 13th century that have been the staple of the town's economy ever since. Ceramics are still made in Montelupo and the best way to see them is to visit the market held on the third Sunday of the month.

The Town of Prato, 15th-century fresco.

Essential information

Visiting the Museums and Churches

Opening times are given in the main text, but they are subject to frequent last minute changes, particularly in winter (November to Easter/May) when many museums decide to reduce their opening hours. To avoid disappointment, it's a good idea to pick up a list of the latest opening times from the tourist office, especially if you're going out of your way to visit a smaller museum or church.

Admission charges range from around €2 for the smaller church museums and refectories to between €6.50 and €8.50 for the major collections.

State museums

All the museums featured in the Major Collections chapter are state-run *(musei statali)*. The "big three" – the Uffizi, the Accademia and the Palatine Gallery (Pitti Palace) – are open all day from 8.15 or 8.30am–6.50pm, with late opening on summer Saturdays until 10pm. The Bargello opens for just half a day until 1.50pm. The ticket offices to all major museums close 45 minutes before the museum itself.

Other state-run museums in Florence include the Pitti Palace museums, the Bargello, the Cappelle Medicee, Museo Archeologico, Museo Davanzati, Museo di San Marco and Opificio delle Pietre Dure. Many of these are open in the morning only and their ticket offices close half an hour before closing time.

Most state museums are closed on Monday, or alternate Mondays, and either close or have restricted opening times on public holidays. All are free for under-18s and over-65s, and half price for 18–25 year-olds, provided you show proof of identity.

To avoid queues, you can book your visit a few days ahead by ringing the State Museums Reservation Line: *tel: 055-294883 (Mon–Fri 8.30am–6.30pm, Sat 8.30am–noon)*. For a small fee you will be given a fixed entry time slot. This is well worth considering for the major collections, particularly during peak season, which is more or less all year round these days.

Each year in April or December, Florence offers a free museum week – La Settimana di Beni Culturali – when all state museums are open free of charge. Contact the Florence tourist office for further details.

In summer, the Friends of Florentine Museums Association *(Via degli Alfani 39; tel: 055-293007, fax: 055-215852)* arrange museum visits in the evening between 9pm and 11pm, often with orchestral recitals.

Municipal and private museums

The remaining museums and monuments are either run by the city council (Comune di Firenze) or are privately owned. These include the Cathedral monuments (the Campanile, Battistero, Duomo, Cupola, Museo dell' Opera del Duomo), the Palazzo Vecchio, Museo di Santa Maria Novella, Museo dell' Opera di Santa Croce, Cappella Brancacci, Cenacolo di Santo Spirito, Spedale degli Innocenti, Palazzo Medici Riccardi, Casa Buonarroti, Museo di "Firenze Com'era", Museo Horne, Museo Bardini, Museo Stibbert, Museo di Storia della Scienza, Museo di Zoologia La Specola, Museo Marino Marini and Raccolta della Ragione. Opening times and days of closure vary enormously *(see individual entries)*.

Churches

Entry to most churches (but not their adjoining museums) is free. Tourists are expected to dress respectfully. Shorts and bare shoulders are frowned upon and in some churches, if your clothing is not considered modest enough, you will be given a plastic cape to wear. However, the city can get very hot and stuffy in summer, so if you are wearing skimpy clothing, it's always a good idea to carry a scarf or a light jacket to wrap around your shoulders, not only out of respect, but also because church interiors can feel chilly after the heat of the street. Churches often close for lunch from around 12.30am until 3–4pm.

Another useful item to keep in your bag is a small pair of binoculars. These come in handy for viewing frescoes and paintings, many of which are too high up to make out in detail.

When to visit

Although Florence is an all-year-round destination, the heat and crowds of July and August are best avoided, and at Easter the crowds and queues can be unbearable. May is probably the best month to see Florence, but June, late September and October are also relatively cool and peaceful. November to March can be wetter and colder than you would believe possible in a Mediterranean climate but, to compensate, the city will be far less crowded (except for during the Christmas period) and you will probably find bargain-price air fares and hotel rooms. If you want to visit Florence during the Calcio in Costume festival *(see below)* you would be wise to book at least six months in advance. If you are visiting for just a few days, try to avoid Sunday afternoon and Monday when many of the city's museums, shops and restaurants are closed.

Holidays and Festivals

Public holidays

1 January, *Capodanno* (New Year's Day); 6 January, *La Befana* (Epiphany); *Venerdì Santo* (Good Friday); *Pasquetta* (Easter Monday); 25 April, *Anniversario*

della Liberazione (Liberation Day); 1 May, *Festa del Lavoro* (Labour Day); 15 August, *Ferragosto* (Feast of the Assumption); 1 November, *Ognissanti* (All Saints' Day); 8 December, *Immacolata Concezione* (Immaculate Conception); 25 December, *Natale* (Christmas Day); 26 December, *Santo Stefano* (Boxing Day).

Banks and post offices close on these dates and many museums either close or reduce their opening hours *(see individual entries)*. In addition to these public holidays, many businesses close on and around June 24 when the city celebrates the feast of San Giovanni (St John the Baptist), the patron saint of Florence. In August many small shops and restaurants close as Florentines leave the city for their annual holiday.

Florentine festivals
Easter Day: *Scoppio del Carro*, the "explosion of the carriage" (fireworks on a float) and the emergence of a dove followed by colourful musical processions.
Ascension Day: *Festa del Grillo*, Festival of the Crickets in the Cascine park. Sale of crickets and sweets.
End of April: Flower Show, near Piazza Libertà.
May and June: *Maggio Musicale Fiorentino* – performances of opera, ballet and concerts to a high standard.
24 June: *San Giovanni* – Florence's patron saint's day, with a holiday in the city and an evening firework display near Piazzale Michelangelo. *Calcio in Costume* – football in medieval costume in Piazza Santa Croce. Three other matches are also played in June/July.
7 September: night festival of the *Rificolona* (lanterns) – procession of carts, lanterns and singers.

Tourist Offices

There are three **APT** *(Azienda di Promozione Turistica)* tourist information offices in central Florence *(Via Cavour, 1r, tel: 055-290832/3, fax: 055-2760383; Piazza Stazione tel: 055-212245, fax: 055-2381226; Borgo Santa Croce, 29r tel: 055-2340444, fax: 055-2264524)* and one in Fiesole *(Piazza Mino, 37. tel: 055-598720, fax: 055-598822)*.

Most Tuscan towns have an **Ufficio Informizioni Turistiche** (tourist office). Look out for the yellow "i" sign.

Getting Around

Florence's main station is Santa Maria Novella, which is the hub of the city transport network *(for train information anywhere in Italy tel: 1478-88088, 7am–9pm)*. Most buses can be caught alongside the station and there is an official taxi rank at the front. However, once you're in the compact city centre, walking is by far the best and most efficient way of getting around. Cars belonging to non-residents are not permitted in the *centro storico* and must be left in one of the peripheral car parks.

Buses
Florence's bright orange buses are run by ATAF. Bus numbers and routes are clearly displayed at each bus stop, and the tourist office also supplies a book of bus routes. Most buses pass through and can be caught from Santa Maria Novella station, Piazza del Duomo and Piazza San Marco.

Bus drivers do not sell tickets, which must be bought in advance from one of the ticket kiosks or vending machines at the main bus stops, or from bars and tobacconists displaying the ATAF sticker. Each ticket is valid for 60 minutes travel, during which time you can get on and off buses as often as you please. Three-hour and 24-hour tickets are also available. Remember to stamp your ticket in the machine at the rear of the bus.

Taxis
The main taxi ranks are located in front of the station and in Piazza Santa Trinità, Piazza del Duomo, Piazza della Repubblica and Piazza San Marco. It's advisable to pick up official taxis (white with the taxi sign on the roof) at taxi ranks and avoid the station touts that pounce on you the minute you set foot outside the station. Supplements are payable for luggage and for journeys to and from the airport. For a radio taxi, *tel: 055-4390/4242/4798*.

Maps
A recommended supplement to the maps in this book is the laminated *Insight Fleximap to Florence*. If you are venturing further afield there is also an *Insight Fleximap to Tuscany*. For a very detailed map of the city, look for *Firenze: Pianta della Città*, published by LAC (Litografia Artistica Cartografica).

Telecommunications

Telephones
Coin-operated phones can be found in many streets and squares; you can phone from a bar if it displays the sign of a red telephone handset in a red circle. Many public phones accept phone cards *(carta telefonica)* that can be bought in tobacconists.

Telephone booths for long-distance or overseas calls are located in the central post office *(open 24 hours, Via Pelliceria 160)* and the railway station *(open Mon–Sat 8am–9.45pm)*.

When dialling any number you must include the area code, even when making a call from within the area or city itself. You should also always include the initial zero. The code for Florence is 055.

To call other countries from Italy, first dial the international access code (00), then the relevant country code: e.g. UK 44, US and Canada 1, Australia 61, followed by the subscriber number. The country code for Italy is 39.

E-Mail

There are a surprising number of internet cafés in the city centre and you are bound to stumble across one as you wander the streets. Internet Train has branches all over town *(www.internettrain.it)*. Most open around 10am and close at around midnight. Many of the cyber cafés also offer international phone and courier services, and some even rent out mobile phones.

Post

The bad reputation of the Italian postal system is well-deserved. Letters can take days, and postcards can take weeks to reach their destination both within Italy and abroad. If you want to send something urgently it's worth paying the extra to use the "express" service. Stamps *(francobolli)* can be bought from any tobacconist (with the black and white "T" sign outside) and from post offices. The main post office in Florence is on Via Pellicceria, off Piazza della Repubblica and is open Mon–Fri 8.15am–7pm; until 12.30pm on Saturday. Other post offices are open 8.30am–2pm on weekdays and until midday on Saturdays.

Emergency and Medical Services

General SOS (fire, police or ambulance with replies in foreign languages): 113
Medical emergencies/ambulance: 118
Fire department: 115
Police emergency: 112
Traffic police: 055-50551
Associazione Volontari Ospedalieri: 0550-234 4567. A voluntary association that offers a free interpreting service for non-Italian speaking visitors in need of medical assistance.
Farmacia Comunale: 055-216761. A 24-hour pharmacy at Santa Maria Novella station.
Automobile Club d'Italia (ACI): 24-hour breakdown: 116; 24-hour information line in English: 06-4477.
Police headquarters: the place to visit in the event of theft, lost passports, etc. Via Zara, 2; tel: 055-49771.

Newspaper and Magazine Listings

Firenze Spettacolo is the main monthly listings magazine (with some listings also in English) with information on concerts, exhibitions and museums, and recommendations for clubs, bars, restaurants and cafés. The Italian dailies *La Nazione* and *La Repubblica* also have details of local entertainment and events.

Florence Today and *Florence Concierge Information* are two English-language events magazines specially produced for tourists. They are generally available in hotels or from tourist information offices. The tourist office also produces a monthly calendar of events *(available from the APT, Via Cavour 1, beside the Palazzo Medici Riccardi)*.

Useful Websites

www.enit.it Official Italian State Tourist Board site with information on hotels, sights, events, exhibitions, etc.
www. comune.firenze.it Site run by the city council with up-to-the-minute information on everything, including the local weather.
www.firenze.turismo.toscana.it General tourist information site with the latest information on exhibitions and cultural events.
www.uffizi.firenze.it The Uffizi gallery's official site.
www.cosi.it/principe The Palazzo Vecchio site.
www.museionline.it Italian museums site.
www.mangiafirenze.com Florence for foodies.
www.paginegialle.it Italy's yellow pages.
www.meteo.it Weather in Italy.

For the latest news on Florence's museums and recommended exhibitions, visit the Insight website **www.insightguides.com**.

Tours

Walking Tours of Florence *(Piazza Santo Stefano 2 – by the Ponte Vecchio; open 8am–8pm, tel: 055-2645033; www.artviva.com)* organise laid-back tours in English around Florence and Tuscany, including the Uffizi. They also run workshops and theatrical events in the Palazzo Vecchio.

The **Centro Guide Turismo** *(Palazzo Borghese, Via Ghibellina 110; tel: 055-288448; fax 055-288476; website: www.webcom97.com/centroguide)*, the Florentine guides association, conducts well-informed personalised gallery and museum tours in most languages. Classic visits cover the minor collectors' museums, private palaces, the *cenacoli* (refectories), and the Medici villas and gardens.

Banks and Money

Most banks are open Mon–Fri 8.20am–1.20pm. Some banks re-open for a short while in the afternoon from 2.30–3.45pm. The Banco Nazionale at the railway station is open all day Mon–Sat 8.20am–7.20pm. All banks are closed on public holidays, often from noon the day before. ATM machines outside banks and post offices will allow you to withdraw euros using your own debit or credit card (remember your PIN number). The accepted cards are marked on the machines.

Several banks in Florence also have automatic exchange machines into which you can feed bank notes and receive euros in return. Instructions are given in several languages and the exchange rate is the same as that offered by banks; these machines are, however, apt to reject any notes that are creased or damaged. Travellers' cheques (obtainable in euros) are easy to cash, but remember that you will be required to present your passport.

Further Reading

Art & Architecture

The Architecture of Michelangelo, James A. Ackerman (Penguin/University of Chicago, 1986)

The Architecture of the Italian Renaissance, Peter Murray (Thames and Hudson, 1986)

Architecture of the Renaissance from Brunelleschi to Palladio, Bertrand Jestaz (Thames and Hudson/New Horizons, 1995)

Artists on Art, compiled by Robert Goldwater and Marco Treves (John Murray, 1980)

Botticelli, Bettina Wadia (Hamlyn, 1985)

Donatello, Bonnie Bennett and Ornella Casazza (Phaidon Press, 1984)

Brunelleschi's Dome, Ross King (Penguin, 2000)

A Concise Encyclopaedia of the Italian Renaissance edited by J.R. Hale (Thames and Hudson, 1981).

The Drawings of Leonardo da Vinci, A.E. Popham (Pimlico, 1994)

The High Renaissance and Mannerism, Linda Murray (Thames and Hudson, 1978)

The Horne Museum – A Florentine House of the Renaissance, Licia Bertani (in English or Italian; Edizione della Meridiana)

From Giotto to Cézanne, Michael Levey (Thames and Hudson, 1962)

The Italian Painters of the Renaissance, Bernard Berenson (Phaidon Press, 1968)

Mannerism, John Shearman (Penguin, 1970)

Palaces of Florence, Patrizia Fabbri (in English or Italian, Arsenale Editrice, 2001)

The Stones of Florence and Venice Observed, Mary McCarthy (Penguin, 1972)

Vasari, Lives of the Artists, Giorgio Vasari (volumes I and II, various editions, including Oxford Paperbacks, 1998)

Guides to the Main Collections

The Accademia, Franca Falletti (Firenze Musei, Giunti; 1998)

National Museum of the Bargello, Giovanna Gaeta Bertelà (Firenze Musei, Giunti; 1999)

The Pitti Palace – Modern Art Gallery, Carlo Sisi (Firenze Musei, Giunti; 1999)

The Pitti Palace: Palatine Gallery & Royal Apartments, Marco Chiarini (Firenze Musei, Giunti; 1998)

The Uffizi, Gloria Fossi (Firenze Musei, Giunti; 1998)

Italian Painting, the Uffizi (Taschen, 2000)

Florence & Tuscany Guides & Travel Companions

Florence: A Traveller's Companion, Harold Acton (Constable, UK, 2002)

Florence Explored, Rupert Scott (The Bodley Head, 1987)

Italian Hours, Henry James (Penguin, 1995)

Pictures from Italy, Charles Dickens (Penguin, 1998)

The Villas of Tuscany, Harold Acton (Thames and Hudson, 1984)

History & Society

The Civilization of the Renaissance in Italy, Jacob Burckhardt (Phaidon Press, 1995)

Sketches of Etruscan Places and Other Italian Essays, DH Lawrence (Penguin, 1999)

Florence: The Biography of a City, Christopher Hibbert (Penguin/Morrow, 1994)

Florence and the Medici, J.R. Hale (Thames and Hudson, 1983)

The Florentine Renaissance, Vincent Cronin (Pimlico, 1992)

The Flowering of the Renaissance, Vincent Cronin (Pimlico, 1992)

Italy, The Unfinished Revolution, Matt Frei (Mandarin, 1996)

Italy, A Difficult Democracy, Spotts and Weisser (Cambridge, 1986)

The New Italians, Charles Richards (Penguin, 1995)

The Italians, Luigi Barzini (Penguin, 1968)

Italian Journeys, Jonathan Keates (Picador, 1992)

Italian Neighbours, Tim Parks (Vintage, 2002)

Machiavelli, Sydney Anglo (Paladin, 1971)

The Prince, Niccolò Macchiavelli (various publishers)

The Rise and Fall of the House of Medici, Christopher Hibbert (Penguin/Morrow, 1979)

Style and Civilization: Early Renaissance, Michael Levey (Penguin, 1991)

Style and Civilization: High Renaissance, Michael Levey (Penguin, 1991)

A Traveller's History of Italy, Valerio Lintner (Interlink Books, 1995)

Literature

The Agony and the Ecstasy, Irving Stone (Arrow, 1990)

Death in Springtime, Magdalen Nabb (Collins, 1986)

The Decameron, Giovanni Boccaccio (various editions)

The Divine Comedy, Dante Alighieri (various editions)

A Room with a View, E.M. Forster (Penguin, 2000)

Other Insight Guides

Insight Guide Italy is the major book in the Italian series covering the whole country, with features on food and drink, culture and the arts. Other Insight Guide titles include *Florence, Tuscany, Northern Italy, Southern Italy, Rome, Sardinia, Sicily* and *Venice*.

There are also numerous Italian titles in the smaller *Pocket Guide* and *Compact Guide* series, including *Florence*. The foldable *Insight Fleximap to Florence* is a useful, easy-to-use companion to this guide.

Other cities in the *Museums and Galleries* series include New York, Paris and London.

Artists' Biographies

Alberti, Leon Battista (1404–72)
The archetypal Renaissance man, Alberti was a humanist, painter, sculptor and architect. His treatises on painting and sculpture are the earliest written records of the theories of perspective first laid down by Brunelleschi, and were very influential on 15th-century architectural design. Buildings by Alberti in Florence include the Palazzo Rucellai and the façade of Santa Maria Novella.

Ammannati, Bartolomeo (1511–92)
A Mannerist sculptor influenced by Michelangelo. His best-known work is the *Neptune Fountain* in Piazza della Signoria. He was also an architect and designed and landscaped parts of the Pitti Palace and the Boboli Gardens.

Andrea del Sarto (1486–1530)
Prominent and influential painter of the High Renaissance, most famous for his frescoes in Santissima Annunziata *(Nativity and the Visitation of the Magi)* and the Chiostro dello Scalzo *(Scenes from the Life of St John the Baptist* and *The Four Virtues)*. Other key works in Florence include: *Madonna of the Harpies, Portrait of a Lady*, Uffizi; *Last Supper*, San Salvi; *St John the Baptist*, Palazzo Pitti.

Botticelli, Sandro (*c.* 1445–1510)
Botticelli was a pupil of Fra' Filippo Lippi, whose influence is clear in the lyricism and delicacy of line of his two masterpieces, *Primavera* and the *Birth of Venus*, both in the Uffizi. Other key works in Florence include: *Virgin and Child*, Accademia; *Coronation of the Virgin*, the Sant' Ambrogio altarpiece, *Madonna of the Magnificat, Virgin and Child with Angels, The Adoration of the Magi, Annunciation, Portrait of a Young Man*, Uffizi; *Saint Augustine*, Ognissanti.

Bronzino, Agnolo (1503–1572)
After time spent in Rome, where he came into contact with the work of Michelangelo, Bronzino was elected court painter to the Medici. He was a pupil of Pontormo and became one of the most important Mannerist portrait painters. Works in Florence include: *Portrait of Lucrezia Panciatichi, Portrait of Eleanor of Toledo,* Uffizi; *The Martyrdom of St Lawrence*, San Lorenzo.

Brunelleschi, Filippo (1377–1446)
Brunelleschi trained as a goldsmith and sculptor, but turned to architecture after losing the competition for the Baptistery doors to Ghiberti, and quickly established himself as the foremost architect and engineer of his day. His greatest achievement was the cathedral dome, built entirely without scaffolding. He was also the first artist to lay down the rules of central perspective representation. Other buildings in Florence by Brunelleschi include: San Lorenzo church and the Old Sacristy, Spedale degli Innocenti and Santo Spirito.

Caravaggio (1571–1610)
After his apprenticeship in Milan, Caravaggio went to work in Rome. He received many commissions from the Vatican, but his religious paintings were widely criticised for their vivid realism. His work is characterised by his attention to detail and use of strong chiaroscuro. Works in Florence include: *Bacchus, Sacrifice of Isaac,* Uffizi; *Sleeping Cupid*, Palazzo Pitti.

Cellini, Benvenuto (1500–71)
Florentine sculptor who began his career as a goldsmith in Rome. Cellini worked as an artist in the courts of François I in France and Cosimo I de' Medici in Florence. Though he lived in the shadow of his idol, Michelangelo, he was an accomplished master of bronze and produced many expressive works. Key works in Florence include: *Perseus,* Piazza della Signoria; *Mercury, Narcissus, Ganymede*, the Bargello.

Cimabue (*c.* 1240–1302)
A Florentine painter in the Byzantine tradition whose work heralds the beginning of Renaissance art. The few mosaics, panel-paintings and frescoes that survive may still appear stylised, but the movement and expression in his figures was revolutionary. He was much admired by Dante and it is widely believed that he was Giotto's teacher. Works in Florence: *Crucifix*, Santa Croce; *Madonna and Child*, Uffizi.

Della Robbia, Luca (*c.* 1399–1482)
Sculptor who developed a terracotta-glazing technique which he used mainly for the decoration of tondi and lunettes. Works in Florence include: *Virgin with an Apple*, Bargello; *Madonna Enthroned*, Orsanmichele.

Donatello (*c.* 1386–1466)
One of the greatest Renaissance sculptors, second only to Michelangelo. He produced a vast body of work and his heroic style influenced greatly the artists of the time. After a brief training in Ghiberti's workshop, he was commissioned to make statues for the cathedral façade. His early figures were marble, but most of his later work was produced in bronze. Works in Florence include: *Judith and Holofernes*, Palazzo Vecchio; *St George, David*, Bargello; *Crucifixion*, Santa Croce; *Deposition* and *Resurrection*, San Lorenzo (pulpits).

Fra' Angelico (*c.* 1387–1455)
A Dominican friar who dedicated his life to painting religious subjects. He was based at the monastery of San Marco where, with the help of his assistants, he painted each of the friars' cells. His direct and simple style is rooted in the Gothic, yet his concern with realism and perspective is characteristic of the Early Renaissance. San Marco has the largest collection of his works including the *Annunciation* and *Crucifixion* frescoes.

Ghiberti, Lorenzo (1378–1455)
His workshop and bronze foundry were in constant demand, but Ghiberti himself spent most of his working life producing the Baptistery doors, an outstanding example of Early Renaissance art.

Ghirlandaio, Domenico (1449–94)
Leading fresco painter of the 15th century together with Botticelli. One of Ghirlandaio's trademarks was the use

of the crowd scene in his religious paintings into which he integrated Florentine nobles. Works in Florence include: *The Last Supper*, San Marco Refectory; *Adoration*, Spedale degli Innocenti; *St Jerome*, *Last Supper*, Ognissanti; *Life of St Francis*, Santa Trinità.

Giambologna (1529–1608)
Flemish-born Mannerist sculptor, Giambologna went to Rome to study ancient sculpture and the work of Michelangelo, then to Florence where he worked as court sculptor to the Medici. In accordance with Mannerist principles, his marble sculptures can be viewed from all angles and not just a fixed point. Works in Florence include: *Rape of the Sabine Women*, Loggia dei Lanzi; *Mercury*, Bargello; *Venus*, Boboli Gardens.

Giotto di Bondone (*c.* 1266–1337)
Florentine artist associated with Cimabue and probably his pupil, considered one of the key figures in the history of Western art. By abandoning the formal Byzantine tradition in favour of a more expressive style, he paved the way for the freedom of Renaissance art. Works in Florence include: *Ognissanti Madonna*, Uffizi; *St Stephen*, Museo Horne; *Crucifix*, Santa Maria Novella

Gozzoli, Benozzo (*c.* 1421–97)
A panel and fresco painter, he worked both with Ghiberti and Fra' Angelico. He is best known for the *Journey of the Magi* in the Palazzo Medici Riccardi, a lively fresco cycle full of colour and detail, with a freshness characteristic of 15th-century Florentine fresco painting. Other works in Florence include: *The Deposition*, Museo Horne.

Leonardo da Vinci (1452–1519)
Painter, sculptor, architect and engineer, a scholar in natural sciences, medicine and philosophy, he was the embodiment of the Renaissance ideal of a "universal man". Key works in Florence include: *Annunciation*, *Baptism of Christ*, *Adoration of the Magi*, Uffizi.

Lippi, Filippino (*c.* 1457–1504)
Son and pupil of Fra' Filippo Lippi, he was an outstanding fresco painter and completed the Brancacci Chapel frescoes left unfinished by Masolino and Masaccio. The influence of his contemporary, Botticelli, in his work is clear. Other works in Florence include: *Adoration of the Child*, *Adoration of the Magi*, Uffizi; *Virgin Appearing to St Bernard*, Badia Fiorentina; Santa Maria Novella frescoes; Nerli altarpiece, Santo Spirito; *Pietà* and *cassone* panel, Horne.

Lippi, Fra' Filippo (*c.* 1406–69)
Carmelite friar influenced by Masaccio whom he observed painting the Brancacci chapel. He received several commissions for the Medici. Works in Florence include: *Madonna with Angels*, Uffizi; *Madonna and Child (Tondo Bartolini)*, Palazzo Pitti; *Annunciation*, San Lorenzo.

Masaccio (1401–*c.* 1428)
Regarded as one of the founders of modern painting, Masaccio was influenced by his predecessor, Giotto and his contemporary Donatello, to create expressive, true-to-life figures set in a clearly understood perspective. His *Trinity* fresco in Santa Maria Novella was a ground-breaking work. He is best known for his frescoes in the Brancacci chapel.

Michelangelo Buonarroti (1475–1564)
The greatest sculptor of the High Renaissance and precursor of Mannerist and Baroque art. His heroic statue of *David* is one of the last masterpieces of the Renaissance produced in Florence. Key works in Florence include: *Deposition*, Museo Dell'Opera del Duomo; *Doni Tondo*, Uffizi; *Bacchus*, Bargello; *Night, Day, Dawn, Dusk, Madonna and Child*, San Lorenzo; *Four Slaves*, Galleria dell' Accademia.

Pontormo, Jacopo (1494–1556)
Along with Rosso Fiorentino, Pontormo is considered the master of early Mannerism. Works in Florence include: *Portrait of Cosimo the Elder*, Uffizi; *Deposition*, Santa Felicità

Raphael (1483–1520)
Quintessential High Renaissance painter who produced a vast body of work during his short life, Raphael studied with Perugino and when in Florence came under the influence of da Vinci and Michelangelo. Key works in Florence include: *Madonna dell'Impannata*, *Madonna della Seggiola*, the Doni portraits, Palazzo Pitti, *Madonna of the Goldfinch*, *Portrait of a Man*, Uffizi.

Titian (*c.* 1487–1576)
Greatest 16th-century painter of the Venetian school, noted for his religious and mythological paintings. Works in Florence include: *Mary Magdalene*, *Portrait of a Gentleman*, *Concert*, Pitti Palace; *Venus of Urbino*, *Flora*, Uffizi.

Uccello, Paolo (1397–1475)
An apprentice in the workshop of Ghiberti and influenced by the work of Masaccio and Donatello, Uccello became a master of perspective and one of the most versatile painters of the Early Renaissance. Works in Florence include: *Sir John Hawkwood*, Duomo; *Battle of San Romano*, Uffizi; *The Deluge*, Santa Maria Novella.

Vasari, Giorgio (1511–1574)
Painter, draughtsman, art historian and architect who received many commissions from the Medici, including the design of the Uffizi. He is best remembered for his book *The Lives of the Artists* (1550).

Veronese (*c.* 1528–88)
Virtuoso painter whose classical style was more akin to the High Renaissance style of Titian than his contemporary Mannerists. *Man in Furs*, Pitti Palace; *The Holy Family with St Catherine and St John*, Uffizi.

Verrochio, Andrea del (1435–88)
Painter, sculptor and goldsmith who became da Vinci's master and Donatello's successor in the service of the Medici. Key works in Florence: *Noblewoman with Bouquet*, *Crucifix*, Bargello; *Baptism of Christ*, Uffizi.

Art & Photo Credits

Permissions

Every effort has been made to trace copyright holders, and we apologise in advance for any unintentional omissions.

All works of art below have been reproduced with the permission of the following copyright holders:

Giorgio de Chirico, *Les Bains Mysterieux,* 1934 © DACS 2002: 172

Renato Guttuso, *Basket with Flask,* 1941© DACS 2002: 173

Marino Marini, *L'Attesa,* 1986 © DACS 2002: 168b

Marino Marini, *La Comparsa,* 1952 © DACS 2002: 164

Marino Marini, *Rider,* 1947 © DACS 2002: 168t

Credits

AKG London; 17, 33t, 106t, 113t, 148, 187t, 187b, 199, 208
AKG London/Orsi Battaglini: 26b, 27, 116, 161, 194–195
AKG London/S. Domingié: 10–11, 21b, 60r, 101, 108, 114t, 137, 140, 142l, 144, 147b, 153, 178t, 179
AKG London/S. Domingié-M. Rabatti: 21t, 51, 73, 103, 107, 114b, 142r, 154–155, 177, 180, 181t, 189,196b
AKG London/Erich Lessing: 25b, 26t, 28, 71, 159, 184
Roger Antrobus/Getty Images: 40–41
The Art Archive/Daglo Orti: 96, 212t
The Art Archive/Bargello

Museum/Dagli Orti: 3, 5l, 58, 60l
The Art Archive/Baroncelli Chapel Santa Croce, Florence/Daglio Orti: inside front cover, 118t
The Art Archive/Museo Civico San Gimignano/Dagli Orti: 210b
The Art Archive/Diocesan Museo Cortona/Dagli Orti: 200
The Art Archive/Duomo Florence/Dagli Orti: 19t, 99
The Art Archive Galleria degli Uffizi Florence/Dagli Orti: Title page, 12, 14, 18, 48, 81, 82
The Art Archive/Galleria d'Arte Moderna Florence/Dagli Orti: 166
The Art Archive/Museo Storico Topografico Firenze Com'era Florence/Dagli Orti: 16, 182, 190
The Art Archive/Palazzo Pubblico Siena/Dagli Orti: 198, 211
The Art Archive/Pitti Palazzo, Florence/Dagli Orti: 65, 68, 69t
The Art Archive/San Lorenzo, Florence/Dagli Orti: 110b
The Art Archive/San Marco Florence/Dagli Orti: 111
The Art Archive/Santa Croce, Florence/Dagli Orti: 2, 119
The Art Archive/Santa Maria del Carmine, Florence/Dagli Orti: 123
The Art Archive/Palazzo Vecchio, Florence/Dagli Orti: 145
The Bridgeman Art Library: 4l, 4m, 4r, 5r, 6–7, 8–9, 13, 15, 16b, 19b, 20, 22t, 22b, 23, 25t, 29t, 30t, 33b, 36, 37t, 49, 50, 53t, 52–53, 54, 55, 57, 59, 61, 63l, 63r , 66l, 66r, 67, 69b, 70l, 70r, 72, 74, 77, 79, 80l, 80r, 83l, 83r, 84, 85, 86–87, 87t, 88, 89, 90, 91, 92l, 92rt, 92rb, 93, 95, 97, 98l, 100,

102t, 102b, 104, 105t, 105b, 109, 110t, 112, 113b, 115, 117, 118b, 120, 121, 122, 125, 126l, 126r, 127, 128, 129, 130, 133l, 133r, 138–139, 141, 143, 147t, 149, 154tl, 154tr, 156, 157, 158t, 162, 167, 176, 178b, 181m, 181b, 183, 192b, 194, 196, 203, 213
The Bridgeman Art Library/Christie Images, London: 56
The Bridgeman Art Library/K & B News Photo, Florence: 29b
The Bridgeman Art Library/Ruskin Museum: 31
Cosmo Condina/Getty Images: 46
Jerry Dennis/Apa: 37b, 75t, 76t, 76b, 94, 98r, 106b, 131, 132, 135, 146, 158b, 197
Courtesy of the Galleria d'Arte Moderna: 165
Guglielmo Galvin & George Taylor/Apa: 201, 205, 207, 209t, 210t
John Heseltine Archive: 206t, 206b
David Lees/Corbis: 35
Mary Evans Picture Library: 32, 75b, 151
Courtesy of Mills College: 150
Courtesy of the Museo d Geologia e Paleontologia: 185
Courtesy of the Museo Guarnacci: 212t, 212b
Courtesy of the Museo Marino Marini: 164, 168t, 168b
Courtesy of the Museo Nazionale di Antropologia e Etnologia: 185
Courtesy of the Museo dell'Opificio delle Pietre Dure: 169, 170
Courtesy of the Museo Salvatore Ferragamo: 171
Museo di Storia della Scienza: 188
Cathy Muscat:136, 209b
Palazzo Medici-Riccardi,

Florence, Italy: 160
Andrea Pistolesi: 62, 191, 192t, 193
Courtesy of the Raccolta di Arte Moderna Alberto della Ragione/Comune di Firenze: 172, 173
Guido Alberto Rossi/Getty Images: 38–39
Santa Maria Maddalena dei Pazzi: 124
Topham Picturepoint: 24t, 24b 31b, 33b, 34t, 152

Map and Plan Production: Stephen Ramsay
© 2002 Apa Publications GmbH & Co. Verlag KG (Singapore branch)

Cover concept and design: Klaus Geisler
Cover illustration created from works of art inside this book.

※INSIGHT GUIDE   MUSEUMS &
GALLERIES

FLORENCE

Art Director and Designer
Klaus Geisler
Production **Sylvia George**
Cartographic Editor **Zoë Goodwin**

Index

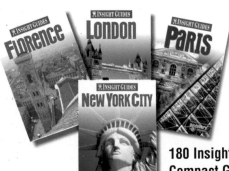